More ...
Patriot Hearts

God Bless America!

W.T. Coffey Jr.

Credits:

Production and Composition: LJEditing, LLC, Monument, Colorado
Wendy Lapsevich and Linda Windnagel

Desktop Publishing: Wendy Lapsevich, wendy@lapsevich.com

Editor: Linda J. Windnagel, Project Manager and Editor,
LJ Editing, LLC, Monument, Colorado. www.ljediting.com

Cover Design: Sergio Miller, Art Director, Berimbau Visual
Communication. www.berimbau.com

Printing: Bang Printing, Brainerd, Minnesota, www.bangprinting.com

Purple Mountain Publishing & Books Research and Marketing Analyst:
Colonel (Retired) William T. Coffey, Sr.

Authors: Colonel (Retired) William T. Coffey, Sr. and
Major William T. Coffey, Jr.

*Printed in the Land of the Free and the Home of the Brave
... the United States of America*

Published by Purple Mountain Publishing & Books

**Purple Mountain
Publishing & Books**

Ordering information for this book and its predecessor, *Patriot Hearts*,
can be found at the back of this book.

ISBN: 0-9704124-3-6 (hardback)
        0-9704124-4-4 (paperback)

DEDICATION

This book is dedicated to those great Americans who lost their lives on and since September 11, 2001 in the Global War on Terrorism. Their examples of service, selflessness, courage and patriotism set a standard for Americans to follow.

For those of us who continue this fight, we must ensure their sacrifice was not in vain.

CONTENTS

AUTHORS' INTRODUCTION

The development and release of this book's predecessor, *Patriot Hearts*, in December 2000 helped to widen and deepen our understanding and appreciation of patriotism in America. Since then, in a continuing effort to explore patriotism in America, we researched, analyzed, compiled and edited uncommon words from common patriots to develop this book. Our intent with this book is to develop within each of us a better understanding of our individual relationship with America and to inspire all of us to higher standards of citizenship.

Like *Patriot Hearts*, this book is a compilation of words spoken and written by Americans about America, or in some cases from foreigners about America. These words reflect our values, character and strength as a nation. They reflect our sense of country, our commonality, our love of country and our vision for a better America and a better world.

This book speaks to the intangibles of patriotism such as love, liberty, selflessness, honor, integrity, duty, courage and compassion. These intangibles can be witnessed throughout our country in many subtle ways. These include: the young child reciting our Pledge of Allegiance; the family clapping at curbside as veterans march by in a Veterans Day parade; the young American warrior who sweats during training and sacrifices during combat; the first responders who race toward tragedy to help those in need of help; the clergyman who speaks about our nation's Christian roots; the citizen who eloquently writes from the heart about their profound feelings of love for America; the teacher who instructs their students on the history of our great nation; and the millions of volunteers who provide their time, talent and part of their wealth in support of causes throughout the full spectrum of our society. The intangibles of American patriotism are all these things and much, much more. American patriotism is freedom in action. This book attempts to capture these intangibles and these expressions of patriotism, as spoken and written from the hearts of our Nation's patriots.

From our hearts to yours,
Colonel (Retired) William T. Coffey, Sr. - Plainville, Connecticut
Major William T. Coffey, Jr. - Colorado Springs, Colorado
July 20, 2003

B-25B *Mitchell* Bombers. The first of 16 to take off from the *USS Hornet* for the *Doolittle Raid* on Tokyo, 18 April 1942.

The 80 crewmen knew they did not have enough fuel to return to the carrier; so, they planned to fly to airfields in China after dropping 64, 500-pound bombs on Tokyo and surrounding areas. None of the planes actually reached the designated airfields in China and all crews had to bail out. Four were killed during the mission. Of the eight airmen captured, three were executed, one died as a POW.

Nothing is as strong as the heart of a volunteer.

LTC James Harold *Jimmy* Doolittle (1896–1993),
speaking of the men of his bombing crews, April 1942

We've got to teach history based not on what's in fashion but what's important ...

President Ronald Reagan

*Democracy doesn't thrive in darkness, and
neither does history. Both need sunlight.*

Paul Greenberg

*A morsel of genuine history is a thing
so rare as to be always valuable.*

President Thomas Jefferson

*History is the geology of human experience,
a study, as it were, of tragedy and comedy
laid down in the strata of past lives.
In death there are no winners or losers,
merely people who once lived but can never live again.
What they thought, what they believed,
what they hoped, is largely lost.
That which remains is history.*

Robert Goddard, Extracted from his book *Sea Change*
published by Bantam Press

*Only human beings guide their behavior
by a knowledge of what happened
before they were born and
a preconception of what may happen after they are dead;
thus only humans find their way by a light
that illuminates more than the patch of ground they stand on.*

J.S. Medawar

*History is to the nation ... as memory is to the individual.
An individual deprived of memory becomes disoriented
and lost, not knowing where he has been or where he is going,
so a nation denied a conception of its past
will be disabled in dealing with its present and future.*

Arthur M. Schlesinger

*P*eace is not made at the council table,
or by treaties, but in the hearts of men.

President Herbert Hoover

*T*he patriot volunteer, fighting for his country and his rights,
makes the most reliable soldier upon earth.

General Thomas J. *Stonewall* Jackson

*T*o be a successful soldier you must know history,
what you must know is how man reacts to win battles,
you do not beat weapons you beat the soul of man.

General George S. Patton, Jr.

*W*hen you lose your national memory,
you risk losing what you need
for understanding your own time–and
you risk losing the future as well as the past.

Thomas Sowell

*T*here is nothing new in the world
except the history you do not know.

President Harry S. Truman

A nation which does not remember what it was yesterday,
does not know what it is today,
nor what it is trying to do.
We are trying to do a futile thing
if we do not know where we came from
or what we have been about.

President Woodrow Wilson

We pay a price when we deprive children
of the exposure to the values, principles, and education
they need to make them good citizens.

Sandra Day O'Conner, U.S. Supreme Court Justice

There are good men and bad men
of all nationalities, creeds and colors;
and if this world of ours is ever to become
what we hope some day it may become,
it must be by the general recognition that
the man's heart and soul,
the man's worth and actions,
determine his standing.

President Theodore Roosevelt, 1 September 1903

It's what's under the left nipple that counts.

Coach Norm Van Brocklin, Atlanta Falcons

CHAPTER 1

DUTY AND SERVICE

Duty is the responsibility to fulfill one's obligations. This chapter explores America's sense of duty, service and citizenship to our country. This duty compels Americans to serve something greater than themselves, their family, their community and their nation. A firm acceptance of duty and service to country in each patriot's heart has been the cornerstone of America's survival and prosperity.

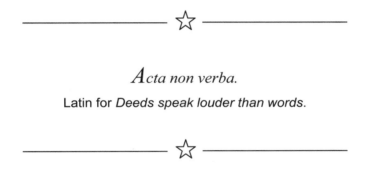

Acta non verba.

Latin for *Deeds speak louder than words.*

THE IDEALS AND VALUES THAT MAKE THIS COUNTRY GREAT

Good citizenship is vitally important if democracy is to survive and flourish. It means keeping abreast of the important issues of the day and knowing the stakes involved in the great conflicts of our time. It means bearing arms when necessary to fight for your country, for right, and for freedom. Good citizenship and defending democracy means living up to the ideals and values that make this country great.

President Ronald Reagan

I'M HERE TO SERVE

By Maj. George Mitchell, 22nd Logistics Group, 14 March 2002, McConnell Air Force Base, Kansas. Courtesy of Air Mobility Command News Service and the Armed Forces Press Network.

I needed a job, and I was thinking about enlisting. My father, a retired Navy chief, recommended the Air Force. He's never said if he was looking out for me or the Navy. He also talked about it not being a regular job, and about the importance of country; the significance of duty, sacrifice and honor; of living with a purpose; and the seriousness of weapons. It was over my head at the time, but I've gained an understanding of those words. I got to basic training and enjoyed the many exercises in futility you endure that first night. Sometime the following morning, I opened my eyes to see a very large man in a Smokey-the-Bear hat leaning over me asking if I planned on getting out of bed that day. I looked around at 49 other guys looking equally incoherent, but at least they were vertical, and wondered, *Who is he and why am I here?* That *duty* word my father had used came back to me. I don't think I understood it, but keeping it in the front of my mind allowed me to do some things I may not have otherwise accomplished. Then I got settled into my first duty station. I needed a job and now I had one. We worked long hours and, like many people who don't know why they're in the military, I became disenchanted and figured I'd do four years and get back to the real world. There are many good reasons for coming into the military. I joined for a paycheck. Some people come in for an education, others to travel and a number of other reasons. However, those reasons don't suffice when it comes down to the challenges we face daily in service to our country. We were recalled dark and early one morning to hear that the U.S. embassy, in a country I couldn't have found on a map, had been taken. The hours became longer and days off became less frequent, but that *duty* word my father had used came back. It made a little more sense this time, but I was still grasping. Later we got word of the Desert One accident and that *sacrifice* word started to take shape. I was working harder than I had ever worked in my life and loved every sleepless minute of it. I still didn't understand all the words, but I was starting to understand the importance of *service* and understood that I was here to serve. Years later, one country invaded another country I hadn't heard of. I again found myself asking, *Why am I here?* This time my problem with *here* was being in a tech school and not out in the *real Air Force*, where every day you have the opportunity to make a difference; where every day I'm allowed to serve. I now understood that this is in fact an honor. A couple of years ago I was part of an exchange program with an Allied Air Force. It was a challenge to be productive in an unfamiliar environment, and it was frustrating. But whenever I had a reason to visit the U.S. Embassy, I could feel exhausted and confused, but when I walked through the embassy gate and saw the flag, I was home. It was an amazing feeling. One day I was walking through town in uniform when a man called to me by my rank. I stopped and he told me about his experiences working with the U.S. military during World War II. He didn't speak English, so it took several attempts to communicate, but he told me how much he had enjoyed working with the Americans and how much he respected our nation. He saluted, I saluted, and we each went on our way. He reminded me why I was there. I was there to serve my country and its Allies, whether procuring parts for airplanes or helping an old man remember who Americans are. On Sept. 11, I, like many others, stood in front of a television and watched as sacrifice was again explained in very understandable terms. These days I don't often wonder why I'm here. After 23 years in uniform, I still can't define what my father's words meant, but I understand. Everyone in uniform came in for his or her reasons, but the only real reason to be here is to serve. To serve your God, your country, and other people, but always to serve. Why am I here? I'm here to serve.

I slept, and dreamed that life was Beauty;
I woke, and found that life was Duty.

Ellen Sturgis Hooper

Placing the line of duty above the line of self interest is all
that distinguishes the soldier from the civilian.

S.L.A. Marshall

Men cannot for long live hopefully unless
they are embarked upon some great unifying enterprise,
one for which they may pledge their lives,
their fortunes and their honor.

C.A. Dykstra

Today you make the change from peacetime pursuits to
wartime tasks. From the individualism of civilian life to the
anonymity of mass military life. You have given up
comfortable homes, highly paid positions, leisure. You have
taken off silk and put on khaki. And all for essentially the
same reason—you have a debt and a date.
A debt to democracy, and a date with destiny.

Colonel Oveta Culp Hobby
First Director, Women's Army Corps, July 1942

A Debt and a Date. American Women take the
Oath of Enlistment, World War II.

WHY MOM STILL WEARS THE UNIFORM

By Colonel Cheryl Zadlo, 95th Air Base Wing commander, 10 May 2002, Edwards Air Force Base, California. Courtesy of the Armed Forces Press Network.

To my daughters:

Remember when I wrote to you during the time I was deployed a few years back? You asked me then, *Why do you do the things you do?* As Mother's Day approaches, I find myself wanting to express to you again why your mom is still wearing the uniform.

Today you see many more people wearing military uniforms in the airports, around bases and in cities, and see even more in the media going to obscure places we didn't even know about a few years ago.

Now, more than ever, there is a vital need for what the Air Force does, and there are many moms dedicating themselves to the task of ensuring our nation's security.

I feel compelled to tell you again, how much being your mom means to me. You both are such a tremendous source of pride! As daughters of an Air Force mom, your passion for life, for your studies and your very real sacrifices warm my heart every day. The way you handle being a *brat* is a positive example to many others. I am proud of you.

I truly hope that as you try to understand my calling and why it is so important, you feel the same pride I carry with me.

I've watched you grow from *sweet and sassy* little girls to responsible, young women. You've had the opportunity to see, do and live things many only read about in books or see on television. These opportunities do not celebrate selfishness.

We value service before self to secure the safety and freedom we enjoy as Americans. We pursue our dreams and aspirations

Mom in Uniform. Colonel Cheryl Zadlo, U.S. Air Force.

without persecution or curtailed civil liberties. That is why I still strive so hard to do my part in making the Air Force stronger, more responsive and the absolute best–so we can continue defending our way of life and our land by combating terrorism, providing humanitarian assistance, and developing future capabilities that will enable us to flourish into this new century and beyond.

I choose to do my part in a uniform because I know the sacrifice is worthy of our goal. I do this for you and America. What I do is no less important now than my last deployment. Freedom is still under attack, and our nation must respond.

Mothers lost their children on Sept. 11 when the spineless attacks occurred in New York and on the Pentagon. Children lost, and continue to lose, their moms in terrorist actions today.

Will I, as one individual, make a difference? I believe I must, and I believe I do make a difference. I join thousands of others with this same attitude and aptitude, teaming to ensure we protect that which is precious to our nation–the strength, the resolve, and the freedoms Americans experience today.

It is not easy, girls. The commitment required often leaves little left over for you and what is important to you. I am always with you in spirit while I'm away from you. Wherever you are, whether at a school or church function, you are in my thoughts; you are my motivation. I don't for a moment regret what I represent–100 percent unfaltering commitment to preserve a way of life for you, me and those we love.

You both mean that much to me. I love you, and that is why I do what I do.

I shall endeavor to do my duty and fight to the last.

General Robert E. Lee
9 April 1865, Confederate General, 1807-1870

IT WAS MY WAR

WWII Recruiting Poster. 1944.

*It wasn't just my brother's country, or my husband's
country, it was my country as well. And so this war wasn't
just their war, it was my war, and I needed to serve in it.*

Beatrice Hood Stroup, Women's Army Corps

Giving back involves a certain amount of giving up.

Secretary of State Colin Powell,
in an open letter to America's youth

*Always do right.
This will gratify some people, and astonish the rest.*

Mark Twain

SOMETIMES I FORGET

By Airman First Class Joshua Wilks, 796th Civil Engineer Squadron, 29 January 2002, Eglin Air Force Base, Florida. Courtesy of Air Force Materiel Command News Service and the Armed Forces Press Network.

When I dress in the morning, I try to remember I wear the uniform of a military that protects the greatest symbol of democracy and freedom in the world.

But sometimes, I forget.

I also try to remember people who dress as I do every morning, the ones who have dressed this way so many days before me, and those who will follow me.

But sometimes, I forget.

I try to keep in mind just one of the fallen heroes who wore this very same uniform. The ones who lost their lives in it, and the ones who still wear it as they lie in their final resting places in a national cemetery.

But sometimes, I forget.

Every morning, when I go to work, I try to remember to say good morning to my co-workers—military and civilian. I try to remember these people protect my freedom as I work beside them each day.

But sometimes, I forget.

I try to remember that my job is the greatest in the world.

But sometimes, I forget.

I try to remember that although this uniform may be a little too warm in the summer and just not warm enough in the

Airman First Class Joshua Wilks.

*winter, thousands of my comrades remain missing in action,
and others were imprisoned for years on foreign soil,
suffering torture and abuse inconceivable to humanity–all
this while wearing this uniform.*

But sometimes, I forget.

*During the day, when I think of all the other things I would
rather be doing with my life, I try to remember the role I
take part in while wearing this uniform. I try to remember
this world is still a dangerous place, and we must work
extremely hard to safeguard the freedom we take for granted
so our children will know the freedom
we have always known.*

But sometimes, I forget.

*I try to remember as I pledge my allegiance to Old Glory,
this awe-inspiring symbol of freedom and democracy, that
others entrust my comrades and me with her safekeeping.*

But sometimes, I forget.

*At bedtime, as I kneel in prayer before God, I try to
remember the hundreds of thousands of families who lost
their loved ones in the defense of this great land.*

But sometimes, I forget.

*I try to remember that I would die for this country, but I
would much rather live for it.*

But sometimes, I forget.

*Yet at times (of war) like this, when I remember to take
these things into account, there is no way I can explain the
pride I feel and the honor I embrace while wearing this
uniform and serving this country. And when I leave this
world, my spirit will echo words known to me since
childhood, 'One nation, under God, indivisible,
with liberty and justice for all.'*

*Our obligations to our country never cease
but with our lives.*

President John Adams

*All that is needed for the forces of evil to triumph is for
enough good people to do nothing.*

Edmund Burke

Duty be ours, consequences be God's.

General Thomas J. *Stonewall* Jackson
Confederate General, 1824-1863

THIS RANGER IS LONE IN HIS WAYS

In case you weren't aware, Pat Tillman exchanged a four million dollar National Football League (NFL) contract in favor of a three-year tour in the infantry at a salary of $18,000 a year. *The Washington Post* sports writer, Sally Jenkins, wrote him a letter. © 2002 *The Washington Post.* Reprinted with Permission.

By: Sally Jenkins, 23 November 2002
To: Specialist Pat Tillman, 75th Ranger Regiment
        Ranger Training Brigade, Fort Benning, Georgia

Dear Pat,
They say that soldiers, between duress and boredom, look forward to mail call; so, I thought I would write. While I don't know you personally, I know of you: how you left your career as a strong safety for the Arizona Cardinals to enlist in the infantry, with the intention of becoming a Ranger.

Congratulations on your graduation from Airborne School this week. I wonder if you have any regret, if learning to parachute from a plane, with 80 pounds of gear on your back, at night, under fire, makes you wish you were back in the NFL defending hitch routes?

Actually, I was tempted to start my letter this way, for laughs, seeing as how you might need some, what with all you're going through:

> Dear Pat, You think you've got it tough, crawling through mud and climbing up rope ladders? Tiger Woods has it tough, too. Every day there's another story about how tough it is to be him–knowing, that any moment, someone else might ask him about Augusta. Always having to bite his nails, and wonder what lies ahead, around the next dogleg.

Or:

> Dear Pat, Don't be afraid. You think you have fears? Allen Iverson has fears, too. He's afraid to live in Philadelphia.

Or:

> Dear Pat, I know you're tired and hurting. Shaq is, too. We all hope his big toe will be healed in time for the next Olympics.

Anyhow, the public affairs people at Fort Benning say you got through basic training with distinction, and now you and your brother Kevin, who left his own career as a minor leaguer with the Cleveland Indians organization, will go through another 18-day boot camp called the Ranger Indoctrination Program. You'll be eligible for deployment sometime after the first of the year. Just about the time we could be at war with Iraq.

They say you want to be just another foot soldier, which is why you've refused all interviews since you joined. This is a nice idea in theory, but I would argue with it. The fact is you aren't another grunt. Your behavior is singular; as far as anyone can ascertain, you're the first pro athlete since World War II to enlist. Others have served, like Rocky Bleier, who was drafted and almost lost a leg to shrapnel in Vietnam, but none has volunteered.

Everybody wants to know why you did it. Are you some crackpot, gung-ho, thrill-seeking dope who should leave things to the real soldiers? It doesn't sound like it. You're a lawyer's son and cum laude graduate of Arizona

State. Bet the Army wishes it was an ordinary thing to exchange a $4 million NFL contract in favor of a three-year tour in the infantry at a salary of $18,000 a year.

I wonder if you've found that as an athlete you're more suited to military service, or less? Athletes visit physical extremes, but they're rewarded with surfeit. I can't think of many who would put up with food deprivation and a 10-mile run with a rucksack. NFL players are certainly possessed of toughness–the injury rate is harrowing–but exactly what brand of toughness is it? Outward strength doesn't reflect inner strength, as we've seen. The boxer Riddick Bowe decided to join the Marines in mid-career and washed out after eight days of boot camp, citing the loss of control over his life. None of this is to say athletes like Woods, Iverson and O'Neal aren't meaningful or marvelous; they explore, they establish values and they divert whole communities from their problems. But the contests are essentially make believe.

The Ranger program is designed to seek hidden stress points in even the most ostensibly strong. The Rangers are arguably the most highly trained branch of the infantry—it was the Rangers who stormed the gun emplacements at Point du Hoc on D-Day and established the motto, *Rangers Lead the Way*.

From what I hear, this is what you can look forward to in the next phase of your training: First they'll make you walk off a diving board with a blindfold on. Then they'll strap you full of gear and throw you in a pool and make you shed it without panicking. That's just the prelim, before they leave you in a swamp for days with no sleep and a bad map.

You seem to be putting up with it fine. All I really know is what you wrote your position coach with the Cardinals, Larry Marmie, in a handwritten letter from basic training a couple of months ago. *He said now he understood a lot of things*, Marmie says. *That he had been in a bit of a cocoon in football.*

It's hard to guess what you mean by that. Marmie says you had a quiet distaste for the more self-absorbed types in the NFL, which may have something to do with your enlistment. *In pro football there's a certain amount of ego involved,* Marmie says. *Maybe some guys have an exaggerated idea of what they mean to the game. Pat always had things in balance.*

You've suggested to friends that you didn't feel right fighting fake battles on the field when other Americans were fighting real ones on other fields. Sept. 11 was a Tuesday, a day off around the league, but as usual you showed up for a workout. You never got the workout in, because the news bulletins interrupted you. You sat in a room in front of the television, staring at it for three straight hours.

That spring when you became an unrestricted free agent, you called Marmie and asked to meet him at a coffee shop, and told him they better draft a safety because you were joining up. Anyhow, it's interesting to think about what you're doing right now, as opposed to your old teammates. Ernest Becker, in the Pulitzer Prize winning book *Denial of Death*, a study of mortality and heroism, writes that the threat of death can lead one to a more purposeful and authentic life. He writes of *inauthentic men,* who *follow out the styles of automatic and uncritical living ... they are one-dimensional men totally immersed in the fictional games being played in their society.* Does this explain you?

Dr. Johnson suggested that nothing concentrates the mind like the prospect of death. Lance Armstrong says that the experience of losing something, whether a career or an old sense of self, is actually enhancing, because unrealized capacities emerge only in crisis. I wonder if you felt wasted, unrealized, because an NFL game could only approximate a crisis?

According to your former teammates, you were always restless. At Arizona State, when head coach Bruce Snyder told you he might redshirt you, you replied that he could do whatever he wanted, *But I'm only going to be here for four years, because I got things to do.* There is an interesting rumor that when you enlisted, you told the Army something similar: You said your three-year tour of duty had to end in the spring, so that you would have time to prepare for the NFL season when you mustered out.

I wonder if the military will alter you, and especially your ideas about heroism. Becker says we've made *animal courage into a cult,* and that heroism is *first and foremost a reflex of the terror of death.* As a culture, we make heroes out of athletes simply for being athletes—in part because they aren't what Becker calls *the automatic cultural man, who imagines he has control over his life if he pays an insurance premium. If he guns his car and runs his electric toothbrush.*

It will be interesting to see what kind of soldier you turn out to be, and whether in the end, you find that soldiering has made you a more authentic man.

Yours truly …

GOD GIVE US MEN

God, give us men! A time like this demands;
Strong minds, great hearts, true faith and ready hand;
Men whom the lust of office does not kill;
Men whom the spoils of office cannot buy;
Men who possess opinions and a will;
Men who have honor; men who will not lie;
Men who can stand before a demagogue and damn
His Treacherous flatteries without winking!
Tall men, sun-crowned, who live above the fog
In public duty and in private thinking.

By Josiah Gilbert Holland

The essence of duty is acting in the absence of orders or direction from others, based on an inner sense of what is morally and professionally right ...

General John A. Wickham, Jr.; Army Chief of Staff 1983-1987

Give the American people
a good cause and there's nothing they can't lick.

John Wayne

THE LAST DANCE

These eight Air Force Reservists, ages 53 to 58, are assigned to the 320th Expeditionary Civil Engineer Squadron in Afghanistan and are all veterans of the Vietnam War. Not one was drafted to serve in Vietnam–all joined the service of their choice when their country needed them most. *Nobody appreciates what all went on*, Cannon said. *It wasn't that the soldiers agreed with the war; it was the fact that they went in and did their duty.* Despite the way they were treated, all opted to serve their country again. Each of these civil engineers has the warrior spirit. They have served in foreign lands and fought for the freedoms every American enjoys. Each knows the price of freedom, and knows even more it is worth fighting for. They call this their *Last Dance.*

Eight of the 315th Civil Engineer Squadron Reservists.
Senior Master Sgt. Sonny Cannon, Chief Master Sgt.
Merritt Porter, Tech. Sgt. George Frazier and Master Sgt.
George Aldrich. Back: Master Sgt. Ronald Gore, Master
Sgt. John Murray, Senior Master Sgt. Tim Hiott and Senior
Master Sgt. Gerald Gullett. All are currently deployed for
Operation Enduring Freedom. Photo by Staff Sgt. Sonny Cohrs.

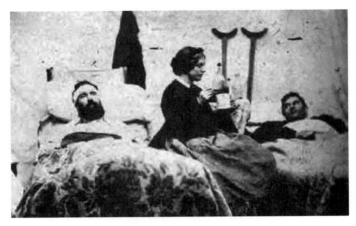

Nashville Hospital. Civil War.

*No, the hospital work never felt burdensome, even when
there was only a board with a blanket for a mattress,
or food—hardtack, bacon and coffee day after day—and
no pay, for no provision was made for that.
It was a work of love of native land and humanity.*

Clarissa Emerly, Civil War Nurse

*Make it a point to do something every day
that you don't want to do. This is the golden rule for
acquiring a habit of doing your duty without pain.*

Mark Twain

*If you succeed here, the president of the United States
will repose special trust and confidence
in your patriotism, valor, fidelity, and abilities
and therefore grant you responsibilities and privileges
which you must always be worthy.*

Sign outside of an Officer Candidate School building,
Quantico Marine Base, Quantico, Virginia

For us in the life of action, of strenuous performance of duty; let us live in the harness, striving mightily; let us rather run the risk of wearing out than rusting out.

President Theodore Roosevelt

The Army really cannot fulfill its mission without a civilian workforce that is every bit as dedicated to duty and to service as the uniformed people.

General John A. Wickham, Jr.

A sense of duty is moral glue, constantly subject to stress.

William Safire, Writer

AN OATH, A SOLEMN PROMISE

Following are the remarks given at the U.S. Navy Pensacola Officer Candidate School Graduation, 11 October 2002, by the Commanding Officer of the *USS John F. Kennedy* (CV 67), Captain Ronald H. Henderson, Jr.

Twenty-six years ago I was sitting in one of those seats. I remember that I was tired, happy, and proud. I was tired from a long week of frenetic activity leading up to the actual graduation. I was happy that it was all soon to be over. As soon as that old guy was finished talking, I could become a Naval officer! Mostly, I was proud, proud that I had accomplished a major step on the road to my goal of serving my country as a Naval Aviator. I suspect that you candidate officers feel some of these same emotions. Realizing that I am the only thing standing between you and a commission, I will be brief and, I hope, offer a little encouragement and inspiration for the trials that lie before you.

In a few moments you will take an oath, a solemn promise. All military members–Army, Navy, Marines, and Air Force, officer and enlisted, male and female–take this oath of service. I would like to examine that oath for a moment.

We swear to *support and defend the Constitution of the United States of America*. Consider this, how unique it is. We do not swear an oath to a President, a Congress, a Supreme Court, or a nation. We do not swear an oath to Democracy, a Republic, a State, a form of government, or an idea. We swear an oath to the Constitution, a piece of paper. It was written during a long hot summer in 1789 in Philadelphia. The founders were mostly white, rich, landholding males. The crafting of this document was not without controversy. The debate lasted all summer and its acrimony on several occasions nearly tore the constitutional convention apart. The document they produced was, without exception, the greatest document on self-government in the history of man. It was not perfect–it did not give women the right to vote, and, in one of the mostly hotly contested debates, it allowed the abomination of slavery to continue. This defect led to our greatest national crisis, our great civil war, which resulted in more deaths in combat and from disease than all our other wars combined. And yet, this document, since amended several times to correct its deficiencies and reflect our modern times, remains today the envy of our world. It is this document that we serve, and which we are sworn to *support and defend*. Like the founding fathers, who pledged their lives, their fortunes, and their sacred honor, we too, as military members, are prepared to give our lives, if necessary, for this *piece of paper*. Consider also, the rest of the oath. We swear to *obey the orders of the President, and all officers appointed over me*. What blind faith this is! How extraordinary this is! While we know who the President is, we swear to obey an unseen list of officers about whom we may know nothing at all. For some of us, you about to be Ensigns, the list is longer than for us old guys. Nevertheless, even we accept as blind faith the competence and dedication of men and women we know nothing of, and in fact we have sworn to follow their orders even at peril to our lives, if necessary. If we did nothing else in the military, we would be extraordinary people by reason of the oath that we swear when we enter service. And of course, you are those extraordinary people. You have survived rigorous screening to be selected to attempt to become officers in the United States Navy. You have further survived a difficult and challenging training program, designed to weed out the soft body and the feeble mind but more importantly, the weak of heart. Your drill instructors, Marine and Navy, have given their best to challenge you, to motivate you, and to instill in you those values that guide our service: Our Honor, our Courage and our Commitment. You all have learned what these mean, but I would like to offer to you what they mean to me:

Honor ... simply means always telling the truth and holding your integrity as your most cherished possession. Honor is truly the bedrock of our organization. It is something that cannot be taken from you; it can only give it away. If you compromise your integrity it will be difficult, if not impossible, to regain it. On the other hand, your honor is the most basic assumption people will make about you; you are honorable unless you prove otherwise. Honor means simply telling the truth, not part of the truth, and not dealing in legalities and artful evasions. Honor means having the self-discipline to do the right thing, whether or not someone is watching. It means admitting a mistake; the benefits that accrue from simply admitting a mistake is one of life's fundamental secrets. We honor ourselves and our teammates when we judge a teammate purely by his or her performance vice by ethnic background, gender or religion. A team member's honor is his or her single most important personal trait. We will be enormously powerful if we are able to simply and confidently assume every one of our Sailors and Marines is acting honorably.

Courage ... comes in two forms. Physical courage is what it takes to enter a burning space to fight a fire or save a shipmate. Moral courage is choosing the difficult right over the easy wrong, whether on liberty or at work. Courage is a prerequisite for honor; having the courage to pay the price that sometimes comes with maintaining one's honor.

Courage is also a prerequisite for commitment; having the courage to step across the line and be an enthusiastic leader vice responding to negative peer pressure, something especially critical for our younger Sailors. We often find in our business that physical courage is something we can rely on, while moral courage is not. Too often the attitude of, *it's only wrong if you get caught*, prevails among our younger Sailors; instilling moral courage in those Sailors is the most important way we can develop them as young men and women and I would propose to you, is one of your sacred duties as Naval leaders.

Commitment ... means always giving one's best effort and never giving up. To be fully committed to something, to struggle in detail all the way to the end, never giving up where others have compromised, combining flashes of insight with sheer hard work, striving for both substance and style and then finding success is one of the truly rewarding things in life. Commitment means quality workmanship, going to sea with the ship and not whining. It means ship, shipmate, and then self. It means division officers and chiefs who are deeply involved with their Sailors vice managing from the desk. It means doing things right the first time. Commitment means always being there when we need you, but it does not mean ignoring your family's needs. It means never walking past something that is wrong even though it may be unpopular to fix the problem on the spot. Understanding the true meaning of *service* is a major part of commitment. Service is what distinguishes what we do in the Navy from that done by pay-by-the-hour labor. We are willing to go to extraordinary lengths, including *the last full measure of devotion*, to support our team even though we receive little or no extra pay for it. We do so because being part of something bigger than our own selfish interests. Service is also what prevents us from resenting the fact that we are held to a higher standard than rest of our nation's citizens. So courage, honor, and commitment. This is your code of values which define you as a Naval Officer. To these ideals you must be true and from which you must never waver. In a few moments you will swear an oath and accept the challenge of what you must be in order to preserve this nation and this Navy. What about this Navy? You will be asked to sacrifice for it over and over again. You will forgo simple pleasures that civilians take for granted and expect as entitlements. Whether you remain in the Navy beyond your initial commitment, or take your service as a life experience and translate your talents to our nation as a civilian, for the next few years, at least, you can take enormous pride and satisfaction in being part of the greatest Navy in the world. I say this not out of arrogance or idle boast. I have seen and worked with most of the world's important naval forces, and I will tell you we are the envy of them all. None can touch us in maritime competency, airmanship, seamanship, professionalism, power, and most importantly, our commitment to the ideals of our nation. Indeed, you are about to become officers in the greatest Navy in the history of the world, a Navy which history has graced with many moments of public glory, but many more hours of quiet and unnoticed duty in service to our country and the cause of freedom. Our naval power has been the key to our freedom from the earliest days, and will continue to be so as long as there are men and women like you, who assume the Blue and Gold and become officers of honor, courage, and commitment. And what of the nation and the cause we serve? Are we indeed an arrogant superpower, the bully of the world, intent on conquest and power for the sake of cheap oil and the right to build a Wal-Mart everywhere? Some say this and many believe it, but I remain an optimist. I believe Abraham Lincoln was right when he called the United States the *last, best, hope for the world*. I believe that history will be kind to America and marvel at our generosity and magnanimity in victory. We are a beacon unto the world, and many who seek justice, peace and prosperity risk everything to come here to be part of our great adventure. Our forefathers pledged their lives, their fortunes and their sacred honor to establish these United States. We have maintained that ideal with the blood, sweat and tears of patriots; including the Greatest generation, passing now quickly from our view, who saved Democracy from fascism and communism and gave us the prosperity we enjoy today. That responsibility to preserve what they paid for so dearly will shortly come to rest on your shoulders as our Republic faces new and deeper dangers.

Now could not be a better time for you to join us. Religious fanatics are intent on destroying everything good about us. They twist the meaning of a great religion to justify their madness and their hate. They do not hate us for things we do. They hate us for what we are. They hate that we are happy. They hate that we are prosperous. They hate that we are tolerant. They hate us because we are free. This is precisely why we will overcome them and ultimately destroy them because these are our strengths as a nation, as a people and as a civilization. This war we are now engaged in will not be short, easy or without sacrifice. We will suffer more tragic loss, and weep again at the graves of the innocent.

Plato was right 2000 years ago when he predicted, *Only the dead have seen the end of war*. Despite this, I remain hopeful and confident, because we have men and women like you, and because we are happy, prosperous, tolerant, and most of all, free. President John F. Kennedy inspired us when he said, ...*let every nation know, whether it wishes us well or ill, that we shall pay any price, bear any burden, meet any hardship, support any friend or oppose any foe to assure the survival and success of liberty.* He was talking to your forefathers then, and he is speaking to all of us now. You have chosen to serve and are about to embark on a great adventure for a noble cause in the most respected profession of arms. You are now part of a great tradition bearing the sword in defense of freedom. Serve with honor, serve with courage and serve with commitment. I welcome you aboard and am honored to have you with me in the struggle. Good luck, God speed, and may God bless you in all your future endeavors in service to our country as officers of the United States Navy.

*T*hose who expect to reap the blessings of freedom, must,
like men, undergo the fatigues of supporting it.

Thomas Paine

*H*onor, Justice, and Humanity call upon us to hold, and to
transmit to our posterity, that liberty which we received
from our ancestors. It is not our duty to leave wealth to our
children ... but, it is our duty to leave liberty to them.

John Dickenson, 1774

*T*he price of greatness is responsibility.

Sir Winston Churchill

*Y*ou cannot be saved by devotion to your ancestors. To each
generation comes its patriotic duty, and upon your
willingness to sacrifice and endure, as those before you
have sacrificed and endured, rests the national hope.

Charles Evans Hughes, Supreme Court Justice

*If we fouled up, it
would have been a
black mark against
black women and
women in general,
but we didn't foul up.
We did our job.*

Janice Stovall Taylor,
Women's Army Corps

Servicing a Truck. Auxiliaries Ruth
Wade (on left) and Lucille Mayo
servicing a truck at Fort Huachuca,
Arizona. 8 December 1942.

The nation today needs men who think in terms of service to their country and not in terms of their country's debt to them.

General Omar N. Bradley, Army

BECAUSE I SAID I WOULD

*Oh, I guess I signed up for a whole lot of reasons–
Pay, thrills, the job–When I add it up, though,
I'm expected to put it all on the line to defend this country
(that's mom and schools and the chance for a job and to go
to church and all the rest.) When I signed up, I agreed
to go where I was sent and do my job. I've got to work with
a lot of other people to make it work. It won't be easy.
I've got to pay attention and do it right all the way.
Tomorrow, I've got to do it better than I did it today.
Because I said I would. Because I'm a professional.*

Author Unknown

I believe that every right implies a responsibility; every opportunity, an obligation; every possession, a duty.

John D. Rockefeller, Jr.

This is our turn to walk as sentries on the walls of freedom.

BG B.J. Butler

*Our foreign policy is based on goals of freedom
and justice. It is in the interest of these goals that
we ask you to serve your country overseas. Your Nation
depends on you and your colleagues, not just for the
execution of American foreign policy, but for the
embodiment of the spirit and ideals of our country.*

President John F. Kennedy

*I will not trade freedom for beneficence nor my dignity
for a handout. I will never cower before any master
nor bend to any threat. It is my heritage to stand erect,
proud, and unafraid; to think and act for myself,
enjoy the benefit of my creations, and to face the world
boldly and say, this I have done.*

Dean Alfange

*I'm glad I'm in the Army, not only for the people
who are in it and for the breadth of experience
which it offers, but because of the feeling I have of
belonging to an outfit which really matters, one which has a
mission of tremendous significance.*

General Maxwell D. Taylor

I PUT ON MY UNIFORM TODAY

A Chief Master Sergeant sat behind his desk, just down the hall from his commander's office at Ennee AFB, America. As the Chief started on a second cup of coffee and finished the last of the morning messages, the commander stepped into the office. *Chief,* the Colonel said, *I hate to ask you this, but you are needed in Southwest Asia in six days for a 90-day rotation. Can you go?* With no voiced emotion and without looking up, the Chief replied, *Ma'am, I put on my uniform this morning.* The Colonel, somewhat taken a-back, thought to herself, *The Chief doesn't usually talk in riddles. Has this veteran of 24 years gone off of the deep end?* The wise old protector of the enlisted corps smiled and began to explain.

Ma'am, I made a promise to myself more than 20 years ago, that I would only put this uniform on as long as I'm available for duty. You see, while it is obvious to most Air Force members, it seems to completely escape others. 'Available for duty' means more than the desire to negotiate and select the premium assignments or choicest TDYs [Temporary Duty]. It requires us to go any place in the world the president or officers appointed over us determines, at any given time. This doesn't mean we shouldn't want or receive our preferences. It does mean we'll go when and where we are needed and called. Now this may seem overly simplistic, but, I think everyone can agree: when it comes to defining service to our country, the answer is just that simple. In today's world of 'What can you do for me?' it's very easy to lose sight of what 'service to country' is all about. Service goes far beyond the individual; it affects the well being of our nation. Sitting in comfortable surroundings, at your dream base in CONUS, it's easy to forget the sacrifices we agreed to endure in service to our country. Sitting in Saudi, Italy, Bosnia, or maybe Korea, the sacrifices become much clearer. The bottom line today is that we are an all-volunteer force, and though our force has been reduced by 30 percent in the last five years, it remains a highly mobilized, continually-tasked *corporation*. Everyone is vital to its continued success.

The Chief continued by saying,

The Air Force will go on tomorrow with or without any single one of us; however, the efficiency of any one of its specific units may be adversely effected by the loss of only a few. All of us have the responsibility to report our availability for duty. If someone has a family problem or special circumstances that precludes them from being available, they need to report it immediately and especially prior to being deployed. If any member does not deploy when called upon, another member must fill that slot. So, any time someone cannot or will not deploy, the ripple effect is felt throughout the Air Force. Everyone's family would like them to be home for the holidays. I can't think of a single person who would intentionally miss their child's graduation. And we're all aware of the pain of losing a loved one and know how the grief can be compounded by not being at their side in the final moments. Yes, we are all continually asked to make sacrifices. Yet some seem to forget that we are serving our nation, and that we are all volunteers. Who said it was going to be easy? The leadership of our country depends upon us for being good and true to our word. Every day, each of us needs to look into the mirror before getting into uniform and ask, 'Am I available for duty?' If the answer is *No*, then we need to notify our supervisor, first sergeant, or commander immediately! Then the next step is to determine if the non-availability is temporary or permanent. Then the toughest question must be asked–should that person resign, separate, or retire? There are no gray areas. Everyone must decide for themselves.

Finally, the Chief looked at his commander and said, *Ma'am, as I said earlier, I put on my uniform today, and I'm available for duty. Do you still need a 'yes' or 'no' answer to your question?*

I pray daily to do my duty.

General George S. Patton, Jr. *Old Blood and Guts*
Army General, World War I, World War II, 1895-1945

*Duty is not collective, it is personal.
Let every individual make known his determination to
support law and order. That duty is supreme.*

President Calvin Coolidge

Many free countries have lost their liberty, and ours may lose hers; but if she shall, be it my proudest plume, not that I was the last to desert; but that I never deserted her.

President Abraham Lincoln, *Honest Abe* 1809-1865

Far and away the best prize that life offers is the chance to work hard at work worth doing.

President Theodore Roosevelt

We will not tire, we will not falter and we will not fail.

President George W. Bush

I'd do anything for this country ... As a paralyzed veteran, I'm proud to be able to say ... If I could go back in time and serve my country, I'd do it, even knowing what the consequences would be.

James J. Peters, Disabled American Veteran

WE WILL BE THE NEXT PATROL

By Nikki Mendicino, 14 years old, 20 September 2001.

Today we attend this vigil not only to remember our POW/MIA's, but also to remember the date of the signing of the agreement that sealed their fate. January 27, 1973, twenty-nine years ago tomorrow, the Paris Peace Accords were signed and stated that all POW/MIA's would be released within 60 days. Twenty-nine years later, there are over 1900 soldiers who remain missing and we still have questions that have never been answered. In part, the Paris Peace Accords stated that *The Parties shall help each other to get information about those military personnel and foreign civilians missing in action, to determine the location and take care of the graves of the dead so as to facilitate the exhumation of the remains, and to take any such other measures as may be required to get information about those still considered missing in action.* What I really don't understand is when did this agreement end? Did it have a deadline that we missed and if not then why in 1978, only five years after the signing of the Paris Peace Accords, did our government declare all of the POW/MIA's killed in action and our efforts turned from rescue to recovery. I think it is about time that we hold our government accountable to this agreement that they entered into and even after 29 years, they must take such other measures as may be required to get information about those still considered MIA.

I would like also to speak about the events that have happened, that have changed our lives forever. September 11, 2001, a new day of infamy, a day of tragedy. We have learned that our very freedom, that all of you so bravely protected, is not immune from terrorist attacks. For the first time in our history, our county was shut down from coast to coast, and from border to border. As a nation, we must look to the future and understand what this means to our way of life. And to defeat this terrorism, we must rally behind our President, our military, our country and each other. We must stand as one, to prove to the world that we will not be controlled by fear. The politics of this country cannot be divided any longer. Once again, our country is at war and once again we could have POW/MIA's who never come home. I stand here before each and every one of you and ask, what you have done to help my generation understand that no soldier gets left behind and have you helped us learn that our freedom is not really free. You must teach us the past, so that we may lead the future. Kids my age don't know about Pearl Harbor, D-Day, or Iwo Jima. We've never heard about the Battle of the Bulge, the Freedom Bridge, or the TET Offenses and Desert Storm is ancient history, something that we were too young to remember. To us, the letters POW/MIA stand for *Powmia* a word we can pronounce, although we have no idea what it means and we don't really understand what a Veteran is. In my 8th grade Social Studies class we have learned about the Civil war, but we will never have time to reach any of the events of the 20th Century. Without you we may never know about WWI, WWII, Korea, Vietnam, the Persian Gulf, Somalia, Beirut, Kosovo or anywhere else that our country has deployed troops, including Afghanistan. September 11th will always be remembered, but to kids younger than me, the sacrifices of our troops in Afghanistan will be ancient history.

Please don't let your sacrifices be forgotten and please don't blame us because we don't know. Visit the schools, share your stories with us, tell us about the love, honor and duty you have for our country and our flag, help us honor those who served, help us honor the POW/MIA's who are still serving, help us honor those who died so that we can live in a free country and help us to understand the price that was paid for every freedom that we enjoy today. This new day of infamy, September 11, 2001, along with you teaching us about the events, and wars and sacrifices of the 20th Century can be the building blocks for kids like me to become the next *Greatest Generation*. If you guide us, share your stories with us and teach us, we will make a difference. My generation will care, we will never forget, and we will bring them home. We will be the Next Patrol. And hopefully, this new day of infamy will be the last this country ever sees.

I have taken a stance to support our troops, our veterans and our POW/MIA's all because one veteran told me his story about landing at Utah Beach on D-Day. If he had not shared that story with me I might not be speaking here today and I probably still wouldn't know what a veteran is. I'm not sure how much help I have been or how much of a difference I can make, but by the Grace of God, if I ever make it to the White House no soldier will ever be left behind, our POW/MIA's will be brought home and I would uphold the very first veterans benefit ever enacted, in the year 1636, which states if a soldier serves his country he shall be compensated for his sacrifices and his losses by the colonies for the rest of his natural lifetime. One simple sentence, four hundred years old that the politicians of today just don't seem to understand.

I would like to end with a short poem that has a very significant meaning, from a book titled *Patriot Hearts* that was sent to me by the author, Major William Coffey, Jr. God Bless you, God Bless the U.S.A. and Godspeed to all of our troops who have been called to defend our nation.

For us it was the six o'clock news
For them it was reality.
We called for pizza
They called for medics.
We watched children play
They watched children die.
We learned of life
They learned of death.
We served dinner
They served their country.
Our passion was success
Theirs was survival.
We forgot
They can't.
Author of Poem Unknown

Since we are sole depositories of the human liberty, our duty to ourselves, to posterity, and to mankind calls on us by every motive which is sacred or honorable, to watch over the safety of our beloved country during the troubles which agitate and convulse the residue of the world.

President Thomas Jefferson

Americans, indeed, all free men, remember that in the final choice a soldier's pack is not so heavy a burden as a prisoner's chain.

General Dwight D. *Ike* Eisenhower
Army General and U.S. President, 1890-1969

HERE I AM, SEND ME

The following speech was given by Navy Seaman Anthony McCarty at the graduation of the U.S. Navy's Information Specialist (IS) *A* School Class 90 on 31 May 2002.

Today I was asked to speak to you all, as a representative of Class 90. I was asked to speak on our reasons for joining, our inspiration, our spirit, and any wisdom we've picked up along the way. These are heart-felt subjects, full of emotion for all of us. Bear with me if I get a little corny.

I believe we all joined for our own reasons. After all, we came into the Navy as individuals. Whether it be because of money for college, patriotism, family tradition, need to prove oneself, or that Wendy's wasn't hiring, we all came into the service with our own hopes and dreams and desires. For whatever reasons we had, we all made the same decision, heard the same promises from our recruiter, signed on the same dotted line, and took the same oath. From that moment on, we were united by that choice, the choice to leave our friends, family and lives, and literally sail off to distant shores.

Joining when I did, I'd always asked if September 11th was the reason I joined the Navy. For more than a few of the sailors in the audience, I'm sure it was the reason. It was hard not to look at the scenes on TV and not want to do something, anything, to stop the things we all saw from ever happening again. I had already joined by then, I was in DEP (Delayed Entry Program) at the time. I was staring at the TV, and it slowly dawned on me that what I was seeing was what I would be up against for the next four years of my life. I realized that I would, more than likely, be going up against the people who did this.

Staring at the scene of the airliners ramming into the World Trade Center again and again, I felt like a kid who had been called out on a dare. I realized I would be responsible to stop things like this from happening again.

More than anything else here today, I hope that you grasp the fact that you matter. One day, or even everyday, you will be asked to make decisions that will change the world in some way. You will be asked to make a difference in someone's life, or the world in general. If you do a good job, then good things will happen. Do a bad job, and someone, somewhere, will pay for it.

Here at *A* School, we've heard time and again that we are at war. But it's a war unlike anything the Navy has fought before. It's not a war at sea, they have no Navy, and we have the greatest fleet that's ever been afloat.

It's not a war in the air, they have no air force, and we would fly circles around them even if they did. It's not a war on the land, they have no standing army as such, and when we do meet them on the ground, it's a matter of how few causalities we might take, not a matter of if we will win. This is a war fought in the caves of third world countries, in the streets of our major cities, in the communications in the airwaves, in the depths of the internet, in quiet nighttime covert operations, and on the screens of CNN. The only way they can beat us is by being smarter than us, trickier than us, by coming up with something we hadn't thought of, or hadn't prepared for. The only way they can beat us is by having better intelligence than us. In short, as the newest members of the Intelligence Community, the war is ours to win or lose.

Instead of running from this responsibility, I hope you embrace it. In the civilian world people do astounding things to prove to themselves that they matter, that the choices they make affect the world. They do almost anything to feel excitement and be challenged. They go to movies, they ride roller coasters, they abuse alcohol, they marry someone they shouldn't, they climb mountains, they join motorcycle clubs, and do anything at all to feel like their life has consequences and excitement in it. I think it would amaze most IS *A* students to find out how many people truly do envy you.

You're young, you're intelligent, you're in a war with a horrible enemy that needs to be stopped, and you're in a position to truly affect that conflict. You have the love and thanks of a grateful country. You have a job that can lead you to anywhere on Earth, doing anything. You have all the elements of a great story in your life. Without taking away from the seriousness of what you do, or sounding like a recruiting commercial, you truly have the chance to live an adventure, if you choose to look for it.

By far the greatest challenge in writing this speech was trying to define the spirit I've seen in both my class, *A* School, and the Navy as a whole. I've met so many people who give of themselves selflessly and seemingly on instinct. One person in particular I would like to thank is Chief Jordan, on behalf of all the BUD/S (Basic Underwater Demolition / School) candidates.

This is a man who wakes up every morning at 0330, Monday through Friday, and leads us in two hours of intense PT (Physical Training). He does this for no other reason than he doesn't want a group of young men to give their all and fail. But he is by no means the only person I've seen give themselves in small acts of heroism everyday.

I've seen the staff and instructors teach their trade with patience, humor, and devotion. I've seen it in my classmates and shipmates. It's humbling to look around you and see so many people who give of themselves. It makes you want to try harder to be a better person, just to fit in. I realize I don't have the words to grasp the spirit I've met in many of the people here at *A* School. There are some Eastern philosophies that teach that some ideas are too big for words, that we should never try to explain some truths, because one is doomed to never to be able to do them justice. All you do is demean it, turn it into some little sound bite. I feel that applies here. I'm not that poetic, I don't have the words. So, like any good writer with nothing to say, I plagiarized. There's one quote I have kept with me since I joined the Navy. Months before I left for Boot camp, I had the chance to go to Coronado, CA and tour the BUD/S facility. My recruiter was a SEAL and a BUD/S instructor, and he pulled some strings for me. There is a T-shirt shop in Coronado, one that sells shirts to all the members of various BUD/S classes. Each class has their own T-shirt design, and there is a book filled with all the patterns of the T-shirts, some of them going back decades. Most of them were Hoo-yah macho stuff, or funny little witticisms, but there was one that stood out in my mind. I memorized it, and put up in my locker at BUD/S.

It came the closest to capturing for me what it is to be in the Navy, and to do the job all of us in *A* School will start to do. On the back of the T-shirt was a silhouette of a lone man, holding a rifle, standing watch on a hill. Above him was a small quote, and these are the words I'll leave you with. It was quote from the Bible, Isaiah 6:8: *And I heard the voice of the Lord say, 'Whom shall I send, and whom will go for us?' Then I said, Here I am. Send Me.*

THE NATIONAL GUARD WIFE

Author Unknown.

A National Guard wife is mostly girl. But there are times, such as when her husband is away and she is mowing the lawn or fixing a flat tire on a youngster's bike that she begins to suspect she is also boy.

She usually comes in three sizes: petite, plump and pregnant. During the early years of her marriage, it is often hard to determine which size is her normal one.

At least one of her babies was born during annual summer training. This causes her to suspect that her husband planned it that way.

An ideal National Guard wife has the patience of an angel, the flexibility of putty, the wisdom of a scholar and the stamina of a horse. If she dislikes money, it helps.

One might say she is as bigamist, sharing her husband with a demanding entity called *duty*. When duty calls, she becomes No. 2 Wife. Until she accepts this fact, her life can be miserable. When she does accept it, she becomes a member of the Guard!

THE HAPPINESS AND LIBERTY OF MILLIONS

The Battle of Bunker Hill. 17 June 1775.

'Our country is in danger now, but not to be despaired of,'
the doctor encouraged the men of Massachusetts. 'On you
depends the fortunes of America. You are to decide the
important questions upon which rest the happiness and the
liberty of millions yet to be born. Act worthy of yourselves.'

Dr. Joseph Warren, 17 June 1775

ALWAYS, ALWAYS FOLLOW YOUR HEART

**Master Sergeant
Gary I. Gordon.**

In 1993, Master Sergeant Gary Gordon was killed trying to rescue a fellow soldier in Mogadishu, Somalia. For his heroic act he was posthumously awarded the Medal of Honor. His widow, Carmen, and their two children, Ian, 6, and Brittany, 3, live in Southern Pines, N.C. The following is Carmen's letter to her children explaining their father's responsibility:

My dearest Ian and Brittany,

I hope that in the final moments of your father's life, his last thoughts were not of us. As he lay dying, I wanted him to think only of the mission to which he pledged himself. As you grow older, if I can show you the love and responsibility he felt for his family, you will understand my feelings. I did not want him to think of me, or of you, because I did not want his heart to break.

Children were meant to have someone responsible for them. No father ever took that more seriously than your Dad. Responsibility was a natural part of him, an easy path to follow. Each day after work his truck pulled into our driveway. I watched the two of you run to him, feet pounding across the painted boards of our porch, yelling, *Daddy!* Every day, I saw his face when he saw you. You were the center of his life.

Ian, when you turned one-year-old, your father was beside himself with excitement, baking you a cake in the shape of a train. On your last birthday, Brittany, he sent you a hand-made birthday card from Somalia. But your father had two families. One was us, and the other was his comrades. He was true to both.

He loved his job. Quiet and serious adventure filled some part of him I could never fully know. After his death, one of his comrades told me that on a foreign mission, your dad led his men across a snow-covered ridge that began to collapse. Racing across a yawning crevasse to safety, he grinned wildly and yelled, *Wasn't that great?*

You will hear many times about how your father died. Your will read what the President of the United States said when he awarded the Medal of Honor: *Gary Gordon ... died in the most courageous and selfless way any human being can act.* But you may still ask why. You may ask how he could have been devoted to two families so equally, dying for one but leaving the other.

For your father, there were no hard choices in life. Once he committed to something, the way was clear. He chose to be a husband and father, and never wavered in those roles. He chose the military, and *I shall not fail those with whom I serve* became his simple religion, he did not hesitate, as he would not have hesitated for us. It may not have been the best thing for us, but it was the right thing for your Dad.

There are times now when that image of him coming home comes back to me. I see him scoop you up, Ian, and see you, Brittany, bury your head in his chest. I dread the day when you stop talking and asking about him, when he seems so long ago. So now I must take responsibility for keeping his life entwined with yours. It is a responsibility I never wanted.

But I know what your father would say, *Nothing you can do about it, Carmen. Just keep going.* Those times when the crying came, as I stood at the kitchen counter, were never long enough. You came in the front door, Brittany, saying, *Mommy, you sad? You miss Daddy?* You reminded me I had to keep going.

The ceremonies honoring your dad were hard. When they put his photo in the Hall of Heroes at the Pentagon, I thought, *can this be all that is left, a picture?* Then General Sullivan read from the letter General Sherman wrote to General Grant after the Civil War, words so tender that we all broke down. *Throughout the war, you were always in my mind. I always knew if I were in trouble and you were still alive you would come to my assistance.*

One night before either of you were born, your dad and I had a funny little talk about dying. I teased that I would now know where to bury him. Very quietly, he said, *Up home. In my uniform.* Your dad never liked to wear a uniform. And *up home*, Maine, was so far away from us.

Only after he was laid to rest in a tiny flag-filled graveyard in Lincoln, Maine, did I understand. His parents, burying their only son, could come tomorrow and the day after that. You and I would not have to pass his grave on the way to the grocery store, to Little League games, to ballet recitals. Our lives would go on. And to the men he loved and died for, the uniform was a silent salute, a final repeat of his vows. Once again, he had taken care of all of us.

On a spring afternoon, a soldier from your dad's unit brought me the things from his military locker. At the bottom of a cardboard box, beneath his boots, I found a letter. Written on a small, ruled tablet, it was his voice, quiet but confident in the words he wanted us to have if something should happen to him. I'll save it for you, but so much of him is already inside you both. Let it grow with you. Choose your own responsibilities in life but always, always follow your heart. Your dad will be watching over you, just as he always did.

Love,

Mom

The rest of the story, by Former Sergeant Major of the Army William Connelly stated:

During a raid in Mogadishu in October 1993, MSG Gary Gordon and SFC Randall Shughart, leader and member of a sniper team with Task Force Ranger in Somalia, were providing precision and suppressive fires from helicopters above two helicopter crash sites. Learning that no ground forces were available to rescue one of the downed aircrews and aware that a growing number of enemy were closing in on the site, MSG Gordon and SFC Shughart volunteered to be inserted to protect their critically wounded comrades. Their initial request was turned down because of the danger of the situation. They asked a second time; permission was denied. Only after their third request were they inserted. MSG Gordon and SFC Shughart were inserted one hundred meters south of the downed chopper. Armed only with their personal weapons, the two NCOs fought their way to the downed fliers through intense small arms fire, a maze of shanties and shacks, and the enemy converging on the site. After MSG Gordon and SFC Shughart pulled the wounded from the wreckage, they established a perimeter, put themselves in the most dangerous position, and fought off a series of attacks. The two NCOs continued to protect their comrades until they had depleted their ammunition and were themselves fatally wounded. Their actions saved the life of an Army pilot. No one will ever know what was running through the minds of MSG Gordon and SFC Shughart as they left the comparative safety of their helicopter to go to the aid of the downed aircrew. The two NCOs knew there was no ground rescue force available, and they certainly knew there was no going back to their helicopter. They may have suspected that things would turn out as they did; nonetheless, they did what they believed to be the right thing. They acted based on Army values, which they had clearly made their own: loyalty to their fellow soldiers; the duty to stand by them, regardless of the circumstances; the personal courage to act, even in the face of great danger; selfless service, the willingness to give their all. MSG Gary I. Gordon and SFC Randall D. Shughart lived Army values to the end; they were posthumously awarded Medals of Honor. The concept of professional courage does not always mean being as tough as nails either. It also suggests a willingness to listen to the soldiers' problems, to go to bat for them in a tough situation, and it means knowing just how far they can go. It also means being willing to tell the boss when he's wrong.

TO THE GOOD PEOPLE I WILL HELP

To the Morning Show with Ross & Mo, KILO 94.3:

I was fortunate enough to have been listening to your show this morning, February 19, 2003, when a man by the name of Carlton Manning called in to speak to you about the protests in Colorado Springs and the ensuing riot that occurred last week. If I understand correctly, Mr. Manning now has intentions to sue the City of Colorado Springs after having been gassed or shot by rubber bullets when he or his colleagues spit on a soldier or attacked a police officer, the details of which I missed. I could not listen to the course of the discussion, as I had a meeting to which I had to attend.

I took great interest in listening to the comments that Mr. Manning made about the current world situation, his views on the military, and even his comments toward the listeners and callers on the show. While most of the other callers had many negative things to say about Mr. Manning, or what should happen to him, I think that his comments were generally valid and his claims arguably just, albeit not entirely accurate. You see, I am a First Class Cadet, or Senior, at the United States Air Force Academy. For the sake of anonymity, I will not identify myself outside of that, for my views may not represent the Air Force as a whole. For the last four years I have been secluded from the world around me, protected from the hatred that has consumed men like Mr. Manning, so that I might better prepare my mind and body to one day fight and die for him and the principles and ideals that have shaped our great nation.

Because of this, and this may come as a surprise to many, I appreciate Mr. Manning's right to voice his opinion. While I may not agree with his actions and find his overly passionate statements to be ill conceived and lacking in reason, I understand that his ability to express himself is what makes our nation so great. The opportunity to speak out so freely against the government, its policies, and the military soldiers who fight to protect us is testament to the freedom that we have and cherish: freedom from tyranny, freedom from terror, freedom to speak one's mind, and freedom to live in a manner that allows each of us to reach his or her potential. And it is this right that I, along with the thousands of men and women of the armed forces of the United States, will fight for and risk our lives to protect. Mr. Manning is an American. And like him or not, I am privileged and duty-bound to protect him and other Americans from the evils that consume so much of this planet! It was, after all, no less an American than Thomas Jefferson who once stated that *the tree of liberty must be refreshed from time to time with the blood of patriots and tyrants.*

After being lambasted by a U.S. Marine from Fort Carson, an obviously passionate and patriotic soldier, Mr. Manning responded by stating *these people are uneducated and must always resort to violence.* His generalization could not have been more wrong. You see, military personnel are highly trained and its members highly educated. For example, service academy cadets receive a *classic liberal* education by being exposed to the humanities and sciences in an effort to produce well-rounded leaders. We spend countless days in class becoming educated in the ways of the world through the study of history, philosophy, leadership, and psychology. In fact, it is reputed that we cadets take more college courses than students at any other college in the nation. Perhaps it is for this reason that the Princeton Review ranks the Air Force Academy number three in the nation for *Best Overall Academic Experience for Undergraduates*. Many of my friends here were accepted to schools such as Harvard and Stanford, yet they chose to come here, not simply for an education, but due to a higher calling.

Mr. Manning is correct when he states that it has been his tax dollars that have given me such an exceptional education and opportunity for service. But it has not been his money, or his parent's money, alone, as all of the good people of this nation, including you and your listeners, have given your hard-earned dollar to buy a certain peace of mind. My education has been paid for by the allowances that you sacrifice for daily, putting up with long commutes, demanding bosses, and difficult deadlines. It has been your tax money that has allowed me to improve my mind and body so that I may better serve you and our nation.

In a matter of 100 days, I will be commissioned an officer in the United States Air Force. Shortly thereafter, I may be called to arms, as so many of my comrades in the military have been, with the prospect of risking life and limb on some foreign soil so that people like Mr. Manning can enjoy the luxury that my life has afforded them. This war will not be about oil, or better gas prices, or proving that America is the *tough guy on the block*. This war that I will fight essentially is one of good versus evil. Period. The nations that have been labeled the *axis of evil*, the nations that we stand and oppose, do not care about our just cause; they do not care about our good intentions; they care only about themselves and their *cause*. They see us as evil, wrong as this may be, and they have targeted America and our allies. They have targeted the citizens of this country, women, children, sons and daughters, even you, Mr. Manning. If given the opportunity, any opportunity, they will kill you, no matter your cause - because you are an American. And for you to assault the very peacemakers that now protect you and your cause boggles the mind. If you are so against this, then leave. Try voicing your protests in another country, see how well they'll respond to that. Because what I do must be done to ensure that the American people, no, the people of the world may rest well at night knowing that they are safe. It is this freedom that America will give to the world. It is this promise that I make to Mr. Manning.

In closing, I would like to leave you with two quotes that have summed up the sacrifices that others have made and that I will make so that people like Mr. Manning can call on one snowy Wednesday morning to exercise his freedoms. His words this morning have given these two quotes new meaning to me, and I will take this lesson to the far places that I will travel, to the good people I will help. Thank you for the great things that you had to say, you have reaffirmed my faith in the American people and the cause for which I chose to fight so that others like Mr. Manning do not have to. Thank you for your hope, and may God bless America and the world that we protect.

Very Respectfully,

Service Before Self

It is the soldier,
not the reporter who has
given us freedom of the press.

It is the soldier,
not the poet who has
given us freedom of speech.

It is the soldier,
not the campus organizer who has
given us freedom to demonstrate.

It is the soldier,
who salutes the flag,
who serves beneath the flag, and
whose coffin is draped by the flag
who allows the protester to burn the flag.

Father Dennis O'Brien, U.S. Marine Corps

A professional soldier understands that
war means killing people,
war means maiming people,
war means families left without fathers and brothers.
All you have to do is
hold your first dying soldier in your arms, and
have that terrible futile feeling that
his life is flowing out and
you can't do anything about it.
Then you understand the horror of war.
Any soldier worth his salt should be antiwar.
And still there are things worth fighting for.

General H. Norman Schwarzkopf, U.S. Army

I didn't know we still had people like this,
people who would sacrifice everything for their country.

President Jimmy Carter, speaking to Colonel Charles Beckwith
about his Special Forces soldiers in April 1980

*U*nder our institutions
each individual is born to sovereignty.
Whatever he may adopt as a means of livelihood,
his real business is serving his country.
He cannot hold himself above his fellow man.
The greatest place of command
is really the place of obedience,
and the greatest place of honor
is really the place of service.

President Calvin Coolidge

I SERVE BECAUSE …

Captain Clemens S. Kruse, U.S. Army, 2 July 2001. At the time this letter was written, Captain Kruse was a company commander at McDonald Army Community Hospital, Fort Eustis, Virginia. Courtesy of Army News Service.

I serve because a royal concept of mercantilism digressed into taxation without representation.

I serve because a common farmer, a colonial militia officer, a decent, ordinary man faced with extraordinary circumstances risked his life and livelihood when he entered a basement chamber in Philadelphia in the fall of 1774 to join the Continental Congress and became the father of our country.

I serve because a first lieutenant brought me coffee at 2 a.m. while I was on guard duty and asked me to talk through my concerns about accepting my nomination to a service academy.

*I serve because of the chills I felt during reveille
as a Boy Scout at Lake Arrowhead,
as a basic trainee at Fort Benning,
and as a new cadet at West Point.*

*I serve because of the chills I feel each day I have the
opportunity to honor my nation's colors at retreat.*

*I serve because of seven articles and 27 amendments that
serve as a 225-year-old experiment in government that
King George wrote off as a doomed system—that is today
emulated by every country introducing free trade.*

*I serve because I know my leaders will never ask me to
march into our legislative branch to establish new law,
as Oliver Cromwell's example.*

*I serve because my country's tremendous
wealth of resources and creativity
is balanced by philanthropic gestures
at home and abroad.*

*I serve to equally protect the idealisms of both
The Honorable Tom Daschle and Rush Limbaugh;
both Billy Graham and Larry Flint;
both Bill Gates and John Doe;
both Al Gore and Charlton Heston.*

*I serve to strengthen George Orwell's statement,
'We sleep safe in our beds because
rough men stand ready in the night
to visit violence on those who would do us harm.'*

*I serve because one million lawyers working today
constantly question and strengthen
the limits of our law—when our law becomes
unquestionable, I will have cause for concern.*

*I serve because
Khomeini, Qaddafi, Hitler,
Noriega, Hussein, Aidid, and Milosevic
are seldom satisfied without introducing
their tyranny and imperialism.*

*I serve because I want my children
to describe their father's job as defending their freedom.*

*I serve because the American public
has high expectations of protection and sanctity.*

*I serve because somebody has to, and
I feel I can do it better than most.*

BACKBONE OF THE NAVY

Author Unknown.

One day a Naval Officer passed by a work station and spotted a Chief Petty Officer (CPO) who had just given the command, *Fall-out, carry out the Plan of the Day.* Impressed by the CPO's command presence he asked, *Have you ever thought about becoming an officer?* In response, the Chief asked:

> Do you know who I am? Do you really know who I am and what I do? I am the backbone of the Navy. My fellow enlisted Sailors and I keep our Navy running. Without us, you don't have a Navy ... you have a group of officers with no one to lead, delegate to, or command. I am more than 100,000 strong. In times of need I've done your job, especially during times of war. Without me, you can't go to war.
>
> The next time you ask a Chief Petty Officer about becoming an officer, ask yourself, Can the Navy afford to lose this CPO from its ranks? I'm all for the *grow your own* concept, but

sometimes robbing one pot to fill another is not the right way to do things.

And if you still feel the need to ask the question of a Chief Petty Officer, be careful how you ask it because sometimes, intentionally or not, it comes off condescending and insulting. I don't know how many times an officer has asked me, 'Why didn't you ever apply for an officer program? It's not too late.' As if by not doing this, I have somehow wasted my time in the Navy or settled for less.

I've settled for nothing and worked damn hard to get where I am. I aspire to be exactly what I am, and strive daily to improve myself, and those around me. I have never regretted being an enlisted Sailor.

So, again I ask, *Do you know who I am?* Obviously you don't or you never would have asked me about becoming an officer. You would have known that you were asking me to give all this up for a salute and a bigger paycheck. For many of us, the price of becoming an officer is just too high.

Now, let me ask you a question, *Have you ever thought of giving up your commission and becoming a Chief?* If that offends you, think about how I feel when you ask me the same thing.

CHAPTER 2
Selflessness, Sacrifice and Compassion

The willingness to put the welfare of this nation before one's own welfare is the focus of this chapter. This chapter also discusses the selfless sacrifices America made and the compassion felt for those who sacrificed themselves for our nation.

1st Brigade, 101st Airborne Division (Air Assault). Soldiers mourn the loss of Capt. Christopher Seifert, ceremony 24 March 2003, Camp Pennsylvania, Kuwait, Operation Iraqi Freedom. Photo by PFC James Matise.

They summed up and perfected, by one supreme act, the highest virtues of men and citizens. For love of country they accepted death, and thus resolved all doubts, and made immortal their patriotism and virtue.

General James A. Garfield

We make a living by what we do ...but we make a life by what we give.

Sir Winston Churchill

WELCOME HOME WARRIORS

Chattanooga Girls Choir. Singing to a group of about 200 Marines who were on their way home from combat in Iraq.

While our military personnel may not be welcomed home by ticker-tape parades in this era, the welcomes they do get are often more meaningful. For example, on June 6, 2003, in the Atlanta airport, amid all the hustle in this massive hub, members of the Chattanooga Girls Choir were waiting for their connecting flight to Vienna when they noticed a couple hundred Marines in a staging area. After spending six months fighting in Iraq, the warriors were in transit from Iraq to their home base in California. To show their appreciation, the choir group went to the staging area where they spontaneously and proudly performed *America the Beautiful.* When they finished, the Marines responded with uproarious approval. The young performers noted, *The sound was so loud that it startled us and it was a moment we will remember and cherish all our lives.* After the Marines said *thank you,* in only a way Marines can, many of the choir girls spoke with the Marines and said *thank you* back to the Marines for their service to our country.

THE NIGHT THEY BROUGHT CAPTAIN WASKOW DOWN

The following is the full text of the winning entry of the U.S. Army Writing Contest, sponsored by the Army Chief of Staff. It is a story written by Major Forrest W. Aurentz, S-2/S-3 of the 4th Training Brigade. The story was inspired by correspondence from the World War II writer, Ernie Pyle. It was originally written while Aurentz was enrolled in the Armed Forces Staff College, Norfolk, Virginia. He was required to write a paper explaining his personal philosophies on leadership. This was published in *The Turret*, Fort Knox, Kentucky, November 1986.

This one is Captain Waskow, one of them said quietly. Two men unlashed his body from the mule and lifted it off and laid it in the shadow beside the stone wall. The men in the lead seemed reluctant to leave. They stood around, and gradually I could sense them moving, one by one, close to Captain Waskow's body. Not so much to look I think, as to say something in finality to him and to themselves. I stood close by and I could hear. One soldier came and looked down, and he said out loud, *God damn it*. Another man came. I think he was an officer. It was hard to tell officers from enlisted men in the dim light, for everybody was bearded and grimy. The man looked down into the dead captain's face and spoke directly to him, as though he were alive, *I'm sorry, old man*. Then a soldier came and stood beside the officer and bent over, and he too spoke to his dead captain, not in a whisper but awfully tenderly, and he said, *I sure am sorry, sir*. Then the first man squatted down, and he sat there for a full five minutes holding the dead hand in his own and looking intently into the dead face. And he never uttered a sound all the time he sat there.

Finally, he put the hand down. He reached over and gently straightened the point of the captain's shirt collar, and then he sort of rearranged the tattered edges of the uniform around the wound, and then he got up and walked down the road in the moonlight, all alone.

Ernie Pyle, Italy–1944.

I remember the Captain. I was a very young soldier in the Continental Line.

All was dark and silent as we stood close to the river's edge waiting for our call to move forward. As a private, I knew little of where we were going. Our clothes, not really uniforms, were turning white as a fine sprinkling of snow fell upon us. We could look down from our positions in the column on the riverbank and see murky figures steadying long, strange-looking boats as ragged soldiers boarded. They huddled forlornly in the bitter cold.

In uneasy shuffles, we moved closer to what we all dreaded. Regardless of where it would happen, we knew that within a few hours the calm would vanish in terrible shouts and exploding flashes. Men would die—we were all very afraid.

While we waited our turn to enter the boats, I saw the Captain near a group of finely dressed officers. A tattered piece of white ribbon in his hat was the only visible sign that he was an officer in the Continental Army. His skinny legs were shaking violently from the cold wind coming from the river.

We continued to move carefully down the slopes that hundreds of men had transformed into a muddy mire. As we got closer, I could see that the Captain was with our regimental commander and several staff officers. Although the Captain was near this small group of important men, he was paying little attention to their fitful gestures and low-toned commands.

He was smiling, at least we all thought he was smiling, and his voice quivered with excitement. He greeted each of us in turn. We knew that he was making a final effort to relieve our fear. As I approached, I could hear him say to the man in front of me how proud he was of our company. Still, due to the cold, I was not paying much attention to his encouragements. I had a gaping hole in the bottom of my right shoe, and the freezing mud was my main concern.

I stepped forward and felt his uncovered hand on my shoulder. I could just make out his face as he asked in a quiet voice whether I had gotten the hole in my shoe fixed. I lied and said that I had. There were other men in other companies who had wrapped linen around their feet to serve as shoes, so I was not about to complain.

Fine, no soldier in our company should go without good shoes, he answered in a firm voice. *Merry Christmas, Captain*, I said. *Merry Christmas*, he replied.

Trenton was our destination. We won a crucial victory for our faltering revolution. Many things happened in that battle, but the things I remember most were the Captain's hand on my shoulder, his smile, and his concern for us as individuals. We were afraid and he was concerned. Officers sometimes spend too much time looking up the chain of command and not enough down it. Not my Captain.

Texas–1877.

I remember the Captain. I was a corporal in his cavalry troop. He was courageous, forthright, competent, and possessed a quick mind; but he was not a person you would pick out from a crowd as a born leader. He had all the qualities of a good officer, but he was also rather quiet.

I remember the time we conducted a patrol in the New Mexico territory. One of the sergeants described our location as 100 miles from trees, 50 miles from water, and 1 mile from hell. We were all filthy, bearded, hungry, and thirsty from the grueling pursuit of a small raiding party of Comanches.

Congress had not seen fit to pay the Army for over five months, so the men were not too anxious to find, much less fight, any Indians. As we were returning to Fort Davis, the Captain rode down the column to check on us. One young trooper immediately in front of me couldn't control his built-up anger and frustrations. He shouted out as the Captain rode past, *Cap'n, we could die out here and nobody would give a damn.*

The Captain wheeled his horse and rode beside the young soldier. He never said a word for over twenty miles. He brushed the dust from his uniform and adjusted his yellow scarf. He always liked to keep his uniform in perfect order.

I could tell the trooper was getting anxious. He gave the Captain nervous, fleeting glances and began adjusting perfectly situated items on his saddle.

Finally, the Captain said, *I would. Is that enough?*

Yes sir, the trooper meekly responded.

I think, the Captain began. Then he paused, and remained silent for a moment. He removed his hat and mopped his brow. I noticed how blond his hair was in the bright sunlight.

I think you're an awfully brave soldier, he said.

I saw a faint smile on the young soldier's face as their eyes met. The Captain then returned to the head of the column.

I remember the Captain. I remember how he could have told that trooper to keep quiet or have given him some long patriotic harangue. He could have been impatient; instead, he took the time to tell an impetuous recruit what we veterans already knew. Some captains merely tell soldier to be quiet. Not my Captain.

France–1918.

I remember the Captain. I was the administrative sergeant in his company. *Rock of the Marne* is what the newspapers called us.

Bewildered and exhausted, we had settled into the village of Passelle only two days prior. After fighting for three straight weeks, rest was our main need.

The Captain had slept the first day, but he had been drafting letters to mothers, fathers, and wives since then. He was new at writing condolence letters, and he was not making much progress. There were so many letters to write.

I read the first letter that he wrote. It contained a lot of phrases such as *finest traditions of the United States Army, sacrifice above and beyond,* and *I was proud to lead him into battle.* After writing that letter, he asked me to make copies of it for his signature. He said that it would serve as the pattern for all others.

As I was about to finish the first copy, the Captain entered my tent and politely asked me to return the letter. He left and began to write again. I never copied another letter for him.

I saw one of his later letters. You should listen carefully to his words.

7 July 1918
Dear Mr. and Mrs. Haroldson,

I have the very sad task of informing you of the death of your son SGT Steven Haroldson on July 2, 1918, near Vaux, France. We will all miss him dearly.

I know that these few words will do little to help you bear the grief of Steven's death, but I would like to share some of my thoughts of him.

Steven did not like soldiering. I knew that. He was, however, proud to be a soldier. I remember his wide-eyed excitement at being in France, his roaring laughter, and his sincere concern for the soldiers of his squad. I remember his love of poetry. Only last week, he gave me a book of poetry by Rudyard Kipling. I shall always treasure it.

The saddest thing is for a soldier to die anonymously. To die is hard enough, but to give your life for others and not be

individually recognized is truly sad. I want you to know that we have not forgotten Steven. None of us ever will.
Company Commander

I remember that Captain. We all knew that he would not let us be forgotten. That means a lot to young soldiers, and old ones too. He could have sent a standard letter, or no letter at all. Not my Captain.

Norfolk–1986.

I remember the Captain. I was his First Sergeant. I first met him at Kasserine Pass in North Africa when he was a lieutenant and I was his platoon sergeant. We were getting our butts kicked, and several of the men were running anywhere the Germans weren't. I looked up from my foxhole and saw two skinny legs attached to a second looie's bar standing in front of me.

Sergeant, he said to me in a calm voice, *good men are acting like cowards. We only have men in our platoon–not cowards. Now get up from there and let's remind them of that.*

He was as scared as the rest of us, but we believed that he was brave. I asked him about it later. He smiled and quoted a Frenchman–something about realizing that courage of troops must be reborn daily. But, you should have seen those skinny legs shaking after the battle was over.

I also remember the high standards of appearance, discipline, and training that he set for us. We were just plain *dogface* infantrymen–nothing special like the Marines or airborne. But, he made us think that we were special; and we all knew that he was someone very special.

He could have used his rank for privilege; instead, he served with us. He was firm, but also fair; he was proud, but not vain; he was courteous, but not timid. He was an extraordinary leader of ordinary men.

The Captain always carried a small book of poems by Rudyard Kipling. I found it on his body when they brought him down from the mountains. Marking the poem *If* was an old tattered white ribbon and a torn piece of yellow cloth with crossed cavalry sabers on it. I later found out that they were relics from his father and grandfathers who had served as soldiers all the way back to the Revolution. I sent them, along with his captain's bars, to his son.

Yes, I remember that night in Italy over forty-two years ago when they brought his body down. I held his hand, gazed into his face, and silently thanked him for being such a fine soldier. I had never done that when he was alive. I hope he somehow heard my thoughts that night. *Thanks my Captain—thanks for caring.*

THOUGHTS FROM A FATHER'S HEART

From Robert B. Hager.

It's been about a week since the day that has changed our lives [September 11, 2001]. I'm wondering if you too are wrestling with these thoughts ... When I pause & realize the full impact of what that event has caused, what this declaration of war (which was rightly called in my opinion) may require of us in personal sacrifices, as a nation and as individuals, I find myself pondering whether this generation has the metal to muster up to the call. Oh, I suspect they will. Yet, I also find myself watching our four boys as they play with their friends and can't help but recall the movie *The Patriot* and the price of this precious gift of freedom. And, watching our boys playing in their innocence, I reflect on the book *Flags of Our Fathers*. Ya know, it wasn't but a few years before, that those Marines who raised that flag at Iwo Jima were merely young boys like ours. Going to school, delivering papers, playing baseball and other games late into the evenings with their friends. Then rising to the call of our country, as I did when I was called. But that call was for me to be a warrior. I wonder ... I wonder if *I* will be able to muster up to the personal sacrifices that may be extracted from me now, as a father. As I deal with these fatherly heart pangs, I let them enjoy the naiveté of their boyhood, laughing and playing into the twilight with their neighborhood friends. Perhaps allowing them a few more minutes than I should before calling them in to start their homework. *For those who have fought for it, Freedom has a flavor the protected will never know ....*

... That man will not merely endure, he will prevail,
because he alone among the creatures has a spirit capable of
compassion, of sacrifice and endurance.

William Faulkner

IF I SHOULD DIE TOMORROW

If I should die tomorrow,
Let it not be said I died forgotten,
For I have done what I can do.
My country called.
I served in uniform.
World War I. World War II. Korea. Vietnam. The Cold War.
And hot spots around the globe.
I served with pride, fear, dreams of glory, heroism,
determination, and hope.
I fought beside some of the best men I ever knew.
Not all of us made it home.
I carry those I knew in my mind and heart, and soul.
I came home to cheers or jeers or silence.
But I'll never forget.
It changed my life forever.
Will anyone remember?
I must believe they will.
For those long days and endless nights
Shaped how I see the world
And, I think, how the world sees me.
My actions alone changed nothing.
In concert with my fellow soldiers we changed, and made, history.
Duty, Honor, Country.
If I should die tomorrow
Let it not be said I died forgotten,
For I have done what I can do.

Author Unknown

A MOTHER'S PRAYER

God, Father of Freedom, look after that boy of mine, wherever he may be. Walk in upon him. Keep his mind stayed on Thee. Talk with him during the silent watches of the night, and spur him to bravery whenever called upon to face the cruel foe. Transfer my prayer to his heart, that he may know the lingering love I have bequeathed to him as an everlasting gift. Keep my boy contented and inspired by the never dying faith in his mother's God. He is my gift to freedom. May that freedom forever remain untarnished, God. Through the lonely and confusing hours of training and combat, and throughout all the long days of a hopeful victory, keep his spirit high and his purpose unwavering. Make him a proud pal to all with whom he comes in contact and make his influence a noonday light wherever his duty takes him. Satisfy the hunger of his soul with the knowledge of this daily prayer of mine. To my country, O Heavenly Father, have I bequeathed this boy of mine. He is my choicest treasure. Take care of him, God. Keep him in health and sustain him under every possible circumstance of events. Warm him anew under his shelter and under the stars. Touch him with my smile of cheer and comfort and my full confidence in his every brave pursuit. Silent and alone, I pray, God, but I am only one of millions of mothers, whose prayers stream day and night to You. This is our Gethsemani. Lead us victoriously through it, God. And lead that boy of mine through this. Fail him not … and may he not fail You, his country, nor his mother. God, our Father, look after that boy of mine.

*T*he soldier prays
for peace above all,
because it is the soldier
that pays the greatest price.

General Douglas MacArthur, Army General
World War I, World War II, Korean War 1880-1964

HE ASKED TO JOIN THE ARMY FAMILY

Ten-Year-Old Army Sergeant Loses Battle, Wins Hearts, by Specialist Chuck Wagner, Army News Service, 15 January 2003.

Sgt. Justin Bryce made the most of his time as a soldier during his visit to the Pentagon and Fort Belvoir, Va., in October. The headstone will be inscribed *Sgt. Justin Bryce*, even though the dates will show he was much too young to enlist.

His teary-eyed mother's description of him explains how a ten-year-old deserved every chevron.

He was a brave little boy. It didn't matter what struggle he had to go through, he just faced them. I think the way he used to look at it was that no matter how tough life seems, you can still overcome everything. And he always had a smile, said Mary Bryce from the family's Grene, N.Y. home.

Justin knew something about struggles. He spent months battling liver cancer, which spread and wracked his small body.

Justin's request to the Make-A-Wish foundation was to outrank his brother, Pvt. Raymond Bryce of 10th Mountain Division, Fort Drum, N.Y. Secretary of Defense Donald Rumsfeld told the Army to make it happen.

Over a few blustery November days, Justin enlisted and was promoted at the Pentagon, climbed around inside an opulent limousine on his way to Fort Belvoir where he shot an M-16 with night-vision goggles and commanded an M-111 personnel carrier. Near day's end, the Army whisked him over Washington aboard a Blackhawk in a last-minute, unscheduled flight because soldiers heard him ask, *Can I fly in a helicopter?*

He rested that evening looking out over Baltimore Harbor aboard a Coast Guard ship. Ships, you see, were another of Justin's passions.

Even up to a couple of days before, he was still calling himself sergeant, his mother said.

Justin, unresponsive over Christmas Eve, died at home Christmas day surrounded by the entire extended family.

Scores of friends visited him during calling hours on December 28. Six National Guard soldiers from a local armory took turns standing vigil for four hours. The family dressed Justin in the battle dress uniform issued to him and hung his ID tags around his neck. His mother shined his boots.

Services were held for the family the next day. Justin's formal burial is planned in spring.

Instead of seeing Disney World, Justin had asked to join the Army family. His mother says he quickly realized how the Army takes care of its own.

More than 40,000 people have logged on the Web site www.caringbridge.org/ny/justinbryce, to read about Justin and leave messages for him and his family. Many of the messages, as well as hundreds of e-mails to his mother, are from service members. More arrive every day.

Sgt. Justin, keep fighting and it was my honor to get to know you and my pleasure to serve with you in the Army, wrote 1st Sgt. Lee Branham before Christmas.

May God give you strength to carry on each passing day. God Bless You, Staff Sgt. Gerald Canada wrote to the family after Justin's funeral.

His mother prints out e-mailed letters from service members to put in Justin's keepsake book, which is bulging with notes, autographs, and pictures of a proud, bald, freckled sergeant surrounded by his Army buddies.

It touches my heart. You guys are very, very caring. Justin picked the right group of people, Mary said.

Sergeant Justin Bryce. Photo taken during his day touring the Pentagon by Peter Cihelka, Fort Myer, Virginia.

It should be the highest ambition of every American to extend his views beyond himself, and to bear in mind that his conduct will not only affect himself, his country, and his immediate posterity; but that its influence may be co-extensive with the world, and stamp political happiness or misery on ages yet unborn.

President George Washington
Continental Army General

Americans have always made sacrifices in the service of their country ... Americans like both of my grandfathers– one a paratrooper on D-Day in Normandy, the other a 20-year veteran of the Air Force–two cousins who are serving in the Marines, and my uncle who is flying an AC-130 gunship in Afghanistan. I'm ready, too.

Seventeen-year-old Luke Davis, 2002

The ultimate test of a man's conscience may be his willingness to sacrifice something today for future generations whose words of thanks will not be heard.

Gaylord Nelson

Far and away the best prize that life offers is the chance to work hard at work worth doing.

President Theodore Roosevelt

The greatest high you can get in life is by helping somebody.

Timothy Stackpole, New York City firefighter who perished while rescuing people in the World Trade Center attacks

THE CHRISTMAS CARD MYSTERY

Every Christmas since 1945, the parents of a young soldier killed at Okinawa had received an unsigned card. It read only, *I, too, have not forgotten*. Then in 1950, they received a letter explaining the mystery with a most heartwarming document. The letter read:

This year I am not sending a card, but an explanation. Perhaps I have been too mysterious, but I was ashamed to sign those cards. You see, your son Carl gave his life to save mine. He was a wonderful guy and had so much to live for. For five years I have searched for the reason: I knew there must be some purpose I was to fulfill. Some months ago I found the answer. I had gone back into the Army a year ago, and two months back I received some replacement in my company. One of them was Carl's kid brother, your youngest boy, Edward. Out of millions that might have been sent, I got Eddie. I feel better, I'll fight better, and let me tell you—I'll take care of that boy. Carl knows it, and I wanted you to know.

From The Executive Speechwriter Newsletter

PRESIDENT BUSH'S STATE OF THE UNION LETTER TO CHILDREN

January 29, 2002

Dear Young Americans:

Since September 11, 2001, many of you have sent cards, letters, and drawings to express your love for our great Nation and for the families of the victims. Thank you for sharing your thoughts and ideas with me. I asked you to send a dollar to help the children of Afghanistan in October. I was moved by the response of our children, and I was particularly touched by an eight-year-old's desire to *help heal their hearts* by baking and selling heart-shaped cookies to raise money for the Afghan children. More than $2 million has been raised so far, and the first shipment of tents, clothing, and school supplies arrived in Afghanistan in December. Thank you for your efforts to

help those in need. I am proud of you. The events of last September have reminded us of the value of the things that matter most in life: our faith, our love for family and friends, and our Nation's freedoms. I particularly want you to understand that the war we are fighting against terrorism is about your future, and the future of our country. We fight to protect America, so that you and other young Americans can pursue your dreams and grow up in peace and freedom. We fight for all freedom-loving people throughout the world. I recently gave my State of the Union message to Congress, and this is my message to you: Work hard. Read. Make the right choices, and follow your dreams. Mrs. Bush joins me in sending our warmest wishes to you, your family, and friends. God bless you, and God bless America.
Sincerely, George W. Bush

THE FIRST LADY'S LETTER TO THE CHILDREN OF AMERICA

September 12, 2001

Dear Children:

Many Americans were injured or lost their lives in the recent national tragedy. All their friends and loved ones are feeling very sad, and you may be feeling sad, frightened, or confused, too.

I want to reassure you that many people–including your family, your teachers, and your school counselor–love and care about you and are looking out for your safety. You can talk with them and ask them questions. You can also write down your thoughts or draw a picture that shows how you are feeling and share that with the adults in your life. When sad or frightening things happen, all of us have an opportunity to become better people by thinking about others. We can show them we care about them by saying so and by doing nice things for them. Helping others will make you feel better, too. I want you to know how much I care about all of you. Be kind to each other, take care of each other, and show your love for each other.
With best wishes, Laura Bush

THE SULLIVAN BROTHERS

**Brothers, Joseph, Francis, Albert,
Madison and George.** From Waterloo, Iowa.

President Roosevelt sent the following letter. All were killed when their ship was sunk by a Japanese submarine, 13 November 1942.

February 1, 1943
Dear Mr. and Mrs. Sullivan:

The knowledge that your five gallant sons are missing in action against the enemy inspires me to write you this personal message. I realize full well there is little I can say to assuage your grief.

As Commander-in-Chief of the Army and Navy, I want you to know that the entire nation shares in your sorrow. I offer you the gratitude of our country. We who remain to carry on the fight will maintain a courageous spirit, in the knowledge that such sacrifice is not in vain.

The Navy Department has informed me of the expressed desire of your sons, George Thomas, Francis Henry, Joseph Eugene, Madison Abel, and Albert Leo, to serve on the same ship. I am sure that we all take heart in the knowledge that they fought side by side. As one of your sons wrote, *We will make a team together that can't be beat.* It is this spirit which in the end must triumph.

I send you my deepest sympathy in our hour of trial and pray that in Almighty God you will find the comfort and help that only He can bring.

Very Sincerely yours, Franklin D. Roosevelt

*I may be compelled to face danger, but never
fear it, and while our soldiers can stand and fight,
I can stand and feed and nurse them.*

Clara Barton, *The Angel of the Battlefield*
Founder of the American Red Cross

*We worked long, arduous hours with little recreation,
doing the job we were sent to do. We mended our boys'
broken bodies, comforted, loved, and laughed with them ...
Our country needed us. It was simple as that.*

Marjorie LaPalme Faneuf

*The ones that didn't make it were never left alone.
One of us would make sure they were as comfortable as possible
and just sit next to them and hold their hand as they died.
To the best of our ability, none of our guys died alone.*

Army Nurse, Author Unknown

*The loss of one human life is intolerable to any of us
who are in the military. But, I would tell you that casualties
of that order of magnitude [Operation Desert Storm], considering
the job that's been done and the number of forces that are
involved, is almost miraculous ... It will never be miraculous for
the families of those people, but it is miraculous.*

General H. Norman Schwarzkopf

*People fight honorably for what they believe in,
and they lose their lives. No one has the right to say that those
lives were wasted. I think that would be a travesty.*

President William Clinton

THEY DIED FOR US

Memorial Service for Fallen Comrades.
Landing Zone Betty, Vietnam.

These heroes are dead.
They died for liberty–they died for us. They are at rest.
They sleep in the land they made free, under the flag
they rendered stainless, under the solemn pines,
the sad hemlocks, the tearful willows, the embracing vines.
They sleep beneath the shadows of the clouds,
careless alike of sunshine or storm,
each in the windowless palace of rest.
Earth may run red with other wars–they are at peace.
In the midst of battles, in the roar of conflict,
they found the serenity of death.

R.G. Ingersoll

Flight 93 redefined sacrifice for me. If a handful of people will
drive an airplane into the ground to save either me, or the
White House, or the Congress, you know others in our country will
make the sacrifice to save us down the road.

President George W. Bush

COMMANDANT'S LETTER TO A PILOT'S SON

General James Jones.

Below is a letter from General James L. Jones, Commandant of the Marine Corps, to a thirteen-year-old boy who lost his Marine Corps aviator father to a plane crash ten years ago. These words of caring and compassion are hard to beat. The sacrifices we as a nation must continue to make are immense, yet imperative.

There can never be a substitute for the loss of a father. But this goes far (I believe) in putting the tragic loss in perspective. As this young boy continues to grow and mature, I believe the letter will continue to generate emotional strength and support for him. The original sender of this letter notes: *Experienced a rich blessing today. I met my wife in 1988 through a Marine pilot married to her sister. He died in a crash in October 1991, just weeks after returning from Desert Storm. The crash was caused by a maintenance contractor using a batch of oil that had caused a previous crash and was supposed to have been destroyed. Senseless tragedy. I was able to give their son Sean, now 13, a tour of the Pentagon today. The best part was when the Marines gave him a tour of the Commandant's office, then presented him with the letter below, signed by the Commandant. Sean says it was the best part of a two-week trip to the East and on the way to the airport was treating that letter like it was the Hope diamond. I'm just awestruck once again, by the human compassion, grace and goodness displayed by the Marines.*

16 July 2001
Dear Sean,

You have lived ten years–most of your boyhood–without your father's presence. You and your mother are commended for a difficult job well done. In the next ten years you will face the greater challenge of becoming a man. Your father loved to fly and it was his dream to be a good pilot and a good Marine.

In the coming years, you must also discover what you love and strive to do it with excellence. Marines are built through the ethos of struggle and sacrifice. Many, like your father, have sacrificed all.

The nation expects her Marines to succeed under the most trying conditions in some of the toughest places on earth.

From deserts, to jungles, to mountains and war-torn cities, we must be rugged and strong to persevere, but we don't stand alone. We persevere and succeed as a team.

As you grow up without your father, you too live daily with struggle and sacrifice. I charge you to grow rugged and strong through this, but with the knowledge that you don't face these struggles alone.

Walk with people who help you learn to thrive in the tough places. Your father succeeded in becoming a good pilot, a good Marine, and a good man. As you grow into manhood, seek out and listen to good men who can help you along the path you have chosen.

Find friends who are also committed to becoming good men, friends that can walk the path with you. Your father loved, respected and cared for your mother. He was the man of your family, and your mother trusted him above all men. Now you are the man of the family and are charged with loving, respecting and caring for your mother, and earning and guarding the trust she places in you.

Remain faithful to the service and sacrifice and courage your father valued. That is his dream for you. Semper Fidelis.
James L. Jones, General, U.S. Marine Corps, Commandant

Now, we have inscribed a new memory alongside those others.
It's a memory of tragedy and shock, of loss and mourning.
But not only of loss and mourning. It's also a memory of bravery
and self-sacrifice, and the love that lays down its life
for a friend—even a friend whose name it never knew.

President George W. Bush, 11 December 2001

Those who have long enjoyed such privileges as we enjoy
forget in time that men have died to win them.

President Franklin D. Roosevelt

American World War II Poster.

The currency with which you pay for peace is made up of manly courage, fearless virility, readiness to serve justice and honor at any cost, and a heart attuned to sacrifice.

Frank Knox

THANK YOU, MARINES

From PO1 Stewart, formerly of the *USS Cole, Thank you, Marines.*

Good morning, ladies and gentlemen:

Yesterday afternoon around 15:10, some of you may have seen me standing in front of my office with a female Navy Petty Officer 1st Class (PO1). She was wearing her dungaree uniform. She was shaking, she was crying, and it was obvious that she was in severe emotional pain. You may have seen me hug her, you may have seen us talk for about four minutes until she turned and left the building. Four minutes is not very long, but those were four of the most eye-opening minutes I have ever experienced as a U.S. Marine.

The Petty Officer entered the front hatch of MATSG-33 looking confused and distraught. Thinking she was just another sailor looking for directions somewhere aboard NAS Oceana, I walked out of my office and greeted her and asked if I could help her. The name on her shirt said *Stewart*. PO1 Stewart remained silent and stationary, staring blankly at the deck. I asked her if everything was okay. Her hands started shaking and her bottom lip started to quiver as tears started streaming down her face. She just stood there, clutching her cover tightly in both hands as she cried silently for about twenty seconds before she could manage to get a word out. I was feeling helpless at this point because I had no idea what to say to her without knowing what was wrong. After she told me, I still had no idea what to say. I was just proud to be a Marine.

Through choked-back tears, PO1 Stewart told me why she came to MATSG-33. She said she was talking with four of her closest friends one day while they were on ship last October. Their ship was the *USS Cole*. She said that it all happened so quickly. One moment they were talking as usual and the next moment, all four of her friends were lying beside her, and she was the only one alive. PO1 Stewart said the real terror sunk in moments after the explosion, after she saw the dead, soot covered bodies of her friends, when she realized that at any moment, another explosion may take the lives of more of her shipmates or her own. She said she was so afraid that the terrorists weren't finished with them yet. Then she saw the Marines. The Marines came and secured the area. The Marines came and secured the survivors. PO1 Stewart said that she knew, and everyone on the *USS Cole* knew, that the terrorists had got their one deadly shot in, but no more lives would be lost that day while the Marines were there.

I know that it was one of the FAST companies that responded that day. PO1 Stewart only knows that it was the Marines. I used to be an infantryman and part of the Marine Security Force, but that was five years ago. I have never set foot on the *USS Cole* or patrolled its surrounding waters. The day the *USS Cole* was bombed, I was sitting at a desk doing paperwork on a quiet Navy Base in Virginia Beach. Yet on an ordinary summer day, a Navy Petty Officer 1st Class who felt the explosion of the *USS Cole* and saw her shipmates die before her, walked into

Marine Aviation Training Support Group-33 to find any Marine who she could look in the face and say thank you.

I was choked up and absolutely stunned by what I had just heard. I hugged PO1 Stewart and I offered to contact the FAST companies to locate the Marines who responded that day, but she told me that she was retiring this week and this was closure for her. By saying thank you to a Marine, she is ready to try and move on from her nightmare. I told her that I would extend her thanks. PO1 Stewart said thank you once more, turned and walked out of MATSG-33. I sat back down in the chair of my quiet office and continued my paperwork–with a much better view of the big picture.

THE DIFFERENCE

Over the years, I've talked a lot about military spouses ... how special they are and the price they pay for freedom too. The funny thing is most military spouses don't consider themselves different from other spouses. They do what they have to do, bound together not by blood or merely friendship, but with a shared spirit whose origin is in the very essence of what love truly is. Is there truly a difference? I think there is. You have to decide for yourself.

Other spouses get married and look forward to building equity in a home and putting down family roots. Military spouses get married and know they'll live in base housing or rent, and their roots must be short so they can be transplanted frequently.

Other spouses decorate a home with flair and personality that will last a lifetime. Military spouses decorate a home with flare tempered with the knowledge that no two base houses have the same size windows or same size rooms. Curtains have to be flexible and multiple sets are a plus. Furniture must fit like puzzle pieces.

Other spouses have living rooms that are immaculate and seldom used. Military spouses have immaculate living room/dining room combos. The coffee table got a scratch or two moving from Germany, but it still looks pretty good.

Other spouses say good-bye to their spouse for a business trip and know they won't see them for a week. They are lonely, but can survive. Military spouses say good-bye to their deploying spouse and know they won't see them for months, or for a remote, a year. They are lonely, but will survive.

Other spouses, when a washer hose blows off, call Maytag and then write a check out for getting the hose reconnected. Military spouses will cut the water off and fix it themselves.

Other spouses get used to saying *hello* to friends they see all the time. Military spouses get used to saying *good-bye* to friends made the last two years.

Other spouses worry about whether their child will be class president next year. Military spouses worry about whether their child will be accepted in yet another new school next year and whether that school will be the worst in the city ... again.

Other spouses can count on spouse participation in special events ... birthdays, anniversaries, concerts, football games, graduation, and even the birth of a child. Military spouses only count on each other; because they realize that the Flag has to come first if freedom is to survive. It has to be that way.

Other spouses put up yellow ribbons when the troops are imperiled across the globe and take them down when the troops come home. Military spouses wear yellow ribbons around their hearts and they never go away.

Other spouses worry about being late for mom's Thanksgiving dinner. Military spouses worry about getting back from Japan in time for dad's funeral.

And other spouses are touched by the television program showing an elderly lady putting a card down in front of a long, black wall that has names on it. The card simply says *Happy Birthday, Sweetheart. You would have been 60 today.* A military spouse is the lady with the card. And the wall is the Vietnam Memorial.

Goodbye. A sailor's wife waves to her husband's departing ship.

I would never say military spouses are better or worse than other spouses are. But I will say there is a difference. And I will say that our country asks more of military spouses than is asked of other spouses. And I will say, without hesitation, that military spouses pay just as high a price for freedom as do their active duty husbands or wives. Perhaps the price they pay is even higher. Dying in service to our country isn't near as hard as loving someone who has died in service to our country, and having to live without them. God bless our military spouses for all they freely give. And God bless America.

By Colonel Steven Arrington
17th Training Wing Vice Commander
Goodfellow Air Force Base, San Angelo, Texas

ARMY OF ONE–I AM AN ARMY WIFE

Author Unknown.

I've noticed in my present job, there is a tiny quirk. There's no respect at all and it's not considered work! Well, I am here to show you another point of view, and give you an idea of what I really do! Here's my job description and to better understand, it's written in the language of the Army Man.

I'm the IG [Inspector General], complaints come to me.

I am the Medic, I bandage skinned knees.

I'm the Legal Office and the courts-martial, too. I decide the punishment, how much and on who.

I'm Health & Welfare, inspecting for junk, and the 1SG checking the bunk.

I'm also Supply, in charge of food, clothes, housewares, diapers, toys, heaven only knows.

I'm the MP [Military Police] who secures the door.

I'm also the Private who GI's the floor.

I'm the Mess SGT who cooks all the meals.

I'm TMP [Temporary Motor Pool] in charge of the wheels.

I'm MWR [Morale, Welfare, Recreation] planning all the fun and I am the Bugler, announcing the *day is done.*

I'm the KP [Kitchen Police] who does all the dishes.

I am the DA [Department of the Army] who hears all you wishes.

I'm the CQ [Charge of Quarters] and the Fireguard, too, there isn't that much that I don't do.

I'm the instructor too, you see, because what is learned is taught by me.

I'm the Squad Leader who knows his troops well, sometimes the Drill Sergeant who really can yell.

I'm the S1, S2, 3, 4, just about everything must come through me.

Appropriations, taskings, commitments too, I'm responsible for all we do.

I never go to battle, an Army Regulation of some sort, but you can count on me to bravely guard the fort.

I'm ALWAYS on duty, I never take leave, no Holidays off, it's hard to believe!

I can never ETS [Expiration of Term of Service], I signed for life, my primary MOS [Military Occupational Specialty] is Mother, my secondary is Army Wife.

For all my devotion, to duty, my LES [Leave and Earnings Statement] says *NO PAY DUE* because I'm not paid in money, but in the words of *I LOVE YOU.* I AM AN ARMY WIFE!

YOU BET I'LL KISS YOU

Author Unknown, February, 2003.

Dear Friends:

I have just returned from doing a small part in our efforts against world conflict. Just got home early from Frankfurt after having picked up a planeload of troops in Alexandria, Louisiana and taking them one leg of their trip ... onward. They had just gotten word 24 hours earlier that full alert was *on* and they were getting ready to be transported.

We arrived in Alexandria on the military airfield in our 777, and the busses were waiting. The troops started to appear from the busses and they were all dressed in their desert uniforms. They looked so clean! Everything was new, including the weapons. Every soldier had a big gun, and some had knives hanging off their belts, too. They were young.

We were told that all weapons were unloaded, and that all the ammo was in the belly. Upon arrival at their destination, they would be given ammo, and they were on full alert and active duty as of the moment of landing at their destination. They had camel packs on their backs, too, and we were told that each soldier had two liters of water in those. Each soldier was also given three K ration packages to get them through the journey. (We fed and watered them with a good meal and lots of soft drinks, too.)

First class was filled with the rank, and also some very young men and women. We figured it out fast ... they had won a prize ... and another right guess ... they were all sharpshooters. Business class was filled with the best of the sharpshooters, too. Even though all got the same food and the same service, these soldiers were thrilled to be in a big seat on an airliner, and they kidded each other about getting to sit in the better cabins. Camaraderie filled the air in every cabin and there was lots of intermingling as they explored who got what, and how wonderful it was to be transported on an airliner with a crew and service! I never heard so many people say *ma'am* in my life. They treated us with respect, and boy, we treated them that way, too. We couldn't do enough for them. *No* was not in our vocabulary! If we had it ... they got it. Without exception, all the crew felt the same way.

We all felt that it was a great honor to be able to participate in getting these troops over there. Some of the flight crew had to step into the lavs and cry occasionally. I had a lump in my throat the entire flight. I was proud to be part of this ... so proud! We stepped over guns, we served cokes, we listened to stories, we served a meal, and then the soldiers took over. They got out in the aisle in their desert uniforms and passed out water and candy. They seemed to get a charge out of taking over from us, and maybe they had an ulterior motive, too, because those guys got every crumb of extra food that we had. They were young men and they were hungry!

I could go on and on about some of the stories I heard, but I will just close by saying that when we landed, we all had tears. A few of the guys passed out the door with, *would you mind kissing me, ma'am?* My response was, *You bet I'll kiss you.* I put lots of lipstick on lots of cheeks, and the guys just grinned.

The pride in country and uniform is overwhelming in a situation like this. I remember my Dad, the three wars he fought in, the pride with which he wore his uniform, his patriotism, his absolute belief that the United States was worth giving your life for, and that he survived it all.

God Bless America. I am so grateful to have been able to do something … anything … for our servicemen and women, too. Let's hope against all hope that every single one of them comes home to their families.

THE MEMORIES THAT HAUNT

*I always thought dying for your country
was the worst thing that could happen to you,
and I don't think it is,*

Senator Robert Kerrey told The New York Times, as he grappled with revelations that his squad of commandos killed unarmed women and children during a nighttime mission in Vietnam 1969.

I think killing for your country can be a lot worse,

Senator Kerrey said.

That's the memory that haunts.

CHAPTER 3
America and Americans

Americans are a blend of people bound by courage, diversity and character. Their common value is freedom; their common bond is pride; their common goal is peace. America is a great country because of its depth of diversity and its common bond of pride. This chapter is dedicated to all who proclaim *I am proud to be an American.*

Why should we become frightened? No people who have ever lived on this earth have fought harder, paid a higher price for freedom, or done more to advance the dignity of man than the living Americans–the Americans living in this land today. There isn't any problem we can't solve if government will give us the facts. Tell us what needs to be done. Then, get out of the way and let us have at it.

President Ronald Reagan, 1976

America is best described by one word: Freedom.

President Dwight D. Eisenhower
In his address to congress, 9 January 1959

America has never been united by blood or birth or soil. We are bound by ideals that move us beyond our backgrounds, lift us above our interests and teach us what it means to be citizens. Every child must be taught these principles. Every citizen must uphold them. And every immigrant, by embracing these ideals, makes our country more, not less, American.

President George W. Bush

CAN YOU NAME ANOTHER COUNTRY …

Look at America; the country they exult at having wounded so grievously. Can you name a country that ever amassed more power and abused it less? Can you name a country that ever amassed more wealth and distributed it more fairly? Can you name another country that was ever attacked by surprise as America was in 1941, rallied to defeat both powerful enemies, and wound up with LESS land than it had previously? (America gave the Philippines its independence after victory in World War II.) Can you name another country that, after victory, treated its allies and enemies alike to massive rehabilitation and rebuilding? Instead of rape and plunder we gave Germany and Japan democracy implants. They're both strong and prosperous democracies today. And you call that 'satanic'?

Barry Farber

A NATION OF CHARACTER

*America, at its best, is a place where personal responsibility is valued and expected. Encouraging responsibility is not a search for scapegoats; it is a call to conscience …
Our public interest depends on private character; on civic duty and family bonds and basic fairness; on uncounted, unhonored acts of decency which give direction to our freedom. …
I ask you to seek a common good beyond your comfort and I ask you to be citizens. Citizens, not spectators. Citizens, not subjects. Responsible citizens, building communities of service and a nation of character … Americans are generous and strong and decent, not because we believe in ourselves, but because we hold beliefs beyond ourselves. When this spirit of citizenship is missing, no government program can replace it.
When this spirit is present, no wrong can stand against it.*

President George Bush

I AM AN AMERICAN AND I STAND PROUD

I am an American and I stand proud,
You may have wounded me But I won't fall down
I may stagger and shake I may sway and rock
But I've got sisters and brothers with whose arms I will lock

I will cry for the dead those you've taken from me
But what you have done right now you can't see
You think that I'll fold like a coward and run but
You have touched my heart something you shouldn't have done

You think that I'm weak for the love I have shown
In all others tragedies far from my home
I've reached out in compassion to those hurting souls
And for you that's a reason to slay my own ...

You don't know the giant you've awoken inside...
In the past I've stood silent now it's your turn to hide
Although I'll forgive you as my Lord says I should
What goes around comes around and this time it's for good ...

So with pity I write this for I know your fates been set ...
You'll get what you've given from America's best
You'll see that although, in love we do walk ...
If you hurt our brethren you will pay the cost ...

The giant's awoken yet another time
He's awoken before and rode on wings from high
He'll sniff you out like a rat in a trap ...
For your destinies sealed you cannot run from that

So enjoy your laughter your toasts as you dine ...
For the giants are coming and you cannot hide.
Your fate has been sealed and as you look behind ...
You'll see that our flag is still flying high!

Author Unknown

AMERICANS ARE FREEDOM

By Alan Keyes, Ph.D., public official, author, Radio Talk Show Host and 1996 Presidential candidate.

Americans are a people who have realized a dream of freedom, who have taken it from an abstract hope and turned it into a living reality. What made this possible was a founding generation that understood the essential principles of liberty, and acknowledged from the very beginning that the basis for human justice, human dignity and human rights is no more–nor less–than the will and authority of our Creator, God.

The importance of this principle is definitive, because it allows us to understand that since we claim our rights by virtue of the authority of God, we must exercise our rights with respect for the authority of God. This truth becomes a sound foundation for discipline in our use of our freedoms. It becomes a bulwark against the abuse of our powers. It becomes also the ground for our confidence that, when we claim those rights, and when we exercise them, we do not have to fear the consequences, because we are a people who exercise our rights in the fear of God.

This means that as American citizens, we can have confidence in our capacity, ability and character to take care of our own families. We can trust ourselves to raise our own children, to direct our own schools, to run our own communities and states, to do honest business together, and to generally take care of the things that need to be done for our nation and its people.

I AM AN AMERICAN

By Clifford C. Spencer, U.S. Marine, World War II.

America is finally responding to a wake up call, very late but hopeful none the less. There is just a moment of time, in historical terms, before the final closing for the World War Two and Great Depression generation.

Taps, that final bugle call to judgment is sounding over 35,000, or more, graves each month. As the new century dawns over this great country called America, our brave men and women, whose entire lives were spent defending and building this Nation, are passing into history. Building and changing this country from a vast island of isolationism into the most powerful world leader in history.

What is even more wonderful about this generation is they were unaware that with an almost magical mixture of opportunity, a constant work ethic, love of family and unwavering patriotism, they were creating a country such as this. A country so solid that it has withstood forty years of ever-increasing assault. Yes, assault on family values, on the teaching of history and patriotism in our schools, on the art of conversation without vulgarity and without shouting, and the lack of teaching the constant quest for knowledge as a fulfilling method of satisfying our curious nature.

Presently the isolationism of the pre-war years has given way to tribal fragmentation of our diverse cultural and ethnic population.

In the 1920s and 30s the Italian, German, Polish, Jewish, Irish and many other ethnic groups cherished and maintained their heritage. Many even lived in neighborhoods made up of families from their same national or religious origins.

However, overriding all their cultural mores they were very, very proud of being Americans, American to the core!

In spite of the slurs and prejudice, and yes there was prejudice, they aspired to send their children to school up to and including college, if possible. Always with the admonition to study hard and *someday you may be President of the U.S. of America!* The goal of this great melting pot of citizens was to just be called an American. Not an African American, or Italian American, or a Japanese American ... Just an American!

The original Anglo/Saxon settlers had only grudgingly accepted each new pulse of immigrants and not without insulting names and ostracizing them for a generation, sometimes longer. With time, each group was included in the mix. Intermarriage, education and familiarity eventually made each succeeding group just Americans.

Surprisingly, minorities already accepted into the mainstream were, at times, more prejudiced toward the subsequent newcomers. It was somewhat like the hazing of underclassmen in college; when they became upperclassmen, they were very mean to the *frosh* enrollees.

Does all this sound familiar? Yes, it was very much like it is today, except for a few important differences. Those ethnic groups knew the ground rules. They knew from experience that it was much better to live in their adopted homeland than where they came from. They also knew that even their detractors respected hard work and will to learn. It was harsh and not the way it should have been, but a sacrifice they were more than willing to make.

Even more important they knew that everyone, including themselves, were proud to be American citizens. That catalyst held the country together in good times and bad. Somehow everyone, recent immigrant or the descendants of the Mayflower voyage, knew that a country without knowledge of its history and pride in the past was just a wasteland. A wasteland where life had no grand plan, only an aimless drifting toward anarchy.

Man is a fallible species; so, rather than highlighting his negatives and faults, it is imperative that the history of one's country be glorified. Not ignoring its faults but highlighting the many good attributes and taught to the extent necessary to train young minds to love their country. Not only to love it but want to protect it and add to its perceived greatness by deeds of their own.

I am reminded of a part I once played in a play written and directed by Severino Montana, titled *I AM AN AMERICAN*. Produced in the auditorium on American University Campus in Washington, D. C. where I was a student. The cast was made up of actual combat veterans of the war still raging on two fronts, cast as veterans of all ethnic and cultural backgrounds. My role was that of a wounded Mexican American soldier. It was a three act Greek/Spartan drama, no sets only a bare stage, all sound effects were vocalized and scenes were set by an off-stage narrator.

I remember well the effort to become that soldier, to feel his mental attitude of having been wounded while fighting for a country wherein most of its citizens called him *Spic* or worse. The war still engulfed the world outside that auditorium but inside we and our often distinguished audience were being taught that to be an American one must believe fervently that *I am an American!*

For forty or fifty years it has been, for many, embarrassing to be a proud patriot. But through all the years of not being taught love of country, each generation had parents and grandparents to teach by recounting that their land of birth had a great and glorious history. A history to be proud of and to aspire to perpetuate.

What must be taught to today's youth is the generation that Tom Brokaw named the *Greatest Generation* was and is not some specific group of greater privilege. This fast disappearing generation was made up of their Grandfathers/Grandmothers, Great Uncle Carlos or Great Aunt Katherine, ordinary people whom in spite of their differences loved their country and were very proud of its history.

OLD GEEZERS

Geezers are easy to spot; this is slang for an old man. But, at sporting events, during the playing of the National Anthem, they hold their caps over their hearts and sing without embarrassment. They know the words and believe in them.

They remember World War I, the Depression, World War II, Pearl Harbor, Guadalcanal, Normandy and Hitler. They remember the Atomic Age, the Korean War, The Cold War, the Jet Age and the Moon Landing, not to mention Vietnam.

If you bump into a *Geezer* on the sidewalk, he'll apologize; pass a *Geezer* on the street, he'll nod, or tip his cap to a lady.

Geezers trust strangers and are courtly to women. They hold the door for the next person and always, when walking, make sure the lady is on the inside for protection.

Battalion Crest. Semi-Old Farts.

Geezers get embarrassed if someone curses in front of women and children and they don't like violence and filth on TV and in movies.

Geezers have moral courage.

Geezers seldom brag unless it's about the grandchildren in Little League or music recitals. This country needs *Geezers* with their decent values and common sense. We need them now more than ever. It's the *Geezers* who know our great country is protected, not by politicians or police, but by the young men and women in the military serving their country in foreign lands, just as they did, without a thought except to do a good job, the best you can and to get home to loved ones.

Thank God for *OLD GEEZERS.*

THIS TIDE OF THE FUTURE IS OURS

This remarkable speech was delivered during an *I am an American* day meeting in New York's Central Park by Harold Ickes, President Franklin D. Roosevelt's Secretary of the Interior. It came at a perilous moment in history, May of 1941, when Adolf Hitler and the Nazis seemed headed toward possible world domination. By this time, countries that had fallen to the Nazis included: Austria, Czechoslovakia, Poland, Norway, Denmark, France, Belgium, Luxembourg, the Netherlands, and areas in North Africa. Airfields and cities in England were now under ferocious air attack from the German Luftwaffe while wolf-packs of Nazi U-boats attempted to blockade the British Isles. Many Americans, however, still questioned the wisdom and necessity of direct U.S. involvement in the European War. Pacifist sentiment was growing, while at the same time Fascism was sometimes referred to as the *wave of the future* by respected Americans, amid the onslaught of effective anti-democratic Fascist propaganda. In this speech, Harold Ickes counters that propaganda, defines what it means to be a free American, and offers a blunt assessment of the perilous future the U.S. would face standing alone against a victorious Hitler. By Harold Ickes, 18 May 1941.

I want to ask a few simple questions. And then I shall answer them. What has happened to our vaunted idealism? Why have some of us been behaving like scared chickens? Where is the million-throated, democratic voice of America?

For years it has been drummed into us that we are a weak nation; that we are an inefficient people; that we are simple-minded. For years we have been told that we are beaten, decayed, and that no part of the world belongs to us any longer.

Some amongst us have fallen for this carefully pickled tripe. Some amongst us have fallen for this calculated poison.

Some amongst us have begun to preach that the *wave of the future* has passed over us and left us a wet, dead fish.

They shout–from public platforms in printed pages, through the microphones–that it is futile to oppose the *wave of the future*. They cry that we Americans, we free Americans nourished on Magna Carta and the Declaration of Independence, hold moth-eaten ideas. They exclaim that there is no room for free men in the world any more and that only the slaves will inherit the earth. America–the America of Washington and Jefferson and Lincoln and Walt Whitman–they say, is waiting for the undertaker and all the hopes and aspirations that have gone into the making of America are dead too.

However, my fellow citizens, this is not the real point of the story. The real point–the shameful point–is that many of us are listening to them and some of us almost believe them.

I say that it is time for the great American people to raise its voice and cry out in mighty triumph what it is to be an American. And why it is that only Americans, with the aid of our brave allies–yes, let's call them *allies*–the British, can and will build the only future worth having. I mean a future, not of concentration camps, not of physical torture and mental straitjackets, not of sawdust bread or of sawdust Caesars–I mean a future when free men will live free lives in dignity and in security.

This tide of the future, the democratic future, is ours. It is ours if we show ourselves worthy of our culture and of our heritage. But make no mistake about it; the tide of the democratic future is not like the ocean tide–regular, relentless, and inevitable. Nothing in human affairs is mechanical or inevitable. Nor are Americans mechanical. They are very human indeed.

What constitutes an American? Not color nor race nor religion. Not the pedigree of his family nor the place of his birth. Not the coincidence of his citizenship. Not his social status nor his bank account. Not his trade nor his profession. An American is one who loves justice and believes in the dignity of man. An American is one who will fight for his freedom and that of his neighbor. An American is one who will sacrifice property, ease and security in order that he and his children may retain the rights of free men. An American is one in whose heart is engraved with the immortal second sentence of the Declaration of Independence.

Americans have always known how to fight for their rights and their way of life. Americans are not afraid to fight. They fight joyously in a just cause.

We Americans know that freedom, like peace, is indivisible. We cannot retain our liberty if three-fourths of the world is enslaved. Brutality, injustice and slavery, if practiced, as dictators would have them, universally and systematically, in the long run would destroy us as surely as a fire raging in our nearby neighbor's house would burn ours if we didn't help to put out his.

If we are to retain our own freedom, we must do everything within our power to aid Britain. We must also do everything to restore to the conquered peoples their freedom. This means the Germans too.

Such a program, if you stop to think, is selfishness on our part. It is the sort of enlightened selfishness that makes the wheels of history go around. It is the sort of enlightened selfishness that wins victories.

Do you know why? Because we cannot live in the world alone, without friends and without allies. If Britain should be defeated, then the totalitarian undertaker will prepare to hang crepe on the door of our own independence.

Perhaps you wonder how this could come about? Perhaps you have heard *them*–the wavers of the future–cry, with calculated malice, that even if Britain were defeated we could live alone and defend ourselves single handed, even against the whole world.

I tell you that this is a cold-blooded lie.

We would be alone in the world, facing an unscrupulous military-economic bloc that would dominate all of Europe, all of Africa, most of Asia, and perhaps even Russia and South America. Even to do that, we would have to spend most of our national income on tanks and guns and planes and ships. Nor would this be all. We would have to live perpetually as an armed camp, maintaining a huge standing army, a gigantic air force, two vast navies. And we could not do this without endangering our freedom, our democracy, our way of life.

Perhaps such is the America *they*–the wavers of the future–foresee. Perhaps such is the America that a certain aviator, with his contempt for democracy, would prefer. Perhaps such is the

America that a certain Senator desires. Perhaps such is the America that a certain mail order executive longs for.

But a perpetually militarized, isolated and impoverished America is not the America that our fathers came here to build.

It is not the America that has been the dream and the hope of countless generations in all parts of the world.

It is not the America that one hundred and thirty million of us would care to live in.

The continued security of our country demands that we aid the enslaved millions of Europe–yes, even of Germany–to win back their liberty and independence. I am convinced that if we do not embark upon such a program we will lose our own freedom.

We should be clear on this point. What is convulsing the world today is not merely another old-fashioned war. It is a counter-revolution against our ideas and ideals, against our sense of justice and our human values.

Three systems today compete for world domination. Communism, fascism, and democracy are struggling for social-economic-political world control. As the conflict sharpens, it becomes clear that the other two, fascism and communism, are merging into one. They have one common enemy, democracy. They have one common goal, the destruction of democracy.

This is why this war is not an ordinary war. It is not a conflict for markets or territories. It is a desperate struggle for the possession of the souls of men.

This is why the British are not fighting for themselves alone. They are fighting to preserve freedom for mankind. For the moment, the battleground is the British Isles. But they are fighting our war; they are the first soldiers in trenches that are also our front-line trenches.

In this world war of ideas and of loyalties we believers in democracy must do two things. We must unite our forces to form one great democratic international. We must offer a clear program to freedom-loving peoples throughout the world.

Freedom-loving men and women in every land must organize and tighten their ranks. The masses everywhere must be helped to fight their oppressors and conquerors.

We, free, democratic Americans are in a position to help. We know that the spirit of freedom never dies. We know that men have fought and bled for freedom since time immemorial. We realize that the liberty-loving German people are only temporarily enslaved. We do not doubt that the Italian people are looking forward to the appearance of another Garibaldi. We know how the Poles have for centuries maintained a heroic resistance against tyranny. We remember the brave struggle of the Hungarians under Kossuth and other leaders. We recall the heroic figure of Masaryk and the gallant fight for freedom of the Czech people. The story of the Yugoslavs, especially the Serbs blows for liberty and independence is a saga of extraordinary heroism. The Greeks will stand again at Thermopylae, as they have in the past. The annals of our American sister-republics, too, are glorious with freedom-inspiring exploits. The noble figure of Simon Bolivar, the great South American liberator, has naturally been compared with that of George Washington.

No, liberty never dies. The Genghis Khans come and go. The Attilas come and go. The Hitlers flash and sputter out. But freedom endures. Destroy a whole generation of those who have known how to walk with heads erect in God's free air, and the next generation will rise against the oppressors and restore freedom. Today in Europe, the Nazi Attila may gloat that he has destroyed democracy. He is wrong. In small farmhouses all over Central Europe, in the shops of Germany and Italy, on the docks of Holland and Belgium, freedom still lives in the hearts of men. It will endure like a hardy tree gone into the wintertime, awaiting the spring.

And, like spring, spreading from the South into Scandinavia, the democratic revolution will come. And men with democratic hearts will experience comradeship across artificial boundaries.

These men and women, hundreds of millions of them, now in bondage or threatened with slavery, are our comrades and our allies. They are only waiting for our leadership and our encouragement, for the spark that we can supply.

These hundreds of millions, of liberty-loving people, now oppressed, constitute the greatest sixth column in history. They have the will to destroy the Nazi gangsters.

We have always helped in struggles for human freedom. And we will help again. But our hundreds of millions of liberty-loving allies would despair if we did not provide aid and encouragement. The quicker we help them the sooner this dreadful revolution will be over. We cannot, we must not, we dare not delay much longer.

The fight for Britain is in its crucial stages. We must give the British everything we have. And by everything, I mean everything needed to beat the life out of our common enemy.

The second step must be to aid and encourage our friends and allies everywhere. And by everywhere I mean Europe and Asia and Africa and America.

And finally, the most important of all, we Americans must gird spiritually for the battle. We must dispel the fog of uncertainty and vacillation. We must greet with raucous laughter the corroding arguments of our appeasers and fascists. They doubt democracy. We affirm it triumphantly so that all the world may hear.

Here in America we have something so worth living for that it is worth dying for! The so-called *wave of the future* is but the slimy backwash of the past. We have not heaved from our necks the tyrant's crushing heel, only to stretch our necks out again for its weight. Not only will we fight for democracy, we will make it more worth fighting for. Under our free institutions, we will work for the good of mankind, including Hitler's victims in Germany, so that all may have plenty and security.

We American democrats know that when good will prevails among men there will be a world of plenty and a world of security.

In the words of Winston Churchill, *'Are we downhearted,'* No, we are not! But someone is downhearted! Witness the terrified flight of Hess, Hitler's Number Three Man. And listen to this– listen carefully:

> The British nation can be counted upon to carry through to victory any struggle that it once enters upon no matter how long such a struggle may last or however great the sacrifices that may be necessary or whatever the means that have to be employed; and all this even though the actual military equipment at hand may be utterly inadequate when compared with that of other nations.

Do you know who wrote that? Adolf Hitler in Mein Kampf. And do you know who took down that dictation? Rudolf Hess.

We will help to make Hitler's prophecy come true. We will help brave England drive back the hordes from Hell who besiege her and then we will join for the destruction of savage and bloodthirsty dictators everywhere. But we must be firm and decisive. We must know our will and make it felt. And we must hurry.

THE IRON HAND, A BRITISH VIEW

A British View of the U.S./Bin Ladin affair, by Andrew Sullivan, as printed in the London Times.

No eloquence can match the impact of their evil. Americans' critical weakness in the past two decades has been their reluctance to shed blood for their goals. They believed they could construct a huge military and never have it fight real wars and suffer real casualties. They thought they could alter history and advance their interests from the air alone. With the exception of the Gulf War, which they hesitated to finish, they have shrunk from the fight. When the current enemy struck again and again throughout the 1990s, Bill Clinton responded without real credibility, struck back without real endurance, enraged the terrorists without truly hurting them. We are now living with the consequences of his appeasement, and of his refusal to challenge Americans beyond what the polls said they already wanted to do. Whoever launched this war on Americans has now accomplished the task Clinton didn't dare embark on. America has been bloodied as it has never been bloodied before. I would be a fool to predict what happens next. But it is clear that Bush will not do a Clinton. This will not be a surgical strike. It will not be a gesture. It may not even begin in earnest soon. But it will be deadly serious. It is clear that there is no way that the United States can achieve its goals without the cooperation of many other states–an alliance as deep and as broad as that which won the Gulf War. It is also clear that this cannot be done by airpower alone. As in 1941, the neglect of the military under Bill Clinton and the parsimony of its financing even under Bush must now not merely be ended but reversed. We may see the biggest defense build-up since the early 1980s–and not just in weaponry but in manpower. It is also quite clear that the U.S. military presence in the Middle East must be ramped up exponentially, its intelligence overhauled, its vigilance heightened exponentially. In some ways, Bush has already assembled the ideal team for such a task: Powell for the diplomatic dance, Rumsfeld for the deep reforms he will now have the opportunity to enact, Cheney as his most trusted aide in what has become to all intents and purposes a war cabinet. The terrorists have done the rest. The middle part of the country–the great red zone that voted for Bush– is clearly ready for war. But by striking at the heart of New York City, the terrorists ensured that at least one deep segment of the country ill-disposed toward a new president is now the most passionate in his defense. Anyone who has ever tried to get one over on a New Yorker knows what I mean. The demons who started this have no idea about the kind of people they have taken on. But what the terrorists are also counting on is that Americans will not have the stomach for the long haul. They clearly know that the coming retaliation will not be the end but the beginning. And when the terrorists strike back again, they have let us know that the results could make the assault on the World Trade Center look puny. They are banking that Americans will then cave. They have seen a great country quarrel to the edge of constitutional crisis over a razor-close presidential election. They have seen it respond to real threats in the last few years with squeamish restraint or surgical strikes. They have seen that, as Israel has been pounded by the same murderous thugs, the United States has responded with equanimity. They have seen a great nation at the height of its power obsess for a whole summer over a missing intern and a randy Congressman. They have good reason to believe that this country is soft, that it has no appetite for the war that has now begun. They have gambled that in response to unprecedented terror, the Americans will abandon Israel to the barbarians who would annihilate every Jew on the planet, and trade away their freedom for a respite from terror in their own land. We cannot foresee the future. But we know the past. And that past tells us that these people who destroyed the heart of New York City have made a terrible mistake. This country is at its heart a peaceful one. It has done more to help the world than any other actor in world history. It saved the world from the two greatest evils of the last century n Nazism and Soviet Communism. It responded to its victories in the last war by pouring aid into Europe and Japan. In the Middle East, America alone has ensured that the last hope of the Jewish people is not extinguished and has given more aid to Egypt than to any other country. It risked its own people to save the Middle East from the pseudo-Hitler in Baghdad. America need not have done any of this. Its world hegemony has been less violent and less imperial than any other comparable power in history. In the depths of its soul, it wants its dream to itself, to be left alone, to prosper among others, and to welcome them to the freedom America has helped secure. But whenever Americans have been challenged, they have risen to the task. In some awful way, these evil thugs may have done us a favor. America may have woken up forever. The rage that will follow from this grief and shock may be deeper and greater than anyone now can imagine. Think of what the United States ultimately did to the enemy that bombed Pearl Harbor. Now recall that American power in the world is all but unchallenged by any other state. Recall that America has never been wealthier, and is at the end of one of the biggest booms in its history. And now consider the extent of this wound–the greatest civilian casualties since the Civil War, an assault not just on Americans but on the meaning of America itself. When you take a step back, it is hard not to believe that we are now in the quiet moment before the whirlwind. Americans will recover their dead, and they will mourn them, and then they will get down to business. Their sadness will be mingled with an anger that will make the hatred of these evil fanatics seem mild. I am reminded of a great American poem written by Herman Melville after the death of Abraham Lincoln, the second founder of the country:

There is sobbing of the strong,
And a pall upon the land
But the People in their weeping
Bare the iron hand;
Beware the People weeping
When they bare the iron hand.

THE FUTURE WILL ALWAYS BE OURS

By President Ronald Reagan.

In all of that time I won a nickname, the *Great communicator*. But I never thought it was my style or the words I used that made a difference: It was the content. I wasn't a great communicator, but I communicated great things, and they didn't spring full bloom from my brow; they came from the heart of a great nation–from our experience, our wisdom and our belief in the principles that have guided us for two centuries. They called it the Reagan revolution. Well, I'll accept that, but for me it always seemed like the Great Rediscovery–a rediscovery of our values and our common sense. ... Because we're a great nation our challenges seem complex. It will always be that way. But as long as we remember our first principles and believe in ourselves, the future will always be ours. And something else we learned: Once you begin a great movement, there's no telling where it will end. We meant to change a nation, and instead we changed a world. ... I never thought of myself as a great man, just a man committed to great ideas. I've always believed that individuals should take priority over the state. History has taught me that this is what sets America apart–not to remake the world in our image, but to inspire people everywhere with a sense of their own boundless possibilities. There's no question I am an idealist, which is another way of saying I am an American.

WHAT MAKES AMERICA STRONG?

Americans have rallied around not just a flag and not just symbols of America, but we have begun to understand that the country needs each one of us to move forward from this point. We have started to understand that what makes America strong is not a constitution, not a flag and not a building; it's the backbone of those Americans who support all of these things.

Montel Williams, Talk-Show host, Actor, former Naval Officer

*I believe the years that I stayed here and even before I stayed here,
when I lived in Brazil, I admired the patriotism of the Americans.
And that's what makes everyone strong over here,
in my opinion ... everybody sticks together, and it's fantastic.*

Helio Castroneves, 2002 Indianapolis 500 winner

*Hold on, my friends, to the Constitution and to the Republic for
which it stands. Miracles do not cluster, and what has happened
once in 6000 years, may not happen again. Hold on to the
Constitution, for if the American Constitution should fail, there
will be anarchy throughout the world.*

Daniel Webster, Statesman, State Representative, Senator,
Secretary of State. 1782-1852

*Freedom. The limits on your life in this country are basically
self-imposed. You can do anything and be anything you want to be,
which is not something that many people born outside
of this country have the ability to do ... When you look back you
find a wealth of people who did what people said couldn't be done.
I think that's what makes us stand out as a nation.*

Curt Schilling, Arizona Diamondbacks, Pitcher
2001 World Series Co-MVP

WHO ARE AMERICANS?

Letter from Major David Balmer, United States Army Task Force
Rakkasan, 101st Air Assault Division, Operation Enduring
Freedom, Kandahar, Afghanistan, 29 March 2002.

To my friends and contacts:

This is my second update to you from Kandahar. I have
been on the ground here for about 2.5 months now. The cold
weather has given way to hot temperatures–90s during the day and
50s at night. Operation Anaconda was a big success, but we are
somber about the 8 KIAs and 26 wounded from that operation. I

Major David Balmer. Kandahar, Afghanistan.

am working 7 days a week–very busy, but still cannot discuss details because of security clearance issues.

I want to thank you for your wonderful cards and packages–I have shared them with my tent buddies. We have built underground bunkers around our tents to protect against mortar attacks. Most of the direct-fire attacks on our perimeter have stopped now, but we remain on a high level of alert. To go outside, I must wear my helmet, flak vest, ammunition belt and carry my weapon–stringent force-protection rules. We have grown used to that lifestyle.

Please allow me to share a minute from my heart. The more time I spend here the more impressed am I with the men and women who wear our uniform. We have over 5,000 troops here in Kandahar (all 50 states are represented). We come from various ethnic and economic backgrounds, but we all are Americans–we all proudly display the American flag on our right sleeve.

This war has proven once again that America's military is the strongest in the world. We are trained well, utilize the best equipment, employ the most powerful weapons; but weapons and training are NOT the real source of our strength. The American military is the best because it is comprised of Americans.

Who are Americans? We are a group of people inspired by God to embrace the purest of freedoms. We have been taught freedom by many patriots who spilled their blood from Bunker Hill to Cemetery Ridge to Pearl Harbor to Normandy to Inchon to Hamburger Hill to Desert Storm to the Twin Towers to the caves of Afghanistan.

Nevertheless, learning freedom from history books is not the same as living it. We all felt our hearts break as the Twin Towers collapsed down on thousands of helpless souls. We went into shock from the horror of it. We watched and hoped as firefighters dug through the rubble. Then, the *sleeping giant* awakened in each of us. Flags appeared on every car, and we all knew that America would respond. From President Bush on down, we stood shoulder to shoulder to fight this war on terrorism. Every American has contributed in some way.

The support from back home has poured into this airport—countless boxes of Girl Scout cookies, for example. We have received thousands of letters and hand-colored banners from elementary school children across America. The letters and banners have been taped up everywhere covering almost every inch of wall space in the corridors of this bombed out airport. When I have time, I walk along and read some of the letters. Most of them start, *Dear Soldier*. As I read further, I get to travel into the minds and hearts of small American children–to listen to their ideas of war, of sacrifice and of freedom. Each time I read these letters I end up crying.

Let me tell you about another occasion when I had to fight back tears. Just three weeks ago I stood at attention on the runway as the flag-draped coffins from Operation Anaconda were loaded on an Air Force C-17 to return home to a grateful nation. At that moment, I experienced freedom in my own life. We all are learning the new meaning of freedom by living in these times.

Five American Warriors. Killed in Action, Afghanistan, are prepared for return to the United States. Kadena Air Force Base, Japan.

I have come to know many Americans here, and this experience has renewed my faith in our country and its love for freedom. I pray that God will continue to strengthen our American resolve to defend freedom across the world. Thank you for all your encouragement and support.

Unfortunately, I still cannot offer you my e-mail address– we only get about 15 minutes on-line per day–time that I use to e-mail my wife, Karen and daughter, Laura. I miss them so much. Please do NOT reply back to Amy Brady at Cherokee–she is just sending this e-mail out for me.

Thanks again for your personal sacrifice for our collective American freedom.

AMERICA!

By Barry Loudermilk.

Broken Arrow, Oklahoma School officials remove *God Bless America* signs from schools in fear that someone might be offended. Channel 12 News in Long Island, New York orders flags removed from the newsroom and red, white, and blue ribbons removed from the lapels of reporters. Why? Management did not want to appear biased and felt that our nation's flag might give the appearance that *they lean one way or another*. Berkeley, California bans U.S. Flags from being displayed on city fire trucks because they didn't want to offend anyone in the community. In an *act of tolerance* the head of the public library at Florida Gulf Coast University ordered all *Proud to be an American* signs removed so as to not offend international students.

I, for one, am quite disturbed by these actions of so-called American citizens; and I am tired of this nation worrying about whether or not we are offending some individual or their culture. Since the terrorist attacks on September 11, we have experienced a surge in patriotism by the majority of Americans. However, the dust from the attacks had barely settled in New York and Washington, D.C. when the *politically correct* crowd began complaining about the possibility that our patriotism was offending others. I am not against immigration, nor do I hold a grudge against anyone who is seeking a better life by coming to America. In fact, our country's population is almost entirely comprised of descendants of immigrants; however, there are a few things that those who have recently come to our country, and apparently some native Americans, need to understand.

First of all, it is not our responsibility to continually try not to offend you in any way. This idea of America being a multi-cultural community has served only to dilute our sovereignty and our national identity. As Americans, we have our own culture, our own society, our own language, and our own lifestyle. This culture, called the *American Way* has been developed over centuries of struggles, trials, and victories by millions of men and women who have sought freedom.

Our forefathers fought, bled, and died at places such as Bunker Hill, Antietem, San Juan, Iwo Jima, Normandy, Korea, Vietnam. We speak English, not Spanish, Arabic, Chinese, Japanese, Russian, or any other language. Therefore, if you wish to become part of our society—learn our language! *In God We Trust* is our national motto. This is not some off-the-wall, Christian, Right Wing, political slogan; it is our national motto. It is engraved in stone in the House of Representatives in our Capitol and it is printed on our currency.

We adopted this motto because Christian men and women, on Christian principles, founded this nation; and this is clearly documented throughout our history. If it is appropriate for our motto to be inscribed in the halls of our highest level of Government, then it is certainly appropriate to display it on the walls of our schools. God is in our pledge, our National Anthem, nearly every patriotic song, and in our founding documents. We honor His birth, death, and resurrection as holidays, and we turn to Him in prayer in times of crisis. If God offends you, then, I suggest you consider another part of the world as your new home, because God is part of our culture and we are proud to have Him. We are proud of our heritage and those who have so honorably defended our freedoms. We celebrate Independence Day, Memorial Day, Veterans Day, and Flag Day.

We have parades, picnics, and barbecues where we proudly wave our flag. As an American, I have the right to wave my flag, sing my national anthem, quote my national motto, and cite my pledge whenever and wherever I choose. If the Stars and Stripes offend you, or you don't like Uncle Sam, then you should seriously consider a move to another part of this planet. The American culture is our way of life, our heritage, and we are proud of it. We are happy with our culture and have no desire to change, and we really don't care how you did things where you came from, if it was so superior, go home. We are Americans; like it or not, this is our country, our land, and our lifestyle. Our First Amendment gives every citizen the right to express his opinion about our government, culture, or society, and we will allow you every opportunity to do so. But once you are done complaining, whining, and griping about our flag, our pledge, our national motto, or our way of life, I highly encourage you take advantage of one other great American freedom, the right to leave.

THE UNITED STATES ONE DOLLAR BILL

Take out a one dollar bill, and look at it. The one dollar bill you're looking at first came off the presses in 1957 in its present design. This so-called paper money is in fact a cotton and linen blend, with red and blue minute silk fibers running through it. It is actually material. We've all washed it without it falling apart. A special blend of ink is used, the contents we will never know. It is overprinted with symbols and then it is starched to make it water resistant and pressed to give it that nice crisp look.

On the front of the bill, you will see the U.S. Treasury Seal. On the top you will see the scales for a balanced budget, in the center a carpenter's square, a tool used for an even cut, and underneath the Key to the U.S. Treasury. That's all pretty easy to figure out, but the back is something we should all know.

If you turn the bill over, you will see two circles. Both circles, together, comprise the Great Seal of the United States. The First Continental Congress requested that Benjamin Franklin and a group of men come up with a Seal. It took them four years to accomplish this task and another two years to get it approved.

If you look at the left-hand circle, you will see a Pyramid. Notice the face is lighted, and the western side is dark. This country was just beginning. We had not begun to explore the West or decided what we could do for Western Civilization. The Pyramid is uncapped, again signifying that we were not even close to being finished. Inside the capstone you have the all-seeing eye, an ancient symbol for divinity. It was Franklin's belief that one man couldn't do it alone, but a group of men, with the help of God, could do anything. *IN GOD WE TRUST* is on this currency. The Latin above the pyramid, ANNUIT COEPTIS, means, *God has favored our undertaking*. The Latin below the pyramid, NOVUS ORDO SECLORUM, means, *a new order has begun*. At the base of the pyramid is the Roman Numeral for 1776.

If you look at the right-hand circle, and check it carefully, you will learn that it is on every National Cemetery in the United States. It is also on the Parade of Flags Walkway at the Bushnell, Florida National Cemetery, and is the centerpiece of most hero's monuments. Slightly modified, it is the seal of the President of the United States, and it is always visible whenever he speaks, yet very few people know what the symbols mean. The Bald Eagle was selected as a symbol for victory for two reasons: First, he is not afraid of a storm; he is strong, and he is smart enough to soar above it. Secondly, he wears no material crown. We had just broken from the King of England. Also, notice the shield is unsupported. This country can now stand on its own. At the top of that shield you have a white bar signifying congress, a unifying factor. We were coming together as one nation. In the Eagle's beak you will read, *E PLURIBUS UNUM*, meaning, *one nation from many people*. Above the Eagle, you have thirteen stars, representing the thirteen original colonies, and any clouds of misunderstanding rolling away. Again, we were coming together as one. Notice what the Eagle holds in his talons. He holds an olive branch and arrows. This country wants peace, but we will never be afraid to fight to preserve peace. The Eagle always wants to face the olive branch, but in time of war, his gaze turns toward the arrows.

They say that the number 13 is an unlucky number. This is almost a worldwide belief. You will usually never see a room numbered 13, or any hotels or motels with a 13th floor. But think about this: 13 original colonies, 13 signers of the Declaration of Independence, 13 stripes on our flag, 13 steps on the Pyramid, 13 letters in the Latin above, 13 letters in *E PLURIBUS UNUM*, 13 stars above the Eagle, 13 bars on that shield, 13 leaves on the olive branch, 13 fruits, and if you look closely, 13 arrows. And, for minorities: the 13th Amendment.

I always ask people, *Why don't you know this?* Your children don't know this, and their history teachers don't know this. Too many veterans have given up too much to ever let the meaning fade. Many veterans remember coming home to an America that didn't care. Too many veterans never came home at all.

THE 13 FOLDS ON OLD GLORY

Why the American flag is folded 13 times. Author Unknown.

Have you ever wondered why the flag of the United States of America is folded 13 times when it is lowered or when it is folded and handed to the widow at the burial of a veteran? Here is the meaning of each of those folds and what it means:

The first fold of our flag is a symbol of life.

The second fold is a symbol of our belief in eternal life.

The third fold is made in honor and remembrance of the veterans departing our ranks who gave a portion of their lives for the defense of our country to attain peace throughout the world.

The fourth fold represents our weaker nature, for as American citizens trusting in God, it is to Him we turn in times of peace as well as in time of war for His divine guidance.

The fifth fold is a tribute to our country, for in the words of Stephen Decatur, *Our Country, in dealing with other countries may she always be right; but it is still our country, right or wrong.*

The sixth fold is for where our hearts lie. It is with our heart that we pledge allegiance to the flag of the United States of America, and to the Republic for which it stands, one Nation under God, indivisible, with Liberty and Justice for all.

The seventh fold is a tribute to our Armed Forces, for it is through the Armed Forces that we protect our country and our flag against all her enemies, whether they be found within or without the boundaries of our republic.

The eighth fold is a tribute to the one who entered into the valley of the shadow of death, that we might see the light of day, and to honor mother, for whom it flies on Mother's Day.

The ninth fold is a tribute to womanhood; for it has been through their faith, their love, loyalty and devotion that the

Folding the American Flag. Two Airmen fold
the American Flag in the traditional way.

character of the men and women who have made this country great
has been molded.

The tenth fold is a tribute to the father, for he, too, has
given his sons and daughters for the defense of our country since
they were first born.

The eleventh fold, in the eyes of a Hebrew citizen
represents the lower portion of the seal of King David and King
Solomon, and glorifies in their eyes, the God of Abraham, Isaac,
and Jacob.

The twelfth fold, in the eyes of a Christian citizen,
represents an emblem of eternity and glorifies, in their eyes, God
the Father, the Son, and Holy Spirit.

The thirteenth fold, when the flag is completely folded, the
stars are uppermost reminding us of our nation's motto, *In God We
Trust*.

After the flag is completely folded, the remaining portion
of the flag, the flap, is tucked in. It now takes on the appearance of
a cocked hat, ever reminding us of the soldiers who served under
General George Washington, and the sailors and Marines who
served under Captain John Paul Jones, who were followed by their
comrades and shipmates in the Armed Forces of the United States,
preserving for us the rights, privileges, and freedoms we enjoy
today.

The next time you see a flag ceremony honoring someone
that has served our country, either in the Armed Forces or in our
civilian services such as the Police Force or Fire Department, keep

in mind all the important reasons behind each and every movement. They have paid the ultimate sacrifice for all of us by honoring our flag and our Country.

STRUCK DOWN, BUT NOT DESTROYED

Brian Shul was an Air Force fighter pilot for 20 years. Shot down in Vietnam, he spent one year in military hospitals recovering from his injuries and miraculously was able to return to active flying duty. He culminated his flying career with assignment to the prestigious SR-71, the world's fastest, highest flying jet. As a Blackbird pilot, Brian participated in over-flights of Libya during the Libyan Crisis in 1986, providing key reconnaissance for the destruction of terrorist sites.

Retired from the Air Force in 1990, Brian pursued his writing and photographic interests and now owns Gallery One Publishing (www.sleddriver.com). He has authored five books on aviation for which he does all the writing, flying, and photography. His remarkable story of perseverance is shared with numerous audiences annually, as Brian is in demand as a keynote speaker nationwide. Brian Shul gave the following speech in Chico, California on October 3, 2001.

Thank you for the opportunity to address this rally today. It is not often that a fighter pilot is asked to be the keynote speaker. There is a rumor that they are unable to put two sentences together coherently. I'd like to dispel that rumor today by saying that I can do that, and in fact that I have written several books. I always wanted to be an author, and I ARE one now.

I'm a pretty lucky person really. I'm like the little boy who tells his father that when he grows up he wants to be a jet pilot, and his father replies, *Sorry son, you can't do both*. I made that choice a long time ago and flew the jets. I was fortunate to live my dream, and then some. I survived something I shouldn't have, and today, tell people that I am 28 years old, as it has been that long since I was released from the hospital. It was like I received a second life, and in the past 28 years, I have gotten to see and do much, so much that I would not have thought possible.

Returning to fly jets in the Air Force, flying the SR-71 on spy missions, spending a year with the Blue Angels, running my own photo studio ... and so much more ... and now, seeing our country attacked in such a heinous way.

Some of you here today have heard me speak before, and know that I enjoy sharing my aviation slide show. I have brought no slides to show you, as I feel compelled today, to address different issues concerning this very difficult time in our nation's history. I stand before you today, not as some famous person, or war hero. I am far from that.

You know, they say a good landing is one you can walk away from, and a really great one is when you can use the airplane again. Well, I did neither ... and I speak to you today as simply a fellow American citizen. Like you, I was horrified at the events of September 11th. But I was not totally surprised that such a thing could happen, or that there were people in the world who would perpetrate such deeds, willingly, against us. Having sat through many classified briefings while in the Air Force, I was all too aware of the threat, and I can assure you, it has always been there in one form or another. And those of you, who have served in the defense of this nation, know all too well the response that is needed. In every fighter squadron I was in, there was a saying that we knew to be true, that said, when there was a true enemy, you negotiate with that enemy with your knee in his chest and your knife at his throat. Many people are unfamiliar with this way of thinking, and shrink from its ramifications.

War is such a messy business, and there are many who want no part of it, but rush to bask in the security blanket of its victory. I spent an entire military career fighting Communism and was very proud to do so. We won that war; we beat one of the worst scourges to humankind the world has known. But it took a great effort, over many years of sustained vigilance and much sacrifice by so many whose names you will never know. And perhaps our nation, so weary from so long a cold war, relaxed too much and felt the world was a safer place with the demise of the Soviet Union.

We indulged ourselves in our own lives and gave little thought to the threats to our national security. You know, normally, my talks are laced with numerous jokes as I share my stories, but I have very few jokes to tell this afternoon. These murdering fanatics came into our land, lived amongst our people, flew on our planes, crashed them into our buildings, and killed thousands of our citizens. And nowhere along their gruesome path were they questioned or stopped.

The joke is on us. We allowed this country to become soft. We shouldn't really be too surprised that this could happen. Did we really think that we could keep electing officials who put self above nation and this would make us stronger? Did we really think that a strong economy adequately replaced a strong intelligence community? Did we imagine that a President who practically gave away the store on his watch, was insuring national security?

While our country was mired in the wasted excess of a White House sex scandal, the drums of war beat loudly in foreign lands, and we were deaf. Our response was to give the man two terms in office, and even then barely half the American public exercised their right to vote. We have only ourselves to blame. Our elected officials are merely a reflection of our own values and what we deem important. Did we not realize that America had become a laughing stock around the world? We had lost credibility, even amongst our allies. To our enemies we had no resolve. We made a lot of money, watched a lot of TV, and understood little about what was happening beyond our shores. We were, simply, an easy target.

But we are a country awakened now. We have been attacked in our homeland. We have now felt the reality of what an unstable and dangerous world it truly is. And still, in the face of this unprecedented carnage in our most prominent city, there are those who choose to take this opportunity to protest, and even burn the flag.

If I were the regents or alumni of certain large universities in this county, I would be embarrassed to be producing students of such ignorance and naive notions. Like mindless sheep, they march with painted faces and trite sayings on signs, blissfully ignorant of the world they live in, and the system that protects them, hoping maybe to make the evening news. Perhaps, if they had spent more time in class, they would have learned that those who forget the past are condemned to repeat it. They might have learned that all it takes for evil to succeed in the world is for good people to stand by and do nothing. If they had simply gone back in history as recently as the Vietnam War, they would have learned that an enemy who knows it can never defeat us militarily will persist as long as there is dissension and disruption in our land. Their ignorance can be understood, as their young empty minds have been filled with the rewritten history tripe that tenured leftist professors can spew out with no fear of removal. But the unwitting aid they provide the enemy, in disrupting the national resolve, is unforgivable.

I think this is a wonderful country, though, that gives everyone their voice of dissension. I am all for people expressing their views publicly because it makes it much easier for us to identify the truly foolish, and to know who cannot be counted on in times of crisis. These are the weak and cowardly who, when the enemy is crashing through the front door, will cower in the back room, counting on better men than themselves to make and keep them free. Well, the enemy is at our front door, and isn't it interesting those who cry loudest and most often for their rights, are usually those least willing to defend it.

I heard a student on TV the other day say that this war just wasn't in his plans and he would simply head to Canada if a draft occurred. *Just wasn't in his plans*. I wonder what *plans* the young men at the beaches of Normandy had that they never got to live. I wonder if it was in the plans of 19-year-old boys in Vietnam to lie dying in a jungle far from home. I guess the men and women at Pearl Harbor one morning had their plans slightly rearranged too. Gee, I hope we haven't inconvenienced this student. Those people in the World Trade Center have no more plans. It is up to us to have a plan now. It isn't going to be easy. Who ever said it would?

Just what part of our history spoke of how easy it was to form a free nation? It has never been easy and has always required vigilance and sacrifice, and sometimes war, to preserve this union. If it were easy, everyone would have done it. But no one else has, and we stand alone as the most unique country on earth. And isn't it amazing that we have spent a generation stamping God out of our schools and government, and now as a nation, have collectively turned to God in memorial services, prayer vigils and churches around this country.

I am also very disturbed to hear that there are people in this country, at this particular time, who feel it inappropriate to wear the flag on their lapel because they are on the news or in a public job, and school officials who want to remove pro-American stickers so as not to offend foreign students. Well I am offended that these people call themselves Americans. I am offended that innocent people were killed in a mass attack of unthinkable proportions. And I am offended at listening to TV broadcasters speak to me condescendingly, with a bias that screams of their drowning in a cesspool of political correctness. I pity the person who thinks they are going to remove this flag from my lapel. This flag of ours is the symbol of all that is good about this country.

America is an idea. It is an idea lived, and fought for, by a people. We are America, and this is our symbol. We are imperfect in many ways, but we continue to strive toward the ideal our forefathers laid down for us over 225 years ago. I could never imagine desecrating that symbol. Perhaps there are many people in this nation who have never been abroad, or in harms way, and seen the flag upon their return. Those poor souls can never know the deep pride and honor one feels to see it wave, to know that there is still a good ol' U.S.A. With all our warts we are still the greatest nation on earth, and the flag is the most powerful symbol of that greatness.

When I was in grade school, we used to say the Pledge of Allegiance every morning. It is something I never forgot. I wonder how many children even know that pledge today. This flag is our history, our dreams, our accomplishments, indelibly expressed in bright red, white, and blue. This flag was carried in our Revolutionary War, although it had many less stars. But it persevered and evolved throughout a war we had no right to believe we could win. But we did, and built a country around it. This flag, tattered and battle worn, waved proudly from the mast, as John Paul Jones showed the enemy what true resolve was. This banner was raised by the hands of brave men on a godforsaken island called Iwo Jima, and became a part of the most famous photo of the 20th Century. Those men are all dead now, but their legacy lives on in the Marine Memorial in Washington, DC. Those of you who have seen it will recall that inscribed within the stone monument are the words—*When Uncommon Valor, Was A Common Virtue*—I don't believe you'll see the words, *it was easy*, anywhere on it.

This flag has even been to the moon, planted there for all time by men with a vision, and the courage to see it through. I personally know what it is to see the flag, and feel something deep inside that makes you feel you are a part of something much bigger than yourself. Laying in a hospital bed, I can vividly recall looking out the only window in the room and on Sundays, seeing that big garrison flag flying proudly in the breeze. It filled the entire window, and filled my heart with a motivation that helped me leave that bed, and enabled me to be standing here today. And many years later, while fighting another terrorist over Libya, my backseater and I outraced Khaddafi's missiles in our SR-71 as we headed for the Mediterranean, and I can still clearly see that American flag patch on the shoulder of my space suit, staring at me in the rear view mirror as we headed west, and it was a good feeling. Now don't ask me why we had rear view mirrors in the world's fastest jet, I assure you, no one was gaining on us that day.

I am so happy to see so many flags out here today. Long may it wave.

History will judge us. How we confront this chapter of American history will be important for the future of this great nation. This will be a war like none other we have endured. The combatants will not just be the soldier on the battlefront, but will be fought by us the citizens. We are on the battlefield now; the war has been brought to us. We will determine the outcome of this war by how well we remain vigilant, how patient we are with tightened security, how well we support the economy, and most importantly, in the resolve we show the enemy. There are some things worth fighting for, and this country is one of them. I pray for our leaders at this time.

In the Pacific, during WWII, Admiral Bull Halsey said, *There are no great men, just great circumstances, and how they handle those circumstances will determine the outcome of history.*

Our future and the future of coming generations are in our hands. Wars are not won just on military fronts, but by the resolve of the people. We must remain tenaciously strong in the pursuit of this enemy that threatens free people everywhere. I am encouraged that we will win this war. Even before the first shot was finished being fired, there were brave Americans on Flight 93, fighting back. These people were the first true heroes of this conflict, and gave their lives to save their fellow countrymen. This nation, this melting pot of humanity, this free republic, must be preserved. This idea that is America is important enough to be defended. Fought for. Even die for. The enemy fears what you have, for if their people ever become liberated into a free society, tyrannical dictatorships will cease and he will lose power. How can they ever understand this country of ours, so self-indulgent and diverse, yet when attacked, so united in the defense of its principles.

This is the greatest country in the world because brave people sacrificed to make it that way. We are a collective mix of greatness and greed, hi-tech and heartland. We are the country of Mickey Mouse and Mickey Mantle; from John Smith and Pocahontas to John Glenn and an Atlas booster; from Charles Lindbergh to Charley Brown; from Moby Dick to Microsoft; we are a nation that went from Kitty Hawk to Tranquility Base in less than 70 years; we are rock and roll, and the Bill of Rights; we are where everyone else wants to be, the greatest nation in the world.

The enemy does not understand the dichotomy of our society, but they should understand this: we will bandage our wounds, we will bury our dead; and then we will come for you … and we will destroy you and all you stand for.

I read this quote recently and would like to share it with you: *We are pressed on every side, but not crushed, Perplexed, but not in despair, Persecuted, but not abandoned, Struck down, but not destroyed.* That is from II Corinthians. Not too long ago it would have been politically incorrect to quote from the Bible. I am so happy to be politically INCORRECT. And I am so proud to be an American.

Thank you all for coming today and showing your support for your government, and your nation. You are the true patriots, you are the soldiers of this war, you are the strength of America.

WHAT IS AN AMERICAN?

By Mr. Peter Ferrara, Executive Director and Treasurer, American Civil Rights Union.

You probably missed it in the rush of news last week, but there was actually a report that someone in Pakistan had published in a newspaper an offer of a reward to anyone who killed an American, any American. So I just thought I would write to let them know what an American is, so they would know when they found one.

An American is English, or French, or Italian, Irish, German, Spanish, Polish, Russian or Greek. An American may also be Mexican, African, Indian, Chinese, Japanese, Australian, Iranian, Asian, or Arab, or Pakistani, or Afghan. An American may also be a Cherokee, Osage, Blackfoot, Navaho, Apache, or one of the many other tribes known as Native Americans.

An American is Christian, or he could be Jewish, or Buddhist, or Muslim. In fact, there are more Muslims in America than in Afghanistan. The only difference is that in America they are free to worship as each of them choose. An American is also free to believe in no religion. For that he will answer only to God, not to the government, or to armed thugs claiming to speak for the government and for God.

An American is from the most prosperous land in the history of the world. The root of that prosperity can be found in the Declaration of Independence, which recognizes the God given right of each man and woman to the pursuit of happiness.

An American is generous. Americans have helped out just about every other nation in the world in their time of need. When Afghanistan was overrun by the Soviet army 20 years ago, Americans came with arms and supplies to enable the people to win back their country. As of the morning of September 11, Americans had given more than any other nation to the poor in Afghanistan.

Americans welcome the best, the best products, the best books, the best music, the best food and the best athletes. But they also welcome the least. The national symbol of America welcomes your tired and your poor, the wretched refuse of your teeming shores, the homeless, tempest tossed. These in fact are the people who built America. Some of them were working in the Twin Towers on the morning of September 11, earning a better life for their families.

So you can try to kill an American if you must. Hitler did. So did General Tojo, and Stalin, and Mao Tse-Tung, and every bloodthirsty tyrant in the history of the world. But in doing so you would just be killing yourself. Because Americans are not a particular people from a particular place. They are the embodiment of the human spirit of freedom. Everyone who holds to that spirit, everywhere, is an American.

So look around you. You may find more Americans in your land than you thought were there. One day they will rise up and overthrow the old, ignorant, tired tyrants that trouble too many lands. Then those lands too will join the community of free and prosperous nations. And America will welcome them!

WHAT IT MEANS TO BE AN AMERICAN

By Lauren Provini, Grade 5, Green Acres School, May 2001, North Haven, Connecticut.

We hold these truths to be self-evident, that all men are equal ... These words, as stated in the Declaration of Independence, guarantee us equality. Freedom is one of the most important parts of life. The colors of the American flag connect to me in a way that gives me strength and courage. The humans in our country are endowed with citizenship.

To be free is to have a right to do anything you want, like all of us in America have. We have freedom of speech and opinion to express our feelings about issues, policies and laws. We have the right to be educated and to learn ways to solve problems and enjoy the responsibilities of growing up. All Americans have freedom of religion, to believe in any creator. Informing us about news issues in newspapers and magazines–that's freedom of press. America gives us freedoms and the right to be you and me.

Red, White and Blue are the colors of our flag. They play such an important part in the story of our country. Red stands for blood from the soldiers at war. White stands for doves, representing American peace. Blue represents water and the thirst for our country's needs. We need to stand up and defend our country's flag. We must pass along its historical importance to new generations.

As an American, it is our responsibility to be good citizens for our country. We need to be honest and respect others for who they are. Following traditions is very important, too. We need to show service to others and help to show the ways of our country.

Our country is a very important part of my life. I have freedom, our flag and citizenship. America is my Home, Sweet Home. God Bless America!

THE NEW COLOSSUS

Written in 1883 by New York City poet Emma Lazarus, *The New Colossus* was published nearly three years before the Statue of Liberty was erected in 1886 as a gift to the United States from France. After its initial publication, the poem fell into obscurity until 1901, 14 years after Lazarus' death, when it was placed on a bronze plaque at the base of the statue. As the 20th Century unfolded, the poet's words resonated and became synonymous with hope and freedom for immigrants who would pass through Ellis Island and ultimately stitch together much of America's tapestry of cultures.

Not like the brazen giant of Greek fame,
With conquering limbs astride from land to land;
Here at our sea-washed, sunset gates Shall stand
A mighty woman with a torch, whose flame
Is the imprisoned lightning, and her name
Mother of Exiles. From her beacon-hand
Glows world-wide welcome; her mile eyes command
The air-bridged harbor that twin cities frame.
'Keep, ancient lands, your storied pomp!' cries she
With silent lips. 'Give me your tired, your poor,
Your huddled masses yearning to breathe free,
The wretched refuse of your teeming shore.
Send these, the homeless, tempest-tost to me.
I lift my lamp beside the golden door!'

*A*mericanism means the virtues of courage, honor, justice, truth, sincerity, and hardihood–the virtues that made America.

President Theodore Roosevelt

*M*adam, don't bring up your sons to detest the United States Government. Recollect that we form one country now. Abandon all these local animosities and make your sons American.

General Robert E. Lee

*T*his nation is seated on a continent flanked by two great oceans. It is composed of men who are descendants of pioneers, or, in a sense, pioneers themselves, of men winnowed out from among the nations of the old world by the energy, boldness, and love of adventure found in their own eager hearts. Such a nation, so placed, will surely wrest success from fortune.

President Theodore Roosevelt

*L*et the American youth never forget, that they possess a noble inheritance, bought by the toils, and sufferings, and blood of their ancestors; and capacity, if wisely improved, and faithfully guarded, of transmitting to their latest posterity all the substantial blessings of life, the peaceful enjoyment of liberty, property, religion, and independence.

Joseph Story

*T*he family has always been the cornerstone of American society. Our families nurture, preserve, and pass on to each succeeding generation the values we share and cherish, values that are the foundation for our freedoms. In the family we learn our first lessons of God and man, love and discipline, rights and responsibilities ... Families maintain the spiritual strength of religious commitment among our people ... It is essential .... That each of us remembers that the strength of our families is vital to the strength of our nation.

President Ronald Reagan

WHAT IS AMERICA? WHAT IS THE U.S.A.?

From Genius at work #141, Published at Intervals, by Kano Laboratories.

Well, it is purple mountains and fruited plains–but it's
smokestacks And railroad ties too.
It's airplanes and ice cream sodas–Rock and roll and symphonies
It's Christmas stockings and plush hotels
Production lines and space shuttles
It's video games and antique shops
Advertising signs and factory whistles
You can put all that together–and add a million bags of fertilizer–
A thousand juke boxes–a hundred Diesel locomotives but the
Inventory isn't even started.
For America's also the country preacher's warm handclasp
The quick come-back of the smart-looking secretary
It's the set jaw of the high school halfback–
The sharp eyes of the farmer
It's the soft quiet talk of mother to her baby–the big laugh at the
Bowling alley–the close harmony at the wiener roast
It's the crackle of ham and eggs frying
The smell of gasoline exhausts and popcorn.
But America isn't just the sum and substance of all things you see
And hear and touch.
America is ideals–beliefs–feelings–the opportunity to work your
Way through college selling magazines–
To invent and sell a million new can openers–
To get a job or quit one–
To open a hot dog stand or farm your land.
It's the freedom to talk back to a cop or boo a politician–
To invest your money or hide it under the mattress–
To worship God in your own way–To run your own life.
But, you have to look ahead to see America
For, most of all, America is a state of mind–a point of view–
A love of moving on–beyond the next hill–the next gas station–
The next frontier. Expanding–growing–living–
Beyond the horizon.
That's America! That's the U.S. A.!

TEN GREAT REASONS TO CELEBRATE

This article was derived from Dinesh D'Souza's latest book What's So Great About America, published by Regnery. Mr. D'Souza is a Rishwain Fellow at the Hoover Institution at Stanford University.

In the aftermath of last September's terrorist attack, we have heard a great deal about *why they hate us* and about why America is so bad. We've endured lengthy lectures about America's history of slavery, about the defects of American foreign policy, about the materialism of American life, and about the excesses of American culture. In the view of many critics at home and abroad, America can do no right. This indictment, which undermines the patriotism of Americans, is based on a narrow and distorted understanding of America. It exaggerates America's faults, and it ignores what is good and even great about America. As an immigrant who has chosen to become a U.S. citizen, I feel especially qualified to say what is special about this country. Having grown up in a different society–in my case, Mumbai, India–I am not only able to identify aspects of America that are invisible to people who have always lived here, but I am also acutely conscious of the daily blessings I enjoy in America.

Here, then, is my list of the 10 great things about America.

(1) America provides an amazingly good life for the ordinary guy: Rich people live well everywhere. But what distinguishes America is that it provides an incomparably high standard of living for the *common man*. We now live in a country where construction workers regularly pay $4 for a nonfat latte, where maids drive nice cars, and where plumbers take their families on vacation to Europe. Indeed newcomers to the United States are struck by the amenities enjoyed by *poor* people in the United States. This fact was dramatized in the 1980s when CBS television broadcast a documentary, *People Like Us*, which was intended to show the miseries of the poor during an ongoing recession. The Soviet Union also broadcast the documentary, with a view to embarrassing the Reagan administration. But by the testimony of former Soviet leaders, it had the opposite effect. Ordinary people across the Soviet Union saw that the poorest Americans

have TV sets, microwave ovens and cars. They arrived at the same perception that I witnessed in an acquaintance of mine from Bombay who has been unsuccessfully trying to move to the United States. I asked him, *Why are you so eager to come to America?* He replied, *I really want to live in a country where the poor people are fat.*

(2) America offers more opportunity and social mobility than any other country, including the countries of Europe: America is the only country that has created a population of *self-made tycoons.* Only in America could Pierre Omidyar, whose parents are Iranian and who grew up in Paris, have started a company like eBay. Only in America could Vinod Khosla, the son of an Indian army officer, become a leading venture capitalist, the shaper of the technology industry and a billionaire to boot. Admittedly tycoons are not typical, but no country has created a better ladder than America for people to ascend from modest circumstances to success.

(3) Work and trade are respectable in America, which is not true elsewhere: Historically, most cultures have despised the merchant and the laborer, regarding the former as vile and corrupt and the latter as degraded and vulgar. Some cultures, such as that of ancient Greece and medieval Islam, even held it is better to acquire things through plunder than through trade or contract labor. But the American Founders altered this moral hierarchy. They established a society in which the life of the businessman, and of the people who worked for him, would be a noble calling. In the American view, there is nothing vile or degraded about serving your customers either as a CEO or as a waiter. The ordinary life of production and supporting a family is more highly valued in the United States than in any other country. Indeed America is the only country in the world where we call the waiter *sir*, as if he were a knight.

(4) America has achieved greater social equality than any other society: True, there are large inequalities of income and wealth in America. In purely economic terms, Europe is more egalitarian. But Americans are socially more equal than any other people, and this is unaffected by economic disparities. Alexis de

Tocqueville noticed this egalitarianism a century and a half ago, but it is if anything more prevalent today. For all his riches, Bill Gates could not approach the typical American and say, *Here's a $100 bill. I'll give it to you if you kiss my feet.* Most likely the person would tell Mr. Gates where to go. The American view is that the rich guy may have more money, but he isn't in any fundamental sense better than anyone else.

(5) People live longer, fuller lives in America: Although protesters rail against the American version of technological capitalism at trade meetings around the world, in reality, the American system has given citizens many more years of life and the means to live more intensely and actively. In 1900, the life expectancy in America was around 50 years; today, it is more than 75 years. Advances in medicine and agriculture are mainly responsible for the change. This extension of the lifespan means more years to enjoy life, more free time to devote to a good cause, and more occasions to do things with the grandchildren. In many countries, people who are old seem to have nothing to do: they just wait to die. In America the old are incredibly vigorous, and people in their 70s pursue the pleasures of life, including remarriage and sexual gratification, with a zeal that I find unnerving.

(6) In America the destiny of the young is not given to them but created by them. Not long ago, I asked myself, *What would my life have been like if I had never come to the United States?* If I had remained in India, I would probably have lived my whole life within a 5-mile radius of where I was born. I would undoubtedly have married a woman of my identical religious and socioeconomic background. I would almost certainly have become a medical doctor, or an engineer or a computer programmer. I would have socialized entirely within my ethic community. I would have a whole set of opinions that could be predicted in advance; indeed, they would not be very different from what my father believed, or his father before him. In sum, my destiny would to a large degree have been given to me. In America, I have seen my life take a radically different course. In college, I became interested in literature and

politics, and I resolved to make a career as a writer. I married a woman whose ancestry is English, French, Scotch-Irish, German, and American Indian. In my 20s I found myself working as a policy analyst in the White House, even though I was not an American citizen. No other country, I am sure, would have permitted a foreigner to work in its inner citadel of government. In most countries in the world, your fate and your identity are handed to you; in America, you determine them for yourself. America is a country where you get to write the script of your own life. Your life is like a blank sheet of paper, and you are the artist. This notion of being the architect of your own destiny is the incredibly powerful idea that is behind the worldwide appeal of America. Young people especially find irresistible the prospect of authoring the narrative of their own lives.

(7) America has gone further than any other society in establishing equality of rights: There is nothing distinctively American about slavery or bigotry. Slavery has existed in virtually every culture, and xenophobia, prejudice and discrimination are worldwide phenomena. Western civilization is the only civilization to mount a principled campaign against slavery; no country expended more treasure and blood to get rid of slavery than the United States. While racism remains a problem in America, this country has made strenuous efforts to eradicate discrimination, even to the extent of enacting policies that give legal preference in university admissions, jobs and government contracts to members of minority groups. Such policies remain controversial, but the point is that it is extremely unlikely that a racist society would have permitted such policies in the first place. And surely African-Americans like Jesse Jackson are vastly better off living in America than they would be if they were to live in, say, Ethiopia or Somalia.

(8) America has found a solution to the problem of religious and ethnic conflict that continues to divide and terrorize much of the world: Visitors to places like New York are amazed to see the way in which Serbs and Croatians, Sikhs and Hindus, Irish Catholics and Irish Protestants, Jews and Palestinians, all seem to work and live together in harmony. How is this possible when

these same groups are spearing each other and burning each other's homes in so many places in the world? The American answer is twofold. First, separate the spheres of religion and government so no religion is given official preference but all are free to practice their faith as they wish. Second, do not extend rights to racial or ethnic groups but only to individuals; in this way, all are equal in the eyes of the law, opportunity is open to anyone who can take advantage of it, and everybody who embraces the American way of life can *become American*. Of course there are exceptions to these core principles, even in America. Racial preferences are one such exception, which explains why they are controversial. But in general America is the only country in the world that extends full membership to outsiders. The typical American could come to India, live for 40 years, and take Indian citizenship. But he could not *become Indian*. He wouldn't see himself that way, nor would most Indians see him that way. In America, by contrast, hundreds of millions have come from far-flung shores and over time they, or at least their children, have in a profound and full sense *become American*.

(9) America has the kindest, gentlest foreign policy of any great power in world history: Critics of the U.S. are likely to react to this truth with sputtering outrage. They will point to longstanding American support for a Latin or Middle Eastern despot, or the unjust internment of the Japanese during World War II, or America's reluctance to impose sanctions on South Africa's apartheid regime. However one feels about these particular cases, let us concede to the critics the point that America is not always in the right. What the critics leave out is the other side of the ledger. Twice in the 20th Century, the United States saved the world: first from the Nazi threat, then from Soviet totalitarianism. What would have been the world's fate if America had not existed? After destroying Germany and Japan in World War II, the U.S. proceeded to rebuild both countries, and today they are American allies. Now we are doing the same thing with Afghanistan. Consider, too, how magnanimous the U.S. has been to the former Soviet Union after its victory in the Cold War. For the

most part America is an abstaining superpower: It shows no real interest in conquering and subjugating the rest of the world. (Imagine how the Soviets would have acted if they had won the Cold War.) On occasion, America intervenes to overthrow a tyrannical regime or to halt massive human-rights abuses in another country, but it never stays to rule that country. In Grenada, Haiti and Bosnia, the U.S. got in and then it got out. Moreover, when America does get into a war, it is supremely careful to avoid targeting civilians and to minimize collateral damage. Even as America bombed the Taliban infrastructure and hideouts, its planes dropped rations of food to avert hardship and starvation of Afghan civilians. What other country does these things?

(10) America, the freest nation on Earth, is also the most virtuous nation on Earth: This point seems counterintuitive, given the amount of conspicuous vulgarity, vice and immorality in America. Indeed some Islamic fundamentalists argue that their regimes are morally superior to the United States because they seek to foster virtue among the citizens. Virtue, these fundamentalists argue, is a higher principle than liberty. Indeed it is. And let us admit that in a free society, freedom will frequently be used badly. Freedom, by definition, includes the freedom to do good or evil, to act nobly or basely. But if freedom brings out the worst in people, it also brings out the best. The millions of Americans who live decent, praiseworthy lives desire our highest admiration because they have opted for the good when the good is not the only available option. Even amidst the temptations of a rich and free society, they have remained on the straight path. Their virtue has special luster because it is freely chosen. By contrast, the societies that many Islamic fundamentalists seek would eliminate the possibility of virtue. If the supply of virtue is insufficient in a free society like America, it is almost nonexistent in an unfree society like Iran. The reason is that coerced virtues are not virtues at all. Consider the woman who is required to wear a veil. There is no modesty in this, because she is being compelled. Compulsion cannot produce virtue; it can only produce the outward semblance of virtue. Thus a free society like

America is not merely more prosperous, more varied, more peaceful, and more tolerant–it is also morally superior to the theocratic and authoritarian regimes that America's enemies advocate. *To make us love our country*, Edmund Burke once said, *our country ought to be lovely*. Burke's point is that we should love our country not just because it is ours, but also because it is good. America is far from perfect, and there is lots of room for improvement. Despite its flaws, however, the American life as it is lived today is the best life our world has to offer. Ultimately, America is worthy of our love and sacrifice because, more than any other society, it makes possible the good life and the life that is good.

I AM THE NATION

By Otto Whittaker, Jr. Originally written in 1955 as a public relations advertisement for the Norfolk & Western Railway, now the Norfolk Southern Corporation. This article originally did not contain the phase *the steaming jungle of Vietnam*, which was added later. This article has been widely reprinted, generally without attribution, has been set to music, is reprinted in some newspapers every Independence Day, and has been read into the Congressional Record several times.

I was born on July 4, 1776, and the Declaration of Independence is my birth certificate. The bloodlines of the world run in my veins, because I offered freedom to the oppressed. I am many things and many people. I am the nation.

I am 250 million living souls–and the ghost of millions who have lived and died for me. I am Nathan Hale and Paul Revere. I stood at Lexington and fired the shot heard around the world. I am Washington, Jefferson and Patrick Henry. I am John Paul Jones, the Green Mountain Boys and Davy Crockett. I am Lee and Grant and Abe Lincoln.

I remember the Alamo, the Maine and Pearl Harbor. When freedom called, I answered and stayed until it was over, over there. I left my heroic dead in Flanders Field, on the rock of Corregidor, on the bleak slopes of Korea and in the steaming jungle of Vietnam.

I am the Brooklyn Bridge, the wheat lands of Kansas and the granite hills of Vermont. I am the coal fields of the Virginias and Pennsylvania, the fertile lands of the West, the Golden Gate and the Grand Canyon. I am Independence Hall, the Monitor and the Merrimac.

I am big. I sprawl from the Atlantic to the Pacific—my arms reach out to embrace Alaska and Hawaii. I am more than five million farms. I am forest, field, mountain and desert. I am quiet villages—and cities that never sleep.

You can look at me and see Ben Franklin walking down the streets of Philadelphia with his bread loaf under his arm. You can see Betsy Ross with her needle. You can see the lights of Christmas and hear the strains of *Auld Lang Syne* as the calendar turns.

I am Babe Ruth and the World Series. I am 110,000 schools and colleges and 330,000 churches where my people worship God as they think best. I am a ballot dropped into a box, the roar of a crowd in a stadium and the voice of a choir in a cathedral. I am an editorial in a newspaper and a letter to a congressman.

I am Eli Whitney and Stephen Foster. I am Tom Edison, Albert Einstein and Billy Graham. I am Horace Greeley, Will Rogers and the Wright Brothers. I am George Washington Carver, Jonas Salk and Martin Luther King, Jr.

I am Longfellow, Harriet Beecher Stowe, Walt Whitman and Thomas Paine.

Yes, I am the nation, and these are the things that I am. I was conceived in Freedom and, God willing, in freedom I will spend the rest of my days. May I possess always the integrity, the courage and the strength to keep myself unshackled, to remain a citadel of freedom and a beacon of hope to the world.

OLD GLORY

The name *Old Glory* was first applied to the U.S. flag by a young sea captain who lived in Salem, Massachusetts. On his twenty-first birthday, March 17, 1824, Captain William Driver was presented a beautiful flag by his mother and a group of Salem girls. Driver was delighted with the gift. He exclaimed, *I name her 'Old*

Glory.' Then, Old Glory accompanied the captain on his many voyages.

Captain Driver quit the sea in 1837. He settled in Nashville, Tennessee. On patriotic days he displayed Old Glory proudly from a rope extending from his house to a tree across the street. After Tennessee seceded from the Union in 1861, Captain Driver hid Old Glory. He sewed the flag inside a comforter. When Union soldiers entered

Nashville on February 25, 1862, Driver removed Old Glory from its hiding place. He carried the flag to the state capitol building and raised it.

Shortly before his death, the old sea captain placed a small bundle into the arms of his daughter. He said to her, *Mary Jane, this is my ship flag, Old Glory. It has been my constant companion. I love it as a mother loves her child. Cherish it as I have cherished it.*

The flag remained as a precious heirloom in the Driver family until 1922. Then it was sent to the Smithsonian Institution in Washington, where it is carefully preserved under glass today.

My American Value

By David Bates. Eight-year-old, third grader David Bates of Spanish Fork, Utah won the 2002 Army writing contest with this letter. His letter was selected from over 14,000 other entries. The contest asked *Which of these seven American values–loyalty, duty, respect, selfless service, honor, integrity or courage–is the most important in your daily life? Why?* This contest was sponsored by the Army and the Weekly Reader.

I think selfless service means freely doing things for other people without expecting a reward. It is most important in my every day life because it incorporates all the other virtues. I can help people every day by doing things for them willingly and without having to be asked.

The people fighting for our freedom are providing a great deal of selfless service. By being honest I am serving them with my words. By showing integrity I am serving them with my good choices. By being loyal I am serving them with my commitment. By doing my duty I am serving them with my word that I will do my part. By showing respect I am serving them with my obedience to our beliefs. By being courageous I am serving them with my bravery. So in other words all the virtues come back to the same thing: selfless service.

I know that the soldiers out there are showing all these services and we should too. That is what I think selfless service to our country is.

THIS IS MY COUNTRY

By Major William T. Coffey, Jr., June 2001. This story is presented to you, my countrymen, as my present on our nation's 225th anniversary. It is my hope that as you read this article it helps you reflect on the character of our country and what makes us a proud and united America. Happy Birthday America!

In August 2000 my wife and I took our two children to Santa Fe, New Mexico for a family vacation. We made a long weekend out of it and wanted to experience some of the local history and culture. We learned that the Santa Clara Pueblo Indians, who have been living on the banks of the Rio Grande for centuries, were celebrating their *Feast Days*. Their pride manifests itself during their annual Feast Days with song, art, costume, dance, foods and a complex array of symbols, spirits, chants and colors. My family spent the better part of a day surrounded by their celebrations, song and dance. Their pride, heritage and manner of celebration fascinated me. After witnessing these celebrations, I am convinced they are a proud, noble and decent people.

But one event we watched made me question my own sense of history and heritage. This event consisted of over 400 tribal members dancing in full traditional costume. Their dress consisted of feathers, animal skins and furs, face paint, bells, beads and the like. We watched these dancers continue one dance, The Corn

Dance, for over an hour in stagnant dust and temperatures exceeding 100 degrees. The dancers, men and women, ranged in age from three to well into their eighties. They were all synchronized in their movements, chants and song. Each was espousing their pride, history and their strong sense of identity steeped in ancient traditions. What they were celebrating was obviously quite important to them and to their culture. I watched wearing khaki shorts, sandals, a T-shirt and a baseball cap. A Santa Clara Pueblo Indian I was not! During this dance is when I developed a sense that I had been, in part, *cheated of my heritage*; for at that moment, my heritage didn't seem nearly as colorful and rich as that of the Santa Clara Pueblo people. Since that weekend I have reflected on my own heritage, my own history and the history and heritage of our nation. I think it now appropriate to share with you my pride, our history and our American heritage and explain what I believe is the substantive fiber of our nation.

As Americans: We honor the great Americans who served and sacrificed for us, those who showed the world the caliber of citizenry we as a nation produce. We know many of them simply by their last names: Jefferson, Lincoln, Armstrong, Monroe, King, Patton, Paine, Washington, and countless others. We remember these Americans because we honor their service, sacrifice and contributions to our nation.

We wrote our own unique history with tongue and pen and deed. Our patriotic hearts are touched when we hear our history repeated with words like *Give me liberty or give me death; When in the course of human events; Ask not what your country can do for you ...; Damn the torpedoes, full speed ahead; I shall return; Remember the Alamo; My Country tis of thee, Sweet Land of Liberty;* and *We the people ...* We have learned these simple words and know their meaning because we are Americans.

We honor other great Americans who have lived the American dream as industrialists, capitalists, philanthropists, inventors and motivators, men like Rockefeller, Gates, Perot, Getty, Ford, Edison, DuPont ... to name a few.

We honor our Founding Fathers. Some of these men are the 56 brave men who signed the Declaration of Independence whom *with firm reliance on the protection of divine providence*, mutually pledged their lives, their fortunes, and their sacred honor to secure our nation's freedom.

We embody the bald eagle as our national symbol. The eagle's domain is the sky, his nests are perched on the highest crags, he screams his defiance at the elements and he is a vicious foe to his enemies. We embrace, and are guided by, the Declaration of Independence and the Constitution of the United States and its Bill of Rights.

We learned about our pioneer men, women and children who walked, fought, bled and carved their way westward across our vast, promising and bountiful continent. When we think of them and *The West,* we think of the Oregon and Santa Fe trails; we think of cowboys, indians, cattle drives, tumbleweeds, log cabins, barbed wire, Sutter's Mill, *Pikes Peak or Bust,* covered wagons, and windmills. It's all so American.

We created and celebrate a wide array of holidays. Holidays honoring our nation include: Independence Day, Flag Day, Memorial Day, Armed Forces Day and Veterans Day. We honor great men who helped shape America with Columbus Day, Martin Luther King Day and Presidents Day. We celebrate our blessings and bounty with Thanksgiving; we celebrate our creators, our religions, and our diverse heritage in our own ways with Christmas, Hanukkah, Easter, Saint Patrick's Day, Kwanza and Cinco de Mayo. We celebrate these days because it's who we are.

We invented and listen to the sounds of Jazz, Blues, Bluegrass, Country, Western, Country & Western, Rock & Roll, Native American, Dixieland, Rap and Hip-hop. These are the sounds of America.

We cherish and display the paintings of Frederick Remington who painted the American West and Norman Rockwell who painted the faces and character of America. We treasure R.C. Gorman who honors Native American women with his unique blend of colors and hues. Ansel Adams has shown us how beautiful our land is in simple black and white.

We wrote and adopted national songs like *America The Beautiful, God Bless America, The Battle Hymn of the Republic, My Country 'Tis of Thee, Home on the Range, Dixie, Yankee Doodle Dandy,* and most important of all, *The Star Spangled*

Banner–our National Anthem. We sing these songs because we love our country and are proud of our heritage.

We proudly recite The Pledge of Allegiance, our national pledge to our flag and to the republic for which it stands. We are united as Americans with this pledge.

We include words in our national vocabulary like liberty, freedom, republic, democracy, equality, justice, rights, citizenship and patriotism. We know what these words mean because as Americans we live them!

We cherish and protect our great national lands. Our purple mountains, amber waves and fruited plains include wondrous places like Yellowstone and Yosemite; Niagara Falls and the Great Salt Lake; the Sun Belt, Bible Belt, Wheat Belt and Corn Belt; the Appalachians, Rocky, Sierra Nevada and Cascade mountains; Pikes Peak, New England and the Great American West; the Bad Lands, the Mojave Desert, Key West, the Grand Canyon and the Ozarks. Our amber waves of grain and fruited plains feed us and also much of the world. Our lands bear sequoia, redwood, and joshua trees; saguaro, organ pipe and prickly pear cacti. We cherish these lands because God has blessed this, our home sweet home with such beauty and bounty.

We built great cities out of the untamed wilderness. Out of swampland arose our nation's capital, Washington, D.C. We built New York, Chicago and Los Angeles, Dallas and Denver; Minneapolis and St. Paul; Baltimore, Philadelphia, Miami, Seattle, San Francisco, and countless others.

We created our own unique blend of foods and diet and cuisine. We originated hot dogs, hamburgers, NY style pizza, Bar-B-Q sauce for every conceivable application, Tex-Mex, salad bars, milk shakes, and Tabasco. We made popular T-bone steaks, prime rib, fries, coleslaw, chips and dip, Twinkies and other wondrous forms of sugar. We thrive on sundaes, banana splits, cotton candy, Buffalo wings, the Big Mac, Whopper and the triple burger with everything on it. We eat these foods because this is what we want.

We invented baseball, football, volleyball and basketball. We have the World Series and the Super Bowl, and we have some of the best athletes in the world. We cheer for these athletes because they show us what winning is all about, and we, as Americans, love competition and winning.

We remember those places where our roots of liberty were planted, the places where our freedoms were won and where our Union was preserved. These are places like Lexington and Concord; Bunker Hill and Antietem and Little Big Horn; Fort McHenry, the Alamo, Valley Forge, Pearl Harbor; and the courthouse in the little town of Appomattox. We remember and honor these places because in these places freedom rings loudly.

We sent more of our warriors overseas to fight and die for other peoples' freedoms than any other nation in the history of mankind. We sent our warriors not to conquer lands, but to conquer hearts and to free nations from oppression, genocide and tyranny. Our national obligation is to export peace and freedom—because this is the right thing to do. This obligation has required our youth to shed their blood in places known as Verdun, Omaha Beach, and the Somme. We died at Ia Drang Valley, Inchon, Iwo Jima, Pork Chop Hill, and Anzio. At Midway, Beirut, Hamburger Hill, Somalia, Bastogne, and Guadalcanal, we ensured freedom of all men with our ultimate sacrifice. Saint Mere Eglise, Khe Sahn, Tarawa, Belleau Wood, the Marne, Kasserine Pass, Bosnia, Kosovo, and thousands of other unnamed tracks of land, sky and ocean define and consecrate the American commitment to freedom for all peoples.

We honor the more than 25 million living heroes, each of which raised their youthful right hand and took the Oath of Office or Oath of Enlistment stating, *I do solemnly swear that I will support and defend the Constitution of the United States against all enemies, foreign and domestic* ... We often refer to these American heroes simply as *veterans*. As Americans we honor these heroes because, without them, America could never have survived.

We possess the most honorable, most respected and most feared military in the world today. We maintain this strength because we have to protect our greatest asset and our most valued export to the rest of the world ... Freedom.

We honor the so-called *Greatest Generation* and know deep down that they are *great* because they were brought into this world and raised by the *Greatest Generation* of moms. Moms who taught them right from wrong and instilled in them a sense of national pride, selflessness, discipline, service to our nation, patriotism, courage and character—values that have kept America on the winning side of history. Deep down we know that all of our generations were and still are the greatest because they all raised the next generation of American patriots. We honor them all.

We built great and memorable structures like the St. Louis Arch, the Golden Gate Bridge and the Space Needle; the World Trade Center, Sears Tower and the Empire State building; Mount Vernon, Montecello, and Independence Hall. We have built great monuments like Mount Rushmore and the White House, the U.S. Capitol building, the Washington Monument and memorials to Lincoln and Jefferson. France presented us one of our most beloved monuments, the Statue of Liberty. Her arms comfort and support us. She holds *the lamp beside the golden door*.

We built the world's first airplane and we continue to build the best planes in the world. Our Apollo landings put men on the moon, not once, but several times and we brought them home alive. We have NASA, the Mars Pathfinder, the space shuttle program and the Hubble Telescope. As a nation, we are the driving force in bringing the world together to develop the International Space Station.

We, as a people, can still picture long lines of immigrants in-processing at Ellis Island carrying all their material possessions in one bag while their hearts overflowed with the American Dream. We picture George Washington and the Continental Army crossing the frigid Delaware River to attack the Hessian forces at their winter encampment at Trenton. We picture *Rosie the Riveter* who left her home for the factory, when our fighting men had to leave their homes for the battlefields. And we appreciate the sacrifice of our nation when we picture five Marines and one Navy Corpsman raising Old Glory atop fireswept Mount Suribachi.

We picture these events because they are an integral part of who we are.

Rosie the Riveter.

We created a strong American dollar, the symbol of economic strength and prosperity known around the world. The strength of our currency is the strength of our people, our freedom, and our form of capitalism. Our dollar represents the strength of our workers on whose back, with the sweat of the brow and the grease of the elbow, this country was built.

And most notable of all, We The People, have our national flag, *Old Glory,* the most beautiful flag in the world, whose 50 stars represent our 50 free and independent states, and whose 13 stripes represent our original 13 colonies who stood up against the strongest nation in the world, at the time, and told them we don't want to live under the British Crown anymore.

Oh say does our star spangled banner yet wave? You're damn right it still waves—stronger and prouder than ever. Never have I been prouder of our nation. My pride in our country is not based on what I think; it is based on what I know. I know that America and being an American is a rare and privileged opportunity in the history of the world. We are unique. We set standards for the world to follow and the eyes of the world are upon us. We are not a perfect nation, but we do have perfect ideals and principles that guide us. We are a people with a unique blend of tongues, kindreds, races, religions, colors, creeds and heritages, with a shared future, possessing the perfect ideal of freedom.

We are Americans not because of who we are or where we came from but because of what is in our patriotic hearts. We are not separate from the people of the Santa Clara Pueblo; we are in fact collectively part of the same diverse pool of peoples that provide us our strength and diversity as a nation of Americans. *'We the People'* is all of us, and the U.S. is our home. We are all Americans, and we all deservingly love this great land.

Cheated? Not by an American country mile! I have never been so proud to proclaim that THIS IS MY COUNTRY. July 4th, 2001 marks our nation's 225th birthday. Happy Birthday, America and God Bless our great nation.

CHAPTER 4

HEROES AND COURAGE

It is important for each nation to define and celebrate heroes. America's heroes define who we are, but most importantly, they define who we want to become. The freedom, growth and prosperity of America is the result of the bravery and courage of Americans, our heroes, both sung and unsung, who faced fear, danger and adversity to fight and win. These heroes are the quintessential citizens of our nation. This chapter honors American heroes, and the physical bravery and moral courage that has kept us free.

Deeds, not stones, are the true monuments of the great.

John L. Motley

Heroes may not be braver than anyone else. They're just braver five minutes longer.

President Ronald Reagan

Courage is not simply one of the virtues but the form of every virtue at the testing point.

Lt. Gen. (Retired) Harold G. Moore

True heroism is remarkably sober, very undramatic. It is not the urge to surpass all others at whatever cost, but the urge to serve others at whatever cost.

Arthur Ashe

A hero is someone who over and over does the right thing even though no one is there to witness it.

Bob Kerry, former Senator and recipient of the Medal of Honor

I have always been inspired by America and its heroes–the cowboy, the soldier, and now the firefighters, police officers and rescue workers. There is one common thread in every hero. They are ordinary Americans, they come from nowhere, make their mark, get knocked down, and rise up again.

Ralph Lauren, International Fashion Designer

The republic was not established by cowards, and cowards will not preserve it.

Elmer Davis, U.S. radio announcer and news commentator

THE YOUNG MEN WHO FACED THE ISSUES OF WAR

What is a hero? My heroes are the young men who faced the issues of war and possible death, and then weighed those concerns against obligations to their country. Citizen-soldiers who interrupted their personal and professional lives at their most formative stage, in the timeless phrase of the Confederate Memorial in Arlington National Cemetery,

'not for fame or reward, not for place or for rank, but in simple obedience to duty, as they understood it.'

Who suffered loneliness, disease, and wounds with an often contagious élan. And who deserve a far better place in history than that now offered them by the so-called spokesmen of our so-called generation.

James Webb, Former Secretary of the Navy, awarded the Navy Cross, Silver Star, and Bronze Star medals for heroism as a Marine in Vietnam

We are not weak, if we make proper use of those means which the God of nature hath placed in our power ... The battle sir, is not to the strong alone; it is to the vigilant, the active, the brave.

Patrick Henry

DOWN IN THE ARENA

The galleries are full of critics. They play no ball.
They fight no fights. They make no mistakes
because they attempt nothing.
Down in the arena are the doers.
They make mistakes because they try many things.
The man who makes no mistakes lacks boldness
and the spirit of adventure.
He is the one who never tries anything.
He is the brake on the wheel of progress.
And yet it cannot be truly said he makes no mistakes,
because his is the biggest mistake,
the very fact that he tries nothing, does nothing,
except criticize those who do things.

David M. Shoup, General, U.S. Marine Corps

U.S. Marine. Operation Iraqi Freedom, Iraq, March 2003.

*Courage is the first of human qualities because it is
the quality which guarantees all others.*

Sir Winston Churchill

*Courage comes from a reserve of mind
more powerful than outside circumstances.*

Author Unknown

*I would define true courage
to be a perfect sensibility
of the measure of danger,
and a mental willingness to incur it,
rather than that insensibility
to danger of which I have
heard far more than I have seen.*

General William T. Sherman
Union General, 1820-1891

Courage is being scared to death but saddling up anyway.

John Wayne

––––––––––––––––– –––––––––––––––––

*There are no great men, just great
circumstances, and how they handle
those circumstances will determine
the outcome of history.*

Admiral *Bull* Halsey

THEY ARE THE REAL HEROES

USS Theodore Roosevelt. Sailors on the Flight Deck.

From an e-mail by LCDR JJ Cummings, F-14 Tomcat pilot aboard the *USS Theodore Roosevelt (USS TR)*, November 2001, while supporting Operation Enduring Freedom.

One last thing before I complete my novella ... Please remember in your thoughts and prayers every single enlisted Sailor that is slugging it out here on the *USS TR*. The aviator types have it easy in that we get to leave this ship for six fun-filled hours to fly into a foreign hostile land and blow stuff up. We have variety and excitement in our days. Think of that 19-year-old kid up on the flight deck 17 hours a day, fixing the same jets day in and day out while maintaining the same daily routine. Imagine doing that for over 70 days straight (only two days off in the last six weeks). He looks forward to four things: 1) getting off his feet for five minutes, 2) eating bland Navy chow, 3) sleeping in a cluttered space shared by 239 other Sailors and 4) port calls. His variety and excitement comes mainly during in-port visits and, to date, we have had none and oh, by the way, there isn't one in the near or even distant future. They are the real heroes of Operation Enduring Freedom because it is through their efforts that we are able to launch and ultimately defend American shores. Through it all, you rarely hear one complaint from these kids despite the fact that they are working harder than anyone on this planet in the most dangerous office space on Earth, the flight deck of an aircraft carrier.

Hope this e-mail finds you all safe and having a great Holiday Season. Don't worry about us; we are doing great out here. I can honestly say that there is no other place in the world I'd rather be than right here, right now, sticking it to the Taliban.

Later, JJ

Courage is the price that life exacts for granting peace.

Amelia Earhart

The amazing thing about the winners is that none of them really felt that they were doing anything special. They just felt like it was the right thing to do. And that's something about courage that really all of us have within us, the capacity to do the right thing.

Caroline Kennedy, during annual Profiles in Courage Award interview

They and all who are participating in Operation Enduring Freedom are heroes. They put their lives on the line on behalf of freedom and on behalf of America, and they do it each and every day. I'm so very proud of them and their comrades in arms.

General Richard B. Myers, Chairman, Joint Chiefs of Staff

Sure I was scared, but under the circumstances, I'd have been crazy not to be scared ... There's nothing wrong with fear. Without fear, you can't have acts of courage.

Sergeant Theresa Kristek, Operation Just Cause, Panama

Victory is never final. Defeat is never fatal. It is courage that counts.

Sir Winston Churchill

Physical courage, which despises all danger, will make a man brave in one way; and moral courage, which despises all opinion, will make a man brave in another.

Charles Caleb Colton

*The important things in life
you cannot see–civility, justice, courage, peace.*

Author Unknown

*You gain strength, courage and confidence by every experience
in which you really stop to look fear in the face.
You are able to say to yourself, 'I have lived through
this horror. I can take the next thing that comes along.'
You must do the thing you think you cannot do.*

Eleanor Roosevelt

WE WILL RALLY THE WORLD ...

*Great harm has been done to us. We have suffered great loss.
And in our grief and anger we have found our mission and our
moment. Freedom and fear are at war. The advance of human
freedom–the great achievement of our time, and the great hope of
every time–now depends on us. Our nation–this generation–will
lift a dark threat of violence from our people and our future.
We will rally the world to this cause by our efforts, by our courage.
We will not tire, we will not falter, and we will not fail.*

President George W. Bush, 20 September 2001, Address to a Joint
Session of Congress and the American People

One man with courage makes a majority.

President Andrew Jackson

*Though soldiers have made an unlimited liability contract of
service, courage cannot be instilled by contractual arrangement.*

Major General (Retired) Carroll D. Childers

The concept of professional courage does not always mean being as tough as nails either. It also suggests a willingness to listen to the soldiers' problems, to go to bat for them in a tough situation, and it means knowing just how far they can go. It also means being willing to tell the boss when he's wrong.

Former Sergeant Major of the Army (SMA) William Connelly

Bravery is the capacity to perform properly even when scared half to death.

General Omar N. Bradley

THEY WERE A BIG DEAL

Rather than go into detail now about what I saw that day, let me share how I expressed it during an October [2001] ceremony held to decorate and honor some of the heroes who emerged that day at the Pentagon: 'I saw Americans coming to the aid of their fallen comrades with little regard for their own safety. If I were to ask each of you about your contributions, I'm sure you'd tell me that they were no big deal—but I would tell you that they were a big deal. Not only did you serve your comrades well that day, you provided all of us with examples of honor and courage that will inspire us in the coming years and in the battles that await us in our war on terrorism. The things you showed us that day are what is good and right about our country, our Army, and the things we all stand for.

Sergeant Major of the Army (SMA) Jack Tilley, October 2001

Where there is one brave man, in the thickest of the fight, there is the post of honor.

Henry David Thoreau

Heroism is latent in every human soul ...
However humble or unknown, they (the veterans) have renounced
what are accounted pleasures and cheerfully undertaken all self-
denials; privations, toils, dangers, sufferings, sicknesses,
mutilations, life-long hurts and losses, death itself—For some great
good, dimly seen but dearly held.

Joshua Lawrence Chamberlain, Memorial Day 1897

A TALE OF EIGHT AMERICANS

By Thomas D. Segel a twenty-six year, retired Marine combat correspondent. Twice recognized for valor, he holds the Bronze Star and was also awarded the Vietnamese Cross of Gallantry, in addition to two Purple Hearts and Joint Service Commendation Medal, along with Navy, Army and two Air Force Commendation Medals. In 1973 he was named Military Journalist of the year and received the Thomas Jefferson Award for journalistic excellence. He is the author of four books, including *Men in Space*, which is the biographical coverage of the space program through 1976.

Michael Parenti stood on the platform at Chico State University and basked in the glow of cheers from hundreds of people in the audience. The California Faculty Association had brought him to this affair ... and it had proven to be a rousing success. Throughout his anti-war speech about the conflict being waged in Afghanistan, he had been able to show those in attendance that the United States was really trying to make the world safe for the corporations which owned it. In a land far way and at a time now long ago, another man stood up in front of hundreds of people. With his platoon pinned down by withering fire, Corporal Charles Abrell rushed forward, sustaining multiple wounds. Reaching the enemy machine gun bunker on that Korean hill, Abrell projected his body through the doorway while holding a live grenade in his hands. The bunker was silenced. Maggie Coulter of the Sacramento, California Yolo Peace Action Group knew how to attract attention. She stood on a street corner in that city and screamed out anti-war protests to people who were stopped in their cars, waiting for the light to change. Sometimes the motorists would yell back in anger. Most often they would just stare blankly at her, as Maggie yelled out all the misdeeds her countrymen were performing in their war against terrorism. It was September 4, 1967 when the Second Platoon of M Company was in danger of being overrun by an overwhelming enemy force. Chaplain Vincent Capodanno ran from the security of the company command post without concern for his own safety. He moved back and forth across the battlefield administering last rites to mortally wounded men. The lieutenant, suffering multiple wounds himself, still refused treatment and directed corpsmen to attend their fallen comrades. Finally, seeing a young corpsman fall wounded and still under the direct fire of an enemy machine-gun, the chaplain covered this young sailor with his own body to shield him from the bullets. Michael Smith is an American Studies professor at the University of California at Davis. Protected by his robe of academic freedom, this faculty member writes and speaks extensively about the wrongs of our actions against terrorists and how to advance the peace movement. He can find nothing right about the involvement of the United States in Afghanistan and dedicates his efforts to developing an activist movement against the war. He arrived in Vietnam in July. Three months later they brought him home. Corporal William T. Perkins Jr. was a combat photographer covering the action of C Company, 1st Battalion, 1st Marines at a place called Quang Tri. There was a strong hostile attack and an enemy grenade landed near Perkins and several other Marines. Realizing the danger, he shouted *Incoming grenade* and in a valiant act of heroism hurled himself across it, absorbing the impact of the explosion and saving their lives.

Charles Trentelman has a continuing commentary on what he calls, *The United States barbaric assault on Afghanistan*. From his protective nook in Berkeley, California, this anti-war writer continues to put out statements which inflame those who read his words. *What worries me*, he says, *is when these idiotic patriots actually think killing people will solve a problem*. In March of 1945 Platoon Sergeant Joseph R. Julian and his men were stopped in their advance on Iwo Jima by heavy enemy fire. Determined to force a break-through against a Japanese machine gun and mortar barrage, Julian fearlessly moved forward to execute a one-man assault on a pillbox. With grenades and rifle fire he secured one objective and moved on to a second and a third enemy cave emplacement. As they were silenced he launched an unassisted bazooka attack on still another fortification ... destroying it before he fell under the endless fire of enemy bullets. Four of these Americans are still living. Four of these Americans are no longer with us. Four of these Americans receive the praises and adulation of a newly forming anti-war movement. Four of these Americans were posthumously awarded the Medal of Honor, protecting the right of the first four to speak out in a free society.

You can select your own heroes.

THE HEROES WE CAN NEVER REPAY

President William J. Clinton's remarks in the small French town of Colleville-sur-Mer at Omaha Beach U.S. cemetery, 7 June 1994.

Now we come to this hallowed place that speaks, more than anything else, in silence. Here on this quiet plateau, on this small piece of American soil, we honor those who gave their lives for us 50 crowded years ago. Today, the beaches of Normandy are calm. If you walk these shores on a summer's day, all you might hear is the laughter of children playing on the sand, or the cry of seagulls overhead, or perhaps the ringing of a distant church bell–the simple sounds of freedom barely breaking the silence–peaceful silence, ordinary silence.

But June 6th, 1944 was the least ordinary day of the 20th Century. On that chilled dawn, these beaches echoed with the sounds of staccato gunfire, the roar of aircraft, the thunder of bombardment. And through the wind and the waves came the soldiers, out of their landing craft and into the water, away from their youth and toward a savage place many of them would sadly never leave ... Oh, the veterans may walk with a little less spring in their step

World War II. American GI hugs a French girl.

and their ranks are growing thinner, but let us never forget–when they were young, these men saved the world. But on this field, there are 9,386 who did not return–33 pairs of brothers; a father and his son; 11 men from tiny Bedford, Virginia; and Corporal Frank Elliot, killed near these bluffs by a German shell on D-Day. They were the fathers we never knew, the uncles we never met, the friends who never returned, the heroes we can never repay. They gave us our world. Those simple sounds of freedom we hear today are their voices speaking to us across the years.

The hero is the one who kindles a great light in the world, who sets up blazing torches in the dark streets of life for men to see by. The saint is the man who walks through the dark paths of the world, himself a light.

Felix Adler

We must be willing to deal with the difficult issues. We must have the courage to tell it like it is–good or bad. We must be willing to deal with the challenges that have often just been pushed to someone else to deal with later. Courage to live the Army values is represented by your ability to face your fear, to act on your training and convictions to carry the day. We must possess the strength of character to do the right things.

LTG Roger C. Schultz, Director, Army National Guard, 2002
From *What the Army Guard Should Be*

When it comes to the pinch, human beings are heroic.

George Orwell

... The formidable will and moral courage of free men that is America's exclusive weapon.

President Ronald Reagan

THE TRUE CHARACTER OF HEROISM

Excerpts from an interview of Lee Bergee, by Dan Prindible, III, from *Military History Magazine.*

During World War II, U.S. Marine Lee Bergee served in the steaming jungles of the Philippines and was wounded during that campaign. He arrived back in the United States on December 13, 1945, and reached his home in Iowa on Christmas Eve, with the temperature hovering at 34 degrees below zero. Little did he realize that five years later he would be back in combat as a platoon sergeant in a Marine rifle company–shivering in the subzero cold of North Korea.

Military History: What acts did you witness that you regarded as outstandingly heroic?

Mr. Bergee: Heroism is a quality few of us would have been able to define in words at that time. It is only in retrospect, after time has passed, and in the civilized comfort and safety of your own home, that exploits you witnessed, and sometimes took part in, take on the character of true heroism. At the time, we were too involved in survival to assess that heroism. It was a real characteristic of the Chosin Few–of being a hero and not knowing it at the time. Cowardice is easily defined because it is so unusual; heroism is not, because it is so common. So when I remember Chosin and the men who fought and died there, I do so with awe. I recall the sheer guts of one of the mortar men. The company was being raked with automatic-weapons fire. That man stood up, in full view of the enemy, exposing himself to sudden death, so that the mortar gunners 35 yards behind him could use him as an aiming stake. He continued to do that for more than two hours. The mortars destroyed many targets, and his heroic act allowed us to break out that morning. Yet that man received no award or citation. Another time, one of the patrols drew withering fire from the enemy, this time on the forward slope overlooking the road. Unable to set up a machine gun because the steep slope would not afford enough elevation to reach the enemy, one of our men lay down under the front leg of the tripod, raising it so the gun could be used to return fire. The machine-gun crew only fired off a few bursts before the enemy fire was trained on the exposed gun. The young Marine who was being used as part of the tripod took a direct hit in the temple. Here is a testimony to a brave young man. He was never cited for bravery, either. Fighting all the way back with frozen feet was in itself a heroic act, but no one received a medal for it. It was a situation where everyone involved was fighting for his life. There was no such thing as *rear echelon* troops at Chosin. To romanticize war is folly, for it is not lovely. In no way do I worship at the shrine of those for whom war is great. It is, however, necessary that free men–men of principle–be willing to fight and if necessary die for that freedom and those principles. Some people tell me it would be wise to try and forget those times. They may be right, but I know I cannot forget. I cannot forget that band of brothers who fought and died alongside me during that terrible winter of 1950. I cannot forget that we who were there share a common bond that time can never change.

*In any moment of decision the best thing you can do
is the right thing, the next best thing is the wrong thing,
and the worst thing you can do is nothing.*

President Theodore Roosevelt

*The rescue effort resulting from the September terror
simply shows how far people in our country will go
to try to find those who are missing. It has always been true
of our military, and I think civilian rescue and
recovery efforts show that it is equally true for civilians.*

President George W. Bush

*Real American heroes don't tread fields of sport,
nor walk the halls of Congress. Rather, they lie buried
in the military cemeteries around the world.*

Anonymous

CITIZENS LIKE YOU

General Henry H. Shelton. U.S. Army.

At a luncheon on 19 January 2001, hosted by the Army, General Henry H. Shelton, the Chairman of the Joint Chiefs of Staff, told the Medal of Honor recipients their *exploits and feats of courage have contributed greatly to the longevity of our republic.* He also added, *Your thoughts on courage, duty, leadership, teamwork and camaraderie are priceless pearls of wisdom and experience for our young men and women.* The Chairman speculated about what motivated the recipients to perform their heroic deeds. *Perhaps it was a gut reaction in the heat of battle, or a desire to save a buddy's life. It could have been anger at the opponent or the fear of being captured or dying in a faraway place. Maybe, it was the sheer will to win, or the flashing thought of the alternative. Whatever it was that motivated you, you did something that no one can be sure any other man would have done or could have done. You didn't quit. You didn't give in to your fears. You had the presence of mind and faith in your maker and in your abilities to do what needed to be done ... We as a nation are made stronger by having citizens like you.*

*W*e can't all be heroes. *Some of us have to stand on the curb and clap as they go by.*

Will Rogers, as a tribute to all veterans

Flags-at-Parade. Patriots stand tall while soldiers parade.

HEROES

Ms. Amy Konigsberger's Second Grade Class at Washington Elementary School in Canton, Ohio wrote this poem, which they dedicated to our heroes nationwide.

H is for ... your helping hands and huge hearts,
the hours of hard work, the headaches,
the heartaches, the heroic acts you do,
and the honor you bring to our country.

E is for ... your effort and unending supply of energy,
the excellence in the example that you set,
the eyes that look up to you and look to you for help,
and for the encouragement you give to everyone every day.

R is for ... the real-life role models that you are,
your quick response for help and rescue,
for reassuring, recovering, and returning
without the promise of a personal reward.

O is for ... all you do for others, overcoming fears,
your occupation of helping and saving,
your obvious dedication and bravery, and
your outstanding commitment to bettering our world.

E is for ... each time you endanger your life to help,
exceeding expectations and going the extra mile,
for the hardships you endure in your experience,
and the education and enrichment you provide.

S is for ... the service and the standards you set for society,
the many selfless acts, the sacrifice, the lives you save,
the sadness you see, and all of the small things
that seem to go unnoticed.

YOU ARE HERE FOR US

Remarks prepared by Major William T. Coffey, Jr. for the recipients of the Congressional Medal of Honor at their Annual Convention, Boston, Massachusetts, October, 2001. Delivered on behalf of Major Coffey by a staff member of the Society.

Poor is the nation that has no heroes ...
Shameful is the one that, having them ... forgets.

Fortunately for America, we have heroes, and we remember them. Tonight ... during this week's Convention and throughout the year, our Nation remembers your heroism, your service, your example, and your sacrifice. Collectively, we look to you so that we may learn, and grow, and aspire to serve this nation like you did.

You are here for us. And thank you very, very much for being here. Thank you for not heeding to General MacArthur's notion that *old soldiers just fade away*. You are here because all of us fighting today's war are in need of your examples ... your demonstrated achievements ... and your character. You heroes are here for us, you don't need us ... we need you.

I have noted that those who took up arms in defense of America displayed what I call the *pinnacle of patriotism* ... *American heroes all*. Yet within this group of heroes ... within this group of soldiers, sailors, airmen and Marines ... our nation finds a pearl, a very small group of men who went well beyond the call of duty, well beyond the imaginable horrors and fears of combat to expand our imaginations of achievable levels of courage, selflessness and duty. Our collective recognition and understanding of such accomplishments remain necessary ingredients to our nation's survival.

Today, as our nation continues mobilizing and fighting this new type of global war, my generation and younger generations thirst for the opportunity to serve our nation well and honorably. We ready ourselves for the time when we are called to duty and required to serve our nation in times of war. In preparing for the beachheads and battlefields of today and tomorrow, we are drawn to your example, which reminds us that the ultimate weapon of this nation remains the character of the individual fighting man and woman.

Your recognition as American Heroes is for us. Your status as a *hero* is for us and our nation to define. It is not for you to define your accomplishments, since you are as humble as you are brave.

Let us now and forever recognize your heroism, let us proudly and justifiably call you *heroes*, and let us let you be our heroes. Let us strive to serve our nation as proudly and courageously as you served it. Let us use your example to develop our own inner strength, character and fiber. Please don't tell us you're not a *hero*. Even if you tell us you're not a hero, we won't believe you, because, quite frankly ... your actions have already spoken for you. All of us need heroes, and therefore, all of us need you. Again, you don't need us ... we need you.

Knowing what I know about this audience here tonight, I recall the words of another old soldier, he said ... *Heroes come in many forms, but most come in uniforms.* Tonight's audience ... you guys ... prove this old soldier right.

Is Our National Soul Any Better One Year Later?

By Dr. William Bennett, *Dallas Morning News*, 11 September 2002. William J. Bennett is a co-director at Empower America and the author of *Why We Fight: Moral Clarity and the War on Terrorism*. Excerpt from the article:

These are the new heroes of our generation: firefighters, police officers and bystanders. In recent years, I have made a practice of asking students who their heroes are. Too many had no answer. Now, they have no excuse. Many heroes died, as they were born, on September 11. Their lives, though over, are living instructions and monuments. Let us never forget them nor what they did to minimize the loss of lives not their own. We must teach our young people to know heroic qualities, which are deeper than hairstyle and pop-icon glitz. We must teach indispensable virtues like courage, honor and duty. Time will tell what we, as a society, truly learned that terrible September day. It is my hope that

America learned once more that good and evil–and right and wrong–are real terms with real meanings. It is my hope that a part of America changed forever–and for the better, not for the trivial and not for the worse.

FROM THE HEART OF A REAL HERO

By Colonel (Retired) David Hackworth, U.S. Army. Distributed by King Features Syndicate Inc. Reprinted with permission.

Jim Silva was a draftee in my infantry battalion in Vietnam. He hated the war, the Army and, for a good while, me. By the time his combat tour was up, he'd gone from point man to platoon sergeant and been awarded a chestful of medals for heroism and multiple wounds. Like millions of combat vets before him, he then headed home to try to reclaim the life he'd led before Uncle Sam said, *I want you*. He sent me some words last week that I felt were worth sharing.

The Memorial weekend is supposed to honor the nation's warriors who have fallen. But that doesn't seem to be happening anymore, and those that our country does honor usually aren't really heroes.

If you attended any veterans' memorial service last month, you would have seen that those who took part were mostly veterans and their relatives.

Most Americans have all but eliminated patriotism as a source for celebration. Memorial weekend means that they get an extended vacation, with pay. Few citizens other than those who've served and their families have any idea of the sacrifices their countrymen made in the past so they can do their thing in the freest land in the world.

When a soldier goes off to war, the sacrifice he and his family make is tremendous. It seems today that only those who have gone to war have any idea of what I am talking about.

Again the movie industry has done itself proud. They released *Pearl Harbor* on Memorial Day. Was this date a coincidence? I think not. Was Hollywood concerned about honoring our war dead? I think not. What they did worry about was making the most money possible on this film, which was more fiction than fact.

Hollywood loves making war movies. Kind of ironic that most American actors wouldn't be caught dead wearing our uniform off the set; yet, they love to portray warriors and receive accolades for being a silver-screen war hero.

It would be nice if this country would get back to honoring and respecting our fallen, but that may now be beyond the average citizen's reach. Pride of being an American may also be a thing of the past.

Frequently, politicians comment on why they ran for office, stating that they want to serve their country. Yet truth to tell, most of them never served in our armed services.

A hero is not a politician, basketball star or a movie actor. None of these people come anywhere near the heroes I remember. They may be stars in their own fields, but they are not heroes. To be a hero in my book, one has to do something above and beyond what most anyone else would do, and, at least on the battlefield, it has to involve an act that could result in death.

America owes a great deal to its fallen veterans. Those are the ones who stood tall on our nation's battlefields. Some died doing heroic deeds. Others died just being in the wrong place at the wrong time. But they're all heroes because they sacrificed their most precious gift, their lives. With their loss, their families have endured the pain from that date forward. They never forget those special men, and this nation should never forget them, either.

These heroes came from all nationalities and races, all faiths and from all walks of life. Most certainly weren't extraordinary in any way, except for the fact that they were all wearing our uniform in a dangerous place and did their duty when our nation called.

War is something that only those that actually served in combat will ever understand. The emotions and sacrifices are the same in all the wars. When combat soldiers hear the national anthem and taps, their hearts overflow with tears. They remember their fallen comrades, and they remember their war as though it was yesterday.

Americans need to understand what the difference is between a celebrity and a hero and start respecting our real heroes.

You won't be able to meet these heroes in person, but you can say a little prayer for them at their gravesite and remember the freedom we enjoy isn't free. Since 1775, good men have paid the price.

THOSE GENTLE HEROES YOU LEFT BEHIND

If you are able, save for them a place inside of you and save one backward glance when you are leaving for the places they can no longer go. Be not ashamed to say you loved them, though you may or may not have always. Take what they have taught you with their dying and keep it with your own. And in that time when men decide and feel safe to call the war insane, take one moment to embrace those gentle heroes you left behind.

By Major Michael O'Donnell, Killed In Action,
24 March 1970, Dak To, Vietnam

I'M NOT A HERO

From an Army officer, (alias) *Lieutenant Smash* (author unknown), in the Kuwaiti Theater of Operations, while preparing for Operation Iraqi Freedom, 22 February 2003.

I'm not a hero. That is to say, I don't think of myself that way. I don't seek out danger. I'm not the type of guy who is always looking for the next adrenaline rush, or the latest thrill sport. I generally avoid dangerous activities. I'm not a coward, either.

I'm not fearless. I realize, every day that I am here, that my life is in danger. There is no way to avoid this conclusion. I'm told to wear body armor and a helmet. I carry a weapon. We build fortifications. I lug a pack full of chemical protection gear everywhere I go. I've received so many shots, I feel like a pincushion. Sometimes, when I have a moment or two to think about it, I feel a little bit scared. Frankly, only an idiot would not be afraid under these circumstances. But I do have courage. Courage is not the absence of fear. To the contrary, courage involves recognizing danger, but acting on the realization that danger must be confronted–or it will find you when you are least prepared. I didn't come here looking for a thrill.

I'm here because there is a hole in the ground in New York, where a couple of the world's tallest buildings used to be.

I'm here because I knew some of those people in the Pentagon. I'm here because my seven-year-old nephew has nightmares about terrorists.

I'm here because whether Saddam is responsible or not for those terrorist attacks, he has the will and is developing the means to do much, much worse.

I'm here because if History teaches us anything, it is that evil men cannot be deterred by sanctions, containment strategies, diplomacy, resolutions, or weapons inspections.

I'm here because I don't believe in appeasement. I'm here because someone has to be. I'm here because I was called. I'm here because I have a job to do.

Some people live their whole lives, long lives, without having left anything behind. My sons will be told their whole lives that their father was a hero.

Lisa Beamer, wife of man believed to have taken action against hijackers on Flight 93 over Pennsylvania on 11 September 2001

Todd Beamer. Age 32. Killed aboard Flight 93, his last recorded words were *Let's Roll*.

Lisa Beamer.

CHAPTER 5

LEADERSHIP AND CHARACTER

Leadership in a free society requires a different set of values and attributes than is required in oppressed societies. In many of these societies, the leaders are in power as the result of military force, family ties or inheritance. Some are corrupt, ruthless, tyrannical, and downright murderous–they hold their leadership positions for reasons other than the will and desire of the people. In America, though, leadership is the result of proven character, trust, goodness, integrity, discipline and selflessness. Leadership formed around character and values is the grease on America's cog. It is *grease* that requires many years and much effort to develop and impart. It is an ingredient in America's recipe for greatness and one this nation cannot survive without.

Leadership is the only ship that doesn't pull into a safe port in a storm.

Author Unknown

Bodily vigor is good, and vigor of intellect is even better, but far above both is character. It is true, of course, that a genius may, on certain lines, do more than a brave and manly fellow who is not a genius; and so, in sports, vast physical strength may overcome weakness, even though the puny body may have in it the heart of a lion. But, in the long run, in the great battle of life, no brilliancy of intellect, no perfection of bodily development, will count when weighed in the balance against that assemblage of virtues, active and passive, of moral qualities, which we group together under the name of character; and if between any two contestants, even in college sport or in college work, the difference in character on the right side is as great as the difference of intellect or strength the other way, it is the character side that will win.

President Theodore Roosevelt, 31 March 1900

A helpless dove can drift
with the wind. It takes an
eagle to fly against the storm.

Author Unknown

*N*othing can bring you peace but yourself.
Nothing can bring you peace but the triumph of principles.

Ralph Waldo Emerson, Author, Poet, Philosopher, 1803-1892

*T*he good leader must have ethos, pathos, and logos.
The ethos is his moral character, the source of one's ability to
persuade. The pathos is the ability to touch feelings, to move
people emotionally. The logos is the ability to give solid
reasons for an action, to move people intellectually.

Mortimer Adler, American Professor, Author, Philosopher and
Educational Theorist

AMERICA'S VALUES AND THE AMERICAN CHARACTER

**Representative
Steve Buyer.**

The following is the statement of
Congressman Steve Buyer, Republican from
Indiana, 12 December 1998, to the 105th
Congress's Impeachment inquiry of President
William J. Clinton.

I thank the gentlewoman, Ms. Bono of
California, for yielding. I am going to support
the Gekas amendment. I will vote for
Impeachment Article IV. The President's

responses to the 81 requests for admissions from the Judiciary Committee were a continuation of a pattern of perjury and obstruction of justice.

When we bring up the issues regarding the impeachment of former Federal judges Mr. Claiborne and Mr. Nixon, what is interesting, at the time we had a Democrat Majority on the Judiciary Committee, and they brought forward Articles of Impeachments. They passed the House. We had managers who prosecuted them in trial before the Senate. What I find most interesting is that these judges were prosecuted, and one standard was used: high crimes and misdemeanors. They said one standard that applies to the President and Vice President will also apply to these Federal judges and other civil officers. Yet now, the President's defenders are arguing Judge Claiborne's position that his private misconduct does not rise to the level of an impeachable offense.

You see, in the defense of the Judges Claiborne and Nixon, the defense lawyers in the trial in the Senate argued that the Federal judges should be treated differently, that they could not be impeached for private misbehavior, because it is extrajudicial. The Democrat Majority at the time rejected that proposition as incompatible with common sense and the orderly conduct of government. Federal judges and the President should be treated by the same standard: impeachment for high crimes and misdemeanors. Well, I agree. I think the Republicans and Democrats at the time in the 1980s on both of those cases agreed and had it right. I think the Judiciary Committee needs to follow the precedent and be consistent, and that is what we are trying to do here.

I also want to express my appreciation to Mr. Coble of North Carolina. Mr. Coble expressed some honesty about his own personal conscience, about his gut and how it was being turned over. And I don't believe anyone should make a mockery about someone describing how they personally feel going through this process, because it is not easy. So I am going to speak about my conscience.

You see, I didn't sleep very well last night. So what I did about 2 a.m. this morning is I went out and took a jog. Now some may say that may not be a smart thing to do in Washington at 2 a.m., but I took a jog down the Mall. I first went through the area of the Korean Memorial. I did that because of my father, and then I thought of Mr. Conyers, and I thought of others; I then went over to the Vietnam Memorial, and I walked slowly. I thought of my days back as a cadet at The Citadel.

There was this officer who was a Vietnam veteran, walked up to the blackboard, and his name today is Colonel Trez. He was a young major at the time, carrying the fresh memories of battle. He walked over and he wrote this statement on the blackboard and demanded that his young Citadel cadets memorize this statement. It read: *Those who serve their country on a distant battlefield see life in a dimension that the protected may never know.*

You see, I worked hard to understand what it meant. I thought I did, but it wasn't until years later that I understood the real meaning from my military service in the Gulf War. I had a very dear friend die. I understand the painful tears, and I understand the horrors of war.

As I jogged back, I stopped at the Washington Monument. The Mall is beautiful at night. And then I thought about the World War II veterans. Mr. Hyde and others, a unique generation. They were truly crusaders. They fought for no bounty of their own. They left freedom in their footsteps. And then I thought about something I had read in military history. After D-Day they were policing up the battlefield and lying upon the battlefield was an American soldier who was dead. No one was around to hear his last words, so he wrote them on a pad. Can you imagine the frustration, knowing you are about to die and there is no one around to say your last words to? I don't know what you would write, but this soldier wrote, *Tell them when you go home, I gave this day for their tomorrow.* Of my fallen comrades, if I permit the eyes of my mind to focus, I can see them. And, if I permit the ears of my heart to listen, I can hear them. The echoes of *do not let my sacrifice be in vain. I fell with the guidon in my hand. Pick it up and stake it in the high ground.*

You see, part of my conscience is driven by my military service. I am an individual that not only is principled, but also steeped in virtues, and I use them to guide me through the chaos. Throughout this case, I think about people all across America, about America's values and the American character, and I want to put it in plain-spoken words.

I believe we are to defend the Constitution, America's heritage, and define our Nation's character. So when I think about America's character and commonsense virtues, I think about honesty. What is it? Tell the truth; be sincere; don't deceive, mislead or be devious or use trickery; don't betray a trust. Don't withhold information in relationships of trust. Don't cheat or lie to the detriment of others, nor tolerate such practice. On issues of integrity, exhibit the best in yourself. Choose the harder right over the easy wrong. Walk your talk. Show courage, commitment, and self-discipline.

On issues of promise-keeping, honor your oath and keep your word.

On issues of loyalty, stand by, support and protect your family, your friends, your community, and your country. Don't spread rumors, lies, or distortions to harm others. You don't violate the law and ethical principles to win personal gain, and you don't ask a friend to do something wrong.

On issues of respect, you be courteous and polite. You judge all people on their merits. You be tolerant and appreciative and accepting of individual differences. You don't abuse, demean, or mistrust anyone. You don't use, manipulate, exploit, or take advantage of others. You respect the rights of individuals.

On the issues of acting responsibly and being accountable, think before you act; meaning, consider the possible consequences on all people from your actions. You pursue excellence, you be reliable, be accountable, exercise self control. You don't blame others for your mistakes. You set a good example for those who look up to you.

On the issue of fairness, treat all people fairly. Don't take unfair advantage of others; don't take more than your fair share. Don't be selfish, mean, cruel or insensitive to others. Live by the Golden Rule.

You see, citizens all across American play by the rules, obey the laws, pull their own weight; many do their fair share, and they do so while respecting authority.

I have been disheartened by the facts in this case. It is sad to have the occupant of the White House, an office that I respect so much, riddled with these allegations, and now I have findings of criminal misconduct and unethical behavior. We cannot expect to restore the confidence in government by leaving a perjurious President in office.

I yield back my time.

The greatest homage to truth is to use it.

Ralph Waldo Emerson

... Virtue, morality, and religion. This is the armor, my friend, and this alone that renders us invincible. These are the tactics we should study. If we lose these, we are conquered, fallen indeed ... so long as our manners and principles remain sound, there is no danger.

Patrick Henry

The strongest oak of the forest is not the one that is protected from the storm and hidden from the sun. It's the one that stands in the open where it is compelled to struggle for its existence against the winds and rains and the scorching sun.

Napoleon Hill

He who is void of virtuous attachments in private life, is, or very soon will be, void of all regard for his country.

Author Unknown

In matters of style swim with the current; in matters of principle stand like a rock.

President Thomas Jefferson, (1743-1826), 3rd U.S. President

The ultimate measure of a man is not where he stands in moments of comfort and convenience, but where he stands at times of challenge and controversy.

Dr. Martin Luther King, Jr.

If you have integrity, nothing else matters. If you don't have integrity, nothing else matters.

Alan Simpson, former Senator

I hold the maxim no less applicable to public than to private affairs, that honesty is the best policy.

President George Washington

Good principles, wisely and honestly administered, cannot fail to attach our fellow citizens to the order of things which we espoused.

President Thomas Jefferson

Of all the properties which belong to honorable men, not one is so highly prized as that of character.

Henry Clay

The job of a football coach is to make men do what they don't want to do, in order to achieve what they've always wanted to be.

Tom Landry, Head Coach, Dallas Cowboys football team

Leadership is a great burden. We grow weary of it at times. ... But if we are not to shoulder the burdens of leadership in the free world, then who will? The alternatives are neither pleasant nor acceptable. Great nations which fail to meet their responsibilities are consigned to the dust bin of history. We grew from that small, weak republic which had as its assets spirit, optimism, faith in God and an unshakeable belief that free men and women could govern themselves wisely. We became the leader of the free world, an example for all those who cherish freedom. If we are to continue to be that example–if we are to preserve our own freedom–we must understand those who would dominate us and deal with them with determination. We must shoulder our burden with our eyes fixed on the future, but recognizing the realities of today, not counting on mere hope or wishes. We must be willing to carry out our responsibility as the custodian of individual freedom.
Then we will achieve our destiny to be as a shining city on a hill for all mankind to see.

President Ronald Reagan

Leadership is the art of human response to uncertainty.

Author Unknown

People never improve unless they look to some standard or example higher and better than themselves.

Tyron Edwards

The key to successful leadership today is influence, not authority.

Author Unknown

Morale is the greatest single factor in successful wars.

President Dwight D. Eisenhower

Great necessities call out for great virtues.

Abigail Adams

It is very easy for ignorant people to think that success in war may be gained by the use of some wonderful invention rather than by hard fighting and superior leadership.

General George S. Patton, Jr.

LEADERSHIP

By Major C.A. Bach, U.S. Army, his address delivered to the graduating officers at Fort Sheridan, Wyoming, 1917.

In a short time each of you men will control the lives of a certain number of other men. You will have in your charge loyal but untrained citizens, who look to you for instruction and guidance.

Your word will be their law. Your most casual remark will be remembered. Your mannerism will be aped. Your clothing, your carriage, your vocabulary, your manner of command will be imitated.

When you join your organization you will find there a willing body of men who ask from you nothing more than the qualities that will command their respect, their loyalty, and their obedience.

They are perfectly ready and eager to follow you so long as you can convince them that you have those qualities. When the time comes that they are satisfied you do not possess them, you might as well kiss yourself goodbye. Your usefulness in that organization is at an end.

From the standpoint of society, the world may be divided into leaders and followers. The professions have their leaders; the financial world has its leaders. We have religious leaders, and political leaders, and society leaders. In all this leadership it is difficult, if not impossible, to separate from the element of pure leadership that selfish element of personal gain or advantage to the individual, without which such leadership would lose its value.

It is in the military service only, where men freely sacrifice their lives for a faith, where men are willing to suffer and die for the right or the prevention of a great wrong, that we can hope to realize leadership in its most exalted and disinterested sense. Therefore, when I say leadership, I mean military leadership.

In a few days the great mass of you men will receive commissions as officers. These commissions will not make you leaders; they will merely make you officers. They will place you in a position where you can become leaders if you possess the proper attributes. But you must make good–not so much with the men over you as with the men under you.

Men must and will follow into battle officers who are not leaders, but the driving power behind these men is not enthusiasm but discipline. They go with doubt and trembling, and with an awful fear tugging at their heartstrings that prompts the unspoken question, *What will he do next?*

Such men obey the letter of their orders but no more. Of devotion to their commander, of exalted enthusiasm which scorns personal risk. Of their self-sacrifice to ensure his personal safety, they know nothing. Their legs carry them forward because their brain and their training tell them they must go. Their spirit does not go with them.

Great results are not achieved by cold, passive, unresponsive soldiers. They don't go very far and they stop as soon as they can. Leadership not only demands but receives the willing, unhesitating, unfaltering obedience and loyalty of other men; and a devotion that will cause them, when the time comes, to follow their uncrowned king to hell and back again if necessary.

You will ask yourselves: *Of just what, then, does leadership consist? What must I do to become a leader? What are the attributes of leadership, and how can I cultivate them?*

Leadership is a composite of a number of qualities. Among the most important I would list self-confidence, moral ascendancy, self-sacrifice paternalism, fairness, initiative, decision, dignity, courage.

Let me discuss these with you in detail.

Self-confidence results, first, from exact knowledge; second, the ability to impart that knowledge; and third, the feeling of superiority over others, that naturally follows. All these give the officer poise.

To lead, you must know–you may bluff all your men some of the time but you can't do it all the time. Men will not have confidence in an officer unless he knows his business, and he must know it from the ground up.

The officer should know more about paper work than his first sergeant and company clerk put together; he should be at least as good a shot as any man in his company.

If the officer does not know, and demonstrates the fact that he does not know, it is entirely human for the soldiers to say to himself, *To hell with him. He doesn't know as much about this as I do*, and calmly disregard the instructions received.

There is no substitute for accurate knowledge. Become so well informed that men will hunt you to ask questions–that your brother officers will say to one another, *Ask Smith—he knows*.

And not only should each officer know thoroughly the duties of his own grade, but he should study those of the two grades next above him. A twofold benefit attaches to this. He prepares himself for duties which may fall to his lot at any time during battle; he further gains a broader viewpoint which enables him to appreciate the necessity for the issuance of orders and joins more intelligently in their execution.

Not only must the officer know, but he must be able to put what he knows into grammatical, interesting, forceful English. He must learn to stand on his feet and speak without embarrassment.

I am told that in British training camps student officers are required to deliver 10-minute talks on any subject that they may choose. That is excellent practice. For to speak clearly, one must think clearly; and clear, logical thinking expresses itself in definite positive orders.

While self-confidence is the result of knowing more than your men, moral ascendancy over them is based upon your belief that you are the better man. To gain and maintain this ascendancy, you must have self-control, physical vitality and endurance and moral force.

You must have yourself so well in hand that, even though in battle you be scared stiff, you will never show fear. For if you by so much as a hurried movement or a trembling of the hand, or a change of expression, or a hasty order hastily revoked, indicate your mental condition, it will be reflected in your men in a far greater degree.

In garrison or camp many instances will arise to try your temper and wreck the sweetness of your disposition. If at such time you *fly off the handle* you have no business to be in charge of men. For men in anger say and do things that they almost invariably regret afterward.

An officer should never apologize to his men; also an officer should never be guilty of an act for which his sense of justice tells him he should apologize.

Another element in gaining moral ascendancy lies in the possession of enough physical vitality and endurance to withstand the hardships of which you and your men are subjected, and a dauntless spirit that enables you not only to accept them cheerfully but to minimize their magnitude.

Make light of your troubles, belittle your trials, and you will help vitally to build up within your organization an esprit whose value in time of stress cannot be measured.

Moral force is the third element in gaining moral ascendancy. To exert moral force you must live clean, you must have sufficient brainpower to see the right and the will to do right.

Be an example to your men. An officer can be a power for good or a power for evil. Don't preach to them–that will be worse than useless. Live the kind of life you would have them lead, and you will be surprised to see the number that will imitate you.

A loud-mouthed, profane captain who is careless of his personal appearance will have a loud-mouthed profane, dirty company. Remember what I tell you. Your company will be the reflection of yourself. If you have a rotten company, it will be because you are a rotten captain.

Self-sacrifice is essential to leadership. You will give, give all the time. You will give yourself physically, for the longest hours, the hardest work and the greatest responsibility is the lot of the captain. He is the first man up in the morning and the last man in at night. He works while others sleep.

You will give yourself mentally, in sympathy and appreciation for the troubles of men in your charge. This one's mother had died, and that one has lost all his savings in a bank failure. They may desire help, but more than anything else they desire sympathy.

Don't make the mistake of turning such men down with a statement that you have troubles of your own, for every time that you do, you knock a stone out of the foundation of your house.

Your men are your foundation, and your house leadership will tumble about your ears unless it rests securely upon them.

Finally, you will give your own slender financial resources. You will frequently spend your money to conserve the health and well being of your men or to assist when in trouble. Generally you get your money back. Very infrequently you must charge it to profit and loss.

When I say that paternalism is essential to leadership I use the term in its better sense. I do not now refer to that form of paternalism, which robs men of initiative, self-reliance, and self-respect. I refer to the paternalism that manifests itself in a watchful care for the comfort and welfare of those in your charge.

Soldiers are much like children. You must see that they have shelter, food, and clothing, the best that your utmost efforts can provide. You must be far more solicitous of their comfort than of your own. You must see that they have food to eat before you think of your own; that they have each as good a bed as can be provided before you consider where you will sleep. You must look after their health. You must conserve their strength by not demanding needless exertion or useless labor.

And by doing all these things you are breathing life into what would be otherwise a mere machine. You are creating a soul in your organization that will make the mass respond to you as though it were one man. And that is esprit.

And when your organization has this esprit you will wake up some morning and discover that the tables have been turned; that instead of your constantly looking out for them, they have, without even a hint from you, taken up the task of looking out for you. You will find that a detail is always there to see that your tent, if you have one, is promptly pitched; that the most and cleanest bedding is brought to your tent; that from some mysterious source two eggs have been added to your supper when no one else has any; that an extra man is helping your men give your horse's grooming; that your wishes are anticipated; that every man is Johnny-on-the spot. And then you have arrived.

Fairness is another element without which leadership can neither be built up nor maintained. There must be first that fairness which treats all men justly. I do not say alike, for you cannot treat all men alike–that would be assuming that all men are cut from the same piece; that there is no such thing as an individuality or personal equation.

You cannot treat all men alike; a punishment that could be dismissed by the men with a shrug of the shoulders is mental anguish for another. A company commander who for a given offense had a standard punishment that applies to all is either too indolent or too stupid to study the personality of his men. In his case justice is certainly blind.

Study your men as carefully as a surgeon studies a difficult case. And when you are sure of your diagnosis apply the remedy. And remember that you apply the remedy to effect a cure, not merely to see the victim squirm. It may be necessary to cut deep, but when you're satisfied as to your diagnosis don't be divided from your purpose by any false sympathy for the patient.

Hand in hand with fairness in awarding punishment walks fairness in giving credit. Everybody hates a human hog.

When one of your men has accomplished an especially creditable piece of work see that he gets the proper reward. Turn heaven and earth upside down to get it for him. Don't try to take it away from him and hog it for yourself. You may do this and get away with it, but you have lost the respect and loyalty of your men. Sooner or later your brother will hear of it and shun you like a leper. In war there is glory enough for all. Give the man under you his due. The man who always takes and never gives is not a leader. He is a parasite.

There is another kind of fairness–that which will prevent an officer from abusing the privileges of his rank. When you expect respect from soldiers be sure you treat them with equal respect. Build up their manhood and self-respect. Don't try to pull it down.

For an officer to be overbearing and insulting in the treatment of enlisted men is the act of a coward. He ties the man to the tree with the ropes of discipline and then strikes him in the face, knowing full well that the man cannot strike back.

Consideration, courtesy, and respect from officers toward enlisted men are not incompatible with discipline. They are parts of our discipline. Without initiative and decision no man can expect to lead.

In maneuvers you will frequently see, when an emergency arises, certain men calmly give instant orders which later, on analysis, prove to be if not exactly the right thing, very nearly the right thing to have done. You will see other men in emergency become badly rattled; their brains refuse to work, or they give a hasty order, revoke it, give another, revoke that; in short, show every indication of being in a blue funk.

Regarding the first man you may say: *That man is a genius. He hasn't had time to reason this thing out. He acts intuitively.* Forget it. *Genius is merely the capacity for taking infinite pains.* The man who was ready is the man who has prepared himself. He has studied beforehand the possible situation that might arise; he had made tentative plans covering such situations. When he is configured by the emergency, he is ready to meet it.

He must have sufficient mental alertness to appreciate the problem that confronts him and the power of quick reasoning to determine what changes are necessary in his already formulated plan. He must have also the decision to order the execution and stick to his orders.

Any reasonable order in an emergency is better than no order. The situation is there. Meet it. It is better to do something and do the wrong thing than to hesitate, hunt around for the right thing to do and wind up by doing nothing at all. And, having decided on a line of action, stick to it. Don't vacillate. Men have no confidence in an officer who doesn't know his own mind.

Occasionally, you will be called upon to meet a situation, which no reasonable human being could anticipate. If you have prepared yourself to meet other emergencies which you could anticipate, the mental training you have thereby gained will enable you to act promptly and with calmness.

You must frequently act without orders from higher authority. Time will not permit you to wait for them.

Here again enters the importance of studying the work of officers above you. If you have a comprehensive grasp on the entire situation and can form an idea of the general plan of your superiors, that and your previous emergency training will enable you to determine that the responsibility is yours and to issue the necessary orders without delay.

The element of personal dignity is important in military leadership. Be the friend of your men, but do not become their intimate. Your men should stand in awe of you–not fear. If your men presume to become familiar, it is your fault, not theirs. Your actions have encouraged them to do so.

And above all things don't cheapen you by courting their friendship or currying their favor. They will despise you for it. If you are worthy of their loyalty and respect and devotion, they will surely give all these without asking. If you are not, nothing that you can do will win them.

And then I would mention courage. Moral courage you need as well as physical courage–that kind of moral courage which enables you to adhere without faltering to a determined course of action which your judgment has indicated as the one best suited to secure the desired results.

Every time you change your orders without obvious reason you weaken your authority and impair the confidence of your men. Have the moral courage to stand by your order and see it through.

Moral courage further demands that you assume the responsibility for your own acts. If your subordinates have loyally carried out your orders and the movement you directed is a failure, the failure is yours, not theirs. Yours would have been the honor had it been successful. Take the blame if it results in disaster. Don't try to shift it to a subordinate and make him the goat. That is a cowardly act.

Furthermore, you will need moral courage to determine the fate of those under you. You will frequently be called upon for recommendations for the promotion or demotion of officers and noncommissioned officers in your immediate command.

Keep clearly in mind your personal integrity and the duty you owe your country. Do not let yourself be deflected from a strict sense of justice by feelings of personal friendship. If your own brother is your Second Lieutenant, and you find him unfit to hold his commission, eliminate him. If you don't, your lack of moral courage may result in the loss of valuable lives.

If, on the other hand, you are called upon for a recommendation concerning a man whom, for personal reasons you thoroughly dislike, do not fail to do him full justice. Remember that your aim is the general good, not the satisfaction of an individual grudge.

I am taking it for granted that you have physical courage. I need not tell you how necessary that is. Courage is more than bravery. Bravery is fearless–the absence of fear. The merest dolt may be brave, because he hasn't the mentality to appreciate his danger; he doesn't know enough to be afraid.

Courage, however, is the firmness of the spirit, that moral backbone, which, while fully appreciating the danger involved, nevertheless goes on with the understanding. Bravery is physical; courage is mortal and moral. You may be cold all over, your hands may tremble; your legs may quake; your knees may be ready to give way–that is fear. If, nevertheless, you go forward; if in spite of this physical defection you continue to lead your men against the enemy, you have courage. But physical manifestations of fear will pass away. You may never experience them but once. They are the *buck fever* of the hunter who tries to shoot his first deer. You must not give way to them.

A number of years ago, while taking a course in demolitions, the class of which I was a member was handling dynamite. The instructor said regarding its manipulation: *I must caution you gentlemen to be careful in use of these explosives. One man has but one accident.* And so I would caution you. If you give way to the fear that will doubtless beset you in your first crater, you will never again have the opportunity to lead those men.

Use judgment in calling on your men for display of physical courage or bravery. Don't ask any man to go where you would not go yourself. If your common sense tells you that the place is too dangerous for you to venture into, then, it is too dangerous for him. You know his life is as valuable to him as yours is to you.

Occasionally some of your men must be exposed to danger which you cannot share. A message must be taken across a fire-swept zone. You call for volunteers. If your men know you and know that you are *right*, you will never lack volunteers, for they will know your heart is in your work, that you are giving your country the best you have, that you would willingly carry the message yourself if you could. Your example and enthusiasm will have inspired them.

And, lastly, if you aspire to leadership, I would urge you to study men.

Get under their skins and find out what is inside. Some men are quite different from what they appear to be on the surface. Determine the workings of their minds.

Much of General Robert E. Lee's success as a leader may be ascribed to his ability as a psychologist. He knew most of his opponents from West Point days, knew the workings of their minds, and he believed that they would do certain things under certain circumstances. In nearly every case he was able to anticipate their movements and block the execution.

You do not know your opponent in this war in the same way. But you can know your own men. You can study each to determine wherein lies his strength and his weakness; which man can be relied upon to the last grasp and which cannot.

Know your men, know your business, and know yourself.

I hope I shall always possess firmness and virtue
enough to maintain what I consider
the most enviable of all titles, the
character of an 'honest man.'
President George Washington

*I*ntegrity is the first and last principle of every leader or
he/she will be a leader without followers.
Major General (Retired) Carroll D. Childers

*L*oyalty is the big thing, the greatest battle asset of all.
But no man ever wins the loyalty of troops by preaching loyalty.
It is given to him as he proves his possession of the other virtues.

Brigadier General S.L.A. Marshall, Men Against Fire

*A*n old Company Commander once said something
to the effect that ... you should never pass up an opportunity
to do everything you can for the troops 'cause one day
you're gonna have to order them up that hill!

Author Unknown

*I*t takes three things to succeed: talent, hard work, and
perseverance. And the greatest of these is not talent.

Scott Moulsen

ONLY FIRST-PLACE TROPHIES

Colonel Hal Moore.
Vietnam.

Words LTG Moore imparted to his officers and battalion staff when he took over command of the Infantry battalion back in 1965. These words are from LTG Moore's and Joe Galloway's book, *We Were Soldiers Once and Young.* These simple principles kept many of his men alive.

Only first-place trophies will be displayed, accepted, or presented in this battalion. Second place in our line of work is defeat of the unit on the battlefield, and death for the individual in combat. No fat troops or officers. Decision-making will be decentralized: Push the power down. It pays off in wartime. Loyalty flows down as well. I check up on everything. I am available day or night to talk with any officers of this battalion. Finally, the Sergeant Major works only for me and takes orders only from me. He is my right-hand man.

*The creative leader is one who will rewrite doctrine,
employ new weapons systems, develop new tactics
and who pushes the state of the art.*

John O. Marsh, Jr., Former Secretary of the Army

*A leader takes people where they want to go. A great leader takes
people where they don't necessarily want to go, but ought to be.*

First Lady Rosalynn Carter

Forty percent of the art of command is the ability to improvise.

S.L.A. Marshall

*Leader Development is more than building
good soldiers, it's about building good people.*

Command Sergeant Major Mark Ripka, 25th Infantry Division

*Just as fire tempers iron into fine steel, so does adversity temper
one's character into firmness, tolerance, and determination.*

Margaret Chase Smith, Lieutenant Colonel
U.S. Air Force Reserve and former U.S. Senator

*Mental toughness is many things and rather difficult to explain.
Its qualities are sacrifice and self-denial. Also, most importantly, it
is combined with a perfectly disciplined will that refuses to give in.
It's a state of mind—you could call it character in action.*

Vince Lombardi, Green Bay Packers Football Coach, 1913-1970

*Let each of you look out not only for his own interests,
but also for the interests of others.*

Philippians 2:4

*Character, not circumstances,
makes the man.*

Booker T. Washington

SOLDIER ACTIONS IN COMBAT

On an Army leadership web site (www.companycommand.com), a soldier asked the following question to General (Retired) Barry McCaffrey, 31 October 2002.

Question: My question deals with how soldiers react to combat situations. When people do extraordinary things under fire, are they acting on instinct? Are acts of heroism related to the type of training received or is it that a person is just naturally courageous? Also, is there any way to instill this warrior ethos in your subordinates?

General McCaffrey's response: My personal instinct is that 25 percent of the U.S. male and female population, if given excellent military training, will perform superbly in combat. It helps to come from a family which develops trust in authority, to have played team sports, to be in excellent physical condition (fatigue makes cowards of us all … Vince Lombardi), to have practiced leadership skills, and to have a sense of spiritual faith.

It is essential to have superior battle leaders who are experts at their profession and who lead by example.

I place my ultimate belief in training … you do in battle what you practice in training. These are complex physical and mental tasks organized in team battle skills. Firefights are won by squads, platoons, and companies which have developed an enormous sense of love and trust for each other … and who have confidence that they can handle extreme burdens of misery and violence. Specifically, in training, units must re-create the physical exhaustion, confusion, hunger, exposure, and where possible the fear of the combat environment. Our training tends to do this at the JRTC [Joint Readiness Training Center], NTC [National Training

Center], CMTC [Combat Maneuver Training Centers], Ranger School, etc.

The courage of the American soldier in battle is extraordinary. 640,000 lost their lives in the 20th Century alone ... most died fighting for a set of ideals they could barely articulate. The battle valor of the rifle companies fighting at 9,000-foot altitude in Afghanistan is in line with our history at Bastogne, Heart Break Ridge, the Ia Drang, and countless other fights not recorded by history. The secret that we rarely talk about is that a significant number of us end up volunteering to serve as front line combat leaders. We actually consider it an incredible honor to lead American soldiers in battle. We are fearful of being killed or maimed, sleepless in worry that we will lose our precious soldiers in battle, but proud and determined to be part of these forward combat units.

As the rifle company moves forward down a jungle trail to link up with a surrounded sister unit ... the sound of the firefight grows ... rounds start cracking thru the brush sounding like the snap of a bull whip ... fear starts to grip every soldier ... platoons moving on line, white faces and hammering hearts, suddenly crashing into 30 enemy soldiers of the enemy rear element at a range of five feet ... an enormous roar of automatic weapons fire ... dozens of grenades with huge bangs lancing bodies on both sides ... the roar of U.S. artillery sounding like a freight train going close overhead and banging off with enormous shattering explosions ... the shriek of F4 Phantoms in steep dive dropping napalm putting huge sheets of blistering flame thru the trees, U.S. soldiers screaming as they are manhandled thru blown down trees to med-evac clearings, the terrible thirst for water, the unbelievable exhaustion, totally sweat soaked and ripped uniforms, the incredible stench of filthy bodies and blood, the crackle of dozens of radios reporting the desperate efforts of thousands of unseen supporting air and ground troops now trying to give you the edge to live and win. An infantry platoon leader with two days in country turns to me and says ... *don't worry I can do this* ... a badly wounded soldier insists he must not be medevaced because his squad needs him ... a Buck Sgt. age 19 who shouts some stupid joke at me with two NVA machine guns ripping down brush inches over our heads ... the exhilaration of assaulting on line into the enemy bunkers with the company bugle insanely blowing the charge (Garry Owen), the company determination at night as 30 plus mangled wounded go out and the FNG's come in on the same choppers ... and you realize that you must fight again in the morning. Tough work. You are the ones the American people will depend upon to safeguard us. Trust me ... you will be as effective, courageous, and moral as those who preceded you.

Leadership is not so much about technique and methods as it is about opening the heart. Leadership is about inspiration—of oneself and of others. Great leadership is about human experiences, not processes. Leadership is not a formula or a program, it is a human activity that comes from the heart and considers the hearts of others. It is an attitude, not a routine.

Lance Secretan

For most men, the matter of learning is one of personal preference. But for Army leaders, the obligation to learn, to grow in their profession, is clearly a public duty.

General of the Army Omar N. Bradley
known as *The GI's General* during World War II, 1893-1981

Leadership can be defined in two words ... Follow Me. A quality leader leads from the front ... not the rear.

Author Unknown

All United States military doctrine is based upon reliance on the ingenuity of the individual working on his own initiative as a member of a team and using the most modern weapons and equipment which can be provided him.

General Manton S. Eddy, Commanding General, XII Corps, World War II

*M*an *is and always will be the supreme element in combat, and upon the skill, the courage and endurance, and the fighting heart of the individual soldier the issue will ultimately depend. Soldiers learn to be good leaders from good leaders.*

General Matthew Bunker Ridgway, Former Army Chief of Staff

*G*eorge *C. Marshall learned leadership from John J. Pershing, and Marshall's followers became great captains themselves: Dwight D. Eisenhower, Omar N. Bradley ... among them. Pershing and Marshall each taught their subordinates their profession; and, more importantly, they gave them room to grow.*

General Gordon R. Sullivan, Army Chief of Staff, 1991-1995

... BECAUSE LEADERSHIP POTENTIAL CAN BE DEVELOPED

By Lieutenant General Melvin Zais, U.S. Army, 1975.

When I reflect on the leaders I have known, I find tall and short, noisy and quiet, extrovert and introvert, intellectual and bore. Which reminds me of an efficiency report, which I read when I was serving on a promotion board. The Rater said, *This officer is equally at ease with intellectuals and those in authority.* Another said, *Smith is not a born leader yet.* There seems to be some unknown chemistry, which makes a man an exceptional leader. This applies in other fields of endeavor also. For example, recently I was listening as Richard Burton, the famous actor, was being interviewed by Barbara Howard on *Who's Who.* He offered the view that many actors are as able as he is but by some strange trick of personality he has been more successful. If one wants to learn to be successful this is a strange *Will O' the Wisp* of advice and leaves little to emulate except a certain degree of modesty or self-effacement, neither of which are his long suits. Jon Ruskind said, *I fear uniformity. You cannot manufacture great men any more than you can manufacture gold.*

Despite all the conflicting evidence which I have inflicted on you I do have some advice to offer and certain points to make. If you heed them, you may, and I am cautious to use the qualifying phrase *may,* advance more rapidly and to a higher grade than your fellow officers and you may improve your leadership qualities and your ability to command because leadership potential can be developed. These pearls of wisdom come under the heading of pipe smoking, pot bellied, pontificating profundities and even if you agree with them you may not be able to or care to place them in effect or practice them.

A. Leadership is the ability to get other people to do what you want them to do. How one develops this capability is closer to an art than it is a science. The ability to get others to respond is a primary prerequisite however and the lack of this ability explains why some very able, bright, conscientious young men flourish in their youth and then begin a gradual fade out in their middle years. These are the men who do everything well as long as the results are dependent on their own efforts. While they are young and their tasks are minor, they are judged solely on their own performance. But, as they move up in the hierarchy, they are increasingly required to delegate responsibility and to create in their subordinates a strong desire to do that which has been directed by them. These men are subject to terrible disappointment and often bitterness because they watch as they are passed by contemporaries who in earlier years did not perform as well as they did. It also explains why some slow starters who suffer from impatience with detail and unwillingness to seek perfection in small matters but who have the ability to influence others to perform finally come into their own and advance rapidly. This explains why the class leaders at service academies, colleges and even advance service schools often are not the leaders in the field. One should therefore not be surprised to discover that many of our great leaders stood low in their class. The lesson here is obvious. The least you can learn to do is delegate. The ability to inspire others to perform is more difficult.

B. A young officer can and should learn by observation and imitation of his admired superiors and by rejection of the modus operandi of those he does not respond to. Often, more is to be learned from the latter. However, human nature is such that we tend to treat others as we have been treated even when we did not like the treatment and then we justify the action with the rationale of, *That is how it was for me!* That explains some of the very harsh treatment meted out in recruit training and boot camp. It also has general application. For example, most people who brutalize their children were themselves beaten by their parents. In my career, I was fortunate to serve under only two men whom I considered sadistic or terribly egotistical. I learned a great deal from them. Mostly I had the good fortune to serve under and closely observe the conduct of such men as Matthew B. Ridgway, Maxwell D. Taylor, James M. Gavin, Creighton W. Abrams and many others. I watched these men very closely. My wife is continually astonished at how much I remember about my former commanders and colleagues. I watch them and I try to learn, which brings me to my next point.

C. You must adapt to your commander. He does not adapt to you. This is an issue on which more officers flounder than any other I know. It is also the most difficult advice to live up to when faced with a commander who violates your own sense of justice or code of ethics.

D. My next advice is don't fight higher headquarters. I know that many of you consider the next higher headquarters as your natural enemy. It requires strong willpower and a level head to keep your cool but you will find it counterproductive to engage in a running battle with your boss and his staff. Save your complaints for the very important issues; there is nothing as tiresome as a quibbling, griping, uncooperative subordinate unit commander. Hold your tongue and sweat your man. When you rarely complain, people listen.

E. Next, don't ask for guidance or you will get more than you want; if you are operating within general policy, move out and display initiative. If your boss doesn't like it, he will inform you. His opinion of you drops off with each succeeding C.Y.A. [cover your ass] request for approval.

F. Most successful leaders do more than is expected of them. You must pay the price; it is a conscious choice and I must admit that I have often envied many of my contemporaries who became much better golfers, bridge players, grass cutters and commissary shoppers than I. Even so, you need not become a drudge or a workaholic. I played golf, poker, fished, hunted, drank, danced and generally had a good time.

G. You must be able to establish priorities and meet deadlines. This again is where the perfectionist often becomes a cropper. I replaced a very able man as the G-3 of the 82nd Airborne Division because he tended to work on the top paper in his in-basket rather than the most important or time sensitive. Whichever paper he worked on, you could be sure, was a masterpiece of attention to detail and thoroughness; however he was often late with his effort and while he was laboring with periods and commas the world was passing him by. You must also be able to whip out an effort in the time allotted even though you know that you could do a better job given more time. Your boss will soon learn which of his subordinates can get with the problem in a hurry and come up with something when he needs it.

H. As you move up–you must broaden your perspective. I recall that Sir William Slim, Chief of the British Imperial General Staff was the Kermit Roosevelt Lecturer when I was at the Command and General Staff College in 1947. He talked about the art of high command. He had commanded the 14th Army in Burma and he reduced his hour lecture to three points dealing with the art of high command—it was, *No papers, No details, and No regrets*.

I. Read about our great leaders. I equate this approach to the case history method of teaching at the Harvard Business School. When you read the lives of MacArthur, Marshall, Arnold, Nimitz, King, Bradley, Ridgway and many others, you will learn a great deal. Whether you can or will apply it is another matter, but first must come learning and understanding.

J. Be for, not against. Most great leaders are positive. They establish goals and achieve them or they have an idea and test it or they have a dream and try to fulfill it. Those who are for things are vibrant, filled with electricity, radiating energy and enthusiasm. People who are against things tend to be dull, negative, uninspiring and boring. They cast a pall on every gathering and they are a wet blanket. We try to avoid them. They are not doers. Be a *Forer*–not an *Aginer*! Happiness in the final analysis is something to be enthusiastic about. Charles M. Schwab said, *A man can succeed at almost anything for which he has unlimited enthusiasm.*

K. You must go where the action is. For some, it is to the sound of the guns. For others, it is in support of those who go to the sound of the guns. When I was privileged to deliver the Kermit Roosevelt Lecture Series in England, the title of my talk was: *Your mission is to fight and don't forget it.* I repeat it to you without elaboration. One thing which I know for sure is the fact that most of my success can be attributed to the fact that I went to the sound of the guns and I was lucky enough to survive.

Discipline, which is but mutual trust and confidence, is the key to all success in peace and war.
General George S. Patton, Jr.

I am confident that an army of strong individuals, held together by a sound discipline based on respect for personal initiative and rights and dignity of the individual, will never fail this nation in time of need.
General J. Lawton Collins, Former Army Chief of Staff

Discipline and shared hardship pull people together in powerful ways.
Sergeant Alvin C. York

In any moment of decision, the best thing you can do is the right thing. The worst thing you can do is nothing.
President Theodore Roosevelt

Honesty is the first chapter in the book of wisdom.
President Thomas Jefferson, 1819

And when at some future date the high court of history sits in judgment on each of us, recording whether in our brief span of service we fulfilled our responsibilities to the state, our success or failure in whatever office we hold, will be measured by the answers to four questions: First, were we truly men of courage ... Second, were we truly men of judgment ... Third, were we truly men of integrity ... Finally, were we truly men of dedication?

President John F. Kennedy

I've never known a man worth his salt who in the long run, deep down in his heart, didn't appreciate the grind, the discipline. There is something good in men that really yearns for discipline.

Vince Lombardi

Nobody can take your integrity away from you, you have to give it up yourself.

General Creighton Abrams, Army Chief of Staff

God grant that men of principle shall be our principal men.

President Thomas Jefferson

The core of a soldier is moral discipline. It is intertwined with the discipline of physical and mental achievement. Total discipline overcomes adversity, and physical stamina draws on an inner strength that says 'drive on.'

Former Sergeant Major of the Army, William G. Bainbridge

Military organizations and success in battle depend upon discipline and a high sense of honor.

General Omar N. Bradley

There is only one kind of discipline; perfect discipline. If you do not enforce discipline, you are potential murderers.

General George S. Patton, Jr.

Discipline is based on pride in the profession of arms, on meticulous attention to details, and on mutual respect and confidence. Discipline must be a habit so ingrained that it is stronger than the excitement of battle or fear of death.

General George S. Patton, Jr.

Leadership is action, not position.

Donald H. McGannon

Leadership cannot be exercised by the weak. It demands strength, the strength of this great nation when its people are united in purpose, united in a common fundamental faith, united in their readiness to work for human freedom and peace; this spiritual and economic strength, in turn, must be reinforced in a still armed world by the physical strength necessary for the defense of ourselves and our friends.

President Dwight D. Eisenhower

Making decisions, exercising command, managing, administering—those are the dynamics of our calling. Responsibility is its core.

General Harold K. Johnson, Former Army Chief of Staff

True genius resides in the capacity for evaluation of uncertain, hazardous, and conflicting information.

Sir Winston Churchill, Prime Minister of Great Britain, World War II

MEN OF THE HEART

Leadership must be based on goodwill. Goodwill does not mean posturing and, least of all, pandering to the mob. It means obvious and wholehearted commitment to helping followers. We are tired of leaders we fear, tired of leaders we love, and most tired of leaders who let us take liberties with them. What we need for leaders are men of the heart who are so helpful that they, in effect, do away with the need of their jobs. But leaders like that are never out of a job, never out of followers. Strange as it sounds, great leaders gain authority by giving it away.

Vice Admiral James Bond Stockdale, Military Ethics, *Machiavelli, Management, and Moral Leadership*, 1987

Leaders are people who do the right thing; managers are people who do things right.

Warren Bennis, Training and Development Journal, August 1984

Leaders do not have to be great men or women by being intellectual geniuses or omniscient prophets to succeed, but they do need to have the 'right stuff' and this stuff is not equally present in all people. Leadership is a demanding, unrelenting job with enormous pressures and grave responsibilities. It would be a disservice to leaders to suggest that they are ordinary people who happened to be in the right place at the right time. Maybe the place matters, but it takes a special kind of person to master the challenges of opportunity.

Kirkpatrick and Locke

No man is a leader until his appointment is ratified in the minds and hearts of his men.

The Infantry Journal, August 1948

*T*he development of bold, innovative leaders of character and competence is fundamental to the long-term health of the Army.

General Erik Shinseki, Chief of Staff of the Army (CSA)
Vision Statement, 23 June 1999

THE OLD MAN 'UP THERE'

General Mathew Ridgway wrote:

I held to the old-fashioned idea that it helped the spirits of the men to see the Old Man up there, in the snow and the sleet and the mud, sharing the same cold, miserable existence they had to endure. During this advance, General Ridgway also attempted to tell the men of Eighth Army why they were fighting in Korea. He sought to build a fighting spirit in his men based on unit and soldier pride. In addition, he called on them to defend Western Civilization from Communist degradation, saying: *In the final analysis, the issue now joined right here in Korea is whether Communism or individual freedom shall prevail; whether the flight of the fear-driven people we have witnessed here shall be checked, or shall at some future time, however distant, engulf our own loved ones in all its misery and despair.*

A soldier may not always believe what you say,
but he will never doubt what you do.

The U.S. Army's Battalion Commander's Handbook

*C*haracter can be described as a 'moral compass' within one's self, that helps us make right decisions even in the midst of the shifting winds of adversity. Unwavering character encourages us to pursue honorable ideals. A wise person once declared,
'Ideals are like stars—we may never reach them
but we chart our course by them.'

General Charles C. Krulak
Former Commandant of the Marine Corps, 1996-2000

*T*hought makes action
Action makes habit
Habit makes character
Character makes destiny.

Mary *Mimi* Key Henley

A JANITOR'S 10 LESSONS IN LEADERSHIP

By Colonel James Moschgat, 12th Operations Group Commander, U.S. Air Force, 2001.

William *Bill* Crawford certainly was an unimpressive figure, one you could easily overlook during a hectic day at the U.S. Air Force Academy.

Mr. Crawford, as most of us referred to him back in the late 1970s, was our squadron janitor.

While we cadets busied ourselves preparing for academic exams, athletic events, Saturday morning parades and room inspections, or never-ending leadership classes, Bill quietly moved about the squadron mopping and buffing floors, emptying trash cans, cleaning toilets, or just tidying up the mess 100 college-age kids can leave in a dormitory.

Sadly, and for many years, few of us gave him much notice, rendering little more than a passing nod or throwing a curt, *G'morning*! in his direction as we hurried off to our daily duties.

Why? Perhaps it was because of the way he did his job–he always kept the squadron area spotlessly clean, even the toilets and showers gleamed.

Frankly, he did his job so well, none of us had to notice or get involved.

After all, cleaning toilets was his job, not ours.

Maybe it was his physical appearance that made him disappear into the background. Bill didn't move very quickly and, in fact, you could say he even shuffled a bit, as if he suffered from some sort of injury. His gray hair and wrinkled face made him appear ancient to a group of young cadets. And his crooked smile, well, it looked a little funny. Face it, Bill was an old man working in a young person's world. What did he have to offer us on a personal level?

Finally, maybe it was Mr. Crawford's personality that rendered him almost invisible to the young people around him. Bill was shy, almost painfully so.

He seldom spoke to a cadet unless they addressed him first, and that didn't happen very often. Our janitor always buried himself in his work, moving about with stooped shoulders, a quiet gait, and an averted gaze. If he noticed the hustle and bustle of cadet life around him, it was hard to tell.

So, for whatever reason, Bill blended into the woodwork and became just another fixture around the squadron. The Academy, one of our nation's premier leadership laboratories, kept us busy from dawn till dusk. And Mr. Crawford ... well, he was just a janitor.

That changed one fall Saturday afternoon in 1976. I was reading a book about World War II and the tough Allied ground campaign in Italy, when I stumbled across an incredible story. On September 13, 1943, a Private William Crawford from Colorado, assigned to the 36th Infantry Division, had been involved in some bloody fighting on Hill 424 near Altavilla, Italy.

The words on the page leapt out at me: *in the face of intense and overwhelming hostile fire ... with no regard for personal safety ... on his own initiative, Private Crawford single-handedly attacked fortified enemy positions.* It continued, *for conspicuous gallantry and intrepidity at risk of life above and beyond the call of duty, the President of the United States ...*

Holy cow, I said to my roommate, *you're not going to believe this, but I think our janitor is a Medal of Honor winner.*

We all knew Mr. Crawford was a WWII Army vet, but that didn't keep my friend from looking at me as if I was some sort of alien being. Nonetheless, we couldn't wait to ask Bill about the story on Monday.

We met Mr. Crawford bright and early Monday and showed him the page in question from the book, anticipation and doubt on our faces. He starred at it for a few silent moments and then quietly uttered something like, *Yep, that's me.*

Mouths agape, my roommate and I looked at one another, then at the book, and quickly back at our janitor. Almost at once we both stuttered, *Why didn't you ever tell us about it?*

He slowly replied after some thought, *That was one day in my life and it happened a long time ago.*

I guess we were all at a loss for words after that. We had to hurry off to class and Bill, well, he had chores to attend to. However, after that brief exchange, things were never again the same around our squadron. Word spread like wildfire among the cadets that we had a hero in our midst—Mr. Crawford, our janitor, had won the Medal!

Cadets, who had once passed by Bill with hardly a glance, now greeted him with a smile and a respectful, *Good morning, Mr. Crawford.* Those who had before left a mess for the *janitor* to clean up started taking it upon themselves to put things in order. Most cadets routinely stopped to talk to Bill throughout the day, and we even began inviting him to our formal squadron functions. He'd show up dressed in a conservative dark suit and quietly talk to those who approached him, the only sign of his heroics being a simple blue, star-spangled lapel pin. Almost overnight, Bill went from being a simple fixture in our squadron to one of our teammates. Mr. Crawford changed too, but you had to look closely to notice the difference. After that fall day in 1976, he seemed to move with more purpose; his shoulders didn't seem to be as stooped; he met our greetings with a direct gaze and a stronger *good morning* in return; and he flashed his crooked smile more often.

The squadron gleamed as always, but everyone now seemed to notice it more.

Bill even got to know most of us by our first names, something that didn't happen often at the Academy. While no one ever formally acknowledged the change, I think we became Bill's cadets and his squadron.

As often happens in life, events sweep us away from those in our past.

The last time I saw Bill was on graduation day in June 1977. As I walked out of the squadron for the last time, he shook my hand and simply said, *Good luck, young man.*

With that, I embarked on a career that has been truly lucky and blessed.

Mr. Crawford continued to work at the Academy and eventually retired in his native Colorado where he resides today, one of four Medal of Honor winners living in a small town.

A wise person once said, *It's not life that's important, but those you meet along the way that make the difference.* Bill was one who made a difference for me. While I haven't seen Mr. Crawford in over twenty years, he'd probably be surprised to know I think of him often. Bill Crawford, our janitor, taught me many valuable, unforgettable leadership lessons.

Here are ten I'd like to share with you.

1. Be Cautious of Labels. Labels you place on people may define your relationship to them and bound their potential. Sadly, and for a long time, we labeled Bill as just a janitor, but he was so much more. Therefore, be cautious of a leader who callously says, *Hey, he's just an Airman.* Likewise, don't tolerate the O-1 who says, *I can't do that, I'm just a lieutenant.*

2. Everyone Deserves Respect. Because we hung the *janitor* label on Mr. Crawford, we often wrongly treated him with less respect than others around us. He deserved much more, and not just because he was a Medal of Honor winner. Bill deserved respect because he was a janitor, walked among us, and was a part of our team.

3. Courtesy Makes a Difference. Be courteous to all around you, regardless of rank or position. Military customs, as well as common courtesies, help bond a team. When our daily words to Mr. Crawford turned from perfunctory *hellos* to heartfelt greetings, his demeanor and personality outwardly changed. It made a difference for all of us.

4. Take Time to Know Your People. Life in the military is hectic, but that's no excuse for not knowing the people you work for and with. For years a hero walked among us at the Academy and we never knew it. Who are the heroes that walk in your midst?

5. Anyone Can Be a Hero. Mr. Crawford certainly didn't fit anyone's standard definition of a hero. Moreover, he was just a private on the day he won his Medal. Don't sell your people short, for any one of them may be the hero who rises to the occasion when duty calls. On the other hand, it's easy to turn to your proven

performers when the chips are down, but don't ignore the rest of the team. Today's rookie could and should be tomorrow's superstar.

6. Leaders Should Be Humble. Most modern-day heroes and some leaders are anything but humble, especially if you calibrate your *hero meter* on today's athletic fields. End zone celebrations and self-aggrandizement are what we've come to expect from sports greats. Not Mr. Crawford—he was too busy working to celebrate his past heroics. Leaders would be well served to do the same.

7. Life Won't Always Hand You What You Think You Deserve. We in the military work hard and, dang it, we deserve recognition, right? However, sometimes you just have to persevere, even when accolades don't come your way. Perhaps you weren't nominated for junior officer or airman of the quarter as you thought you should–don't let that stop you.

8. Don't pursue glory; pursue excellence. Private Bill Crawford didn't pursue glory; he did his duty and then swept floors for a living.

9. No Job is Beneath a Leader. If Bill Crawford, a Medal of Honor winner, could clean latrines and smile, is there a job beneath your dignity? Think about it.

10. Pursue Excellence. No matter what task life hands you, do it well. Dr. Martin Luther King said, *If life makes you a street sweeper, be the best street sweeper you can be.* Mr. Crawford modeled that philosophy and helped make our dormitory area a home.

Life is a Leadership Laboratory. All too often we look to some school or PME class to teach us about leadership when, in fact, life is a leadership laboratory. Those you meet everyday will teach you enduring lessons if you just take time to stop, look and listen. I spent four years at the Air Force Academy, took dozens of classes, read hundreds of books, and met thousands of great people. I gleaned leadership skills from all of them, but one of the people I remember most is Mr. Bill Crawford and the lessons he unknowingly taught. Don't miss your opportunity to learn.

Master Sergeant (Retired) William John Crawford.

Bill Crawford was a janitor. However, he was also a teacher, friend, role model and one great American hero. Thanks, Mr. Crawford, for some valuable leadership lessons.

The rest of the story: Private William John Crawford was a platoon scout for 3rd Platoon of Company L 142nd Regiment 36th Division (Texas National Guard) and won the Medal Of Honor (MOH) for his actions on Hill 424, just 4 days after the invasion at Salerno.

On Hill 424, Private Crawford took out three enemy machine guns before darkness fell, halting the platoon's advance. Private Crawford could not be found and was assumed dead. The request for his MOH was quickly approved. MG Terry Allen presented the posthumous MOH to Bill Crawford's father, George, on 11 May 1944 in Camp (now Fort) Carson, in Colorado Springs. Nearly two months after that, it was learned that Private Crawford was alive in a POW camp in Germany. During his captivity, a German guard clubbed him with his rifle. Bill overpowered him, took the rifle away, and beat the guard unconscious. A German doctor's testimony saved him from severe punishment, perhaps death. To stay ahead of the advancing Russian army, the prisoners were marched 500 miles in 52 days in the middle of the German winter, subsisting on one potato a day. An allied tank column liberated the camp in the spring of 1945, and Private Crawford took his first hot shower in 18 months on VE Day. Private Crawford stayed in the Army before retiring as a Master Sergeant and becoming a janitor. In 1984, President Ronald Reagan officially presented the MOH to Bill Crawford.

A lot of people think that as a commander all you do is give a single order and everybody obeys. But you use the same type of leadership in civilian life as in the military–persuasion, education and enthusiasms. And you must believe in your cause. Good leadership involves a sense of duty, value, integrity and morality.

General H. Norman Schwarzkopf

A NEW CULTURE OF RESPONSIBILITY

During these last few months, I've been humbled and privileged to see the true character of this country in a time of testing. Our enemies believed America was weak and materialistic, that we would splinter in fear and selfishness. They were as wrong as they are evil. ... After America was attacked, it was as if our entire country looked into a mirror and saw our better selves. We were reminded that we are citizens, with obligations to each other, to our country, and to history. We began to think less of the goods we can accumulate, and more about the good we can do. For too long our culture has said, 'If it feels good, do it.' Now America is embracing a new ethic and a new creed: 'Let's roll.' In the sacrifice of soldiers, the fierce brotherhood of firefighters, and the bravery and generosity of ordinary citizens, we have glimpsed what a new culture of responsibility could look like. We want to be a nation that serves goals larger than self. We've been offered a unique opportunity, and we must not let this moment pass.

President George W. Bush
excerpts from the State of the Union Address, 29 January 2002

*Do not go where the path may lead,
go instead where there is no path and leave a trail.*

Ralph Waldo Emerson

Character cannot be developed in ease and quiet. Only through experience of trial and suffering can the soul be strengthened, ambition inspired, and success achieved.

Helen Keller

*A good commander is someone who can step
on your boots and still leave a shine.*

A group of American soldiers

THE PENALTY OF LEADERSHIP

This text appeared as an advertisement in the Saturday Evening Post, January 2, 1915, courtesy of Cadillac Motor Car Division.

In every field of human endeavor, he that is first must perpetually live in the white light of publicity. Whether the leadership be vested in a man or in a manufactured product, emulation and envy are ever at work. In art, in literature, in music, in industry, the reward and the punishment are always the same. The reward is widespread recognition, the punishment fierce denial and detraction. When a man's work becomes a standard for the whole world, it also becomes a target for the shafts of the envious few. If his work is merely mediocre, he will be left severely alone. If he achieves a masterpiece, it will set a million tongues awagging. Jealousy does not protrude its forked tongue at the artist who produces a common-place painting. Whatsoever you write, or paint, or play, or sing, or build; no one will strive to surpass or to slander you unless your work be stamped with the seal of genius.

Long after a great work has been done, those who are disappointed or envious continue to cry out that it cannot be done. Spiteful little voices in the domain of art were raised against our own Whistler as a mountebank, long after the big world had acclaimed him its greatest artistic genius.

Multitudes flocked to Bayreuth to worship at the musical shrine of Wagner, while the little group of those whom he had dethroned and displaced argued angrily that he was no musician at all. The little world continued to protest that Fulton could never build a steamboat, while the big world flocked to the river banks to see his boat steam by. The Leader is assailed because he is a Leader, and the effort to equal him is merely added proof of that leadership. Failing to equal or to excel, the follower seeks to depreciate and to destroy, but only confirms once more the superiority of that which he strives to supplant. There is nothing new in this; it is as old as the world and as old as the human passions of envy, fear, greed, ambition, and the desire to surpass. And it all avails nothing. If the leader truly leads, he remains the leader. Master Poet, Master Painter, Master Workman; each in his turn is assailed, and each holds his laurels through the ages. That which is great makes itself known, no matter how loud the clamor of denial. That which deserves to live, Lives.

BLINDING FLASHES OF THE OBVIOUS ABOUT LEADERSHIP

By Major General (Retired) Perry M. Smith, President, Visionary Leadership. MG (Retired) Perry M. Smith is the author of *Rules and Tools for Leaders* and *A Hero Among Heroes.*

1. *Know Yourself*: Each of us is really five people: who we are; who we think we are; who our subordinates think we are; who our peers think we are; and who our boss thinks we are. Those who seek feedback from many sources are more likely to understand their various selves–and be better leaders.

2. *Develop Mental Toughness*: Leaders must be brutally honest with themselves, or they slip into the terrible habit of self-deception. Even the best leaders make mistakes. By acknowledging and correcting them quickly, a good leader can become a superb leader.

3. *Be Magnanimous*: Leaders who share their power and their time can accomplish the extraordinary. Leadership is the liberation of talent; hence, you gain power by constantly giving it away–and not grabbing it back.

4. *Squint with Your Ears*: Listening is the most important leader skill. Introverts have an edge, since they tend to listen quietly. Too many extroverts are thinking about what they will say next, rather than hearing what is being said.

5. *Protect the Innovators*: For three years I had a Vietnam Medal of Honor recipient working for me–most innovative person I have ever known. Although well over half his ideas were awful, buried among the bad was an occasional pearl of great wisdom. I learned to protect him from his bad ideas while encouraging his best suggestions and insights.

6. *Don't Become Indispensable*: We need indispensable organizations but not indispensable people. Leaders should not become indispensable nor let others become so. When that indispensable person gets sick, retires, or transfers, the organization will be damaged badly.

7. Avoid the Cowardice of Silence: So-called leaders often sit on their hands when it is time to speak up. Leadership requires the courage to make waves, the courage to confront bosses when they are wrong, and the courage of one's convictions. Every Lee needs a Longstreet.

8. Don't Waste People's Time: The best question to ask a subordinate during a counseling session is, *How am I wasting your time?* Not everyone will tell you–but cherish the ones that do, for they will help you keep your priorities in order and dramatically reduce wasted time.

9. Reward the Invisible People: Many fine people who do great work seldom get thanked because they are *invisible*. They work so quietly and competently that they are never noticed by the leader. Over time, their morale suffers. Conversely, beware of those who seek too much *face time* with the boss. These are primarily concerned with their ambitions and egos.

10. Avoid Cronyism: Too many bosses promote people out of friendship rather than competence. Not only does this undermine morale, it also moves friends to positions at their level of incompetence, and everyone suffers.

11. Smoke Those of Low Integrity: Leaders must ensure that high standards are maintained. In most large organizations, someone is almost always walking out the back door with something. Expense accounts, personnel records, training reports, and contracts need constant scrutiny. Also, beware of the problems of *integrity once removed*. Just because you and your immediate associates are honest doesn't mean there aren't integrity problems elsewhere.

12. Concentrate on Performance, Not Just Results: How you get results is vitally important–both process and performance. Constantly ask yourself what it took to get those great results.

13. Maintain a Sense of Outrage: Too many super-cool managers concentrate on keeping the boss happy and staying out of trouble. They are never outraged when the system does serious damage to their subordinates. The best leaders get mad occasionally and, using controlled outrage, correct the wrongs levied against their people.

14. Beware of Intimidation: Some bosses allow themselves to be intimidated by their bosses, outsiders, or even their subordinates. An intimidated boss can never be a great leader. Robert McNamara's intimidation of the chiefs of the military services during the Vietnam War is a stark example.

15. *Avoid the Activity Trap*: The overly busy manager seldom plans for the long term; this leads to strategic drift. The micromanager and the workaholic are seldom visionary leaders.

16. *Anticipate Crises*: The very best leaders see problems coming and solve them before they become full-fledged crises. They ask the right questions and perfect their anticipation skills. If a crisis occurs, have a transition plan, make decisions quickly and form an *opportunity team* to exploit the crisis.

17. *Do Serious Reading on Leadership*: Read at least one good book each month. My favorites on leadership include: Killer Angels (Shaara); Leaders (Bennis) Integrity (Carter); and The New Realities (Drucker). Leaders who do not read are slowly but surely going brain dead–not a pleasant sight.

18. *Don't Become a Prisoner of Your Own Paradigm*: While serving as CNN's military analyst during the Gulf War, I noticed that the *New York Times* was unable to grasp how dramatically weapons and warfare had changed. For over 20 years, the *Times* had criticized the military for acquiring systems that were overly complex. It took weeks before the editors grasped the significance of the triple paradigm of reliability, precision, and stealth.

19. *Don't Send 'I Don't Trust You' Messages*: Leaders who say, *I don't like surprises* or *Check with me before you start anything* or *I'll call in every morning for an update* are sending their subordinates *I do not trust you* messages. Such employees never will contribute at their full potential.

20. *Find an Anchor and Hold On To It*: My wife of over 38 years has lifted me when down and eased me down when my ego became inflated. My two adult children have been very helpful, especially on issues of integrity. Close friends and classmates have helped with advice, comfort, solace, and support.

21. *Don't Sweat the Small Stuff*: And its corollary, most everything is small stuff. Leaders who are perfectionists should recall that often *the best is the enemy of the good.*

22. *Fight the Tendency to Clone Yourself*: It is a mistake to hire people who look, act, and think as you do. Always ask if the

person under consideration brings a fresh perspective, background, or point of view. Also, actively resist the tendency to encourage subordinates to act as you do.

23. *Prepare for the Future*: I suggest joining the World Future Society (301-951-0394). At its annual July convention, some of the smartest, long-range thinkers in the world present workshops. I also suggest reading *The Futurist* and *Business Week*.

24. *Remember*: Leadership is not maintaining control, gaining power, keeping the boss happy, avoiding trouble or getting to the bottom of your in-box. Leadership is accomplishing the mission, serving your people, giving power away, allowing yourself to be vulnerable, and raising the level of integrity and dignity in your organization.

I admire men of character, and I judge character not by how men deal with their superiors, but mostly how they deal with their subordinates, and that, to me, is where you find out what the character of a man is.

General H. Norman Schwarzkopf

Leadership is understanding people and involving them to help you do a job. That takes all of the good characteristics, like integrity, dedication of purpose, selflessness, knowledge, skill, implacability, as well as determination not to accept failure.

Admiral Arleigh A. Burke, Naval Leadership:
Voices of Experience, The D-Day Decision

Communications, or the ability to inform people what you expect of them in understandable terms and the ability to transmit to them your interest in them, is the key to successful leadership.

General Harold K. Johnson
from *The Leadership Qualities of Great Generals*

RELATIONS BETWEEN OFFICERS AND MEN

By Lieutenant General John A. Lejeune, 13th Commandant of the Marine Corps, from the Marine Corps Manual, 1921.

Young Marines respond quickly and readily to the exhibition of qualities of leadership on the part of their officers. Each Officer must endeavor by all means in his power to develop within himself those qualities of leadership, including industry, justice, self control, unselfishness, honor and courage, which will fit him to be a real leader of men and which will aid in establishing the relationship described below.

The spirit of comradeship and brotherhood in arms which has traditionally existed throughout the ranks of the Marine Corps is a vital characteristic of the Corps. It must be fostered and kept alive and made the moving force in all Marine Corps organizations. The relationship between officers and enlisted men should in no sense be that of superior and inferior, nor that of master and servant, but rather that of teacher and scholar. In fact, it should partake of the nature of the relations between father and son, to the extent that officers, especially commanders, are responsible for the physical, mental, and moral welfare, as well as the discipline and military training of the men under their command who are serving the nation in the Marine Corps.

The recognition of this responsibility on the part of officers is vital to the well being of the Marine Corps. It is especially so for the reason that so large a proportion of the men enlisted are under 21 years of age. These men are in the formative period of their lives and officers owe it to them, to their parents, and to the nation, that when discharged from the service they should be far better men physically, mentally, and morally than they were when they enlisted.

To accomplish this task, a constant effort must be made by all officers to fill each day with useful and interesting instructions and wholesome recreation for the men. This effort must be intelligent and not perfunctory, the object being not only to eliminate idleness, but to train and cultivate the bodies and minds, and the spirit of our men.

It will be necessary for officers not only to devote their close attention to the many questions affecting the comfort, health, morals, religious guidance, military training and discipline of their men under their command, but also to actively enlist the interest of their men in building up and maintaining their bodies in the finest physical condition; to encourage them to improve their professional knowledge and to make every effort by means of historical, educational and patriotic addresses to cultivate in their hearts a deep abiding love of the Corps and Country.

Our moral compass is not broken. The needle continues to point in the same direction. But 'south' has been mislabeled as 'north.' And for a generation, these reversed compasses have been handed to kids by parents, teachers, government officials, various advocacy groups and–yes–even some clergy. 'Broken moral compass' is a convenient but inaccurate description of the problem. Our moral compass has been altered, inverted and in fact sabotaged by those who are unwilling or unable to follow a legitimate compass, but who conceal their accountability by inducing the rest of us to go along with them. There is still time to repair our moral compass. All that's needed is to compare our compass with a genuine one and re-label the directions. The real difficulty comes in following the corrected compass. The genuine path isn't always easy. Often it leads uphill and over difficult terrain. But it is always straight, and eventually it will get us home again.

Dr. David C. Stolinsky

Every crew of a ship in the U.S. Navy has some really talented individuals. The real test though of a ship is bringing those talented individuals together as a team and making that ship click ...

Admiral Bob Natter, Commander in Chief, Atlantic Fleet

I don't mind being called tough.
It's the tough guys who lead the survivors.

General Curtis E. LeMay, U.S. Air Force

If I place two pieces of material the same size, shape, and
form on an anvil and one is made of granite, the other of leather,
and then hit each with a hammer, what will happen?
The granite will shatter into pieces, precisely, because it is hard.
It is rigid, brittle and weak. The leather is barely dented,
precisely because it is not hard. It is flexible, malleable, resilient,
elastic, durable, supple, and it is tough!

Joe Batten, author of *Tough Minded Leadership*

The way a team plays as a whole determines its success. You may
have the greatest bunch of individual stars in the world, but if they
don't play together, the club won't be worth a dime.

George Herman *Babe* Ruth

A reflective reading of history will show that
no man ever rose to military greatness who could not convince his
troops that he put them first, above all else.

General Maxwell D. Taylor

An Army officer is, above all else, a patriot.
From the moment he is commissioned, he incurs an obligation
which remains with him throughout his military life–to cherish and
protect his country and to develop within himself
that capacity and strength which will enable him to serve his
fellow Americans with wisdom, diligence and patriotic conviction.

Major General Benjamin H. Pochyla

THE D-DAY DECISION

On 4 June 1944, the largest invasion armada ever assembled was poised to strike the Normandy region of France. Weather delays had already caused a 24-hour postponement and another front of bad weather was heading for the area. If the Allies didn't make the landings on 6 June, they would miss the combination of favorable tides, clear flying weather, and moonlight needed for the assault. In addition to his concerns about the weather, General of the Armies (GA) Dwight D. Eisenhower, the Supreme Allied Commander, worried about his soldiers. Every hour they spent jammed aboard crowded ships, tossed about and seasick, degraded their fighting ability. The next possible invasion date was 19 June; however, the optimal tide and visibility conditions would not recur until mid-July. GA Eisenhower was ever mindful that the longer he delayed, the greater chance German intelligence had to discover the Allied plan. The Germans would use any additional time to improve the already formidable coastal defenses. On the evening of 4 June, GA Eisenhower and his staff received word that there would be a window of clear weather on the next night, the night of 5-6 June. If the meteorologists were wrong, GA Eisenhower would be sending seasick men ashore with no air cover or accurate naval gunfire. GA Eisenhower was concerned for his soldiers. *Don't forget,* GA Eisenhower said in an interview 20 years later, *some hundreds of thousands of men were down here around Portsmouth, and many of them had already been loaded for some time, particularly those who were going to make the initial assault. Those people in the ships and ready to go were in cages, you might say. You couldn't call them anything else. They were fenced in. They were crowded up, and everybody was unhappy.* GA Eisenhower continued, *Goodness knows, those fellows meant a lot to me. But these are the decisions that have to be made when you're in a war. You say to yourself, 'I'm going to do something that will be to my country's advantage for the least cost. You can't say without any cost. You know you're going to lose some of them, and it's very difficult.'* A failed invasion would delay the end of a war that had already dragged on for nearly five years. GA Eisenhower paced back and forth as a storm rattled the windows. There were no guarantees, but the time had come to act. He stopped pacing and, facing his subordinates, said quietly but clearly, *OK, let's go.*

CARNATION MILK

In 1989, the associate editor of *Fortune* magazine interviewed the manager of the Los Angeles Dodgers, Tommy Lasorda, about his thoughts on leadership. When asked, *What's the secret?* Tommy Lasorda said: *I can remember when I was 15 years old. I was sitting at home in the kitchen and my mother had a can of Carnation milk. I'll never forget this. It had a slogan on it, which said that contented cows give better milk. And I believe that contented people give better performances.*

Tough standards that mean something develop strong character. ... Whether for soldiers in foxholes, or the rest of our culture, for that matter, arrogance and ego do not hold us together. Rather, we need a commitment to one another, a regard for the common good, and the old-fashioned virtues of 'duty, honor, and country.'

Charles Colson

... A sound body is good; a sound mind is better; but a strong and clean character is better than either.

President Theodore Roosevelt, 24 May 1904

Even with the gifts of human understanding and of professional competence arising from careful training, our military leader will not be complete without the third attribute of greatness; namely, character—character which reflects inner strength and justified confidence in oneself.

General Maxwell D. Taylor

Leadership is not a natural trait, something inherited like the color of eyes or hair ... Leadership is a skill that can be studied, learned, and perfected by practice.

The Non-Commissioned Officer's Guide, 1962

Leadership in the field depends to an important extent on one's legs, and stomach, and nervous system, and on one's ability to withstand hardships, and lack of sleep, and still be disposed energetically and aggressively to command, to dominate on the battlefield.

General George Marshall, Army Chief of Staff 1938-1945, Awarded Nobel Peace Prize in 1953

It is essential to understand that battles are primarily won in the hearts of men. Men respond to leadership in a most remarkable way and once you have won his heart, he will follow you anywhere.

Vince Lombardi

History teaches that when you become indifferent and lose the will to fight someone who has the will to fight will take over.

Colonel Arthur D. *Bull* Simons, Son Tay Raid, 21 November 1970

Leadership in the right direction finds followers and supporters.

Defense Secretary Donald H. Rumsfeld

Character is much easier kept than recovered.

Thomas Paine (1737-1809)

I have said that the Declaration of Independence is the ring-bolt to the chain of your nation's destiny; so, indeed, I regard it. The principles contained in that instrument are saving principles. Stand by those principles, be true to them on all occasions, in all places, against all foes, and at whatever cost.

Frederick Douglass (1817–1895)

CHAPTER 6

DEFENSE AND THE BATTLEFIELD

America's peace, freedom and prosperity are not the result of an election, poll or a gratuity from another nation. Our freedom is the result of American military victory on battlefields throughout the world. Our national defense capabilities were, still are, and always will be our only guarantee, or *insurance policy* for freedom. This chapter is dedicated to our national defense posture and those who made it so, both on and off the battlefields.

Our cause is noble; it is the cause of mankind!

President George Washington

We have an Army for one reason—to win.

Brigadier General Vernon Lewis, Speech to the U.S. Army
Command and General Staff College, 1975

You and I have the courage to say to our enemies
'There is a price we will not pay.' There is a point beyond which
they must not advance. This is the meaning of the phrase
'Peace through strength.'

President Ronald Reagan

If we are strong, our strength will speak for itself.
If we are weak, words will be of no help.

President John F. Kennedy

One sword keeps another in the sheath.

George Herbert

SNATCH IT FROM OUR HANDS AND CARRY ON!

By Second Lieutenant R.B. Thieme, III. U.S. Army Infantry, 1972.

God has ordained the military in order that the human race can survive war. He has ordained the police system and the objective administration of law so that the human race can survive crime. Basic stability of a national entity depends upon having a well-trained, strong military organization, plus an objective set of laws and excellent enforcement of these laws. Both systems for stability have one thing in common: In the operation of the military in combat, the enemy has to be killed in order to protect freedom. The same thing is true with crime: the criminal must be killed– therefore, the necessity for capital punishment. The military executes the enemies from without, while the judicial system executes them from within. Only in this way can the peace and survival of a nation be assured. One of the results of revisionism is neglect of the military. As always, when war comes, it is the Regular Army and its officers who hold the line and are sacrificed until new men can be trained ... and when you finally come, you will find our bleached bones still clutching the guidon ... snatch it from our hands and carry on!

To each of my Nephews, William Augustine Washington, George Lewis, George Steptoe Washington, Bushrod Washington, and Samuel Washington, I give one of my swords or Cutteaux of which I may be Possessed; and they are to choose in the order they are named. These Swords are accompanied with an injunction not to unsheathe them for the purpose of shedding blood, except it be for self defense, or in the defense of their Country and its rights; and in the latter case, to keep them unsheathed, and prefer falling with them in their hands, to the relinquishment thereof.

From the Last Will and Testament of President George Washington

WAR AS WORK

By John Keegan, British historian, from his 1995 book *Fields of Battle*.

The United States continues to elude me. If I understand it at all, it is through the strange profession that has shaped my life, the study of war. War is repugnant to the people of the United States; yet, it is war that has made their nation, and it is through their power to wage war that they dominate the world. Americans are proficient at war in the same way that they are proficient at work. It is a task, sometimes a duty.

Americans have worked at war since the 17th Century, to protect themselves from the Indians, to win their independence from George III, to make themselves one country, to win the whole of their continent, to extinguish autocracy and dictatorship in the world outside. It is not their favoured form of work. Left to themselves, Americans build, cultivate, bridge, dam, canalize, invent, teach, manufacture, think, write, lock themselves in struggle with the eternal challenges that man has chosen to confront, and with an intensity not known elsewhere on the globe. Bidden to make war their work, Americans shoulder the burden with intimidating purpose. There is, I have said, an American mystery, the nature of which I only begin to perceive. If I were obliged to define it, I would say it is the ethos of work as an end in itself. War is a form of work, and America makes war, however reluctantly, however unwillingly, in a particularly workmanlike way. I do not love war; but I love America.

*B*ack in the '20's, Will Rogers had an answer for those who believed that strength invited war. He said, 'I've never seen anyone insult Jack Dempsey' (world heavyweight champion at that time).

President Ronald Reagan

*When under attack, no country is obligated to collect
permission slips from allies to strike back.*

Charles Krauthammer

*War is an uncertain business and yet on every
uncertain day that our nation has had to face the grim business of
defending itself, American women have stepped forward.*

Togo D. West, Jr., Secretary of the Army, October 1997

*Weakness can be provocative simply because it is tempting to a
nation whose imperialist ambitions extend to the ends of the earth.*

President Ronald Reagan

*A just war is in the long run far better for a nation's soul
than the most prosperous peace obtained by acquiescence
in wrong or injustice. Moreover, though it is criminal
for a nation not to prepare for war, so that it may escape
the dreadful consequences of being defeated in war,
yet it must always be remembered that even to be defeated in war
may be better than not to have fought at all.*

President Theodore Roosevelt

*It is our duty still to endeavor to avoid war;
but if it shall actually take place, no matter
by whom brought on, we must defend ourselves.*

President Thomas Jefferson

*Nobody dislikes war more than warriors,
but we value the causes of peace so
highly that we will not duck a war
in an effort to get a lasting peace.*

General Daniel *Chappie* James, Jr. (USAF), 1977

We are not a warlike people. Quite the opposite. We always seek to live in peace. We resort to force infrequently and with great reluctance, and only after we have determined that it is absolutely necessary. We are awed by the forces of destruction loose in the world in the nuclear era, but neither can we be naïve or foolish. Four times in my lifetime America has gone to war, bleeding the lives of its young men into the sands of beachheads, the fields of Europe, and the jungles and rice paddies of Asia. We know only too well that war comes not when the forces of freedom are strong, but when they are weak. It is then that tyrants are tempted.

President Ronald Reagan

Mystify, mislead, and surprise your opponent.

General Thomas J. *Stonewall* Jackson

The belief that public opinion or international public opinion, unbacked by force, had the slightest effect in restraining a powerful military nation in any course of action ... has been shown to be a pathetic fallacy.

President Theodore Roosevelt

Exit strategy applies only to wars of choice. You can choose to quit Vietnam or Somalia or Kosovo. The war on radical Islam is a war of necessity. Wars of necessity have no exit. They must be won. What possible exit strategy can you have against an enemy whose ordinary soldier signs up with the following oath (found among the documents captured from al Qaeda in Afghanistan): 'I state in the presence of God that I will slaughter infidels for my entire life'? There is only one exit strategy in fighting such a man. He dies or you die. No other exit.

Charles Krauthammer

We no longer differentiate in an ultimate sense between the Army, National Guard and Reserve forces. Every energy ... is bent to the development of the Army of the United States. Our purpose is to think only of the American citizen who is to be a soldier in that Army and to prepare him in time of peace for duties in war.

General John J. *Blackjack* Pershing, Army General, Mexican War, World War I, 1860-1948

The cost of freedom is always high, but Americans have always paid it. And the one path we shall never choose ... is the path of surrender, or submission.

President John F. Kennedy

There are no victories at bargain prices.

General of the Army, Dwight D. Eisenhower

There are things worth fighting for. A world in which brutality and lawlessness are allowed to go unchecked isn't the kind of world we're going to want to live in.

Lieutenant General Walter Boomer, USMC

We have learned that we cannot live alone, at peace; that our own well-being is dependent on the well-being of other nations, far away. We have learned that we must live as men, and not as ostriches, nor as dogs in the manger. We have learned to be citizens of the world, members of the human community.

President Franklin D. Roosevelt

*You and I know and do not believe that life is so dear and peace
so sweet as to be purchased at the price of chains and slavery.
Is it worth dying for ... ? Should Moses have told the children of
Israel to live in slavery under the pharaohs? Should Christ have
refused the cross? Should the patriots of Concord Bridge have
thrown down their guns and refused to fire the shot heard round
the world? The martyrs of history were not fools ...*

President Ronald Reagan

*There can be no truly moral choice unless that choice is
made in freedom; similarly, there can be no really
firmly grounded and consistent defense of freedom
unless that defense is rooted in moral principle.*

Murray N. Rothbard

A LOOK I DREAD

*A soldier who has been a long time in the line does have a 'look'
in his eyes that anyone with
practice can discern. It's a look of
dullness, eyes that look without
seeing, eyes that see without
transferring any response to the
mind. It's a look that is the display
room for the thoughts that lie
behind it—exhaustion, lack of sleep,
tension for too long, weariness that
is too great, fear beyond fear,
misery to the point of numbness, a
look of surpassing indifference to
anything anybody can do to you.
It's a look I dread to see on men.*

**Korean War soldier of the 5th
Regimental Combat Team.**
Weary after 31 days of combat.

Ernie Pyle, 5 April 1944, War
Correspondent World War II, Pulitzer
Prize winner, American Folk Hero

THE SECURITY OF FUTURE GENERATIONS

Defense Secretary Donald Rumsfeld.

On September 11, terrorists attacked the symbols of American freedom, prosperity, and military might. They visited violence on thousands of innocent people–small children, mothers and fathers, people of many nationalities and religions. In less than a month, the United States responded. ... Today, one often hears that everything has changed after September 11. While the nation is united in support of the courageous efforts of its Armed Forces, the danger exists that complacency will slowly return. The temptation will arise to return to the old ways of doing things. Free people must be vigilant to not forget or disregard the lessons of September 11. One of those lessons is that dangers are likely to increase, not diminish. Our lives and liberties and those of future generations depend on the contribution of the U.S. Armed Forces. To preserve our freedom, security, and prosperity, we must ensure our men and women in uniform have the resources they need to contribute to peace and security in our still dangerous world. Each generation must bequeath to the next the capabilities to ensure its security. Today, we have the security of future generations of Americans in our hands. We must get it right.

Guard with jealous attention the public liberty.
Suspect everyone who approaches that jewel.
Unfortunately, nothing will preserve it but downright force.
Whenever you give up that force, you are ruined.

Patrick Henry

A nation which can prefer disgrace to danger
is prepared for a master, and deserves one!

Alexander Hamilton

National preparedness means first of all, the moral organization of the people, an organization which creates in the heart of every citizen a sense of his obligation for service to the nation in time of war.

West Point Military History Seminar

We've been blessed with the opportunity to stand for something– for liberty and freedom and fairness. And these are things worth fighting for, worth devoting our lives to.

President Ronald Reagan

Whatever enables us to go to war, secures our peace.

President Thomas Jefferson

TWO SIDES OF THE COIN

The militia is the dread of tyrants and the guard of freemen.

Governor R. Lucas, former Major General of the Ohio Militia, 1832

The United States should get rid of its militias.

Joseph Stalin, 1933

————————————— ☆ —————————————

We view our Nation's strength and security as a trust, upon which rests the hope of free men everywhere.

President Dwight D. Eisenhower

LIARS, FRAUDS AND HYPOCRITES

The anti-warriors must know that their position is a luxury made affordable only by the sure bet that no one in authority will ever accede to their position. The marchers and shouters and flag-burners in Washington pretended to the argument that war should not be waged. What they really mean is that war should not be waged by them. It should be waged by other mothers' sons and daughters. How many pacifists would be willing to accept the logical outcome of their creed of nonviolence even in face of attack–life as a conquered people? Not many, I would think. How many want the (mostly lower-class) men and women of the United States armed forces to continue to fight so that they may enjoy the luxury of preaching against fighting? Nearly all, I would think. Liars. Frauds. Hypocrites.

Michael Kelly

No victory is assured until the man on the ground takes possession by his physical presence on the enemy's soil.

General Omar N. Bradley

You were born to be free. You were also born with a responsibility to contribute to our common defense. For as long as a trace of avarice exists in the hearts of men, there will be a need for the defense of men and their established institutions.

General James M. Gavin

Our Military Establishment is ... more than national. The time for military isolation has passed, as we live in a new world of national interdependence. Our Military Establishment is charged with a trust for the benefit of many other nations.

John Foster Dulles

Happy are all free peoples, too strong to be dispossessed; but blessed are those among nations who dare to be strong for the rest!

E.B. Browning

Those who test our courage will find it strong and those who seek our friendship will find it honorable.

President Lyndon B. Johnson

Armies can not only defend their countries–they can build them.

President John F. Kennedy

I greatly admired the manner in which the American Army was formed. I think it was a prodigy of organization and improvisation. There have been many occasions when a powerful state has wished to raise great armies, and with money and time, and discipline and loyalty that can be accomplished. Nevertheless the rate at which the small American Army of only a few hundred thousand men, not long before the war, created the mighty force of millions of soldiers, is a wonder of military history. I saw the creation of this mighty force–this mighty Army–victorious in every theater against the enemy in so short a time and from such a very small parent stock. This is an achievement which the soldiers of every other country will always study with admiration and envy.

Sir Winston Churchill

The civilian community exists to promote the quality of life but the military community exists to fight and if need be, to die in defense of that quality of life.

General Walter Kerwin, remarks made during his retirement as Vice Chief of Staff of the Army

We did not ask for this present challenge, but we accept it. Like other generations of Americans, we will meet the responsibility of defending human liberty against violence and aggression. By our resolve, we will give strength to others. By our courage, we will give hope to others. And by our actions, we will secure the peace and lead the world to a better day.

President George W. Bush, 7 October 2002

THE BATTLE OF BELLEAU WOODS, WORLD WAR I

Excerpt from Marine Colonel Frederick May Wise's After Action Report.

At the battle's end, the sight was awesome. Two weeks' growth of beard bristled on their faces. Deep lines showed, even beneath beard and dirt. Their eyes were red around the rims, bloodshot, burnt out. They were grimed with earth. Their cartridge belts were almost empty. They were damned near exhausted. Past physical limits. Traveling on their naked nerve. But every one of them was cocky–full of fight.

I lined the men up and looked them over. It was enough to break your heart. I had left Courcelles May 31st with nine hundred and sixty-five men and twenty-six officers–the best battalion I ever saw anywhere. I had taken them, raw recruits for the most. Ten months I had trained them. I had seen them grow into Marines.

Now before me stood three hundred and fifty men and six officers.

Six hundred and fifteen men and nineteen officers were gone. Some had fallen at Les Mares Farm; some in the bottleneck and on the ridge across from the Bois de Belleau. The most of them had gone down that morning we took the woods. Dead, or in hospitals far to the rear.

For seventeen days–since May 31st–they hadn't had a cup of hot coffee or a bite of hot food. They hadn't taken off their shoes. They hadn't had a chance to wash their faces. Even drinking water had been scarce for days. The only place they had found any rest had been on the bare ground. For the last four days they had even been without their packs. They had stood days and nights of terrific shelling without a chance to hit back. Behind an inadequate barrage, they had walked into the muzzles of German machine guns and had taken them. They had driven trained German veterans out of fortified positions by frontal attack. Most of them raw recruits less than a year before, they had walked into the fiercest kind of woods fighting in France. In the face of the military axiom that twenty-five percent casualties justify retreat, they had sustained over sixty percent casualties–and had gone ahead and gained their objectives. Those objectives once gained, they had never given up an inch.

They had stopped the Germans at the nearest point a German with a gun in his hand ever got to Paris after America entered the war. At the Bois de Belleau they had done the impossible.

They had taken nearly twice their own number in German prisoners. They had captured more than fifty German machine guns and half a dozen trench mortars. They had made a record that never was passed in the World War. But they had paid for it.

Our military strength is a prerequisite to peace, but let it be clear we maintain this strength in the hope it will never be used, for the ultimate determinant in the struggle that's now going on in the world will not be bombs and rockets but a test of wills and ideas, a trial of spiritual resolve, the values we hold, the beliefs we cherish, the ideals to which we are dedicated.

President Ronald Reagan, 1982

In the long history of the world, only a few generations have been granted the role of defending freedom in its hour of maximum danger. I do not shrink from this responsibility. I welcome it. ... The energy, the faith, the devotion which we bring to this endeavor will light our country and all who serve it–and the glow from that fire can truly light the world.

President John F. Kennedy, Inaugural Address, 20 January 1961

Yet, finally, war is always the same. It is young men dying in the fullness of their promise. It is trying to kill a man that you do not even know well enough to hate ... therefore, to know war is to know that there is still madness in this world.

President Lyndon Johnson, 12 January 1966, during his State of the Union Address before Congress

There is a rank due to the United States, among nations, which will be withheld, if not absolutely lost, by the reputation of weakness. If we desire to avoid insult, we must be able to repel it; if we desire to secure peace, one of the most powerful instruments of our rising prosperity, it must be known that we are at all times ready for war.

President George Washington

THE COST OF BEING WRONG

Defense Secretary Rumsfeld's Interview with the American Forces Information Service, 29 May 2001, interview with Jim Garamone.

Question:
Mr. Secretary, yesterday at Arlington I heard your speech. You said you contrasted the world at the turn of the 20th Century to today with the idea that the people of that era thought they were beyond war, and Churchill was asked what if you're wrong? Are you in Churchill's role now, asking America what if you're wrong? If you don't think there's a war, but what if you're wrong?

Secretary Rumsfeld:
Well you know, if you think about it, those who were complacent at the turn of the 20th Century in 1900, were wrong. And they weren't wrong a little. They were wrong a lot. And millions of people died. When you get up in the morning in a country that's at peace and you're able to walk out the door and not have to look to the left and look to the right to see if someone's going to machine gun you or throw a grenade, you get used to that. And you begin to feel that, well that's the nature of

things. That's the way it's going to be. We can relax, and we can enjoy ourselves and not be concerned about threats to our freedom or threats to our lives. The problem with that is that the whole sweep of history is to the contrary. But there is a difference today. The difference is that the weapons are vastly more powerful, more deadly, more lethal. The reach of those weapons is vastly greater. In the last century people had to worry about their neighbors, for the most part. Today national bomb rates are really not terribly wrong because of the reach of these weapons. Therefore the penalty, if you will, for being wrong, is enormous. What we need to do as a country is to recognize that, and to recognize the difficulty of seeing the future. I'm struck by the fact that at Dick Cheney's confirmation hearings in 1989 not a single senator asked him about Iraq. The word never came up. And a year later we're at war with Iraq in the Persian Gulf. It made me wonder what word, what name of a country or what word for a military capability wasn't mentioned in my confirmation hearing four months ago that within a year could come up and dominate our lives. That isn't the kind of thing that happens occasionally. That's the kind of thing that happens every five or ten years, period, in my entire lifetime. The Shah of Iran was the regional power that we were helping, supporting and working closely with. A year later the Ayatollah was there and it was the center of anti-Western, anti-American hostility in the world. The violent swings that can take place are breathtaking. And if you think about it, the United States of America for a very modest amount of money, that is to say something like three or three and a half percent of our gross national product, can have an insurance policy that will enable our country to live essentially in a peaceful and stable world where people can go about their business. And if we fail to provide that margin of safety, if we say well, goodness, we don't want to spend 3.5 percent or 3.2 percent, we want to spend 2.5 percent of our gross national product, and we're wrong, the penalty for it is just enormous. The cost in billions and billions and hundreds of billions of dollars to be wrong. The cost in human life to be wrong. That's not a mistake we want to make.

*There is no merit in putting off a war for a year if,
when it comes, it is a far worse war or one much harder to win.*

Sir Winston Churchill

THE MORAL VINDICATION

*What tortures the conscience of anti-war liberals to this day is
that the American public never agreed with them. While Americans
grew to doubt the way the war was prosecuted, they never doubted
the morality of the U.S. purpose in Vietnam. The Cold War was
at its height, and the U.S. had to draw the line somewhere against
Communist aggression. The history of Southeast Asia after
the U.S. pulled out of Vietnam is all the moral vindication
most of us need–the Khmer Rouge genocide, the 'boat people' and
the re-education camps, all compared to the prosperity of those
nations (Thailand, Malaysia, the Philippines) that we defended.*

Wall Street Journal

*The primary reason for the existence of all the
U.S. Armed Forces is to provide the military power
to deter war. Should deterrence fail for reasons beyond
our control, then these forces must be able to fight and win.
There is no cheap way to do this.
There also is no second prize in the business of war today,
nor will there ever be.*

General George H. Decker

*... Word to the Nation:
Guard zealously your right to serve
in the Armed Forces, for without them,
there will be no other rights to guard.*

President John F. Kennedy, 1962

WAR IS A TIME OF TEARS

The following letter was written by Major Vincent Colasuanno, 333 Tactical Fighter Squadron, 355 Tactical Fighter Wing, Takhli, Thailand. It is dated 27 December 1968 and was written in response to letters from Fourth Graders in a parochial school in Wichita, Kansas, where his children attended and his wife was a teacher. This was written before his fatal ejection from an F-105D near Udorn, Thailand.

December 27, 1968
Dear Fourth Graders,

I cannot tell you what great pleasure I received from reading your wonderful letters. Children's thoughts are always honest and sincere, and yours have made this Christmas just a bit more meaningful for me. Your simple prayers for my safety, and hope that I have a Merry Christmas are very comforting.

Some of you asked how it feels to be so far away from my family. Well, it is a terribly lonely feeling, but I have received much comfort through prayer. Our Lord is very kind indeed, and He will help you carry your burden if you but ask. Without His help I do not know what I would do. Not only has He eased my loneliness, but He has given me the courage to face the dangers of war. A few of you asked what war is like—the questions came from boys. I'll tell you what it is not like. It is not a glamorous, daredevil existence where the *good guys* always win. It is not a fearless fighter pilot jumping into his airplane to shoot down the enemy. It is not a game which you play (and which I played as a child) where you go home to a good supper and a warm bed after it is over. War is fought by real human beings, not Hollywood stars—men like your daddy and perhaps older brother. We all face a moment of truth when we must overcome our fears and do what must be done, no matter how difficult. War is a time of tears when we must overcome our sorrow for our fallen comrades and do what must be done, no matter how difficult. War is the curse of mankind because he will not listen to God's will. War is the agony of mankind because he will not love his neighbor, because he is greedy and selfish, because he is proud and arrogant, because he covets what his neighbor has and would rather try to take from him than build it for himself. War is all the horrible things a human being can do to another human being because he has not learned to love–rather, to hate.

And this is the great, and yet unheard message of Christ–to love. If we all did this, there would be no wars, for man does not hurt that which he loves. Perhaps your generation can accomplish this–it seems that mine has failed.

God bless you, dear children. Learn God's message well and do not allow adults to teach you to hate–for no reason, and against no man. And pray for me.

Love, Maj. Colasuanno

*Battle is the ultimate to which the whole life's labor
of an officer should be directed. He may live
to the age of retirement without seeing a battle;
still, he must always be getting ready for it exactly as if he knew
the hour of the day it is to break upon him. And then, whether it
come early or late, he must be willing to fight–he must fight.*

Brigadier General Charles F. Smith, U.S. Army, 1861

MILITARY STRENGTH AND THE OTHER PILLARS

By General James L. Jones, Commandant of the Marine Corps. Excerpts from *The Retired Officer Magazine*, May 2001, article titled, *National Security in the 21st Century*.

Our national power is comprised of various interrelated elements that are best described by the following pillars; economic strength, technological dominance, cultural influence, democratic principles, diplomatic and political leadership, and the strength of our armed forces. The collective strength of these pillars is reflected, ultimately, in the nation's prosperity and security. However, far too often we fail to appreciate their interdependency, particularly the benefits that a strong military bestows upon the other pillars of national power. Indeed, in using our military power, we have made the world a better place for economies to prosper; democratic values to take root; cultures to expand and interrelate; and science, technology, and the arts to blossom on a scale unimagined 50 years ago.

The lack of awareness of the connection between military strength and the other pillars is understandable when one considers that, historically, our armed forces have been viewed principally as an instrument for national defense. Our military traditions and heritage have long been epitomized by the citizen soldier who, in the form of the minuteman or volunteer, answered the nation's call, contributed to the resolution of the threat or contingency, and promptly returned to civilian life.

You may think me transported with enthusiasm, but I am not. I am well aware of the toil and blood and treasure that it will cost to maintain this Declaration, and support and defend these States. Yet through all the gloom I can see the rays of ravishing light and glory. I can see that the end is worth more than all the means.

President John Adams, 2 July 1776, in a letter to his wife Abigail, 2nd U.S. President, 1797-1801

ENOUGH GROUND TO BURY THEM IN

When in England at the World Economic Forum, U.S. Secretary of State Colin Powell was asked by the Archbishop of Canterbury, Mr. George Carey, if our plans for Iraq were just an example of empire building by President George Bush. Part of Mr. Carey's question was as follows:

> And would you not agree, as a very significant political figure in the United States, Colin, that America, at the present time, is in danger of relying too much upon the hard power and not enough upon building the trust from which the soft values, which of course all of

our family life that actually at the bottom, when the bottom line is reached, is what makes human life valuable?

Secretary Powell answered by saying that,

> The United States believes strongly in what you call soft power, the value of democracy, the value of the free economic system, the value of making sure that each citizen is free and free to pursue their own God-given ambitions and to use the talents that they were given by God. And that is what we say to the rest of the world. That is why we participated in establishing a community of democracy within the Western Hemisphere. It's why we participate in all of these great international organizations. There is nothing in American experience or in American political life or in our culture that suggests we want to use hard power. But what we have found over the decades is that unless you do have hard power—and here I think you're referring to military power—then sometimes you are faced with situations that you can't deal with. I mean, it was not soft power that freed Europe. It was hard power. And what followed immediately after hard power? Did the United States ask for dominion over a single nation in Europe? No. Soft power came in the Marshall Plan. Soft power came with American GIs who put their weapons down once the war was over and helped all those nations rebuild. We did the same thing in Japan. So our record of living our values and letting our values be an inspiration to others I think is clear. And I don't think I have anything to be ashamed of or apologize for with respect to what America has done for the world.

(Applause)

> We have gone forth from our shores repeatedly over the last hundred years and we've done this as recently as the last year in Afghanistan and put wonderful young men and women at risk, many of whom have lost their lives, and we have asked for nothing except enough ground to bury them in, and otherwise we have returned home to seek our own, you know, to seek our own lives in peace, to live our own

lives in peace. But there comes a time when soft power or talking with evil will not work where, unfortunately, hard power is the only thing that works.

(It became very quiet in the room.)

KILL RATES

AC-130. Air Force *Spectre* Gunship.

It is a fashionable assertion in these troubled times that nations must focus on economic, not military strength. Over the long run, it is true, no nation can remain militarily strong while economically exhausted. But I would remind you that defeats on the battlefield occur in the short run ... Power still matters. More precisely, economic power is not a replacement for military power. Lest we forget, Kuwait's economic wealth did not protect it from the predatory Saddam Hussein; quite the opposite. Nor was the Iraqi dictator finally driven from Kuwait because his GNP [Gross National Product] was smaller than that of the U.S., Britain or Japan. It is not the industrial productivity of democracies that is feared by ... armed bandits ... but the kill rates of their gunships.

President Ronald Reagan

AMERICANS ON GUARD

American Father and Son.
Photo by Senior Airman Crissy.

Brig. Gen. (Select) Edward *Buster* Ellis, American co-commander of the combined task force for Operation Northern Watch, stands in front of an F-15E Strike Eagle with his son, Capt. Edward Ellis. Both are F-15E pilots on active duty flying combat missions on opposite sides of the globe. In May 2002, BG Ellis was flying over Iraq in support of Operation Northern Watch and Capt. Ellis was flying over America in support of Operation Noble Eagle. BG Ellis's father, Colonel Ellis flew combat missions during the Berlin Airlift and in both the Korean and Vietnam wars. Since the Air Force became a separate service in 1947, there has always been an Air Force pilot named Edward Ellis defending America.

*P*ut *none but Americans on guard tonight.*

General George Washington

*I*t *is an unfortunate fact that we can secure peace only by preparing for war.*

President John F. Kennedy, 6 September 1960

*N*ational Defense *is not a threat to peace; it is the guarantee of peace with freedom.*

President Ronald Reagan

CHAPTER 7

THE WARRIOR SPIRIT

American warriors have won every war they have ever fought, and their battle record is the envy of every military in the world. If there is a single reason for this success, it is a secret that resides deep within the heart of each warrior. This chapter gives a title to this secret, the *warrior spirit*. No attempt is made to define the *warrior spirit*, at least not with any brevity; instead, this chapter attempts to provide examples of the warrior spirit from the hearts of American warriors.

In battle, casualties vary directly with the time you are exposed to effective fires. Your own fire reduces the effectiveness and volume of the enemy's fire. Battles are won by frightening the enemy. Fear is induced by inflicting death and wounds on him. Death and wounds are produced by fire.

General George S. Patton, Jr.

World War II. A German Soldier lies
dead from American firepower.

HAWGDRIVER'S DREAM

A-10 Warthog (*Hawg*). Firing a Maverick Missile.

Make no mistake about it ... this war is gonna be a Hawgdriver's dream ... no more of this sending GPS guided bombs from the ionosphere ... I want to camp out on the enemy's border ... I want to yell across the border, in the immortal words of Wyatt Earp (as portrayed by Kurt Russell), *You tell 'em I'm coming! AND HELL'S COMING WITH ME!*

I wanna punch Bin Laden in the face and say, *You gonna do something? Or just stand there and bleed?* And then, I wanna laugh maniacally, as my 30mm shells decimate his camps.

I ain't talking about the Armor Piercing shells this time, although the thought of poisoning their lungs (if, in the unlikely event, they survived my attack) with the dirty dust of spent uranium is quite refreshing ... that would make the cloud over New York seem like pure Oxygen.

I want High Explosive Incendiary (HEI) rounds ... 1,150 of them, fired two or three hundred at a time ... like three hundred grenades exploding all at once ... and that's just my jet ... the three coming with me brings that total to 16 cans of CBU-87 ... that's 3,232 individual sub munitions for them ... that's what I want.

I want four Maverick missiles per jet ... that's 16 of those things ... and if we run outta trucks and other small things to hit with those missiles, I wanna find out what a maverick will do when it locks onto a terrorist and hits him at just over 1,000 feet per second ... there might not be enough deceleration to detonate the thing but at that speed ... I don't think it would be necessary. And I want two pods of rockets, hanging from my wings. Seven white phosphorous and seven HEI ... I want the 'Willie Petes' to put a cloud of smoke, to climb into the sky, to let everyone following know ... that's where the gettin' is good ... And the HEI ... well, I just want FRAG in the air, tearing apart their greasy, scumbag bodies the same way they tore into our nation ... and then we'll start cleaning up with the almighty General Electric GAU-8/A Avenger cannon ... what a perfect name ... AVENGER CANNON!

If that's all I had, that's all I'd want ... four hawgs, with 4,600 of our little friends ... lock and load, hammer down!

But that's just my personal end ... here's what else I want ... I want John Madden, Terry Bradshaw and Howie Long, to take over CNN, NBC, ABC and every other news network, to provide coverage of this war ... I want Madden, with his electronic chalkboard, out there describing what's going on ... *You see here, across the top of the screen, that ridge line is exactly where the attack is gonna come from ... you'll see the Warthawgs come popping over them and unleash a fury that we haven't seen since Lawrence Taylor was on the prowl ... Speaking of that, here they come and BAM! These guys are great! ... They remind me of linemen ... they don't get much press coverage, but when they hit you, man do you know it!* I want Hank Williams, Jr. and Lee Greenwood belting out, *I'M PROUD TO BE AN AMERICAN*, as the intro to *Monday Night Air Strikes ... Fight night* would have a whole new meaning now ... I want to see Sports Center air, the *HIT OF THE DAY ... Today's strike comes from a flight of two A-10 Warthogs. You'll see here that some terrorist got the wild idea that he could shoot at these guys ... you can see the missile come up and totally miss the two jets ... and here, you see, as they roll in and unleash that awesome gun on the point of origin, ... nothing left there now! And that's our, PLAY OF THE DAY!* I want Mills Lane, in the field, giving play-by-play descriptions. I want *Flight of the Valkaries* playing at full bore, from every mountainside, as we run in at 100 feet ... I want *WELCOME TO THE JUNGLE*, playing after the first bomb hits, and when I'm WINCHESTER ammunition, I wanna land on Bin Laden's personal airstrip, grab him by his twisted, dead neck and poke him in the eyes and say, *YOU JUST GOT KNOCKED OUT!* I want the NFL cheerleaders to send us off to war, and the XFL cheerleaders to welcome us home.

And while we're at it, I don't just want to beat the crap outta these scumbags, I want to humiliate them, too. I want to see Schwarzkopf come outta retirement, to start kicking some butt ... I want a cure for Alzheimer's–right now–to get Reagan back in working order, and like Dennis Leary says, I want a cure for cancer, to thaw out the 'Duke' and see just how pissed off he is right now. I want STUKA terror sirens, mounted to the wings of my Hawg ... although the unique whine of our engines is about all the terror siren we'll need right now ...

All right, Zero ... slow down ... breathe ... in ... out ... ok.

I think the coffee has worn off a bit now, and I should get back to work. You just picked the wrong people to mess with ... not such a good day to be a bad guy.

Do not hit at all if it can be avoided, but never hit softly.
President Theodore Roosevelt

When you stop to think about it, peace merely
for the sake of peace isn't all that inviting.
The easiest way to get and ensure peace
is by surrendering your principles and your freedom.
Most Americans (I hope) don't want that kind of peace.
The United States could have peace if
it contacted Osama bin Laden and asked him his price,
but I suspect whatever it is it's more than we'd be willing to pay.
Ditto Saddam Hussein. The sad–but true–fact is that
the only peace worth having is a peace that's worth fighting for.
Because peace without freedom is not worth having.
And freedom cannot be sustained without
being willing to fight for it.
Lyn Nofziger

THE POWER OF THE USS JOHN F. KENNEDY

Captain Ronald H. Henderson, Jr.

On 11 February 2002, Captain Ronald H. Henderson, Jr. took command of the *USS John F. Kennedy* (CV-67) as the 26th Commanding Officer. On 10 March 2002, just prior to the *JFK* launching her first strikes into Afghanistan, he addressed the crew of the *JFK* with the following remarks:

Good evening onboard *John F. Kennedy*, Carrier Air Wing SEVEN, and Carrier Group Six. We are currently preceding at best speed to our launch point for tonight's strikes, off the coast of Pakistan, nearly 700 miles south of our targets in Afghanistan. At midnight, CVW-7 will launch into the dark night, and strike their first blows of Operation Enduring Freedom, the war on terrorism. For us, this is a culminating point in space, a culminating point in time, and a culminating point in history.

Our enemy is a group of religious fanatics, who pervert the peace of Islam and twist its meaning to justify the murder of thousands of innocents at the Twin Towers of New York, at the Pentagon, and in a field in Pennsylvania. They hate us and attack us because they oppose all that is good about America. They hate us because we are prosperous. They hate us because we are tolerant. They hate us because we are happy. Mostly, they hate us because we are free and because we will *pay any price, bear any burden, meet any hardship, support any friend or oppose any foe to assure the survival and success of liberty*. Make no mistake—this is a fight for Western Civilization. If these monsters are not destroyed, they will destroy us, and our children and children's children will live in fear forever. America is the only nation that can stop them and destroy them. Only America has the strength of character and the vast resources to hunt these fanatics down anywhere in the world. We have friends and Allies but we are the leaders of the world our forefathers made and died for. Our Naval power has been the principal weapon of our resolve. Great ships and great crews have gone before us—*ENTERPRISE, CARL VINSON, KITTY HAWK, TEDDY ROOSEVELT, JOHN STENNIS.*

Tonight, our enemies will feel the power of *USS JOHN F. KENNEDY*. It is now our turn to strike for justice and we will strike hard. Millions of Americans wish they could be here tonight with us. They saw the Twin Towers fall, and watched helplessly, wanting to do something to defend America and our way of life. For us tonight, that wait and that helplessness are over. We have reached the point where we are all part of something so much greater than ourselves. For the rest of our lives, no matter whether we stay in the Navy or move on to civilian life, no matter what we do or where we go, we will remember that on 10 March 2002, we came together and struck a blow for freedom.

All of us are volunteers. Most of us joined the Navy to serve our country and better ourselves. Tonight and in the nights to come we are given the opportunity of a lifetime, a chance to truly make a difference in the world. Our namesake John F. Kennedy wrote that *a single person can make a difference, and every person should try*. Tonight, WE make a difference! We represent America in all its power and diversity. We are men and women, rich and poor, black and white, and all colors of the human rainbow. We are Christian, Jew, and yes, Muslim. WE ARE AMERICA. This war will not be short, pleasant, or easy. It has already required the sacrifice of our firefighters, our policemen, our soldiers, our sailors, our airmen, and our Marines. More sacrifices will be made. In the end we will win, precisely because we are those things that the terrorists hate—prosperous, happy, tolerant, and most of all, free. Those Americans who wish they could be here with us are, in fact, here with us in spirit. Never before in American history has our nation been so completely unified and resolute in purpose. Every one of them is cheering us on, praying for our safety and our success. Our families are behind us 100 percent. We will not let them down. We are, and will be, men and women of honor, courage, and commitment. I believe, as Abraham Lincoln said, that *America is the last, best hope for the world*. Tonight, we hold a shining beacon of that hope. We shall keep it burning brightly.

Stay sharp. Stay focused. Stay safe. Use the training that has made you the best Sailors in the world, the best Sailors in the history of the world. Trust in your faith, and in your shipmates. God bless us all, and God bless America.

*No nation can long endure that does not foster
a military spirit among its young men.*

General John J. Pershing, 5 December 1916

Pile blows on your enemy thick and fast.

General William T. Sherman

FIGHT AND WIN

Admiral Vern Clark, Chief of Naval Operations, gave this speech just prior to the beginning of Operation Iraqi Freedom.

Soon, our nation will call upon you, the men and women of our Navy, to meet the next challenge in the global war on terrorism.

When you raised your right hand, took the oath, and donned the Sailor's uniform, you chose to make a difference in the service of this nation—and you are. Rest assured, your service is unquestioned; you have the support of the citizens of the United States of America and your families. They care, and they believe in you. Make them proud. I couldn't be more proud to serve with you.

You are part of the greatest joint and combined military force ever assembled. If our Commander-in-Chief gives the signal, fight and win!

USS Lincoln. 1,100 Sailors spell *Ready Now*, while deployed for
Operation Enduring Freedom.

NO BETTER FRIEND, NO WORSE ENEMY

Major General J.N. Mattis. Photo by Sergeant Joseph R. Chenelly.

30 March 2003, Central Iraq, U.S. Marines, 1st Marine Division (REIN), James N. Mattis, Major General, Message to All Hands.

For decades, Saddam Hussein has tortured, imprisoned, raped and murdered the Iraqi people; invaded neighboring countries without provocation; and threatened the world with weapons of mass destruction. The time has come to end his reign of terror. On your young shoulders rest the hopes of mankind.

When I give you the word, together we will cross the Line of Departure, close with those forces that choose to fight, and destroy them. Our fight is not with the Iraqi people, nor is it with members of the Iraqi army who choose to surrender. While we will move swiftly and aggressively against those who resist, we will treat all others with decency, demonstrating chivalry and soldierly compassion for people who have endured a lifetime under Saddam's oppression.

Chemical attack, treachery, and use of the innocent as human shields can be expected, as can other unethical tactics. Take it all in stride. Be the hunter, not the hunted; never allow your unit to be caught with its guard down. Use good judgment and act in best interests of our Nation.

You are part of the world's most feared and trusted force. Engage your brain before you engage your weapon. Share your courage with each other as we enter the uncertain terrain north of the Line of Departure. Keep faith in your comrades on your left and right and Marine Air overhead. Fight with a happy heart and strong spirit.

For the mission's sake, our country's sake, and the sake of the men who carried the Division's colors in past battles–who fought for life and never lost their nerve–carry out your mission and keep your honor clean. Demonstrate to the world there is *No Better Friend, No Worse Enemy* than a U.S. Marine.

In December 2002, the Nuclear Aircraft Carrier, *USS Harry S. Truman* departed from Norfolk, Virginia for an extended deployment. Just as the lines were cast off, this announcement was made throughout the ship and topside on the ship's intercom:

Peace on Earth to men of good will—All others, Stand By.

An aircraft carrier is a noble thing. It lacks almost everything that seems to denote nobility, yet deep nobility is there. A carrier has no poise. It has no grace. It is top heavy and lop-sided. It has the line of a well-fed cow ... Yet a carrier is a ferocious thing, and out of its heritage of action has grown its nobility. I believe that every Navy in the world has its Number One priority the destruction of enemy carriers. That's a precarious honor, but a proud one.

Ernie Pyle, Last Chapter, 1945

Resistance to tyrants is obedience to God.

President Thomas Jefferson

You have a comradeship, a rapport that you'll never have again ... There's no competitiveness, no money values. You trust the man on your left and your right with your life.

Captain Audie Murphy, Medal of Honor recipient and most decorated American soldier of World War II

The conduct and weapons of warfare may change, but victory will always result from a soldier imposing his will on the enemy.

General Eric Shinseki, Army Chief of Staff, January 2003

To Fight Me ... Is To Respect Chaos & Death!

They Fight Because ...

*M*en fight, essentially, because of each other. They fight because
they grow to know each other, trust each other, and ultimately, to
love each other. They fight because they are unwilling to let each
other down. That's teamwork, and that's why it's so critical. It's the
foundation for survival and mission accomplishment in combat.
Officers who do not clasp this concept to their hearts, or only pay
lip service to it, should not be permitted to command.

LTC Alfred Dibella, Response to Questionnaire on Teamwork
United States Army Armor School, 1988

I fought in three wars and three more would not be
too many to defend my country. I love America and
as she has weaknesses or ills I'll hold her hand.

General Daniel *Chappie* James

*T*he probability that we may fail in the struggle ought not to
deter us from the support of a cause we believe to be just.

President Abraham Lincoln

TWAS THE NIGHT BEFORE BOMBING

*T*was the night before Payback and all through the Land,
They're running like rabbits in Afghanistan,
Osama's been praying, he's down on his Knees,
He's hoping that Allah will hear all his Pleas.

*H*e thought if he killed us that we'd fall and Shatter,
But all that he's done is just make us Madder.
We ain't yet forgotten our Marines in Beirut,
And we'll kick your butt, with one heavy Boot.

*A*nd yes we remember the USS Cole,
And the lives of our sailors that you bastards stole.
You think you can rule us and cause us to Fear,
You'll soon get the answer if you live to Hear.

*A*nd we ain't forgotten your buddy Saddam,
And he ain't forgotten the sound of our Bombs.
You think that those mountains are somewhere to Hide.
They'll go down in history as the place where you died.

*R*emember Khadhafi and his Line of Death?
He came very close, to his final Breath.
So come out and prove it, that you are a Man,
Cause our soldiers are coming and they have a Plan.

*T*hey're Mothers and Fathers,
Daughters and Sons,
And they sure do carry
some mighty big Guns.

*O*sama I wrote this especially for you,
For airmail delivery by B-52.
You soon will be hearing a thud and a whistle,
Old Glory is coming, attached to a Missile.

I will not be sorry to see your ass Go.
It's Red, White, and Blue that is running this Show.

Lisa Ossman

Nathan Ross Chapman.

*S*tand up and do something.

Personal motto of Green Beret Sergeant First Class Nathan Ross Chapman, 1st Special Forces Group, first American killed by hostile fire in the Gardez area, West of Khost, Operation Enduring Freedom, Afghanistan, 04 January 2002,

*A*mericans know now that we are at war, and will make the sacrifices and show the resolve necessary to prevail, I say to our enemies, we are coming. God may show you mercy. We will not.

John McCain, U.S. Senator (R-AZ)

*T*he cost of freedom is always high, but Americans have always paid it. And one path we shall never choose, ... is the path of surrender, or submission.

President John F. Kennedy

THE NEW YORK CITY FLAG

From Brigadier General Andrew Davis, Director of Public Affairs, Headquarters, U.S. Marine Corps:

You are all familiar with the now-famous flag raised by firefighters in NY City and which now flies over the carrier *USS Theodore Roosevelt* which deployed from here in Norfolk. What you may not know is that the first strike against Afghanistan was made by a United States Marine Corps FA-18 *Hornet*. The pilot carried that flag in the cockpit of his FA-18 when he dropped the first bomb on the Taliban *for the people of New York* Oooohh ... Rahhhh!

SIX TO EIGHT ROUNDS

Sent: 29 August 2001
From: Jones MajGen Thomas S.
To: Hanlon LtGen Edward, Jr.
Subject: General Myers Visit

Sir,

Without exaggeration or hyperbole, the General's visit could not have gone better; the Marines were superb. General Myers [Vice Chairman Joint Chiefs of Staff, at that time] ranks as a *ringer* when it comes to shooting skills, outdone only by his bodyguard. Truly, he fired every weapon VERY well, especially skilled with the pistol, and it was obvious that he's had some trigger time in days past. While working on the 240G, he asked a young Marine how many rounds he should fire at a time, and the immediate response was six to eight. The General then asked the Marine how he could calibrate the number of rounds being fired. The Marine hesitated and then asked the General if he would be offended if he (the Marine) told him how Marines calibrated the right burst when he was in the FMF [Fleet Marine Force]. General Myers said definitely not, and the Marine responded with, *Sir, we use 'die mother f**cker die,' as it takes 6 to 8 rounds to say that.* The General said he was going to share the Marines response with the folks in the Pentagon tomorrow. In short, the General made the Marines feel ten feet tall and bullet proof, giving all those who assisted him a VJCS Coin. It was clear that he was interested in the Marines and what they did. He listened, exchanged dialogue and really embraced the weapons; this doesn't happen with many VIP groups. I wouldn't be surprised if we saw General Myers on another visit in days ahead. He's really excited about General Pace becoming his deputy, stating that he wanted a Marine by his side, as he would be assured of getting an honest perspective. As would be expected, TBS and Weapons Training Battalion did great work; Major Smith of your staff had everything wrapped together very tightly. I served as senior straphanger and hand shaker. All in all, an enjoyable afternoon. S/F

U.S. Machine Gunner. Operation Enduring
Freedom, Afghanistan, 18 September 2002.

THIS GENERATION IS READY!

By Lance Corporal Timothy G. Apel, USMC Machine Gunner.

It was us who signed the contract swearing to *protect this country from enemies foreign and domestic.* This generation thanks you for sparing us the fears of a global nuclear war with the U.S.S.R. We thank you for not having to worry about a raid through Europe by the Warsaw Pact. We thank you for fighting the war against communism and raising us in an almost entirely democratic world. Now this generation has its own fight. This generation is ready.

We will lay down our lives if it comes to that. If it takes me and a thousand or five thousand of my brethren to make that possible, so be it. If that is what it takes to know that when OUR sons and daughters board a plane their biggest fear is turbulence, then it will be done. We will make that sacrifice. Despite what many believe, our generation is aware of what that word means and we will make silence the criticism that has characterized our generation.

Mothers, your sons and daughters fight for you, and for their country. Your sons and daughters love you. Your sons and daughters wish only for what we have wanted since our conception. We wish to make you proud.

All my love,

THE FUNDAMENTALS OF WARTIME NEGOTIATIONS

American B-1 *Lancer* Bomber.

Author Unknown.

The mission of SAC [Strategic Air Command] is to put bombs on target. Everything else, such as MPF, BX, fuel trucks and fighters, is simply support for this mission. You win the war by killing the enemy, by the thousands, on the ground, not one at a time at 20,000 feet.

In wartime, our POWs are not released because the enemy sends representatives to sit smugly at *peace talks*. They are not released because some famous movie actress betrayed her countrymen at arms, and they are not released because the enemy lost five aircraft to certain individuals who became aces. They are released because brave men took their bombers downtown and spoke with the enemy personally, in the only language the enemy understands: iron bombs falling on their heads.

You can shoot down all the MiGs you want, but if you return from the mission and find the Russian tank commander having lunch in your snack bar, you've lost the war, Jack.

These lessons have been forged in blood and steel by all those crews who have gone before you–crews who flew back when men were men, and the rest of the world knew not to fool with the U.S.A. or we would nuke'em off the map; back when SAC patches were twice the size of every other commands'; back when bomber jets were built to be water drinkin', smoke pourin' and BIG, and only quiche-eaten airline pukes flew fans. Times change, the technology changes, but the crew in the cockpit must remain the same brave warriors every age has counted on in times of peril.

Finally, real men fly BOMBERS because they understand the fundamentals of wartime negotiations. You negotiate with the enemy with your knee in his chest and your knife at his throat.

THAT SPIRIT

Paul W. Tibbets. In his bomber, the *Enola Gay*, just before his mission over Hiroshima, Japan, August 1945.

General Paul W. Tibbets spoke before the retired members of the 490th Bomb Group on the opening day of the group's 20th reunion, September 4th, 2001 in New London Connecticut. He was a 29-year-old lieutenant colonel in the Army Air Force when he got the orders in September 1944 to establish a special unit that would drop atomic bombs on Europe and Japan to end World War II.

He closed his remarks by taking questions from the crowd. The last question: Did he ever have any doubts about what he had done? *I've been asked that a lot of times*, Tibbets said. *The answer is, I have never lost a night's sleep. I would do it again, given the same circumstances, without hesitation. That's about all I can say.*

We've all changed, Tibbets said as the audience viewed pictures of the young men in the bomb crew 56 years ago. *But I don't think that spirit has changed one damned bit.*

LEVEL THE PLACE

In October 1954, LTG Chesty Puller was the base commander at Camp Lejeune. I was the commanding officer of A-1-2. In those days (and maybe now) we had a rifle company on each coast that was combat ready and on alert to fly anywhere on a couple of hours' notice. The duty or alert fell to one company for a period of time, then to another. In early October 1954, Able Company was the *clutch company* when the panic button was pushed. I was called to battalion. The battalion CO and I then rushed to regiment. We picked up the regimental CO and sped to division, straight to the war room. In the war room was the division commander, the G3,

G2 and an awful lot of brass. And, in the back of the room sat Chesty Puller. The briefing started. First, one Colonel, then another, briefed on where we would be going and why, how soon we had to be in the aircraft, initial destination, and all that. Maps were brought out, various opinions offered, and contingencies discussed. As I recall, when the division commander asked if I had any questions, I was so overwhelmed that I did not. Then, the division commander turned toward Chesty Puller in the back of the room. *General Puller*, he asked. *Is there anything you would like to say?* Chesty looked at me for what seemed an eternity, then said rather quietly and very seriously, *Son, if they give you any shit, level the place.*

FROM THE HEART OF THE SEVENTH, RESCORLA'S NO MORE

British-born Rick Rescorla was a hero of the Ia Drang and both terrorist attacks on the World Trade Center. By Major Robert L. Bateman, U.S. Army, for *Vietnam Magazine*, June 2002.

I heard his voice long before I ever met him: *Gaaaa-rry Owen, Garry Owen, Garry Owen, / In the Valley of Montana all alone / There'll be better days to be for the 7th Cavalry / When we charge again for dear old Garry Owen* ... It was the summer of 1995. I was a company commander in the 2nd Battalion, 7th Cavalry–George Armstrong Custer's old outfit–and an audiotape made at An Khe in the spring of 1966 had found its way into my hands. *Garry Owen* is the motto of the 7th Cavalry. The voice pounding through on the scratchy tape was a voice out of the pages of history for me–the voice of Rick Rescorla. As a 7th Cavalry man I had heard of Rescorla. He was made famous by the account of his actions during the Battle of the Ia Drang Valley in November 1965, the Americans' first major battle of the Vietnam War. He became a legend in the unit for his behavior in combat, and his face became an American icon when a young reporter named Peter Arnett snapped his photo. That photo became the cover of the book *We Were Soldiers Once ... and Young*, by Hal Moore and Joe Galloway, two who were there. The book, and now the movie, We Were Soldiers, tell the story of the fight.

Rescorla was a second lieutenant then, but was already experienced in combat. Born in Cornwall, on the English coast, Rescorla had seen man's darker side already, first from service with the British army on Cyprus, and later in a *security force* in Rhodesia. The epitome of the young warrior, he was the sort that England seems to have bred in abundance for centuries: the type of young man who in times past went forth from Britain and created an empire upon which the sun never set. England happened to be fresh out of wars in the 1960s, so Rescorla became an American and fought in ours.

In 1965 Rescorla knew war. His men did not, yet. To steady them, to break their concentration away from the fear that may grip a man when he realizes there are hundreds of men very close by who want to kill him, Rescorla sang. Mostly he sang dirty songs that would make a sailor blush. Interspersed with the lyrics was the voice of command: *Fix bayonets ... on liine ... reaa-dy ... forward.* It was a voice straight from Waterloo, from the Somme, implacable, impeccable, impossible to disobey. His men forgot their fear, concentrated on his orders and marched forward as he led them straight into the pages of history: 1st Platoon, Bravo Company, 2nd Battalion, 7th Cavalry ... *Hard Corps.*

When I started interviewing these veterans of my regiment decades later, I was struck by the emotions Rescorla's men still felt for him. His old radio telephone operator (RTO), Sam Fantino, 30 years later still seemed to maintain that constant *where-the-hell-is-the-lieutenant-now* look out of the corner of his eye. When a lieutenant and his RTO click, the radioman takes on a host of new roles–part radioman, part scrounge, part mother hen looking over *his* lieutenant. With Fantino and Rescorla it was something special to watch. Many other survivors of the platoon acted the same way.

Over time, I came to believe that they would have followed Rescorla in an assault upon the gates of Hell, for he did not order, he led. After his time as a rifle platoon leader, Rescorla technically became a liaison officer. But in reality he was running a sort of miniature, brigade-level LRRP (long range reconnaissance patrol) team for Hal Moore, who had by then been promoted from commander of 1-7 Cavalry to commander of the 3rd Brigade, 1st Cavalry Division. They called it a Ground Reconnaissance Infiltration Team, though Rescorla told me they preferred to call his group a GRIT patrol. One hundred fifty men tried out, from whom Rescorla chose 15 for a trial patrol. From those 15, three men were selected to accompany Rick on the ground, one of them a former British SAS member. Walking deep into areas such as the *Crow's Foot*, well ahead of the rest of the brigade, Rescorla and his team bridged the gap between division recon and battalion scouts. That was his idea of a *cushy staff job*.

Twenty-nine years later, the tape made in 1966, in a claptrap officers' club, made its way into my hands, and for the first time I heard the voice that I had only read of in history books. It was a strong voice, booming out the solos and leading the chorus of young American officers trying to forget, or perhaps to remember with honor, their soldiers who now lay still. I doubt there was a sober voice in the pack. In the background there is the recurrent booming of 105mm howitzers firing. This was the 1st Cavalry Division, in war. It was eerie to know that nobody had heard this tape in almost 30 years. I made seven copies so the tape would not disappear into history, and sent one to Rescorla himself.

I am really lucky. Over the course of my life I have met men who, to my eyes, have walked into the room off the pages of a history book. Sometimes I get to meet my heroes. A few months after receiving the tape from An Khe, I had the chance to attend the annual reunion dinner of the veterans of the fighting in the Ia Drang. That weekend I also had the honor of meeting Rick in person. He was bigger now, rounder and downright jolly actually, but in his eye I caught the glint of mischief that so many of his former soldiers talked about. He was now a civilian. After returning to the States in 1966, he had spent a year teaching at Fort Benning and then got out—sort of. He stayed in the Army Reserve, advancing to colonel before he retired in 1990.

Along the way he had picked up a master's degree and a law degree. But something in his makeup would not allow him to entirely abandon the idea behind our profession. Rick Rescorla had become the director of security for Morgan Stanley in their offices at the World Trade Center. Nor had he forgotten his origins as a warrior poet. Approaching him almost as a religious supplicant, I asked him to sign my copy of *We Were Soldiers Once ... and Young*. He asked me to wait a moment, got himself a drink, and sat staring into the middle distance for a moment. When he handed my

Lieutenant Rick Rescorla. Platoon Leader, B Co 2/7 Cavalry in Bayonet Attack, morning of 16 November 1965. Photo by Peter Arnett.

copy back, the inscription read: *To: Captain Bob Bateman / Old Dogs and Wild Geese are Fighting / Head for the Storm / As you faced it before / For where there is the 7th / There's bound to be fighting / And where there's no fighting / It's the 7th no more. / Best, / Rick Rescorla, Hard Corps One-Six* [his radio call sign in Vietnam]. When Islamic fundamentalists bombed the World Trade Center in 1993, Rick was there. Apparently songs don't work as well on civilians as they do with us soldiers, and so Rick had some difficulty in getting people's attention, to stop the panic and get them the hell out of there. And so (or at least so the legend goes), he jumped up onto a desk and bellowed out to the flower of American capitalism and propriety that he would moon them all unless they listened. Nobody I ever met said Rick could not make a statement. People stopped, that's for sure, and Rick proceeded to do his job, saving lives by moving people out of the tower. And that's what he was doing again on September 11. Various employees of Morgan Stanley report his presence across all 20 floors occupied by the company. Just as in combat, he was everywhere—calm, jocular in the face of panic, reassuring in his personal presence.

There is no way to exaggerate the number of human lives he saved that day. Not just the Morgan Stanley employees, but every single person on a floor above theirs owes a nod in his direction. Thanks to him, just about every one of the employees of his company made it out of the building, all 20 floors of them. Of their thousands, all but seven got out. Think about that. His legend in the company helped (people remember when somebody on an executive salary threatens to moon the staff), and that was enough to keep those people moving, which allowed others to follow, to leave—and to live. Rescorla would no more have left that tower before every single person was outside than I would start singing show tunes from Broadway. When he called his wife not long after the first plane hit the other tower, he told her not to worry, he was getting everyone out. Despite the fact that an announcement was made over the building speakers telling everyone to stay put after that first strike, Rescorla apparently said, *Bugger THAT!* and started the evacuation immediately. When it appeared that everyone was out, he went back in, heading up those stairs with the rescue workers. That is where he was last seen. He was inside, being himself, when the tower came down on him. They killed my hero. But heroes never really die. Rick will live on. So long as my pen has ink, and my voice bellows out to your sons manning the ramparts today, he will live on. Rick was a volunteer in a draftee army. In some ways that made it hard for him. It's easy today. Today we are all volunteers, and the young men and women I serve with will hear Rick's story because I will tell them, and they will remember. It is our professional strength: We remember.

This period of global peace has been called *Pax Americana*, just as the peace under the Romans was called *Pax Romana*. It has always been a peace that exacted a cost. Rick knew that. He lived that. I suspect that he's waiting now, down in Fiddler's Green– *halfway down the trail to hell*, where all cavalrymen pull off the road for a drink–composing his next bawdy ballad and telling those men from his platoon whom he last saw in the Ia Drang what they missed over the past 30-plus years. He'll be telling them lies, of course, but they will be magnificent glowing lies, and every one of them will have a punch line to bring tears to your eyes. Shoot, he's probably tending the bar by now.

... So after you read this, get your canteen cup, / And fill it with mead, or scotch, or rotgut, / Then pour it right out, on the ground, on the floor, / For the heart of the Seventh, Rescorla's no more. / Garry Owen.

We have shared the incommunicable experience of war; we have felt, we still feel, the passion of life to its top.

Oliver Wendell Holmes

A TASK THAT DOES NOT END

President George W. Bush holds the badge of a police officer killed in the September attacks. *And I will carry this*, said President Bush during his address to Congress Sept. 20. *It is the police shield of a man named George Howard, who died at the World Trade Center trying to save others. It was given to me by his mom, Arlene, as a proud memorial to her son. This is my reminder of lives that ended, and a task that does not end.*

WHY WE FIGHT

By Major Dave Saville, 27th Component Repair Squadron, 11 April 2002. Courtesy of Armed Forces Press Network and the Air Combat Command News Service.

I discovered one of the most powerful lessons I ever learned in a short book titled *What They Fought For, 1861-1865*, by James M. McPherson, the Pulitzer Prize-winning author of *Battle Cry For Freedom*.

The book was McPherson's summary of hundreds of letters written by soldiers of the Civil War in both the Union and Confederate armies. I had always wondered why so many thousands of Americans would sacrifice themselves on the battlefield, fighting against each other. It baffled me. All other books I have read about the Civil War failed to answer this fundamental question for me. But reading this unique book clarified for me why they fought and why I am ready to fight. The Civil War was the first war in history in which the average foot soldier was literate, and the last war in history in which personal correspondence was free of censorship or security guidelines. Civil War soldiers wrote lots of letters, and many of those letters are available today, preserved by families and museums. In fact, these soldiers wrote descriptively about their experiences and their thoughts, revealing insights into their motivation for fighting. The most common motivation McPherson discovered in the letters, from both sides, was to preserve liberty and government *of the people, by the people, for the people*. They understood they were responsible for preventing it from vanishing from the Earth. How did they develop this sense of global responsibility? McPherson theorizes that most of these soldiers learned their duty to defend the Constitution by sitting on their great-grandfathers' and great-grandmothers' laps and hearing stories of the Revolutionary War.

When the war began in 1861, it had only been 80 years since the capture of Cornwallis at Yorktown and the end of the Revolutionary War. When the Civil War soldiers were children, they learned what the first war was all about from those who lived it. When the Southern states seceded from the Union over issues of state sovereignty and slavery, the stage was set for these young Americans to rise up and serve the Constitution themselves. The South saw the future of America one way while the North saw it another way.

The letters from the soldiers reveal that the average soldier felt a profound burden to personally ensure democracy survived. This sentiment was captured in President Lincoln's Gettysburg address. He said, *We are highly resolved that these dead shall not have died in vain; that this nation, under God, shall have a new birth of freedom; and that government of the people, by the people, for the people shall not perish from the earth*. Like the soldiers who died on that battlefield after writing these letters, Lincoln knew democracy was fragile, and its future hung in the balance, affecting not only Americans, but the whole world. Although America is much stronger now, the ideals of this country based on liberty are still under attack. The terrorist attacks on America over the past few years, including the attacks on Khobar Towers, the *U.S.S. Cole* and the World Trade Center and Pentagon, remind us that we have the same job our forefathers had at Yorktown and Gettysburg.

We have our chance to *ante up*, like our fathers did at Normandy, Inchon and Vietnam. We can now add to that list Kuwait, Kosovo and Afghanistan. It is in these conflicts that we find the stories and lessons we will tell our grandchildren as we bounce them on our knees. Imagine if our children and grandchildren do not learn the same sense of responsibility and patriotism we received from our forefathers? That would be a tragedy too colossal for words to describe. We must ensure the future of a government *of the people, by the people, for the people* or we risk losing it from the Earth.

That is why we fight.

WE GALLANT CAVALIERS

Written by Lieutenant David Hughes, somewhere near Chorwon, Korea. This letter was the winner of the Freedom's Foundation Award, 1951. LT David Hughes won the Distinguished Service Cross (this medal is second to the Medal of Honor) for his heroic actions while serving as a company commander in the 7th Cavalry Regiment. His original company of 169 enlisted men and 6 officers was down to 29 enlisted men and himself after two weeks of continuous combat. With a total of 30 men, he led his company in an uphill attack against a reinforced Chinese Infantry battalion consisting of 650+ men. He was out of sub-machine gun ammunition; so he attacked with grenades; he used his grenades and re-threw those thrown at him. After capturing the hill, only 15 of his men were still standing. They had killed 250 Chinese and captured 192.

Korea, May 1951

Dear Mom:

I was cold, wet, miserable, tired, hungry and discouraged a few minutes ago, when I saw some sturdy soul come trudging up the Mountainside with mail. Now, I am only cold, wet, tired and hungry. Your letter gave me a great lift in the midst of all this chaos and confusion.

I am now well down in a foxhole on the top of the highest– I swear–mountain in all Korea, except, of course, for the one we were over yesterday, and the day before and the day before that. We gallant cavaliers of the First Cavalry are now trying to break the backs of the Chinese right now, and upon the reflection of the last week, I do not see how the bodies and minds of men keep going so long without losing their elements of control and composure.

I do not kick too much for myself, for all I must carry is weapon, ammunition and rations. But these men of my platoon who must stagger up the slopes with 40 pounds of machine-gun ammunition–and the machine guns–and the rockets–only to be shouted at, shot at and cajoled into running the last fifty yards through machine-gun bullets, grenades, mortar fire–are men of the highest discipline. And discipline for what? To be carried off the hill by four other men, and suffer smashed heads and broken bodies, thinking they are the unluckiest men in all the world until they see the dribble of others into the Aid Station, with their heads smashed in a little deeper, and their bodies broken a little more? I do not know. It is a question deeper than all questions, when I look over that hill and watch the placid face of the Chinaman, with the flap-eared cap on his head and the quilted coat, and wonder what he is thinking, and–what is more important–why he is–thinking it.

In an hour or so I will be there where he is, and he will be dead, with a hole in his head much larger than you would expect from my little .30 caliber rifle, that he will be dead, I am very sure; because I have confidence in my men and in myself.

As I have been writing here six men (two from my own platoon) have passed my foxhole, hit by mortar shrapnel. They are on their way down to the Aid Station–and rest–some for weeks, and some for months.

I wonder sometimes how much luck there is to the game. Or is it luck? And is it a game? Back on Big Hill 578 we got pinned down close to a strong position, and they grenaded us. I was lying in the open when they yelled *Grenade*, I rolled over and felt something against my leg–looked down just in time to see the handle of a potato grenade against me, Blam! The handle of the thing gave me a real Charlie-horse and a bum eye for a while. But not a puncture in me anywhere, the next man to me was killed by it.

What is the answer? Luck? Prayer? I won't even hazard a guess. Something is making it possible to live, and yet I would rather be here than anywhere in the world now, it is life in its rawest form, it reduces sham to nothingness, and here men are themselves.

Korean War. Dead Chinese Soldier.

There is no democracy on a hilltop; but as a platoon leader, there is no troop leading quite as intimate or as thorough; and it is a responsibility. There is no officer below to pass the buck to. What more could one ask in the way of service to those of lesser rank? The only guide I must religiously keep is the principle of humility; decide with confidence; lead without fear; listen with compassion; and remain humble.

Korea is tough, but what worthwhile reward is gained without some price?

That's all from Korea today, Love, Dave

DEMAND AND VALUE

The following is a change of command speech by ADM Nathman. He took command of the Naval Air Forces Pacific. Comment from someone who was there, *Short, sweet and to the point ... printed in its entirety below. No hello's, no thank you's. Stood up, gave the speech, sat back down, then released it via Naval message to all PacFleet.* The speech was given the day after VP Al Gore said all was well in the military, and was printed the next day in the San Diego paper. 24 August 2000.

My speech should be and will be short. There are two fundamental issues we should understand—demand and value. Let me explain ...

This nation, its President and its citizens, demand global stability–demand a world inclined to democratic ideals and countries that will protect the rights of their citizens. There is a valid need for a global economy, one that the United States intends to lead. There's a need for constrained oil pricing. There's a need for a community of nations that can deal effectively with rogue states and bullies–this is what the U.S. Navy does. The value of the Naval service is its willingness to do its duty to meet the nation's demands. We will be asked, no ordered, to train, deploy and engage. We engage diplomatically with our forward presence and, if necessary, in combat to sustain those demands. Is it not right then that our men and women have demands too? Isn't it right that pilots and aircrew we send daily into harm's way have modern and capable aircraft? Isn't it right that our young men and women expect to work in efficient, clean, connected and even new hangers and workspaces? Isn't it right that my naval air force be sustained at levels which support our operations and tempo? Isn't it right that our sailors and their families are paid enough to live in dignity? To me, the fact is that we have reached such a low level of funding it will soon be impossible to meet the expectations of this nation in executing our operational tasks and completing the mission. There is a fundamental disconnect between the value we provide and the willingness of the richest nation on earth to pay for its demands. It is obvious–the naval service is undervalued. This is the challenge– it must be resolved.

NEVER BRING A BOX CUTTER TO A JIHAD!

Sent by BG Mattis, Commander, Task Force 58, Operation Enduring Freedom. Remarks at a USMC dinner, 26 April 2002.

From the Anaconda Area of Operations (Afghanistan) ...

Ground war will be run by CINC's man on the spot, the Commander of 10th Mtn Division. (The CINC isn't trying to run the war via video from Tampa–he has a hell of a lot more to run besides Afghanistan, and that is his job and his place.) As any other senior officer who has grown up in a branch culture, the two-star 10th Mtn Division commander is most comfortable with Army and will primarily rely on them to be the lion's share of the offense on the ground. That's the way they are designed and supported. I think the performance during ANACONDA was a bit of an eye opener. Intel very hard to pin down–it's not a perfect world. Afghans often playing both sides of the fence, thus the senior leaders have to be cautious. Don't think they thought resistance would be as bad initially as they found. Al Qaeda were well entrenched and prepared to fight. UK SAS had a significant cave fight on a small complex last fall, and it was a brutal close quarter battle. That should have keyed us to always be thinking they will do the same anytime we find pockets of them, especially if you intend to surround them and provide no *back door* for escape (setting up ambushes to catch them just as they think they've gotten out). ANACONDA AO almost impossible to close off (huge and rough terrain), and locals supported Al Qaeda in many ways. We nailed a lot of them, but a lot got away. We can expect more of the same in the future. Certainly not a failure, and we'll take them out 100 at a time or two at a time, it matters not. The end will be the same, just might take longer.

Special Forces A Teams doing dynamite mixing in with locals and doing their thing. USAF CCT doing incredibly well calling in heavy fire and bombs from above with precision. USAF PJs have been on every hot mission supporting as combat medics. Unfortunately, there's still some mistaken concept out there that SEALs are only comfortable in water. A target is a target, and very few are on water. SEALs learned long ago to conduct raids, ambushes, recon missions, hit buildings, bridges, and encampments anywhere they exist. Multiple units of SEALs are on the ground searching caves, conducting raids, and moving by helo and organic ground combat vehicles (yes they have some), taking the fight to the enemy. (SEALs have had a mountain warfare capability for decades–they just don't advertise everything they can do. Conventional forces and leaders may not have gotten the word) SEALs are raiding alongside other raiding brothers from the Army SF's top unit, UK SAS and SBS, Australian SAS, New Zealand SAS, German KSK, Dutch commandos, and Canadian JTF's Commandos and Infantry. (When the Pentagon doesn't tell you exactly who is conducting some of these raids, there's a reason. They also don't report every action that takes place) We now also need to get the USMC out there raiding also. There's plenty to go around and rotating troops will help keep them fresher. The Marines can move fast, however, and having them offshore on the ships for now allows commanders the option to go into other countries quickly if an intelligence windfall identifies something that needs to be hit quickly, such as in Somalia or Yemen. UK 45 Commando now coming in to help out, with more rough terrain expertise.

Air war has been a beacon of technological genius. Unfortunately, it can't do it alone. Combined with ground forces, it's extremely lethal. Army Apache gunship helos worked well until they got shot up badly at beginning of ANACONDA (but they delivered a hell of a fight where fast movers couldn't go), requiring re-intro of older (but also extremely lethal) USMC Cobras. Underestimation appeared in a couple spots at beginning of ANACONDA, but U.S. was always in the driver's seat and will remain so. All helo pilots, USA, USAF, and USMC, have shown extreme courage in their operations under incredibly difficult circumstances. You have to ride these at night into a brown out situation where they kick up dust until you can't see, on night vision goggles to understand. Throw in RPGs and machine-gun fire, and most people would be shaking in their boots. These guys all eat it up.

As far as the SEAL story goes, the full truth may never actually come out. MH-47 was hit just before landing a recon team by an RPG that failed to detonate, but went through back end. Roberts was either assisting a USAF spec ops guy who fell on the rear ramp as a result of the hit, or was knocked down as he stood on the ramp. When two more RPGs hit the helo, a hydraulic line was severed and the helo went critical, jinxed, and tried to bolt out of there, hydraulic spray all over, peppered by bullets as it flew away. In the confusion in the darkened rear, Roberts fell out off the ramp. He was a SAW gunner and his light machinegun fell inside the helo. He hit the ground with a pistol and 2 hand grenades. The helo, having been shot up badly, was barely able to go 8 kilometers before being put down. They were lucky. Roberts was noted missing en route, but the helo was in an emergency mode, pilots fighting to keep it from crashing at any moment, and in no condition to try to double back at the moment. After landing, the recon team immediately boarded a sister helo and went back to get Roberts, inserted nearby and immediately got in a firefight.

Meanwhile, Roberts crawled from where he fell about 200 feet or yards (not certain which) to hide, activated his emergency beacon. 60 + heavily armed Al Qaeda in the area. When the rescue helo came back, a machinegun opened up on it as it came in. Realizing the gravity of the situation, Roberts totally disregarded his safety and attacked it with a handgun and his grenades.

Navy Petty Officer 1st Class Neil C. Roberts. A Navy SEAL, age 32, of Woodland, California, Killed In Action, 4 March 2002.

He was killed in a close quarter firefight, incredibly outnumbered and outgunned.

The commandos on the ground were able to hold against heavy odds. Another rescue force was launched and flew max speed to the area, inserting a couple hours later. Rangers, CCT, PJs poured out and right into an extremely heavy firefight. That's where the other six got killed, many wounded. This was a brutal slugfest of a firefight. Close air support called in and the fight was on for about 9-12 hours. U.S. commandos finally won, and more helos and forces inserted to recover wounded, KIA. Roberts' body recovered as well.

Predator watched after he was shot as three Al Qaeda dragged his body from where he was shot–he was already dead. For my money, Roberts and the others who came to try to rescue him deserve at least the Silver Star if not more. True heroes, taking it to the enemy, so we can all relax at home in the U.S. safer from terrorist attack. Believe it or not, this incident is only one of several unbelievable combat actions yet untold. SAS is pushing for one of their men to get the Victoria Cross as a result of the cave fight last fall. (And he clearly deserves it from all accounts). UK SBS was in an extremely heavy firefight early in the action last fall. There are other U.S. stories that have not (and may not) be told that are equally incredible, if not more. Stay tuned.

Whether we need heroes or not, the forces are clearly and eagerly going hand to hand and man on man with the Al Qaeda. We may underestimate from time to time in small battles, but the Al Qaeda have clearly underestimated what we were going to be like on the battlefield compared to their Soviet experience.

The other reason we need the appropriate top awards pinned on these heroes is this—Let the message go forth to the Al Qaeda, other terrorists, and those who want to back them anywhere on the globe. Think you're tough? You want to kill our families, blow up civilians? Stand by! We are sending our very best to hunt you down and take you out. These are the guys who are coming to get you. These are the guys who will climb into the mountains and into the darkened caves halfway around the world and look you in the eye, toe to toe, with any weapon at hand (ours or yours), to take you out. These guys have trained longer, are stronger, harder, faster, tougher, and more relentless and lethal than anything you will ever produce. And we will arm them with the best money can buy, from Spectre gun ships and thermo baric bombs to knives sharper than any box cutter you can sneak on a plane. They are now on your trail. They're hunting you down. How's it feel to be a terrorist now? Never bring a box cutter to a Jihad.

No nation can long endure that does not foster a military spirit among its young men.

General John J. Pershing, December 5, 1916

Aggressive fighting for the right is the noblest sport the world affords.

President Theodore Roosevelt. It is also a quote on a bronze plaque on the desk of Secretary of Defense Donald Rumsfeld

Don't fire unless fired upon. But if they want to have a war, let it begin here!

Captain John Parker
19 April 1775, to his company's Minutemen, about 70 soldiers, on the green in Lexington, Massachusetts as they heard and watched the British Grenadiers approach

We'll Fight to the Last 50-Year-Old!

By: Jeff Ackerman. Jeff Ackerman is editor and publisher of the *Nevada Appeal*.

A couple of weeks ago I indicated that if I could, I'd enlist today and help my country track down those responsible for killing thousands of innocent people in New York City and Washington, D.C. But I'm 50 now and the Armed Forces says I'm too old to track down terrorists. You can't be older than 35 to join the Army.

They've got the whole thing backwards. Instead of sending 18-year-olds off to the fight, they ought to take us old guys. You shouldn't be able to join until you're at least 35-years-old.

For starters: Researchers say 18-year-olds think about sex every 10-seconds. Old guys think about sex every 15 seconds, leaving us more than 28,000 additional seconds per day to concentrate on the enemy.

Young guys haven't lived long enough to be cranky and grumpy. A cranky and grumpy soldier is a dangerous soldier. If we can't kill the enemy we'll complain them into submission or surrender. *My back hurts! I'm hungry! Where's the remote control?*

An 18-year-old hasn't had a legal bottle of beer yet, and you shouldn't go to war until you're at least old enough to legally drink beer. An average old guy, on the other hand, has probably consumed at least 126,000 gallons of beer by the time he's 35, and a jaunt through the desert heat with a backpack on and an M-60 over your shoulder would do wonders for a beer belly.

An 18-year-old doesn't like to get up before 10 a.m. Old guys get up early just to show we can [and to steal the neighbor's newspaper]. If old guys got captured we couldn't spill the beans because we'd probably forget where we put them. In fact, name, rank and serial number would be a real brain teaser.

If it wasn't for the age barrier, I'd pretty much be able to get into the Army without a hitch. According to the Army Internet site, I'd need to pass an entrance exam [officially called an ASVAB], but the simple questions I saw weren't exactly headache material.

Boot Camp would actually be easier for old guys. We're used to getting screamed and yelled at, and we actually like soft food. We've also developed a deep appreciation for guns and rifles.

We like them almost better than naps. The Army could lighten up on the obstacle course, however. I've been to the desert and didn't see a single 20-foot wall with a rope hanging over the side. I can hear the Drill Sergeant now. *Get down and give me ... er ... one!*

And the running part seems to be a hell of a waste of good energy. I've never seen anyone outrun a bullet. I'm reminded of the story of the young bull and the old bull standing on a hill looking down at the cows. *Let's run down there and make love to one of those cows*, says the young bull. *How about we WALK down there and make love to ALL those cows*, replies the old bull.

Patience is something most 18-year-olds simply do not have. For good reason too. An 18-year-old has the whole world ahead of him. He's still learning to shave. To actually carry on a conversation. To learn that a pierced tongue catches food particles. And that a 200-watt speaker in the back seat of a Honda Accord can rupture an eardrum. All great reasons to keep our sons at home to learn a little more about life before sending them off to a possible death.

Let us old guys track down those dirty, rotten, filthy, cowards who attacked our country. The last thing they'd want to see right now would be a couple of million old guys with attitudes!

*T*here are certain units in the world, there have been certain units in the history of the world ... when their flags appear on the battlefield–things happen.

General Gordon Sullivan, former Chief of Staff of the Army, talking about the 82nd Airborne Division

*F*ull Victory—nothing else.

General Dwight D. Eisenhower, to paratroopers just before they boarded their airplanes to participate in the first assault in the invasion of Europe, 5 June 1944

FOR EACH OTHER

*To the combat soldier, in the end, nothing held greater
importance than comradeship. Indeed, as protracted campaigning
darkened and dirtied everything else, it provoked
an intensification of comradeship. 'Friendship,' said
Eugene Sledge 'was the only comfort a man had.'
Comradeship–friends' love and loyalty and devotion to one
another–seemed the only redeeming presence in war;
it alone was able to sustain a world in which battle had
reduced their consciousness to 'us.' As Kurt Gabel said,
'We would march in step for us, sing for us, excel for us, endure for
us and ... suffer and die for us. For each other.'*

Gerald R. Linderman, from the book *The World Within War*

*In battle, our world shrank to the man on our left
and the man on our right and the enemy all around.*

From *We Were Soldiers, Once and Young,* Authors Joe Galloway and
Lt. Gen. (Retired) Hal Moore, U.S. Army

Morale is the greatest single factor in successful wars.

President Dwight D. Eisenhower

You don't hurt 'em if you don't hit 'em.

General Lewis *Chesty* Puller

I wish to have no connection with any ship that does not sail fast; for I intend to go in harm's way.

John Paul Jones

A FIGHT FOR FREEDOM

Excerpt (closing statements–as delivered) from speech by Tony Blair, Prime Minister, Labour Party conference, Brighton, England, 3 October 2001.

America has its faults as a society, as we have ours. But I think of the Union of America born out of the defeat of slavery.

I think of its Constitution, with its inalienable rights granted to every citizen still a model for the world.

I think of a black man, born in poverty, who became Chief of their Armed Forces and is now Secretary of State Colin Powell and I wonder whether such a thing could have happened here.

I think of the Statue of Liberty and how many refugees, migrants and the impoverished passed its light and felt that if not for them, for their children, a new world could indeed be theirs.

I think of a country where people who do well, don't have questions asked about their accent, their class, their beginnings but have admiration for what they have done and the success they've achieved.

I think of those New Yorkers I met, still in shock, but resolute; the fire fighters and police, mourning their comrades but still head held high.

I think of all this and I reflect: yes, America has its faults, but it is a free country, a democracy, it is our ally and some of the reaction to 11 September betrays a hatred of America that shames those that feel it.

So I believe this is a fight for freedom. And I want to make it a fight for justice too. Justice not only to punish the guilty. But justice to bring those same values of democracy and freedom to people round the world.

And I mean: freedom, not only in the narrow sense of personal liberty but in the broader sense of each individual having the economic and social freedom to develop their potential to the full. That is what community means, founded on the equal worth of all. The starving, the wretched, the dispossessed, the ignorant, those living in want and squalor from the deserts of Northern Africa to the slums of Gaza, to the mountain ranges of Afghanistan: they too are our cause. This is a moment to seize.

The Kaleidoscope has been shaken. The pieces are in flux. Soon they will settle again.

Before they do, let us re-order this world around us. Today, humankind has the science and technology to destroy itself or to provide prosperity to all. Yet science can't make that choice for us. Only the moral power of a world acting as a community can. *By the strength of our common endeavor we achieve more together than we can alone.*

For those people who lost their lives on 11 September and those that mourn them; now is the time for the strength to build that community. Let that be their memorial.

LOYALTY TO OUR COUNTRY

By SGM (Retired) Paul E. Pritchett, U.S. Army 1951-1971.

11 September 2001

Honorables, Ladies, Gentlemen and Military Retirees:

While I and many of you are in our waning years, we have not lost our loyalty to our Country which has today been attacked by terrorists. I believe that we should reinforce that loyalty by making known that we are ready and willing to again serve our country in its need. We may not be able to pick up weapons and charge any enemy fortifications, but we are still able to offer our services in administrative and other non-combatant services.

It is time for us to let our leaders in Washington know that we, some former warriors, are still warriors at heart. While many of us never served in the line of fire while serving our country, our services were nevertheless services that mattered. Even with our various disabilities and infirmities, WE ARE HERE IF NEEDED!

Send this nationwide to all the peoples of this great land so they will know that although we have been asking that promises made to us be fulfilled, we still have tremendous loyalty to our country.

THE RANGER CREED

Recognizing that I volunteered as a Ranger, fully knowing the hazards of my chosen profession, I will always endeavor to uphold the prestige, honor, and high *esprit de corps* of my Ranger Regiment.

Acknowledging the fact that a Ranger is a more elite soldier who arrives at the cutting edge of battle by land, sea, or air, I accept the fact that as a Ranger my country expects me to move further, faster and fight harder than any other soldier.

Never shall I fail my comrades. I will always keep myself mentally alert, physically strong and morally straight and I will shoulder more than my share of the task whatever it may be. One hundred percent and then some.

Gallantly will I show the world that I'm a specially selected and well-trained soldier. My courtesy to superior officers, neatness of dress and care of equipment shall set the example for others to follow.

Energetically will I meet the enemies of my country. I shall defeat them on the field of battle for I am better trained and will fight with all my might. Surrender is not a Ranger word. I will never leave a fallen comrade to fall into the hands of the enemy and under no circumstances will I never embarrass my country.

Readily will I display the intestinal fortitude required to fight onto the Ranger objective and complete the mission, though I be the lone survivor.

RANGERS LEAD THE WAY!

It takes a remarkable person to not just read a creed,
or memorize a creed, but to live a creed.

Stephanie Shughart said in accepting the Medal of Honor awarded
posthumously to her husband, Army SFC Randall D. Shughart who lived
... and died by the Ranger creed, SFC Shughart died in Mogadishu,
Somalia while protecting a downed American helicopter pilot

HIGH SPIRITED HORSES

In whatever field or profession you may follow, I know you will
continue as civilians with the same spirit and qualities you
demonstrated as a Ranger. No better way can I sum up my feelings
of pride for your splendid achievements than to state this;
commanding the Rangers was like driving a team of very high
spirited horses. No effort was needed to get them to go forward.
The problem was to hold them in check. Good luck 'Rangers' and
may your future be crowned with deserving success.

Colonel William O. Darby's closing remarks to the Earl & Darby's
Rangers (Rangers of the 1st, 3rd and 4th Ranger Battalions), 1945

I believe in the goodness of a free society. And I believe that
society can remain good only as long as we are willing to fight for
it–and to fight against whatever imperfections may exist.

Jackie Robinson

The spirit of man is more important than mere physical strength,
and the spiritual fiber of a nation than its wealth.

President Dwight D. Eisenhower

There exists a special brotherhood among those who stand
shoulder to shoulder to look death in the face and defend not only
each other, but the principles in which they believe.

Author Unknown

SHEER DETERMINATION

American Paratroopers wait for the Drop Zone.

As the 75th Ranger regimental commander on his way to Panama, for Operation Just Cause, December 1989, Army Gen. William *Buck* Kernan found himself at one of the most inspirational moments of his life. Excerpt from article by Jack Dorsey, *The Virginian-Pilot* Newspaper, 2 October 2002.

As a leader I was thinking about all the things I needed to be prepared to do, but I remember when we got ready to jump [into Panama, December 1989, Operation Just Cause], one of the last things we did was read the Ranger's Creed ... just prior to opening the doors. It was more than rote memory at the time. *People were thinking about what the words meant. I saw those doors open and I knew it was a hot DZ (drop zone) because we heard on the aircraft that the enemy knew we were coming ... I looked around at those kids–19, 20, 21, 22 years old–sheer determination. Scared? Yeah. But every one of them jumped, 500 feet, into tracers in the dead of night. What makes them do that? I was proud to be part of it.*

SOLDIER INTANGIBLES AND THE WARRIOR SPIRIT

An email, 2 April 2002, from an Army general to his staff:

Gents, as we work Objective Force Soldier issues, watch our ongoing training, and reflect on what we do with PCC and CTCs, I'm concluding that there are opportunities we ought to seize to better articulate and instill the Warrior Spirit into our BCT and AIT soldiers. I'll expound some more (see FM 22-100 excerpt attached) on how we define and spell out *Warrior Ethos* and Warrior Spirit down the road, but I want you to begin thinking about it, and thinking through how you can begin to instill those warrior attributes inherent in being a soldier into our Soldiers in Training. The bottom line is that we must instill the firm belief in every one of our graduates that every soldier owns and lives the Warrior Spirit—not just a select few. Some aspects of the Warrior Spirit might encompass the following:

We will never leave an American behind—Demonstrated again in Afghanistan I will never leave a fallen comrade ...

We will never quit—we never accept defeat as an option.

Mission First—accomplishment of the unit mission overrides all other priorities.

Every Soldier is a Warrior—I may learn in AIT that I'm a *Finance Warrior* or a *Commo Warrior*, but as Soldiers, we're all Warriors.

Quite frankly, I don't think our Soldiers in Training ever hear these statements today, and I'm not sure that we are making this a clear part of the expectations of being a soldier within the hearts of our graduates. We must fundamentally ask ourselves *if soldiers don't learn this here, where will they learn it?* BCT, OSUT and AIT are about tasks and skills, but perhaps even more importantly about the intangibles of the heart and soul which make up soldiering. In some ways, these expectations may fall within our values instruction, but they are not explicitly covered in values. With our relentless (and correct) focus on standards and tasks, we must not lose sight of the even more important role we play in shaping and changing the hearts of the civilians we receive into the Soldiers whom we graduate. The intangibles of soldiering ... we've got to always be thinking about this, about shaping, growing and demanding adherence to our Soldier culture, our Warrior Spirit.

Recognize also that there is an implied training task here for our leaders–officers, NCOs, Drill Sergeants. Our leaders here come from many sub-cultures within the Army, and some may not have any significant exposure to the intangibles that I'm talking about. We've got to figure out how to educate and inspire them as well as our young Soldiers here in BCT and AIT.

Mull this over in your own minds, and start to look for ways to deliberately instill these Intangibles of Soldiering into your subordinates, your cadre, your Drill Sergeants, and ultimately and most importantly–your soldiers. I'd be most interested in your feedback.

David W. Barno, Major General, Fort Sill, Oklahoma

A WILLINGNESS TO FIGHT AND WIN

From an Army Field Manual on Leadership:

CRITICAL LEADER TASK: Create a willingness to fight and win, despite necessary sacrifices, difficulty or danger.

CONDITIONS: In a garrison or field leadership position, 24 hours a day.

STANDARDS:

1. Lead by example. Share hardships and danger with soldiers. When appropriate, lead from the front.

2. Exhibit a positive, optimistic attitude, despite conditions. Display self-confidence and firm control, especially under stressful conditions. Never complain in front of subordinates.

3. Instill in subordinates the desire to fight aggressively and win. Emphasize there is no second place in combat–those who finish second are dead, wounded, prisoners of war, or fleeing a victorious enemy.

4. Take risks and initiative in order to win. In the absence of orders, or break down of communications, seize every opportunity to fight, capture, or destroy the enemy. Keep subordinates moving and maintain the momentum.

5. Exercise decentralized leadership. If the immediate leader is absent, or a casualty, take action to ensure success and continue to do things right.

6. Enforce discipline and attention to detail. Make on-the-spot corrections and conduct immediate *footlocker* counseling when required. Use chain of command to enforce discipline.

7. Emphasize to all subordinates, through the chain of command and SOPs (Standard Operating Procedures), that it is a moral obligation to recover fellow soldiers who become WIA or KIA.

8. Make every effort to keep soldiers informed of the situation, clearly communicate intent and orders, and obtain feedback to ensure understanding.

9. Encourage boldness, innovation, and initiative. Listen to subordinates and encourage candid ideas on better ways to accomplish the mission and kill the enemy.

10. Teach, coach, counsel that SURRENDER IS DETESTABLE AND DISHONORABLE, whether it be in combat, training, or garrison. Teach and live the philosophy that a soldier who falls out of a difficult PT run or tough road march SURRENDERS HIS PHYSICAL AND MENTAL COURAGE. An Officer who does not train to tough, realistic live-fire standards SURRENDERS HIS MORAL COURAGE AND PRIMARY LEADERSHIP RESPONSIBILITY. A leader in stressful field conditions who complains in front of his men SURRENDERS HIS SELF RESPECT. The idea of surrender, in any form, is made abhorrent by the leader with the will to fight and win.

*H*ave *your musket clean as a whistle, hatchet scoured, 60 rounds of powder and ball, and be ready to march at a moment's notice.*

Major Robert Rogers, Continental Army

*B*oys! *Raise the colors and follow me.*

General Israel D. Richardson

I see that the old flagpole still stands. Have your troops hoist the colors to its peak, and let no enemy haul them down.*

General Douglas MacArthur, returning to the Philippines, World War II

*W*e give up the fort when there is not a man left to defend it.*

Colonel George Croghan

**Major Marie
Therese Rossi.**

*What I am doing is no greater or less than
the man who is flying next to me.*

Major Marie Rossi, Age 32, U.S. Army Company
B, 154th Aviation Battalion, Killed In Action, 1
March 1991, Operation Desert Storm

Put your trust in God, my boys, and keep your powder dry!

Colonel Valentine Blacker, Continental Army

*Soldiers, we are attacking. Advance as long as you can.
When you can no longer advance, hold your position.
When you can no longer hold it, die!*

General J.C. Joffre

WE MUST BEAT THEM TODAY

*There, my boys, are your enemies, the Hessians and the Tories.
We must beat them today—or tonight Molly Stark sleeps a widow.*

General John Stark, Continental Army

General Stark and his soldiers were victorious that day, during the
Battle of Bennington, 16 August 1777. He reported thirty of his
men killed and forty wounded. He estimated over 200 enemy dead
and approximately 700 enemy prisoners. More than 30 years after
this battle, the citizens of Bennington requested the honor of 81-
year-old General Stark's presence at a ceremony commemorating
the victory. Too weak to travel, the ailing General penned his
reply. He issued his *last orders to my volunteers, to look well to
their sentries* ... and in a post script offered *my volunteer toast.
Live free or die. Death is not the worst of evils.* General Stark
passed away in 1822 at the age of 94. His words live on. *Live Free
or Die* was adopted as New Hampshire's state motto in 1945.

SOMEONE WHO KNOWS HOW TO COUNT

The Korean War, in which the Marine Corps fought and won some of its most brutal battles, was not without its humor. During one such conflict a ROK (Republic of Korea) commander, whose unit was fighting with the Marines, called legendary Marine Chesty Puller to report a major Chinese attack in his sector.

How many Chinese are attacking you? asked Puller.

Many, many Chinese! replied the excited Korean officer.

Puller asked for another count and got the same answer,
Many, many Chinese!

Goddammit! swore Puller,
Put my Marine liaison officer on the radio.

In a minute, an American voice came over the air:
Yes sir?

Lieutenant, growled Chesty,
exactly how many Chinese you got up there?

Colonel, we got a whole shitload of Chinese up here!

Thank God, exclaimed Puller,
At least there's someone up there who knows how to count!

The man on top of the mountain didn't fall there.

Vince Lombardi

*You can't help someone get up a hill
without getting closer to the top yourself.*

General H. Norman Schwarzkopf

JUSTICE WILL BE DONE

*Whether we bring our enemies to justice
or bring justice to our enemies,
justice will be done.*

President George W. Bush

THE WARRIOR SPIRIT

This speech, *The Warrior Spirit* was presented on 18 August 2001 by Major William T. Coffey, Jr. at Fort Carson, Colorado during the Colorado Army National Guard (COARNG) Officer Candidate School (OCS) Commissioning Ceremony.

Welcome to tonight's ceremony and thank you for the privilege to speak with you tonight. Eighteen years, three months and three days ago on the campus of the University of Kansas my father had the opportunity to tell his only son to *raise your right hand and repeat after me.* That was an important day for my parents ... and an important day for me. But the one thing I remember over the years more than anything else was how I did not appreciate the contributions that my parents had made in getting me there that day. At this time I would like to have all the parents of the Officer Candidates please stand up (Long applause for parents). A couple of months ago I wrote a story called *This is My Country.* It's a quite lengthy story that talks about what we cherish as a nation, what we protect, what we invented, what we eat, the songs we sing, and our heritage and our history. I would like to share with you one particular paragraph that talks about, specifically in this case, Mothers.

We honor the so-called *Greatest Generation* and know deep down that they are *great* because they were brought into this world and raised by the *Greatest Generation* of moms. Moms who taught them right from wrong and instilled in them a sense of national pride, selflessness, discipline, service to our nation, patriotism, courage and character–values that have kept America on the winning side of history. Deep down we know that all of our generations were ... and still are ... the greatest because they all raised the next generation of American patriots. We honor them all.

And of course this honor extends to the Dads as well, and to the spouses who have picked up the day-to-day chores of keeping soldiers motivated and inspired with their untiring patience, tolerance, PCS moves, deployments ... well you know the rest of it. Tonight, we are really here to specifically thank the parents. We are here to congratulate the Officer Candidates and recognize their accomplishments, but we're not here to *thank* the Officer Candidates; we're here to thank the parents and the spouses who brought the Officer Candidates here tonight and made them young Americans that they are.

Back in the early part of the Civil War the Confederate Army was enjoying a number of victories over the Union Army. In doing so they had the opportunity to march unopposed right through Virginia on their way to invade Maryland. Robert E. Lee was marching his Army through a town one day and there was a Northern woman standing in her front yard watching this procession of soldiers marching by all day. She made a very interesting observation about what she saw. After the Army marched through her town, she wrote:

> This body of men moving along with no order, their guns carried in every fashion, no two dressed alike, the officers barely distinguishable from the privates, were these the men who had driven back, again and again, our splendid legions? They were the dirtiest men I ever saw, the most ragged, lean and hungry set of wolves ... Yet there was a dash about them that the northern men lacked.

Tonight, I would like to talk about that *dash*, what it is ... what it means. Some people call it the *Warrior Ethic*, some call it the *Fighting Spirit*, others the *Warrior's Soul*, but for tonight's purposes I would like to call it the *Warrior Spirit*. Over the last couple of weeks while I was jotting down in my mind, and also on paper, what I thought this Warrior Spirit was. What I ended up with was a list that somewhat resembled a recipe. So I wrote the recipe for the Warrior Spirit Stew. After I read this to you I will talk about what the Warrior Spirit sounds like ... from the battlefield ... and from the soldiers.

You start with one large pot. You then add two gallons of pure Rocky Mountain spring water–which is representative of the purity of our national values and ideals.

Then we start adding ingredients: We begin by adding one large patriotic heart. We simmer over the flame of freedom to achieve a rich, pure and patriotic broth. Then we add a pinch of Physical and Moral Courage. Then:

- A dash of Esprit de Corps
- You have to have a cup of Audacity
- Some Alpha Male Genes
- Some Service to Country
- A handful each of Duty, Love of Country, Loyalty, Integrity, Camaraderie, Selflessness and Honor
- Throw in your Unit Patch, Unit Crest and Unit Motto ... so we don't forget who we are
- Add a sprinkling of Piss and Vinegar–this keeps us going when times get tough
-Sprinkle in liberal amounts of HOOAH
- Add an insatiable appetite for Winning
- And lastly, for the Warrior Spirit Stew, you must add several pounds of Raw Desire to give the enemy the maximum opportunity to die for his country

Once all the ingredients are added, you need to stir with the guidon of leadership–but the secret is that every soldier in your unit needs to put their hand on that guidon and stir the stew. Then you need to cover the pot with the lid of our military heritage to contain all those ingredients and values. And the color of the stew? ... nothing but Red, White and Blue. There is one warning about the stew ... it's highly contagious to anyone who ever smells it or tastes it. And the recommendation for servings: You should serve hefty portions to soldiers who have an appetite for service to our nation. To me, that's what the Warrior Spirit Stew is.

—

So what does the Warrior Spirit sound like?

About a year ago this week I took my family on a vacation down to Santa Fe, and we ended up in this store named *Sherwoods–Spirit of America*. Essentially, the store is a collection of artifacts from American history ... weapons ... Indian artifacts. You could buy a Gattling gun for $175,000. I went over to the rack where they had muskets, and there was one particular musket that caught my eye. So I asked the gentleman if I could go behind the counter and pick it up, and he gave me permission. I picked up this musket from the Revolutionary War ... then I checked the price tag on it: $6,000–so I knew I couldn't afford it. Nonetheless, I was immediately seized with what that musket represented, and I thought about the young man, the young soldier in the Continental Army who carried it. I didn't think about the musket's mechanical perfection, or its maximum effective range, or how many times it had been fired. Instead, I thought about the young soldier who carried it and his Warrior Spirit. This musket reminded me of a story that took place in the early part of the Revolutionary War in Connecticut. There was a call to arms that went out to all citizens of Connecticut to assemble a couple of Infantry companies. There was one particular order for a number of men to meet at a certain town, in the town's green one day. Men came from all around the state, about 45 or 50 of them. They were a dirty bunch. They weren't clothed very well. Not all of them had shoes. A few of them had muskets, others had farm tools, some held ancient swords. General Washington met them on the green; then, he stood in front of those soldiers, up on a podium. Looking at them, with pride, as if they were the finest regiment in the world, he said, *You men of Connecticut, I have total confidence in you.* One of the young Privates wrote home to his mother after this incident and explained what those words meant to him, the words that General Washington spoke. He wrote to his mother, *When I heard General Washington say that, I clasped my musket and I pulled it to my breast and I said to myself 'Let them come on!'* That's the Warrior

Spirit. I wonder if that weapon the young soldier held was the same musket I held, 225 years later, down in Santa Fe last August?

—

In World War I, Sergeant York, the greatest decorated American soldier in that war ... Medal of Honor recipient, said, *War brings out the worst in you. It turns you into a mad fighting animal. But it also brings out something else, something I just don't know how to describe ... a sort of tenderness and love for the fellow fighting with you.* Well ... I call that compassion ... camaraderie ... and love. And that's the Warrior Spirit as well.

—

Also in World War I there was a young man named Martin Treptow. Before the war he was a barber in a small town. He answered this nation's call to arms and enlisted in the Army and was sent to France. While running a message between two units who were getting shelled with artillery, an artillery shell killed him. Later that day, his comrades were able to go out after him to recover his body and to recover his personal belongings that were to be returned to his family. One of the things they found on him was his diary. On the inside flyleaf of that diary, there were two handwritten words, *My Pledge.* Under those two words, he penned *America must win this war. Therefore, I will work, I will save, I will sacrifice, and I will endure. I will fight cheerfully and do my utmost as if the issue of the whole struggle depended on me alone.* Martin Treptow gave his life for this nation. That was his pledge ... and that's the Warrior Spirit.

—

World War II. The U.S. 8th Infantry Division, U.S. Army was advancing across Europe enjoying a number of hard-fought victories against the Germans. The Assistant Division Commander, BG Canham took the surrender of a German general and all of his soldiers. The two had a pre-arranged agreement of where and when they were to meet to conduct the surrender. As the two generals faced each other, all the American troops gathered behind BG Canham to watch the proceedings. Speaking through an interpreter, the German general questioned BG Canham's credentials for accepting his surrender. The American general looked at him, straight into his eyes, and he jerked his thumb behind him, pointing to all his soldiers, and he said, *THEY ARE MY CREDENTIALS!* That's the Warrior Spirit.

———

I'm glad we have a few Marines here tonight. You all know *Chesty* Puller? LTG Lewis Puller. He was fighting down in the South Pacific against Japanese and at one point things were getting pretty tough. He found that the Japanese had a good number of his Marines surrounded. He showed up on the scene, he rallied his men, and this is what he told them: *So they've got us surrounded. Good! Now we can fire in any direction. Those Bastards won't get away this time!* That's the Warrior Spirit.

———

Korean War. Matthew Ridgway, Commander of the U.S. Eight Army, took command at a time when the Chinese were doing a number on US and UN forces. Morale was low and he knew he needed to get up front. It's what I call *Leadership by Walking Around*; it's kind of the reverse of an *Open Door Policy*. He went up front to confront the enemy … find out what the troops were saying … how they were feeling. There was one thing he told all the soldiers. Every soldier he saw up on the front lines, soldiers who went face to face, day to day with the Chinese hordes, he would tell them: *Your job is to point that rifle in the enemy's face and shoot him dead.* That was their mission. And that is the Warrior Spirit.

———

Same timeframe, General Ridgway was standing at the side of a road one day, early early morning, barely at the break of dawn, with three of his staff officers. A column of Marines were marching by under heavy load … each carrying at least 100 pounds on their backs, battle worn and tired. All the Marines could see were four figures, silhouettes, standing at the side of this muddy road. They didn't know who they were. One of the Marines who walked by them had one of his bootlaces undone. He couldn't stop.

General Matthew Ridgway.

He couldn't bend over, the weight was too heavy on his back, so he looked at these four individuals, these four silhouettes, and he said, *Hey, could one of you Son-of-a-Bitches tie my boot?* The Commander of the Eight U.S. Army, LTG Matthew Ridgway, knelt down on the trail, in the mud, and tied that Marine's boot. He didn't say a word. You see, sometimes the Warrior Spirit is silent. Often it is silent. It's actions … actions that matter.

—

In Vietnam, a young Captain, John Hottell, wrote a letter to his wife about what it meant to him to serve in the Army. This letter was not to be opened though, unless he died. He essentially wrote his own obituary. I have his letter in front of me here; I'll read a couple parts of it.

> I'm writing my own obituary because I am quite simply the last authority on my own death. I love the Army, it reared me, it nurtured me, it gave me the most satisfying years of my life. Thanks to it, I have lived an entire lifetime in 26 years. It is only fitting that I should die in its service. We all have but one death to spend and insofar as it can have any meaning, it finds it in the service of comrades in arms.

He goes on and talks about what he did in the Army. His closing paragraph follows:

> I have experienced all these things because I was in the Army and because I was an Army Brat. The Army is my life, it is such a part of what I was, that what happened was the logical outcome of the life I have lived. I never knew what it was to fail; I never knew what it was to be too old, or too tired to do anything. I lived a full life in the Army and it has exacted the price, it is only just.

Unfortunately, his helicopter went down during a tropical storm into the side of a mountain … and he was killed … his wife got that letter.

—

Cadet John Hottell.
United States Military
Academy, West Point.

**Lance Corporal
John Tanney.**

Vietnam, 1967. Lance Corporal John Tanney, 18-years-old, was preparing with his fellow Marines to assault Hill 881 ... a young kid ... Joe American. He wrote a letter to his seven-month-old brother, who he had seen only a couple of times before being shipped off to Vietnam.

Dear Brother Bob,
I know that you won't be able to read this for a while, but I felt the compulsion to write you anyway. I'm waiting to be picked up by a helicopter with the rest of my buddies, to push onto Hills 861, 881, 881 North, and 689. My platoon is spearheading the assault up Hill 881 North. The enemy has many soldiers up top and they are dug in, as well as we are at Khe Sahn (a Viet Cong siege of U.S. Marines). It will be a hard and bitter struggle, but as always, we Marines will take the objective.

He goes on and writes,

I am nearly going crazy thinking about assaulting that hill. But, I am a Marine and I shall not falter. I will be confident in the Lord and in my training as a Marine. Bob–if anything should happen, remember this: I am fighting for what I believe in–you, Mom, Dad, Tom and Cindy. I am fighting for the right to choose my own religion, make my own decisions, and to be my own man. And yes, I am fighting for my flag. My country means a lot to me and I am proud to fight for it. I know that you will be, too.

He closed his letter by writing,

We are United States Marines. We are the best troops in the world. We fight odds that are heavily against us–and win! Our spirit is indomitable, our courage unexcelled, and our loyalty is unquestionable. I felt like writing to you. Perhaps it sounds foolish. Perhaps it is. But you can never imagine what it is like–not knowing if I'm coming back down that hill. I wanted you to have something from me to you. I love you, Bob, but you are too young to know it. Someday you will know. I will leave now– time is short. Love to you, Brother Bob.

John Tanney never came down that mountain alive. He too had the Warrior Spirit.

———

I had the pleasure of working for one of the finest officers I have ever met, over in Korea, a soldier by the name of BG Herbert Lloyd. He enlisted during Vietnam and received a battlefield commission. If there was ever a soldier who had the heart of a warrior, it was him. He always took time to share stories, tell us what it was like to be a soldier, what it was like in combat, what the Warrior Spirit was. He shared a story of the last words made over a radio transmission from a helicopter pilot in Vietnam, to an Army Captain and his unit who were fighting the 174th and 66th North Vietnamese Regiments at Hill 614. This pilot's last words, *Red Hat Six, this is Ghost Rider Two-Seven. I'm sorry I won't be able to help you any more today. I'm gut shot. I'll have to leave you now. Hang on and good luck.* His last words were the words of a Warrior, with a passion in his heart ... and the Warrior Spirit.

———

Another story, two days earlier, same hill, SFC Herbert Lloyd (rank at that time) crawled over to a soldier who had been shot. He was bleeding out, and he knew it. SFC Lloyd said, *How are you doing?* SP4 James K. Stoddard said, *No sweat, sir. You can count on me. We'll stop them.* ... then he died. He had the Warrior Spirit.

———

Back in 1991, I was stationed with the 2nd Infantry Division in Korea. We had the opportunity to bring over some civilian engineers from the Army Materiel Command who had an array of cover, concealment and deception devices–one of the devices they brought over was a camouflage net that was fastened to and around, kind of like a skirt, an Abrams tank, it was designed to break up the silhouette. Picture a tank parked inside of a tree line. This device would just unroll, then you'd put stakes in it, pinning it to the ground, looked like a pretty nice device to break up the silhouette from visual observation. I walked up to this tank, and there was this young E-5 soldier standing beside the tank ... just full of piss and vinegar. I could tell. He had a dash in his eye; he was proud. He saluted me and said:

Good afternoon Sir, How you doing?

Is this your tank? I questioned.

Yes sir it is.

How do you like it?

I love it Sir.

So then I asked, *So what do you think about this camouflage skirt on your tank?*

He said, *Sir, it's a piece of shit.*

So ... what makes you say that?

Sir, the M1A1 Abrams Main Battle Tank is an offensive weapon ... and that makes me an offensive soldier, so I don't have the time to put this thing up.

So I said, *Well what if you have to stop and get some fuel and beans and bullets?*

He replied, *Sir, I'm only stopping as long as it takes to get what I need. Then I'm gonna continue the attack and kick the enemy's ass.*

That's the Warrior Spirit. Now I may not agree with his tactics, but I didn't need to. I have nothing but praise and admiration for his Warrior Spirit, and his attitude, and his aggressiveness.

—

Several months ago I was talking to a young Sergeant who was working here at Fort Carson last summer, rotating some soldiers through what they call *Lane Training*. In this particular case there was a young platoon leader out in the maneuver area where he and his soldiers were in a defensive position and the Opposing Forces (OPFOR), through simulation, were calling in an artillery strike onto the platoon's position. The *White Cell*, or control cell, called down to this Sergeant and said, *You better tell that platoon that the OPFOR is going to send so much artillery their way that it's going to block out the sun.* And that Lieutenant, hearing this statement, without hesitating, turned to his men and said, *Men ... prepare to fight in the dark!* That's the Warrior Spirit.

—

During the conflict in Somalia and Mogadishu, there were a number of fire fights; when they had them, they were pretty bad. One night at Andrews Air Force Base, a C-141 was bringing back a bunch of U.S. soldiers who had been wounded in action. The Chief of Staff of the Army, General Gordon Sullivan, went down there to meet these wounded soldiers on the tarmac. The medics carried one wounded soldier off the plane on a stretcher; he was pretty shot up, a Private. This Private was a Combat Engineer. The difference between a Combat Engineer and other regular Engineer soldiers is like the difference between night and day. Combat Engineers are up front. They actually break things and blow things up–and they call themselves *Sappers*. If you're a Sapper, you want everyone to know it. Those who are not Sappers are the guys who build bridges, do things back in the rear ... combat support type functions. General Sullivan walked up to that soldier and pinned a Purple Heart on his shirt, then he said, *Private Ly, I notice that you're an Engineer with the 41st Engineers.* He looked the Chief of Staff of the Army straight in the eye and said, *Sir, I'm not an Engineer. I'm a Sapper!* He was proud—that's the Warrior Spirit.

—

The Oath of Office ... *The duties of the office upon which I am about to enter. ...* the last four words, *So Help Me God.* That's the Warrior Spirit. You'll be speaking these words tonight, every one of you seven Officer Candidates.

Last Tuesday I was reading through a periodical when I came across a quote; it's kind of funny how you come across quotes sometimes. This particular quote was from one of my heroes, a civilian, a guy named Lance Armstrong. Lance had just won the Tour de France Bike Race, for the third year in a row, AFTER battling cancer that almost killed him. This is what he said, *I recently read that I flew up the mountains in France. Well, I'll tell you, you don't fly up mountains ... you struggle ... slowly ... and painfully. And, if you work really hard at it, you might get to the top before anyone else.*

—

We have a thing in America I like to call *America's Mountain.* It exists in our hearts. It's a mountain that all of us who have served have had to climb. And for you seven Officer

Candidates, you're going to take your first step up that mountain tonight. But I can assure you, it won't be easy. You won't fly up that mountain. You're going to have to struggle, it's going to be slower than you want, and more painful than you want. You are going to have to work harder than you thought. But if you work really hard at it, you might get to the top before anyone else. There's going be times when you walk up that mountain, or march up that mountain with your soldiers, when you are going to come across some tough times. Those of us who served in uniform or who currently serve already know this. I don't really know how to express it to those of you who have not *walked that walk* yet, but I can assure you that you'll know that you've *arrived* as a leader when you're sitting in a situation and you say to yourself, *What the hell did I ever do to get myself in a situation like this?* Those days are coming. And it will be times like that when you need to reach back behind you and find that long hard bone, and remind yourself that you have a spine. Then you need to look down at your collar, and look at that symbol–some people call it rank–I call it a symbol, a symbol of servitude to your soldiers and a symbol of servitude to your nation–and remind yourself of the duties you have as a commissioned officer. And remember the Oath you recite tonight. *... So help me God.*

It is then that you need to seize the guidon of leadership, rally your soldiers and lead them well. You will know what to do when you look into your soldiers' eyes. Their eyes will tell you something. I know what their eyes will be saying. I've seen it in my soldiers' eyes. Their eyes are going to be saying: *Sir* or *Ma'am, Make a decision. Tell us what to do. We trust you. We'll follow you. We'll follow you into hell. We'll die for you ... just make a decision and let's head up the mountain.* That is when you must ignite in your heart and into the hearts of all your soldiers the Warrior Spirit I spoke about, and climb America's Mountain. And when you get to the top, there'll only be one thing at the top of the mountain. Only one thing. At the top will be a pole, and on top of that pole will be that (pointing to the American Flag). Old Glory. It is the only thing on top of that mountain ... because ... when it comes right down to it, that flag is the only thing that really matters. Everything we ever do as soldiers is about that flag and everything it stands for ... I'll see you at the top!

SEE YOU SOON ... SLEEP TIGHT

Dear Terrorists,

I am an Air Force Aviator. I was born and raised in a small town in New England. I come from a family of five. I was raised in a middle class home and taught my values by my mother and father. My dad worked a series of jobs in finance and my mom took care of us kids. We were not an overly religious family but attended church most Sundays. It was a nice small Episcopal Church. I have a brother and sister and I am the youngest in my family. I was the first in many generations to attend college. I have flown Air Force aircraft for 16 years. For me the flying was never a lifelong dream or a *calling*; it just happened. I needed a job and I liked the challenge. I continue to do it today because I feel it is important to give back to a nation which has given so much to me. I do it because although I will never be rich my family will be comfortable. I do it because many of my friends have left for the airlines and someone has to do it. I like baseball but think the players make too much money. I am in awe of firemen and policemen and what they do each day for my community. They don't make enough money. I respect my elders and always use sir or ma'am when addressing a stranger. I'm not sure about kids these days but I think that's normal for every generation. I voted for George Bush because I like him. I think I made a pretty good choice. I tell you all this because when I come for you, I want you to know me. I won't be hiding behind a woman or a child. I won't be disguised or pretending to be something I am not. I will be in a U.S. issue flight suit. I will be wearing standard U.S. issue flight gear, and I will be flying an Air Force aircraft clearly marked as a U.S. warplane. I wish we could meet up close in a small room where I could wrap my hands around your throat and slowly squeeze the life out of you, but unfortunately you're hiding in a hole in the ground so we will have to do this a different way. I want you to know also that I am very good at what I do. I can put a 2,000-pound weapon through a window from 10,000 feet up. I generally only fly at night so you may want to start sleeping during the day. I am not eager to die for my country but I am willing to sacrifice my life to protect it from animals like you. I will do everything in my power to ensure no civilians are hurt as I take aim at you. My countrymen are a forgiving bunch. Many are already forgetting what you did on Sept 11th. But I will not forget, and my President will not forget.

I am coming. I hope you know me a little bit better, see you soon ... sleep tight.

Signed ... a U.S. Air Force Pilot

WISH YOU WERE HERE

By Corporal Joshua Miles and all the Marines from 3rd Battalion 2nd Marines, Kuwait, March 09, 2003. This poem is dedicated to Marine Sergeant Nicholas M. Hodson, age 22, from Smithville, Missouri. SGT Hodson was assigned to the 3rd Battalion 2nd Marine Regiment when he was killed in action, March 23, 2003, Operation Iraqi Freedom, Iraq.

Sergeant Hodson.

For all the free people that still protest.
You're welcome.
We protect you and you are protected by the best.
Your voice is strong and loud, but who will fight for you?
No one standing in your crowd.
We are your fathers, brothers, and sons,
wearing the boots and carrying guns.
We are the ones that leave all we own,
to make sure your future is carved in stone.
We are the ones who fight and die,
We might not be able to save the world, Well, at least we try.
We walked the paths to where we are at
and we want no choice other than that.
so when you rally your group to complain,
take a look in the back of your brain.
In order for that flag you love to fly
wars must be fought and young men must die.
We came here to fight for the ones we hold dear.
If that's not respected, we would rather stay here.

So please stop yelling, put down your signs,
and pray for those behind enemy lines.
When the conflict is over and all is well,
be thankful that we chose to go through hell.

I WILL DEFEND IT

The following is a letter from a Navy corpsman to his mom who was ready to march in an anti-war demonstration. The mother, whose son was in Kuwait, preparing for combat in Iraq, wrote her son asking how he would feel if she joined other relatives of service members in an anti-war demonstration in Hollywood. After reading her son's response, she elected not to participate.

Dear Mom,

It's really your decision to march if you want to or not. You are the one who has to decide if what we are doing out here is right or not. My opinion is not yours.

I do, however, have things I would like for you and Grandma and everyone else at home to know. I am a United States Serviceman. I was sworn to defend my country against all enemies, foreign and domestic. People may not agree with the things we are ordered to do. I would like to address those people by telling them that terrorism is not only a threat to us as Americans, but to many other innocent people in the world.

What type of country would we be if we didn't defend the rights and freedoms of others, not because they're Americans, but how about just because they're human? We live in a country where people feel secure with their daily lives. They do business like usual and don't worry about the thought of terrorism actually happening to them. The people of 9-11 thought the same thing. We now know that it can happen to anyone at any time.

Yet as Americans we're afraid of losing our soldiers to defend our security. I can only speak for myself when I say that my life is an easy expense to ensure that my family and friends can live in peace. I strongly believe in what we are doing and wish you were here to see for yourselves the honor and privilege that American warriors aboard this ship are feeling, knowing that we are going to be a part of something so strong and so meaningful to the safety of our loved ones. Then you would know what this potential war is about. We will stand tall in front of terrorism and defeat it. We, as warriors, are not afraid of what may happen. We are only afraid of Americans not being able to understand why we are here.

I ask for your courage as Americans to be strong for us; I ask for your understanding in what we believe is right. I ask for your support in what we are sworn to do: defend our country and the life of all. We will succeed in our task and will end the threat of terrorism in our back yard. We will also end the threat of terrorism in our neighbors' back yards. We have to remind ourselves of what this country stands for: life, liberty and justice for all. In order to maintain those rights we have to stop the threat of terrorism.

I am proud to be here. I will be coming home, but not until I know that it's going to be safe for all Americans and for everyone I love. My family is first. My country is where they live. I will defend it.

Lonnie J. Lewis, Navy, C Co., 1/4 WPN PLT

An American Soldier. A family photo
on the stock of his M16, Operation
Iraqi Freedom, Iraq, March 2003.

CHAPTER 8

THE AMERICAN WARRIOR

Soldiers, Sailors, Airmen and Marines are collectively referred to as American Warriors. They are the ones who first fired the shots at Concord Bridge and the ones who are continuing the struggle to preserve our freedoms in the mountains of Afghanistan and the deserts of Iraq. They are the singular reason that we enjoy freedom today. The American Warrior is the *tip of America's spear*, and this chapter honors them all.

American Soldiers in Training.

To be a soldier is the noblest act of mankind.

Colonel Mike Malone

I AM AN AMERICAN SOLDIER

*I am an American Soldier, overlooked
and sometimes misunderstood.*

*I serve my country with loyalty, courage,
and unyielding honor.*

*I stand as a shield of hope and protection against all
threats from enemies who bring danger. When I feel fear, I
remember I am a protector, a warrior of justice,
armed with my God and my rifle.*

*I wrap my flag around my heart, say a prayer to God—and
stand with bravery. Tears fall from my eyes,
but those tears are for the country I love.*

*I forfeit my life for my parents, family, wives, sons,
daughters, friends, and of course, for those who fail to
appreciate me, overlook me and misunderstand me; but I
leave behind immortality because a part
of my soul is within every American.*

I transcend color or race, I am an AMERICAN Soldier.

I am the Red, White and Blue.

By Otto Whittaker

*Whoever dares to look upon them as an irregular mob,
will find himself much mistaken. They have men amongst
them who know very well what they are about.*

British *Red Coat* Brigadier Lord Hugh Percy
after returning from the Green at Lexington, Massachusetts
where he heard the *Shot Fired Round the World*
by New England Minutemen, April 19, 1775

THEY'RE JUST NOT IN STEP
WITH TODAY'S SOCIETY

The Annual Daedalian Convention was held in June 2001 in Las Vegas, Nevada. The following benediction just says it all. This benediction was given by Pete Peterson at the Daedalian luncheon in Las Vegas.

My friends, it was once said ... *O lord, we have long known that prayer should include confession.* Therefore on behalf of the aviators and their guests gathered here this afternoon, I confess their sins.

Lord, they're just not in step with today's society. They are unreasonable in clinging to old-fashioned ideas like patriotism, duty, honor and country. They hold radical ideas believing that they are their brothers' keepers and responsible for the aviators on their wing. They have been seen standing when colors pass, singing the National Anthem at ball games, and drinking toasts to fallen comrades. Not only that, they have been observed standing tall; taking charge, and wearing their hair unfashionably short. They have taken Teddy R's and JFK's words too seriously and are overly concerned with what they can do for their service and country instead of what it can do for them. They take the Pledge of Allegiance to heart and believe that their oath is to be honored. And ... they know well what the definition of *'is'* is.

Forgive them, Lord, for being stubborn men and women who hold these values as genuine. They are aware of the price of honor and with total command of their spirit; they have been willing to pay the price. After all, what more can you expect? They're aviators! O Lord our God, bless these men and women, continue to raise up in this nation strong leaders and deliver us from *me first managers and don't ask me leaders.*

Be our honored guest today, Oh Lord, and join with us in laughter, good food, good drink, and telling of tall tales and legends that may occasionally exceed the truth.

We bow our heads to those aviators who were lost to protect our freedom and our ability to praise You.

Watch over and keep safe all those who wear this nation's uniform with special attention to their families and loved ones everywhere.

We thank You for Your grace during this convention and all the days and nights in our future. God bless You, God bless this great nation and God bless the President of the United States of America.

The most impressive thing about any Army is the individual soldier. He will always be the one responsible for taking and holding the ground in support of our foreign policy, mission, goals, and objectives. Even with sophisticated technology and advanced equipment, an Army cannot fight, sustain, and win a war without individual, quality soldiers.

SMA Glen E. Morrell, *The Army as an Institution*
Sergeants' Business, March-April 1987

On a visit to one of our installations, I was shown an automated system which is designed to significantly improve artillery fire support. Being a former tanker, I was impressed by a system which, according to reports, will revolutionize the battlefield. As I was leaving, the young soldier who had operated the control console and had overheard my praise of the system stood up as I walked past him and said, 'Sergeant Major, this sure is a great machine, but it doesn't do anything unless I tell it to.'

SMA William A. Connelly, *The Soldier Remains Our Ultimate Weapon*. U.S. Army, October 1979

I WAS A SOLDIER

By Colonel (Retired) Daniel K. Cedusky, U.S. Army.

I was a Soldier: That's the way it is, that's what we were ... are. We put it, simply, without any swagger, without any brag, in those four plain words. We speak them softly, just to ourselves. Others may have forgotten. They are a manifesto to mankind; speak those four words anywhere in the world–yes, anywhere–and many who hear will recognize their meaning. They are a pledge. A pledge that stems from a document which said: *I solemnly swear, to protect and defend* and goes on from there, and from a Flag called *Old Glory*. Listen, and you can hear the voices echoing through them, words that sprang white-hot from bloody lips, shouts of *medic*, whispers of *Oh God*!, forceful words of *Follow Me*. If you can't hear them, you weren't, if you can you were. *Don't give up the ship! Fight her till she dies ... Damn the torpedoes! Go ahead! ... Do you want to live forever? ... Don't cheer, boys; the poor devils are dying.* Laughing words, and words cold as January ice, words that when spoken, were meant, *Wait till you see the whites of their eyes.* The echo's of I was a Soldier.

You can hear the slow cadences at Gettysburg, or Arlington honoring not a man, but a Soldier, perhaps forgotten by his nation ... Oh! Those Broken Promises.

You can hear those echoes as you have a beer at the *Post*, walk in a parade, go to The Wall, visit a VA hospital, hear the mournful sounds of taps, or gaze upon the white crosses, row upon row.

But they aren't just words; they're a way of life, a pattern of living, or a way of dying. They made the evening, with another day's work done; supper with the wife and kids; and no Gestapo snooping at the door and threatening to kick your teeth in.

They gave you the right to choose who shall run our government for us, the right to a secret vote that counts just as much as the next fellow's in the final tally; and the obligation to use that right, and guard it and keep it clean.

They prove the right to hope, to dream, to pray; the obligation to serve.

These are some of the meanings of those four words, meanings we don't often stop to tally up or even list.

Only in the stillness of a moonless night, or in the quiet of a Sunday afternoon, or in the thin dawn of a new day, when our world is close about us, do they rise up in our memories and stir in our sentimental hearts.

And we are remembering Wake Island, and Bataan, Inchon, and Chu Lai, Knox and Benning, Great Lakes and Paris Island, Travis and Chanute, and many other places long forgotten by our civilian friends.

They're plain words, those four simple words.

You could engrave them on stone; you could carve them on the mountain ranges.

You could sing them, to the tune of *Yankee Doodle*.

But you needn't. You needn't do any of those things, for those words are engraved in the hearts of Veterans; they are familiar to 24,000,000 tongues, every sound and every syllable. If you must write them, put them on my Stone.

But when you speak them, speak them softly, proudly, I will hear you, for I too,

I was a Soldier.

THE QUALITIES OF A GREAT ARMY

President Abraham Lincoln's message to the Army of the Potomac at the Executive Mansion, Washington.

22 December 1862

To the Army of the Potomac: I have just read your Commanding General's preliminary report of the battle of Fredericksburg. Although you were not successful, the attempt was not an error, nor the failure other than an accident. The courage with which you, in an open field, maintained the contest against an entrenched foe, and the consummate skill and success with which you crossed and re-crossed the river, in face of the enemy, show that you possess all the qualities of a great army, which will yet give victory to the cause of the country and of popular government. Condoling with the mourners for the dead, and sympathizing with the severely wounded, I congratulate you that the number of both is comparatively so small. I tender to you, officers and soldiers, the thanks of the nation.

THE LAST WORD

Excerpts from President George W. Bush's Radio Address given to the Nation on Saturday, 15 September 2001.

We will smoke them out of their holes. We'll get them running and we'll bring them to justice. ... This is a conflict without battlefields or beachheads, a conflict with opponents who believe they are invisible. Yet, they are mistaken. They will be exposed, and they will discover what others in the past have learned: Those who make war against the United States have chosen their own destruction. Victory against terrorism will not take place in a single battle, but in a series of decisive actions against terrorist organizations and those who harbor and support them ... We are planning a broad and sustained campaign to secure our country and eradicate the evil of terrorism. And we are determined to see this conflict through. Americans of every faith and background are committed to this goal ... Yesterday I visited the site of the destruction in New York City and saw an amazing spirit of sacrifice and patriotism and defiance ... A terrorist attack designed to tear us apart has instead bound us together as a nation ... Now we honor those who died, and prepare to respond to these attacks on our nation. I will not settle for a token act. Our response must be sweeping, sustained and effective. We have much to do, and much to ask of the American people ... You will be asked for your patience; for, the conflict will not be short. You will be asked for resolve; for, the conflict will not be easy. You will be asked for your strength, because the course to victory may be long … In the past week, we have seen the American people at their very best everywhere in America. Citizens have come together to pray, to give blood, to fly our country's flag. Americans are coming together to share their grief and gain strength from one another … Great tragedy has come to us, and we are meeting it with the best that is in our country, with courage and concern for others. Because this is America. This is who we are. This is what our enemies hate and have attacked. And this is why we will prevail.

BOOTS OF THE NCO

Author Unknown.

In battledress, the NCO wears boots. He always has. Well, almost. Many soldiers at Valley Forge did not have shoes, much less boots. They marched and fought with no more than rags that were wrapped around bleeding, frostbitten feet. These volunteers literally knew the meaning of a *come as you are* war.

Three roses on the boots of Army Staff Sergeant Justin Galewski. An Explosive Ordnance Disposal soldier who was killed, along with three other service members, 15 April 2002, Afghanistan when rockets they were attempting to destroy accidentally exploded. Photo by Specialist Elizabeth Casebeer.

From the crude, rough and soiled moccasins worn by the soldiers more than 225 years ago, to the smooth and polished jump or jungle boots of today, boots have been basic to soldiering. Whether strapped, laced, buttoned, buckled or wrapped by leggings, boots have marched, paced, sloshed, trampled, jumped and charged over or through dirt, mud, snow, brush, rock, sand and water.

In peace and war, the boots of the American soldier have left their prints in many places–Yorktown, Little Big Horn, Shiloh, San Juan Hill, Luzon, Cantigny and Koblenz, Omaha Beach, and Iwo Jima, Inchon, Khe Sanh, St. George's, the Sinai and Gander, Panama City and Kuwait City, to name a few.

With boots on, U.S. soldiers have fought wars, policed cities, stood between hostile forces, provided humanitarian relief, rescued civilians … and died. Boots have been buried with soldiers, removed from bodies, amputated with legs and shattered by mines.

No matter where, or when, or what the mission, and Army NCO was there … wearing boots.

The one thing that makes us a standout among the world's military services is the quality of our NCOs. Don't ever believe it's the officers; it's the noncommissioned officers.

General A. C. Zinni, USMC, Commander in Chief, Central Command Farewell Remarks, July 2000

It has been clearly demonstrated in this war, as in past wars, that noncommissioned officers are the backbone of the Army. All unit commanders must give their personal attention to improving the quality and prestige of noncommissioned officers, especially those who exercise command responsibility.

General George S. Patton, Jr., 18 November 1944

However much we may honor the 'unknown soldier' as the symbol of sacrifice in war, let us not mistake the fact that it is the 'known soldier' who wins battles. Sentiment aside, it is the man whose identity is well known to his fellow soldiers who has the main chance as a battle effective.

S.L.A. Marshall, in the book *Men Against Fire*, 1947

MY FAVORITE QUOTE OF ALL TIME

SFC (Retired) Elijah R. Murphy, Colorado Springs, Colorado.

Once upon a day in February 1988, a 28-year-young SFC Elijah Murphy had just graduated from the SERE (Survival Evasion, Resistance, and Escape) Course at Ft. Bragg, NC. It was three weeks of starvation, degradation and soul searching. The course was designed by Nick Rowe, Author of *Five Years To Freedom* and Dan Pitzer who was captive in Vietnam with Nick. Their escapes from communist control took very different courses. They integrated many items that they fondly remembered from their own captivity into the SERE course. At any rate after this three weeks of *hell* I was certain that they had put the fear of God into me and that ETS (Enlisted Termination of Service) was a certainty in my future. It had scared me silly thinking that this was a game compared to what Russian captors would do to you. I had lost 30 pounds in the three weeks and could damn near touch my backbone through my navel. And it was only an exercise. My team medic had an uncle who was one of Hitler's Polish guests at Auschwitz. He told me, *yea, the fat ones got skinny and the skinny ones died*. I had no end of acquaintances who had first-hand experience at this thing and who had fought in so many *conflicts*. They had a different opinion of the *Police Actions*. If lead is flying and it is pointed in your general direction … it is war. You are fighting for your very life and existence. But there is always the chance of capture. And that scared me to the point of wanting to quit. I had seen the light at last and reality was ugly. The training Company that I was assigned to was commanded by Major Charters who had been in Co C 2-10 SF while I was in Co B. I went over to pay an office call to the man and he wasn't home. I went into his office and sat down at his desk, put my feet up on the desk and contemplated what life would have been like had I gone to West Point when it was offered. All the while examining the memorabilia Major Charters had collected over the years. But the most interesting thing I saw was a simple wooden frame hanging above the door of his office ... and I carefully read the words that it said ... I must have read it ten times.

War is an ugly thing but not the ugliest of things; the decayed and degraded state of moral and patriotic feelings which thinks that nothing is worth war is much worse. A man who has nothing for which he is willing to fight, nothing which is more important than his own personal safety, is a miserable creature and has no chance of being free unless made and kept so by the exertions of better men than himself.

John Stuart Mill

... and that made all the difference. I proudly retired from the military ten years and three *conflicts* later.

SFC Murphy (center). In Northern Iraq, Operation Provide Comfort, 1991 with Kurdish Tribal elders.

SMALL HEROES, BUT HEROES NONETHELESS

Speech given by General John P. Jumper during the Senior Non-Commissioned Officer (SNCO) Academy Graduation Ceremony, Maxwell Air Force Base, Alabama, 27 June 2001.

Thanks for that introduction Sergeant Davis (SMSgt Johnny Davis). Thank you Don (LtGen Donald Lamontagne, Commander, Air University), for your interest in furthering the interests of Aerospace Power. And thank you Chief Ball (CMSgt Ball, Commandant, SNCO Academy), for the invitation to speak here tonight.

On this date in 1950, President Harry S. Truman committed U.S. Air Forces, along with Naval Forces, to their first major conflict following the establishment of our separate service. We stand ready today, as we did over half a century ago, to protect American values at home and abroad. You graduates are already committed to your nation, and are the true leaders of the force. To you falls the responsibility of sustaining the best Air Force on the face of the earth.

Tonight I am going to tell you about heroes–small heroes, but heroes nonetheless; heroes that have been beacons of inspiration in my life and career. My first memory is when I was two years old–sitting in my Dad's lap in the cockpit of a P-51 Mustang. He was a second lieutenant just after WWII. We were stationed at a small base near Tokyo during the occupation of Japan. His job was to take fighter planes that had arrived by barge, and after all the preservatives were removed, to test fly them and ferry them inland to their permanent bases. Before I was three years old I had time in all the great WWII fighters: P-51, P-43, P-38 and British Spitfire. I just wish I could remember more about them than the noise they made.

I grew up in an era of heroes; my Dad's contemporaries were all heroes, like Chuck Yeager who was the first to fly faster than the speed of sound. My Dad commanded an F-106 interceptor squadron at Langley AFB, Virginia and we lived on Eagan Avenue. On the same street were several of the Mercury Seven astronauts.

I was captured in the world of flying, and heroes from an early age. They were larger than life; I knew that even then–but there were other heroes not so large.

When I was the commander of the 33rd Tactical Fighter Wing, Eglin Air Force Base in Florida, we were in the final day of an ORI [Operational Readiness Inspection]. We already had achieved an Outstanding, and had generated 71 of 72 jets. I was sitting back in the command post, ready to knock it off, when the DCM (we had DCM's back then) came in and said, *Boss, before we knock it off, you need to come out and see this.* So we jumped in a truck and went down to the flight line, and there was a group of about five people pushing a jet down the taxiway.

There was that 72nd jet, a jet with an engine write-up, being pushed over to the trim pad, trying to get the last check done to run up the engine and generate the jet. On the way, the tow bar had broken, but these folks were doing what they needed to get the airplane ready to fly. See, it was a matter of pride with that last crew chief that his jet was going to be generated for the ORI. So the DCM and I jumped out, and we started pushing the jet too. And more folks along the flight line started to join in.

People in buildings all around the base started filing out to help get this jet to the trim pad. By the time that the last check was done, and the chief signed off the checklist, there were probably 3,000 people gathered in the area, a lot of them probably had no idea what was going on–and when he signed it off, a cheer arose that was better than anything you have ever heard in the Super Bowl.

When I was commander of the 457th Fighter Wing at Nellis AFB in Nevada, I got an unusual call. The Chairman of the racing division at General Motors called and asked to come out and take a look at our operations. I agreed, and he and some of his folks came out to look around. We had an aircraft out on the flight line and some of our maintenance troops there to talk with the GM team. The Chairman asked the young NCO out there if the aircraft was ready to fly. He said *No, see if you look up here, you can see that the power supply is burned out, but I've got the part over to Sgt Smith in the repair shop, and he'll get it fixed and get it out here; If he doesn't get it out here, I'm gonna go over and kick Sgt Smith's butt. We'll have it installed and ready at about 1400 so it can fly this afternoon.* The GM folks were amazed that this young man would place such personal interest in the mission status of this aircraft. He asked the young Sergeant why he was so motivated to make it happen. And this crew chief replied that *Well, sir, that's my name on the side of the airplane.* It's that kind of professional pride that we have in the Air Force, and you don't always see in the outside world.

Next, I'd like to talk to you about something that happened during Operation ALLIED FORCE. Specifically, let me describe a single night from ALLIED FORCE that I'll never forget, 27 March to be exact. In fact, some of you may also remember this night, because it was the night we lost the F-117 near Belgrade. Now those of us that were in Vietnam learned very early to dread the sound of an aircraft emergency beacon. And as I sat in my office at Ramstein AB, through the marvels of modern technology, I could hear that beacon and knew that we had lost one of our own. An F-117 had been hit, right over the center of downtown Belgrade, and managed to glide to the outskirts of the city before the pilot was able to eject. Well, soon after this, a young Captain named Cherry—an A-10 pilot—scrambled his aircraft and began to organize the search and rescue effort. And I sat there and listened to him do exactly what our nation had trained him to do: direct planes to the tanker, position surveillance aircraft, and coordinate with the helicopters to set up for a very difficult effort to save his fellow airman.

While this was happening, I had one of those red phones you see in the movies, with all the buttons—the first one being the President, and the rest all the way down the chain of command. Well, this thing was ringing off the hook! All the lights are flashing at once, and everyone with the same questions: *Why aren't we in there? When are we going to pick him up?* and so on. In the background, that young Captain Cherry was calmly continuing to marshal the forces, ensuring that every piece was in place prior to executing the rescue. Well, my answer to some high officials in our government was: *Sir, the very best thing we can do is let Captain Cherry do his job. There's nobody better equipped to do what needs to be done.*

When the time came, it was incredible to see a package of 75 aircraft converge on downtown Belgrade, just waiting to pounce on the smallest move from the Serbians. There wasn't a peep! The helicopters then worked their way into the area, picked up a very grateful pilot, and brought him out safely, followed by the rest of the package. It was truly inspiring to watch the spirit, dedication, loyalty and patriotism all come together but what do these stories tell us? What do they mean? These are demonstrations of character–manifestations that attend the character of those able to transcend preoccupation with self–that virtue within us all which elevates the human spirit, compels us to reach beyond our meager selves–commands us to seek more–to attach our spirit to something bigger than we are.

When I was a Rat at VMI, entering in 1962, the cadet Regimental Commander was a fellow named Josiah Bunting [nicknamed *Si*]. Si graduated in the class of 1963, was a Rhoades Scholar, served in the U.S. Army in Vietnam and has since devoted his life to higher education, having been a professor at the United States Military Academy and President of several colleges. He is now the Superintendent at VMI and a noted author. Si Bunting lectures widely on value-based education. I recently heard him render the finest definition of character I have ever heard. He said, *character is integrity projected over time.* And then he reminded his audience that the Indo-European root of the word integrity is *tag*–to touch. Literally translated, the word integrity means *that within us that cannot be touched.* But we went through a period in the decade of the 90s where the AF lost some of its character as an institution. We once had a quality Air Force that was ruined by a concept known as Quality Air Force. During the early '90s, I was in the Pentagon on the Joint Staff and in OSD [Office of the Secretary of Defense] while the Air Force was taking up something called the Quality Air Force. When I was going to take command of 9th Air Force, the QAF had taken root. Now, I had read about Deming and Baldridge, and some of what they said made sense–common sense. The management tools they talked about were good in some cases. We were using them as well–we didn't talk about it though, we just did it.

When I arrived at Shaw, the first guy to meet me was the Quality guy. He said we needed to have an off-site—get the staff together and come up with our *mission, vision and goals* for the future. I understand the off-site idea, get folks focused on planning and get away from the distractions of the office. Then he started talking about how we needed to break down barriers. And this was a little curious, so I asked him how we were going to do that. He said, *Well, we're not going to wear our uniforms–and we are going to call each other by our first names*. It was all about breaking down barriers in his mind. It was bullshit. My plan was a little different. We went off station, but we wore uniforms, and we used ranks and were professional in all we did. We used no coaches, no timekeepers, and we were able to accomplish everything we set out to do, and more. We were told to believe that big business had all the answers. *Quality* was used as a substitute for leadership. It let words and slogans guide our behavior. Words like *empowerment, break down barriers*, etc. We stopped mentoring our people. We lost touch with the fine art of chewing ass.

An example of this is the Blackhawk shoot down. We screwed up with those F-15 pilots. The essential nature of our business is to gain and maintain air superiority by shooting down bad guys. When you visually ID an aircraft and shoot it down, and it's one of ours, you have failed in your primary mission. It's worse than a doctor taking out the wrong lung. Something should have been done. Then

General Fogleman made his video about accountability. He sat there as chief, on the edge of his desk, and with an angry tone talked about how we were going to be accountable for our actions. Scared a lot of people in the fighter community. He said we needed to have our flyers take responsibility for their actions. For starters, a good butt-chewing would have worked. Another example is the Lieutenant Kelly Flynn situation. You remember, she was the one who was caught messing around with an enlisted member's husband. Now, the press tried to make it into an adultery issue. It was never an issue about adultery; it was about lying.

Lying, and taking responsibility for your actions. Now her squadron commander had the opportunity to stop the problem before it got out of hand. If he would have brought young Lieutenant Flynn into his office and said, *I don't know if the stories I'm hearing are true or not, and frankly, I don't care. But I'm giving you one chance, and one chance only to knock it off!* I guarantee that would have been the end of it. That's what our young people today need, a little personal attention and counseling.

So this virtue of character is about institution, but it's also about individuals. The character we seek to define is the fire of conscience that burns within us and superintends our conduct over a lifetime. But character is out of vogue in this world whose standards are set more by the culture of Beavis and Butthead, or the Simpsons, than by the standards of, say, our founding fathers: John Adams, Thomas Jefferson or James Madison. These men were truly unique. They transitioned easily from the pulpit to the plowshare to the musket. They wrote the history of their time with powerful words that will live forever: The Declaration of Independence, The Constitution, The Federalist Papers. And they used words we don't hear today—Words that describe the supreme traits of virtue and character that inspired them. Words like Continence: *Self-restraint; the ability to refrain from impulse.* Also Disinterested: *Free of selfish motive—intellectual curiosity is the lifeblood of real civilization.* Thomas Jefferson once said of John Adams that he was *as disinterested as the being who made him.* It was the supreme compliment for one who was totally devoted to crafting the framework of a new nation.

It is that same dedication we see in the F-15 crew chief, or the A-10 pilot who is determined that we won't leave one of our own stranded deep in enemy territory. Bunting describes the *death of shame.* It is the propensity that exists in today's society to reward the most unconscionable behavior with a *tell-all* book or a movie contract. To hate the sin but love the sinner; to turn the perpetrator into the victim; to deflect blame and responsibility anywhere but on me. But this is not a diagnosis of despair–these traits of culture are turned around by generations that seek the path of higher standards. Such a generation sits before me tonight. You, here, have chosen such a path–the path of most resistance instead of least resistance. The path that can forge the very character we seek to revive. And it will be tested–again and again–as you exercise the power of your choices: To do the right thing and to make it prevail at whatever cost; to always speak the complete truth; to assume responsibility; to be accountable for your mistakes as well as rewarded for accomplishments; and, to make these choices without calculation of risk or reward. It is the sum of that power which gives strength to this nation, and will define the character and integrity of your generation of senior NCOs. You, as future Air Force Leaders, must earn the right to lead our heroes.

Finally, here are a few practical tenets that have served me well for more than 35 years in uniform. Jumper's Rules of Life:

Number 1. Your most meaningful memories will be the times when your character, integrity, endurance, stamina or fortitude were most challenged and you had the courage to do the right thing.

Number 2. The things that make you feel best about yourself will not be things you do for yourself, but the good things you do for others. During the Kosovo war one member of my staff went to a refugee camp where twenty thousand or so Kosovar Albanians were living in tents. As he entered the front gate with several other people they were immediately surrounded by a huge throng of people–none of them could speak English but soon a chant began to arise from the people: *NATO, NATO, NATO.* The people were grateful; they were alive because NATO was protecting them from the Serbian military that had tried to eliminate them.

Number 3. I can tell you exactly how to get ahead–the unfailing key to success: Always do the best at the job you have right now–the rest will take care of itself. How remarkable it is that prosperity, good luck and fortune come to those who work hard.

Number 4. The experiences in your life that truly elevate the human spirit will not come from material rewards, but from moral and spiritual rewards that attend virtues of sacrifice, duty, honor and courage.

So, as you sit here tonight you are ahead in the marathon of life and your goal is to finish. You have already demonstrated the virtues of hard work and success that shape character. Stay on that path–remain the same person that got you where you are today–listen to the wisdom that surrounds you: your seniors, your peers, your spouses, your children all contribute to that wisdom. They have walked the path you are on and they do understand. They are beside you here tonight because they care. Remain united with them into your future. Thank you. God bless the United States of America and the U.S. Air Force.

MY MONTH WITH THE MILITARY

By Dan Juneau, President, Louisiana Association of Business & Industry and father of a U.S. Marine.

It wasn't a good way to start a Sunday morning or a holiday season. My bedside phone rang at 1:45 a.m. on December 10, and I awoke to the voice of a young Marine captain telling me that my 18-year-old son, a Marine recruit in San Diego, was in intensive care at the Camp Pendleton Naval Hospital. A few hours later, I was on a plane. Over the next month, I got to see the U.S. military, up close and personal. I lived on base among the Marines, and I spent countless hours with the Navy personnel at the hospital. The experience taught me much about today's U.S. military, as an institution, and more about the young men and women who make it breathe.

You cannot spend time on a base and not be overwhelmed by how utterly young our military is. Even those in the upper ranks and the *seasoned* noncommissioned officers (NCOs) are, for the most part, twenty and thirty something. As I traveled around the camp, the Marines' penchant for physical fitness was obvious. At the crack of dawn, it seemed that every platoon was either jogging or marching in cadence. By evening, there would be pickup basketball and flag football games breaking out around the base. Calorie burning, it seems, is a sacred ritual in the Marines. Another noticeable trait in this *young nation* within the military is their politeness and respect. If I sought assistance (be it directions or information), I was accorded not only a high degree of civility, but also the utmost in personal attention to ensure that my needs were met. Manners, hospitality and respect are obviously elements instilled in today's enlistees, certainly so in the Marine Corps. The stories about the spartan life and stern training in Marine boot camp are not exaggerations. But the story seldom told publicly is the strong feeling of personal responsibility that Marine Corps officers and NCOs have for those in their charge. The same young captain who called to inform me of my son's serious condition met me at the airport. He had reserved a car and found a place for me to stay at Camp Pendleton before my plane landed. He took me straight to my son and remained with us until late that night. When I told him earlier in the evening that he should go home to his wife and young child, he replied, *Your son is my responsibility, sir.* As my son went through four surgeries, the senior drill instructor for his platoon spent countless hours with us. In those tough first days, he stood at my son's door like a centurion standing guard, a look of genuine concern on his face. Other officers and NCOs from my son's battalion came by to check on him, encourage him, and let him know he was not forgotten. So, too, with the young Navy medical personnel who not only were expert caregivers but also showed constant concern for the person, not just the condition. As fate would have it, my son was leaving San Diego for a 30-day convalescent leave on the same day his training company was graduating. We went to the ceremonies that morning and watched 400 young men do what my son would not now be able to do: become an official member of the U.S. Marine Corps. When the ceremonies were over and mothers had finished hugging their new Marines, I watched my son limp with his heavy splints down to the parade deck and shake hands with the members of his platoon, telling them, *Congratulations, Marine!* He entered boot camp unsure and apprehensive, but he left exhibiting class and confidence. Thank the Marines for that. My own 30 days *in the Marines* has made me proud of those who serve, appreciative of those who lead, and much more confident about our younger generation.

CONFESSIONS OF A NINTENDO SOLDIER

Author Unknown, 2001.

As a soldier, I consider it part of my duty to read the various editorials and opinion columns relating to my profession. I hear this retired General say that, and I read a retired NCO say this, and every column seems to speak of the downward spiral of the modern Army, co-ed Basic Training, the lack of combat readiness, our Chief of Staff's decision to change official headgear. But the favorite topic by far, is the quality of the *new* soldiers, and the weakness, ill training and overall worthlessness of the people filling the Army's ranks. I am not a senior leader. I am not an NCO. I am the center mass of the Army, a Specialist with two years of service, and not an Airborne Ranger, but a combat supporter. Given the MOS demographics of late, this puts me directly in the category of Joe Average, the everyday, stereotypical soldier. I am also one of the *new* soldiers, who attended co-ed Basic, who missed Desert Storm and Somalia by a long shot, and who, if you listen to the consensus, seems to consistently be *weaker* than the soldiers of yesterday. Basically, I'd say I'm at the ground level of everything that the retired Colonels and Sergeants Major seem to write about and despise the very composition of the force that seems to concern them. So I thought I'd put in my two cents, and let everyone know what it's like to be a fabled *Soldier of the Nintendo Generation*. Despite the pictures that are being painted by everybody, my basic wasn't fun. I counted the days till I graduated, and cherished mail, just like the old soldiers did back whenever they were in. I did hundreds of push-ups, I woke up at obscene hours, I was screamed at, despised by Drill Sergeants, called worthless, I did more push-ups, I didn't use the phone every Sunday (try twice), I didn't eat pizza or eat candy, I didn't have a stress card, and I didn't have fun. And that was U.S. Army Basic Combat Training at Fort Jackson, South Carolina in 1999. I don't know how these stories are built, and where all the grizzled veterans are getting their facts. Maybe there are some utopian BCT companies somewhere that exhibits all these soft qualities, but I haven't seen them. I saw professionals, NCOs and Drill Sergeants doing their best to train civilians to be soldiers, to train us to be like them. And believe me, my Drill Sergeant remains my mentor for soldiering to this day. Now, I am at my line unit, my permanent party assignment, out in the big, bad Regular Army. And every time I turn around, I read the articles I have already mentioned, complaining of the *soft* soldiers manning the Army's Divisions. Well I'm here, right in the middle of it all, and what do I see? I see *soft* soldiers who work ridiculous hours, day and night–Privates, Specialists, and Sergeants. I see *soft* soldiers who could be making a lot more in the civilian world, but instead staying in boots, transcending fiscal desires for love of country. I see *soft* soldiers who are preparing to fight and win war, through countless deployments to NTC and JRTC, and experience tough, realistic training on a daily basis. I see *soft* soldiers daily going above and beyond what they are required to do, putting the accomplishment of the mission before all else. The Army is swirling in a mass of controversy, differing opinions, uncertainty and doubt. The last thing we, the soldiers of today, need is to read volumes of documents by you, our predecessors, our mentors, and our fathers, degrading us. If you disagree with the policies, discuss the policymaker. If you disagree with the leadership, discuss the leader. But leave us, the soldiers, out of it. As *soft* and *weak* as you say we are, we remain here, on guard, in Tuzla, Korea, Fort Bragg and Fort Campbell. We don't choose who we perform Basic Training with or what hat we wear. We just serve. I am the rank and file of the new army you all seem to distrust. I ask one thing: next time you put us, the new, *soft* soldiers, in the sights of your verbal lashings, have a little faith, because when the dogs of war are loosed again, we will rise to the challenge just as you did, and continue to uphold the legacy of the American Soldier. You'll see.

A good soldier, whether he leads a platoon or an army, is expected to look backward as well as forward; but he must think only forward.

General of the Army Douglas MacArthur

The American soldier demonstrated that, properly equipped, trained, and led, he has no superior among all the armies of the world.

General Lucian K. Truscott
Former Commanding General, 5th Army

GOD BLESS THE U.S. MARINE CORPS

Marines Always Welcome, Relatives by Appointment.

Good Night Chesty, Wherever You Are.

*To Boldly Go Where A FEW GOOD MEN
Have Gone Before.*

Heroes Get Remembered, Legends Live Forever.

Pappy Boyington.

USMC WWII Ace Fighter pilot with up to 28 aerial *kills*, recipient of the Medal of Honor and the Navy Cross, Ex-POW, Flew with the Black Sheep Squadron *Flying Tigers*, Author of the book *Baa Baa Black Sheep*. 1912-1988.

When It Absolutely, Positively Must Be DESTROYED Overnight—Call The USMC.

Heaven Won't Take Us and Hell Is Afraid We'll Take Over.

There are Two Types of People: MARINES and Those Who Wish They Were.

Marines of Company A. 26th Marine Expeditionary Unit, Afghanistan, 6 January 2002.

South of the DMZ, Vietnam, 1966. Marine gunner
John Wilson, shouldering a rocket launcher, was part
of a U.S. Marines reconnaissance force. He was
killed in action twelve days after this picture was
taken. Photo by Larry Burrows.

More Sweat in Peace, Less Blood in War.

*We Deliver More Destruction Overnight Than
Those Who Deliver Overnight.*

*The Impossible is Done with the Lord's Help
and a Few Good Men and Women.*

Women Marines—Fewer and Prouder.

Pain is Only Temporary, Pride is Forever.

Pain is Weakness Leaving the Body.

The Marine Corps Doesn't Build Character, It Reveals It.

Marines. 1st Battalion, 1st Marine Regiment Scout/Sniper
Platoon, Afghanistan.

USMC Infantry—Taking Out the Garbage.

Once a Marine Always a Marine.

The U.S. Marine Corps.
Eagle, Globe and Anchor.

*And On the Seventh Day
when GOD Rested,
We Overran His Perimeter
and Stole the Globe,
We Stole the Eagle from the
Air Force,
The Anchor from the Navy,
The Rope from the Army,
And have been Protecting
Our Shores Ever Since.*

MARINE

United States Marines!

*You earned the title 'Marine' upon graduation
from boot recruit training. It wasn't willed to you;
it isn't a gift. It is not a government subsidy. Few can claim
the title; no one can take it away. It is yours forever.*

Tom Barlett, from *Leatherneck* Magazine

Marine Lance Corporal Dalton Gunderson.
Sniper, Vietnam.

No Former or Ex Marine here!
Just a Marine no longer on active duty.

The U.S. Air Force Chief-of-Staff
would never be called–Airman.

The Chief-of-Naval Operations
would never be called–Sailor.

The Commanding General of the U.S. Army
would never be called–Soldier.

But the Commandant of the Marine Corps
would be proud to be called a–Marine.

UNITED STATES MARINE CORPS

Leader of men, teller of tall tales, legend in his own mind, U.S. Marine extraordinaire, stream fordable, air droppable, beer fueled, water cooled, author, history maker, lecturer, traveler, freedom fighter, defender of the faith. Wars fought, tigers tamed, revolutions started, bars emptied, alligators castrated. Let me win your hearts and minds or I'll burn your damn hut down!

Marine. World War II.

BREATH OF THE DRAGON

Written to the *Sunday Mail*, London, by Tom Clancy, 14 September 2001.

For Tom Clancy, the world's highest-paid fiction writer–whose thrillers have sold 60 million copies and been turned into blockbuster movies–the events of 11 September 2001 hold a special poignancy. In his best-selling novel *Debt of Honor* in 1994, he created a scenario chillingly similar to the attacks: a Japanese pilot crashes a 747 jet into the U.S. Capitol buildings, killing the President and most of his Cabinet. In the following article, Clancy explains why the mood of his nation is now turning to revenge:

It was a friend of mine formerly of the Royal Navy who first pointed out that the casualty count on this incident exceeds that of Pearl Harbor. Yes, my country has taken a big and costly hit, and somewhere, perhaps in South Asia, some people are exchanging high-fives and having themselves a good laugh. And maybe they're entitled to it. Like Pearl Harbor, it was a well-planned and well-executed black operation. But, you know, they've made the same mistake that Japan made back in 1941. It's remarkable to me that America is so hard for some people to understand. We are the most open of books, after all. Our values and customs are portrayed on TV and movie screens all over the world. Is the character of my country so hard to grasp? Japan figured that they could defeat us not physically, but morally, that America was not tough enough to defeat their death-seeking warriors, that we would be unwilling to absorb the casualties. (In this they were right: we didn't absorb all the casualties they tried to inflict–but that was because we killed their samurai much more efficiently than they were able to kill our men.) An enemy willing to die in the performance of his duty can indeed be a formidable adversary, but, you see, we've dealt with such people before. They die just like everyone else.

Perhaps the American sort of patriotism, like the British sort, just isn't bombastic enough for our enemies to notice. We don't parade about thumping our chests and proclaiming how tough we are, whereas other people like that sort of display. But they don't seem to grasp the fact that they do it because they have to–they evidently need to prove to themselves how formidable they are. Instead, our people, like yours, train and practice their craft every day, out in the field at places like Fort Bragg, North Carolina, and Fort Irwin, California. I've been to both places and seen our people and how they train. The difference between a civilian or a common ruffian and a soldier, you see, is training. A professional soldier is as serious about his work as a surgeon is about his. Such people are not, in my experience, boastful. If you ask what they can do, they will explain it to you, usually in quiet tones, because they do not feel the need to prove anything. Off duty they are like everyone else, watching football on TV and enjoying a quiet beer with their pals. They read books, shop at the local supermarkets, and mow the grass at home. They all enjoy a good laugh. They make the best of friends. They look physically fit–and indeed they are physically fit– because their job requires it, and every day they do something tiresome in the field, working at some more or less demanding field exercise, again and again and again until every aspect of their job is as automatic as zipping one's zipper is for us people in civilian life. But, you know, inside all of these people, such as the 82nd Airborne at Fort Bragg, or the 75th Ranger Regiment at Fort Stewart, Georgia, there burns a little flame. Not a big one–instead like the pilot light in a gas stove. And, when you put more gas there, the flame gets bigger, enough to cook with. Inside every one of these people is something else, something you have to look for—pride. They know that they are good at their work, in the event they ever have to do it for real. This doesn't happen very often, and indeed they do not ordinarily lust to do it because it's a serious, nasty job. The job is the taking of life. Military organizations exist for only one mission: killing people and breaking things. This is not something to be undertaken lightly, because life is a gift from God, and a lot of these people–kids, really–can be found in church on Sunday mornings. But their larger purpose–the reason these kids enlist, both in my country and in yours–is to preserve, protect, and defend their nations and the citizens who live there. It's not an easy job, but someone has to do it, and typically the hardest jobs attract the best of us. Mostly, they never have to kill anybody, and that's okay with them. It's knowing that they are able to do something difficult and dangerous that gives them their pride.

This purpose, defending their country, is something they don't talk much about, but it's always there, and with it comes a quiet, steely look in the eyes. Especially when something like this happens. That's when their sense of self is insulted, and these are people who do not bear insults well. They are protectors, and when those whom they are sworn to protect are hurt, then comes the desire–the lust–to perform their mission. Even then it's quiet. They will not riot or pose before TV cameras or cry aloud for action, because that's not their way. They are the point of the lance, the very breath of the dragon, and at times like this they want to know the taste of blood. Their adversaries just don't appreciate what they are capable of. It's something too divorced from their experience. This isn't like hosing civilians with your machine gun or setting off a bomb somewhere, or killing unarmed people strapped and helpless inside a commercial aircraft. This means facing professional warriors at a time and place of their choosing, and that is something terrorists don't really prepare for. The day of Pearl Harbor, the commander of the Japanese navy told his staff not to exult too much, that all their beautifully executed operation had accomplished was to *awaken* a sleeping dragon and give it a dreadful purpose. Perhaps alone in his country, Isoroku Yamamoto, who had lived briefly in America, knew what his enemy was capable of; and for that reason, perhaps, he was not surprised when the .50-caliber bullet from a P-38 fighter entered his head and ended his life. Whoever initiated last week's operation is probably not quite as appreciative of what he has begun as Yamamoto was. Because the dragon is now fully awake, and its breath is too hot for men to bear. America is now fully awake. Our quiet patriotism is a little louder now, but it will not get too loud. Why spoil the surprise? *We sleep safely in our beds because rough men stand ready in the night to visit violence on those who would harm us.* George Orwell.

THE RIFLEMAN

The Rifleman fights without promise
of either reward or relief. Behind every river there's
another hill—and behind that hill, another river.
After weeks or months in the line only a wound can offer
him the comfort of safety, shelter, and a bed.

Those who are left to fight, fight on, evading death
but knowing that with each day of evasion they have
exhausted one more chance for survival.
Sooner or later, unless victory comes,
this chase must end on the litter or in the grave.

General Omar Bradley

Infantrymen of the 3-15th, U.S. 3rd Infantry Division. Near the Border Between Kuwait and Iraq, March 20, 2003, Operation Iraqi Freedom.

THE REAL LAND WARRIOR, WHAT THE MEDIA MISSED

By Major William T. Coffey, Jr., 15 September 2000, Fort Polk, Louisiana.

In a time when the media's spotlights are focusing on battle command computers, new weapon systems and advanced sensors, there comes a story about our nations ultimate weapon … the character of the American soldier. Last night I was inspired by such a story told by one of our Army's leaders. It is a story worth retelling.

The Army's Joint Contingency Force Advanced War Fighting Experiment (JCF AWE) is currently in full swing here at Fort Polk, Louisiana. This AWE is testing new technologies and gaining insights into new war fighting concepts that leverage Information Age technologies, which are designed to increase the lethality and survivability for our Nation's land force. One of the cornerstone efforts, and an item of great media interest, is the *Land Warrior* initiative. The *Land Warrior* consists of a series of technologies that *digitize* the individual Infantryman, such as a helmet mounted video display, Global Positioning System, and a thermal weapons sight. But the story told was not about the technology on the soldier. Rather, it was a story about one particular soldier behind the technology—a story that the plethora of reporters and cameras completely missed.

Every night supporting organizations gather to provide the JCF Experiment Director, LTG Rigby, an update on the conduct of the AWE. Last night LTG Rigby noted his satisfaction at the way the Army was *telling the story* how we are digitizing our light forces to the daily flow of reporters and cameras chartered to gather such stories on the multitude of battle command computers, next generation weapon systems, and advanced sensors. His story about one particular soldier came at the end of this meeting when he stood and concluded with his account of an incident he witnessed the previous night.

Two nights ago, the *Land Warrior Live Fire* event was conducted at the Fort's live fire weapons range. This event, according to LTG Rigby, was a *media highlight*. Reporters from around the world descended on this event, cameras and microphones in tow, to watch a platoon of about 50 Land Warrior equipped Infantrymen (from the 3rd Battalion, 325th Parachute Infantry Regiment, 82nd Airborne Division) fire and maneuver in total darkness using their advanced capabilities. The Land Warrior Platoon Leader's radio transmissions were wired to a loud speaker allowing reporters a real-time account of all voice commands between the Platoon Leader and his Company Commander. LTG Rigby stated that the young Platoon Leader's voice was stern and confident as he maneuvered his soldiers across the range. The assembled media was able to experience the feel of moving, shooting, and communicating with what is probably the most modernized and lethal Infantry platoon in the world today. I am confident the accounts of this event and its supporting technologies will find their way into forthcoming articles, professional journals, newspapers, and TV broadcasts. Shortly after the conclusion of the live fire event, the Land Warrior Platoon gathered near the media's building to be interviewed, videotaped, and photographed. From LTG Rigby's account, there was a large group of reporters

Land Warrior **Soldiers.** The 3/325th, 82nd Airborne Division, participating in an experiment, Fort Polk, Louisiana, August 2000.

conducting their interviews amid an array of bright camera lights. What the reporters didn't see was one lone Land Warrior soldier off to the side. He was lying on his back receiving medical attention from a couple of medics. The soldier was unable to walk any longer due to an injury to both his legs. As one medic was wrapping both the soldier's knees with ice packs, the other pulled from the soldier's ammo pouch a doctor's *profile* [written instructions from an Army doctor restricting certain physical activities] and proceeded to chastise the soldier with words, to the effect, *Can't you read right here that the doctor said no running, jumping, physical training? What did you think you were doing?* Apparently, the soldier had sustained some type of injury to his knees well before the live fire event and received a medical directive not to conduct any further physical activity. After being chastised by the medic the soldier responded, to the effect, *Hell, we trained hard for this event and I wanted to be there with my platoon. I didn't want to miss this important event.* No doubt, this soldier conducted final preparations of this event and the live fire itself with a great amount of physical pain. He hid his pain by refusing to limp, ran when he had to run and low crawled when he had to low crawl. He did everything his platoon did, when they did it, and to established standards. I suspect he did all this without any sniveling. It is evident that he just *bit the bullet* and remained focused on the mission and committed to his team. No one could have blamed him for heeding the doctor's advice. But he didn't quit. He gave a damn, did what had to be done and got the job done. LTG Rigby closed by saying, *I hope that soldier did not sustain any permanent injury to his knees, I hope he gets better, and I hope he stays in the Army. We need soldiers like him in the Army.*

This injured soldier's personal courage, duty, and selfless service was not lost to anyone in the audience listening to LTG Rigby tell this story. Nonetheless, I think the real story goes beyond the lone injured soldier and his personal character. I believe this story speaks volumes to the soldier's training, the inspiring leadership provided him from his chain of command, his esprit, and the morale in his unit. I believe this story also speaks volumes to the character of the American soldier ... a character that reflects our national character and Army values.

In this era of Army modernization, in a time when we are buying, maintaining, and repairing hundreds of millions of dollars of Information Age equipment, it is important to reflect for a moment on the fundamental aspects of our profession—something our nation's media often misses. We must reflect on how we collectively develop, mentor, lead, motivate, inspire, and train our soldiers to the best of our abilities. We must remain focused on our Army values. We must remember that the ultimate weapon on the battlefield remains the character and skills of our soldiers, it is a weapon our adversaries do not have. Sometimes it takes a land warrior with two swollen knees, unable to walk, laying off to the side away from the frenzy of the media to remind us why we make the sacrifices that we do to protect our country. We can never allow ourselves to get enamored with technology at the expense of the soldier. We must always remember the soldier. Our country deserves and demands nothing less.

Although the Corps contains its share of visible heroes, its triumphs, in an aberration of history, are triumphs of the institution itself and not the attainments of individual Marines. We remember that Marlborough defeated the French, that Togo defeated the Russians, that Scipio defeated Carthage. But we know only that it was the Marines who won at Belleau Wood, the Marines who won at Guadalcanal, the Marines who led the way to Inchon. And that is exactly the way the Corp's heroes–big and small–would have it, for the Corps is less of flesh than of the spirit.

General Krulak, former Commandant of the Marine Corps

*Our society asks much of its warrior soldiers and gives
little back, a fact of life too long lived to be the shame to us
that it ought to be. We very often do not have the decency to
ask. We just expect them to be there when they are needed,
and out of sight when they are not. We examine every
action for flaws and celebrate those flaws for the world to
see, as though the people who wear our uniforms
were enemies instead of friends.*

Tom Clancy, in memoriam to Gerry Carroll, in *No Place to Hide*

AUTUMN 1942: IT CAME DOWN TO ONE MARINE AND ONE SHIP

By Vin Suprynowicz.

October 26 falls on a Thursday this year.

Ask the significance of the date, and you're likely to draw some puzzled looks–five more days to stock up for Halloween? It's a measure of men like Col. Mitchell Paige and Rear Adm. Willis A. *Ching Chong China* Lee that they wouldn't have had it any other way. What they did 58 years ago, they did precisely so their grandchildren could live in a land of peace and plenty. Whether we've properly safeguarded the freedoms they fought to leave us, may be a discussion best left for another day. Today we struggle to envision–or, for a few of us, to remember–how the world must have looked on Oct. 26, 1942. A few thousand lonely American Marines had been put ashore on Guadalcanal, a god-forsaken malarial jungle island which just happened to lie like a speed bump at the end of the long blue-water slot between New Guinea and the Bismarck Archipelago–the very route the Japanese Navy would have to take to reach Australia. On Guadalcanal the Marines built an airfield. And Japanese commander Isoroku Yamamoto immediately grasped what that meant. No effort would be spared to dislodge these upstart Yanks from a position that could endanger his ships during any future operations to the south. Before long, relentless Japanese counterattacks had driven supporting U.S. Navy from inshore waters. The Marines were on their own. World War Two is generally calculated from Hitler's invasion of Poland in 1939. But that's a Eurocentric view. The Japanese had been limbering up their muscles in Korea and Manchuria as early as 1931, and in China by 1934. By 1942 they'd devastated every major Pacific military force or stronghold of the great pre-war powers: Britain, Holland, France, and the United States. The bulk of America's proud Pacific fleet lay beached or rusting on the floor of Pearl Harbor. A few aircraft carriers and submarines remained; though as Mitchell Paige and his 30-odd men were sent out to establish their last, thin defensive line on that ridge southwest of the tiny American bridgehead on Guadalcanal on Oct. 25, he would not have been much encouraged to know how those remaining American aircraft carriers were far off shore.

(The next day, their Mark XV torpedoes–carrying faulty magnetic detonators reverse-engineered from a First World War German design–proved so ineffective that the United States Navy couldn't even scuttle the doomed and listing carrier Hornet with eight carefully aimed torpedoes. Instead, our forces suffered the ignominy of leaving the abandoned ship to be polished off by the enemy ... only after Japanese commanders determined she was damaged too badly to be successfully towed back to Tokyo as a trophy.) As Paige–then a platoon sergeant–and his riflemen set about carefully emplacing their four water-cooled Brownings, it's unlikely anyone thought they were about to provide the definitive answer to that most desperate of questions: How many able-bodied U.S. Marines does it take to hold a hill against 2,000 desperate and motivated attackers? The Japanese Army had not failed in an attempt to seize any major objective since the Russo-Japanese War of 1905. Their commanders certainly did not expect the war to be lost on some God-forsaken jungle ridge manned by one thin line of Yanks in khaki in October of 1942. But in preceding days, Marine commander Vandegrift had defied

War College doctrine, *dangling* his men in exposed positions to draw Japanese attacks, then springing his traps *with the steel vise of firepower and artillery*, in the words of Naval historian David Lippman. The Japanese regiments had been chewed up, good. Still, the American forces had so little to work with that Paige's men would have only the four 30-caliber Brownings to defend the one ridge through which the Japanese opted to launch their final assault against Henderson Field, that fateful night of Oct. 25. By the time the night was over, *The 29th (Japanese) Infantry Regiment has lost 553 killed or missing and 479 wounded among its 2,554 men*, historian Lippman reports. *The 16th (Japanese) Regiment's losses are uncounted, but the 164th's burial parties handle 975 Japanese bodies. ... The American estimate of 2,200 Japanese dead is probably too low.* Among the 90 American dead and wounded that night were all the men in Mitchell Paige's platoon. Every one. As the night wore on, Paige moved up and down his line, pulling his dead and wounded comrades back into their foxholes and firing a few bursts from each of the four Brownings in turn, convincing the Japanese forces down the hill that the positions were still manned.

The citation for Paige's Congressional Medal of Honor picks up the tale: *When the enemy broke through the line directly in front of his position, P/Sgt. Paige, commanding a machinegun section with fearless determination, continued to direct the fire of his gunners until all his men were either killed or wounded. Alone, against the deadly hail of Japanese shells, he fought with his gun and when it was destroyed, took over another, moving from gun to gun, never ceasing his withering fire.* In the end, Sgt. Paige picked up the last of the 40-pound, belt-fed Brownings–the same design which John Moses Browning famously fired for a continuous 25 minutes until it ran out of ammunition at its first U.S. Army trial–and did something for which the weapon was never designed. Sgt. Paige walked down the hill toward the place where he could hear the last Japanese survivors rallying to move around his flank, the gun cradled under his arm, firing as he went. The weapon did not fail. Coming up at dawn, battalion executive officer Major Odell M. Conoley first discovered the answer to our question: How many able-bodied Marines does it take to hold a hill against two regiments of motivated, combat-hardened infantrymen who have never known defeat? On a hill where the bodies were piled like cordwood, Mitchell Paige alone sat upright behind his 30-caliber Browning, waiting to see what the dawn would bring.

One hill: one Marine.

But that was the second problem. Part of the American line had fallen to the last Japanese attack. *In the early morning light, the enemy could be seen a few yards off, and vapor from the barrels of their machine guns was clearly visible*, reports historian Lippman. *It was decided to try to rush the position.* For the task, Major Conoley gathered together *three enlisted communication personnel, several riflemen, a few company runners who were at the point, together with a cook and a few mess men who had brought food to the position the evening before.* Joined by Paige, this ad hoc force of 17 Marines counterattacked at 5:40 a.m., discovering that *the extremely short range allowed the optimum use of grenades.* In the end, *The element of surprise permitted the small force to clear the crest.* And that's where the unstoppable wave of Japanese conquest finally crested, broke, and began to recede. On an unnamed jungle ridge on an insignificant island no one had ever heard of, called Guadalcanal. Because of a handful of U.S. Marines, one of whom, now 82, lives out a quiet retirement with his wife Marilyn in La Quinta, Calif. But while the Marines had won their battle on land, it would be meaningless unless the U.S. Navy could figure out a way to stop losing night battles in *The Slot* to the northwest of the island, through which the Japanese kept sending in barges filled with supplies and reinforcements for their own desperate forces on Guadalcanal. The U.S. Navy had lost so many ships in those dreaded night actions that the waters off Savo were given the grisly sailor's nickname by which they're still known today: Ironbottom Sound. So desperate did things become that finally, 18 days after Mitchell Paige won his Congressional Medal of Honor on that ridge above Henderson Field, Admiral Bull Halsey himself broke a stern War College edict–the one against committing capital ships in restricted waters. Gambling the future of the cut-off troops on Guadalcanal on one final roll of the dice, Halsey dispatched into the Slot his two remaining fast battleships, the USS South Dakota and the USS Washington, escorted by the only four destroyers with enough fuel in their bunkers to get them there and back. In command of the 28-knot battlewagons was the right man at the right place, gunnery expert Rear Adm. Willis A. *Ching Chong China* Lee. Lee's flag flew aboard the Washington, in turn commanded by Captain Glenn Davis. Lee was a nut for gunnery drills. *He tested every gunnery-book rule with exercises*, Lippman writes, *and ordered gunnery drills under odd conditions–turret firing with relief crews, anything that might simulate the freakishness of battle.* As it turned out, the American destroyers need not have worried about carrying enough fuel to get home. By 11 p.m. on Nov. 13, outnumbered better than three-to-one by a massive Japanese task force driving down from the northwest, every one of the four American destroyers had been shot up, sunk, or set aflame, while the *South Dakota*– known throughout the fleet as a jinx ship–managed to damage some lesser Japanese vessels but continued to be plagued with electrical and fire control problems. *Washington was now the only intact ship left in the force*, Lippman writes. *In fact, at that moment Washington was the entire U.S. Pacific Fleet. She was the only barrier between (Admiral) Kondo's ships and Guadalcanal. If this one ship did not stop 14 Japanese ships right then and there, America might lose the war.* ... On Washington's bridge, Lieutenant Ray Hunter still had the conn. He had just heard that South Dakota had gone off the air and had seen (destroyers) Walke and Preston *blow sky high*. Dead ahead lay their burning wreckage, while hundreds of men were swimming in the water and Japanese ships were racing in. Hunter had to do something. The course he took now could decide the war. *Come left,* he said, and Washington straightened out on a course parallel to the one on which she had been steaming. Washington's rudder change put the burning destroyers between her and the enemy, preventing her from being silhouetted by their fires. The move made the Japanese momentarily cease fire. Lacking radar, they could not spot Washington behind the fires. ... Meanwhile, Washington raced through burning seas. Everyone could see dozens of men in the water clinging to floating wreckage. Flag Lieutenant Raymond Thompson said, *Seeing that burning, sinking ship as it passed so close aboard, and realizing that there was nothing I, or anyone, could do about it, was a devastating experience.* Commander Ayrault, Washington's executive officer, clambered down ladders, ran to Bart Stoodley's damage-control post, and ordered Stoodley to cut loose life rafts. That saved a lot of lives. But the men in the water had some fight left in them. One was heard to scream, *Get after them, Washington!* Sacrificing their ships by maneuvering into the path of torpedoes intended for the Washington, the captains of the American destroyers had given China Lee one final chance. The Washington was fast, undamaged, and bristling with 16-inch guns. And, thanks to Lt. Hunter's course change, she was also now invisible to the enemy. Blinded by the smoke and flames, the Japanese battleship Kirishima turned on her searchlights, illuminating the helpless South Dakota, and opened fire. Finally, standing out in the darkness, Lee and Davis could positively identify an enemy target. The Washington's main batteries opened fire at 12 midnight precisely. Her new SG radar fire control system worked perfectly. Between midnight and 12:07 a.m., Nov. 14, the *last ship in the U.S. Pacific Fleet* stunned the battleship Kirishima with 75, 16-inch shells. For those aboard the Kirishima, it rained steel. In seven minutes, the Japanese battleship was reduced to a funeral pyre. She went down at 3:25 a.m., the first enemy sunk by an American battleship since the Spanish-American War. Stunned, the remaining Japanese ships withdrew. Within days, Yamamoto and his staff reviewed their mounting losses and recommended the unthinkable to the emperor–withdrawal from Guadalcanal. But who remembers, today, how close-run a thing it was—the ridge held by a single Marine, the battle won by the last American ship? In the autumn of 1942, when the Hasbro Toy Co. called up some years back, asking permission to put the retired colonel's face on some kid's doll, Mitchell Paige thought they must be joking. But they weren't. That's his mug on the little Marine they call *GI Joe*. And now you know.

THE INFANTRYMAN

The average age of the Infantryman is 19 years. He is a short-haired, tight-muscled kid who, under normal circumstances is considered by society as half man, half boy. Not yet dry behind the ears, but old enough to die for his country. He never really cared much for work and he would rather wax his own car than wash his father's; but he has never collected unemployment either.

He's a recent High School graduate; he was probably an average student, pursued some form of sport activities, drives a ten-year old jalopy, and has a steady girlfriend that either broke up with him when he left, or swears to be waiting when he returns from half a world away.

An Infantryman with the 2nd Platoon, B Company, 1/505th Parachute Infantry Regiment, 82nd Airborne Division, Afghanistan, December 2002, returning from his last combat mission.

**Army Specialist
Jeremy K. Carlton.**

He listens to rock and roll or jazz or swing and 155mm Howitzers. He is 10 or 15 pounds lighter now than when he was at home because he is working or fighting from before dawn to well after dusk.

He has trouble spelling, thus letter writing is a pain for him, but he can field strip a rifle in 30 seconds and reassemble it in less. He can recite to you the nomenclature of a machine gun or grenade launcher and use either one effectively if he must. He digs foxholes and latrines and can apply first aid like a professional. He can march until he is told to stop or stop until he is told to march. He obeys orders instantly and without hesitation, but he is not without spirit or individual dignity.

He is self-sufficient. He has two sets of fatigues: he washes one and wears the other. He keeps his canteens full and his feet dry. He sometimes forgets to brush his teeth, but never to clean his rifle. He can cook his own meals, mend his own clothes, and fix his own hurts. If you're thirsty, he'll share his water with you; if you are hungry, his food. He'll even split his ammunition with you in the midst of battle when you run low. He has learned to use his hands like weapons and his weapons like they were his hands. He can save your life–or take it, because that is his job.

He will often do twice the work of a civilian, draw half the pay and still find ironic humor in it all. He has seen more suffering and death than he should have in his short lifetime. He has stood atop mountains of dead bodies, and helped to create them. He has wept in public and in private, for friends who have fallen in combat and is unashamed. Just as did his father, grandfather, and great-grandfather, he is paying the price for our freedom. Beardless or not, he is not a boy. He is the American Fighting Man that has kept this country free for over 200 years. He has asked nothing in return, except our friendship and understanding. Remember him, always, for he has earned our respect and admiration with his blood.

He is an INFANTRYMAN!

The hallmark of the American soldier since Colonial days has been his individuality and resourcefulness.

General Barksdale Hamlett

He plods and groans, sweats and toils, he growls and curses, and at the end he dies, unknown, uncomplaining, with faith in his heart, and on his lips a prayer for victory.

General Douglas MacArthur

The most precious commodity with which the Army deals is the individual soldier who is the heart and soul of our combat forces.

General J. Lawton Collins

THE HIGHEST OBLIGATION AND PRIVILEGE

Lt. Gen. George S. Patton. U.S. Third Army Commander, pins the Silver Star on Private Ernest A. Jenkins of New York City for his conspicuous gallantry in the liberation of Chateaudun, France. 13 October 1944.

The Soldier is the Army. No Army is better than its soldiers. The soldier is also a citizen. In fact, the highest obligation and privilege of citizenship is that of bearing arms for one's country. Hence it is a proud privilege to be a soldier, a good soldier. To be a good soldier a man must have a discipline, self-respect, pride in his unit and in his country, a high sense of duty and obligation to his comrades and to his superiors, and self-confidence born of demonstrated ability.

General George S. Patton, Jr.

THE FRONTLINE COMBAT SOLDIER

1st Battalion, 187th Infantry Regiment, 101st Airborne Division (Air Assault). An Army Infantryman takes a knee and watches for enemy movement during a pause in a road march during Operation Anaconda, Afghanistan.

While a ship may symbolize the Navy and an airplane or long-missile the Air Force, the only completely adequate symbol of the Army is man—the frontline combat soldier. He doesn't float, fly, or fission. He is not a superman, but he must be a little better than most men, a little tougher in character, with stamina, guts, determination, and discipline, and he must be dedicated to his profession, to ensure that our Army will be victorious in the future as it always has been in the past.

General Paul L. Freeman, Jr.

U.S. Marines: No Finer Friend, No Worst Enemy

Found on Sign at Entrance into Camp Rhino, Afghanistan

*There are only two kinds of people that understand
Marines: Marines and the enemy.
Everyone else has a second-hand opinion.*

*U.S. Marines are the most peculiar breed of human beings
I have ever witnessed. They treat service as if it was some
kind of cult, plastering their emblem on almost everything
they own, making themselves look like insane fanatics with
haircuts to ungentlemanly lengths, worshipping their
Commandant almost as if he was a god, and making weird
animal noises like a gang of savages. They'll fight like
rabid dogs at the drop of a hat just for the sake of a little
action, and are the cockiest sons of bitches I have ever
known. Most have the foulest mouths and drink well beyond
man's normal limits, but their high spirits and sense of
brotherhood set them apart and, generally speaking, the
United States Marines I've come in contact with are the
most professional soldiers and the finest men and women
I have ever had the pleasure to meet ...*

Author Unknown

U.S. Army. Soldier from the 2nd Infantry
Second-to-None Division.

Being a Marine is a state of mind. It's an experience some have likened more to a calling than a profession. Being a Marine is not a job, not a paycheck; it's not an occupational specialty. It's no male or female, majority or minority. Nor is it a rank insignia. Stars, bars, or chevrons are only indicators of the responsibility of authority we hold at a given time. Rather, being a Marine comes from the eagle, globe, and anchor tattooed on the soul of every one of us who wears the Marine Corps uniform. It's a searing mark on our innermost being, which comes after the right of passage through boot camp or Officer Candidate School. When a young man or woman is allowed for the first time to say 'I'm a United States Marine,' unlike physical or psychological scars, which over time will tend to heal and fade in intensity, the eagle, globe, and anchor only grow more defined, more intense the longer you are a Marine.

Lieutenant Colonel Jeffrey Wilkinson
As quoted in the December 1997 issue of *Marine Corps Gazette*

DEFINITION OF A MARINE

By General William Thornson, U.S. Army, 1956.

Marines come all sizes, weights, states of sobriety, misery and confusion. He is sly as a fox, has the nerve of a dope addict, the stories of an old sailor, the sincerity of a liar, and the appetite of a horse. He is unreliable, irresponsible, and indestructible.

A Marine is a magical creature; you can lock him out of your house but not your heart, You can take him off your mailing list, but not your mind.

Marines are found everywhere—in bars, in battle, in love, on leave, and in debt. No one could write so seldom and yet think so much of you. No one else could get so much enjoyment out of one letter, civilian clothes, or a six pack of beer.

A Marine is lazy with a deck of cards, a millionaire without a cent, brave without a brain of sense. He is the protector of America with the latest copy of Playboy in his pocket.

When he wants something it is usually a three day pass, a five dollar bill or a standby at home. Girls love them, mothers tolerate them, the United States supports them, and somehow they manage to live together.

No woman can tame him, no man can beat him. He likes girls, females, ladies, dames and members of the opposite sex.

He dislikes answering letters, wearing uniforms, his superiors, getting up for reveille, Marine Corps chow, basic training, and the week before payday.

You might as well give in. He is your long distance lover, your bright eyes, your bundle of worry. Even all of your shattered dreams become insignificant, when he comes home to you and greets you with those innocent spoken words, *Hi!*

The man who will go where his colors go, without asking; who will fight a phantom foe in jungle and mountain range, without counting; and who will suffer and die in the midst of incredible hardship, without complaint, is still what he has always been from Imperial Rome to sceptered Britain to democratic America. He is the stuff of which legions are made. His pride is his colors and his Regiment, his training hard and thorough and coldly realistic to fit him for what he must face, and his obedience is to his orders. As a legionary, he held the gates of civilization for the classical world ... he has been called United States Marine.

Lieutenant Colonel T.R. Fehrenbach, U.S. Army,
from his book, *This Kind of War*

*A*ll militaries harden their recruits, instill the basics, and
bend young men to their will. But the Marine Corps
provides its members with a secret weapon. It gives them
the unique culture of pride that makes the Marines the
world's premier warrior force. 'The Navy has its ships, the
Air Force has its planes, the Army its detailed doctrine, but
culture–the values and assumptions that shape its
members–is all the Marines have.' They call this culture
esprit de corps. Alone among the U.S. military services, the
Marines have bestowed their name on their enlisted ranks.
The Army has Army officers and soldiers, the Navy has
naval officers and sailors, the Air Force has Air Force
officers and airmen–but the Marines have only Marines.

James Bradley, Author of the book, *Flags of Our Fathers*
and son of John Bradley, one of the six men who raised the
American flag on Mount Suribachi, Iwo Jima

*T*he United States Marine Corps is more than 227 years of
romping, stomping death and destruction. Marines are the
finest fighting force this world has ever known. As a
Marine I was born in a foxhole. My mother is Anger and
my father is Pain. Each moment that I live is a deadly
threat upon the life of my country's enemies. I'm a rough-
looking, tough-talking soldier of the sea, but if you can do
it, it ain't bragging. I'm cocky, self-centered, overbearing,
and I will not know the meaning of fear, for I am fear itself.
I own the very ground upon which I stand. I am a green
amphibious monster made of blood and guts and know-
how, who arose from the sea to prey upon America's
enemies across the globe. I feed upon anti-Americanism
wherever it may arise–their hatred of me only makes me
grow stronger. When my time comes, I will die a glorious
death on either the battlefield of combat or the battlefield of
life, giving all I am for my God, my country, and
my Killer by day, lover by night, drunkard
by choice ... Marine By God!

Author Unknown

*A Marine is a rain cooled, foot powered,
spam fed, semi-automatic fighting machine,
never known to have a stoppage.*

Master Sergeant (Retired) W. Lord, U.S. Marine Corps

HEART, LEADERSHIP AND THE AMERICAN SOLDIER

Remarks by Major (USAR) William T. Coffey, Jr., to about 700 soldiers participating in the Sergeant Audie Murphy Club (SAMC) Induction and the Fort Carson and 7th Infantry Division Soldier and NCO of the Year ceremonies, 1 July 2002, Fort Carson, Colorado.

Thank you for that warm introduction. MG Campbell, Mrs. Campbell, Colonel (Promotable) Reece, Colonel and Mrs. Castle, Sergeants Majors, soldiers of Fort Carson, members of the Colorado Springs military community and special guests.

It is certainly my honor to speak here today. Whenever I get the chance to speak with soldiers I take it, because I cannot think of a greater or more prestigious group to speak to than a group of American soldiers.

President Franklin D. Roosevelt once stated: *We cannot always build the future for our youth, but we can build our youth for the future.* This morning I'd like to talk about the REASON WHY, the REASON WHY we serve, why we build our youthful soldiers for our nation's future, why we recruit, equip, train, lead, motivate, retain, physically and mentally challenge, sacrifice for, inspire and develop great soldiers.

I think it's important to discuss the REASONS WHY. When confronted with this question most people readily answer, *The REASON WHY is to fight and win our nation's wars.* And if you believe that, you are correct. But that's the easy and readily apparent answer. What I'd like to discuss with you this morning is an answer that goes beyond the obvious, one that goes to a greater depth, and it is the harder, less often discussed and less obvious REASON WHY. And I believe we must discuss this REASON WHY since it is absolutely central to what we do as a nation, and what we do as an Army, and it is central to what we do as soldiers. This REASON WHY has produced the greatest soldiers this world has ever seen. Soldiers who comprise an Army that is clearly the best, most respected and most feared ground force in the world today.

In preparing my notes for this morning I had to reflect back about a year and a half ago when I was preparing some notes for a similar presentation for some Air Force Cadets up at the Air Force Academy. I was asked to talk about a topic on leadership, but I didn't want to just talk about leadership in general, what I wanted to talk about was one specific aspect of leadership that is unique to our Army. It is an aspect of leadership that is near and dear to my heart. It was a topic that I felt profoundly compelled to discuss. The topic was *Leaders Who Develop Leaders*. So for about a week and a half I put together my notes, and I had about 10 things I wanted to mention and discuss. But about two days out I was feeling uncomfortable because I could not actually articulate and encapsulate what I was trying to say ... into something like a *slogan* or a *bumper sticker*, or a *takeaway point*. It was two days before the presentation and I was on a TDY [Temporary Duty] trip back at Fort Monroe and I was sitting in my hotel room and I was watching TV, and for some strange reason this commercial came on television and it just captured me. The first thing it showed was two golden retrievers running in slow motion across a field. They looked healthy and happy, and genetically pure, and well groomed. Their hair and the grass were waving ... it was all in slow motion. Then a soft voice came on and said, *People don't raise champion dogs for money ... they do it for the love of the breed.* [It was a Pedigree Dog Food commercial] Immediately I grabbed my pen and a piece of paper and I wrote down these words, and I said, *That's it! That's the takeaway point.* The REASON WHY we do this, the REASON WHY we serve and sacrifice is for the love of the breed. And of course I'm not talking about canine dogs, but rather AMERICAN DOGS OF WAR ... you guys. No, we don't do it for money ... it ain't about money. It's about the love of the breed.

And the type of love I'm talking about is not a sexual or a romantic love, but rather, a deep, unconditional, and abiding love that's based on service and sacrifice, hardship and duty, commitment, loyalty and love, and selflessness. It is the deepest and most profound of all loves. And when we as leaders employ this love towards our soldiers, we do it for the purpose of developing and training great soldiers, and great leaders. Leadership among all soldiers (or as I like to call it, *Leadership at all levels*) is something the other Army's don't have. It is something that is very unique to the American Army. And at the heart of American leadership ... is the heart. In 1993 there was a Sergeant First Class who wrote a letter to the Editor of the NCO Journal, and in that letter she wrote something that is perhaps my favorite quote of all time, since it says so much with so few words. She wrote, *Heart is what makes the American soldier.*

This morning I'd like to share with you a few stories that illustrate the heart, the leadership and the love of the American soldier.

About a year ago I had a conversation with a WWII veteran whom several years ago went over to Germany to celebrate a 50th reunion. Also invited to this reunion were German WWII veterans who fought Americans. So this German comes up to this American Vet and says, *You know, if I had to fight any other army in the world, Americans would be the last ones that I would ever want to fight.* So the American says, *Why's that?* And the German says, *Whenever I'd fight American units, the first thing we would do is shoot off the Captains, and then the Lieutenants would take over, then we'd shoot off the Lieutenants, and then the senior NCOs would take over, and then we'd shoot off the senior NCOs and the junior NCOs would take over.* He said, *No matter what we did, your American units kept on fighting. And that's unfair.*

And of course the American didn't know how to respond. And that's an example of leadership at all levels.

Now let's turn the clock up to the Korean War. One night during the Korean War, Private First Class (PFC) Minelli, a trumpeter assigned as a Division Artillery (DIVARTY) night duty clerk, single-handedly directed a successful artillery battle. The duty officer was exhausted, and PFC Minelli did not want to wake him; so, at 0100, when the battle began with the receipt of the first reports of incoming mortar shell attacks, he responded to each requirement. By 0330 the 54 guns of the division artillery were all in action plus the corps artillery with four battalions was well into its counter battery plan. More than 3,000 artillerymen were hard at work ... The subdued thunder of artillery fire was ... constant and omni directional. The sky was lighted by gun flashes from three quadrants.

During all this the division artillery commander and his staff slept on. Any artilleryman worth his salt can sleep through a fire mission with his cot 50 yards from the gun position, and unless he is purposely awakened will never know that the guns have fired. After the battle, Minelli completed the duty log, and when the duty officer woke, Minelli told him that everything was fine, though he added that he had managed to keep busy all night. By this time the day crew had begun to straggle into the bunker and the duty officer went off to shave ... A few minutes later ... the DIVARTY commander came in and said: *Can anyone here inform me concerning an artillery battle fought last night? ... The division commander ... complimented me on the conduct of this division artillery fight throughout the engagement.*

It took some time to pry the whole story out of PFC Minelli; and after the DIVARTY Commander had been briefed, he drummed his fingers on the desktop and dictated two short memos. The first consisted of additional instructions to the night duty officer ... *The officer in charge will take such steps as are necessary to prevent Private First Class Minelli from assuming command of the division and corps artillery.* ... The second note was a directive to the adjutant ordering Minelli's promotion to Corporal. Again, leadership at all levels.

Now let's turn the clock up to Operation Enduring Freedom. A couple of months ago, a small number of officers from the Pentagon and the Army's Center for Army Lessons Learned (CALL), at Fort Leavenworth, Kansas, took a fact-finding mission over to Afghanistan. And one particular Colonel sent out what was somewhat of an unofficial assessment of what he saw. It was a very interesting and insightful report. I'd like to share with you one paragraph of an observation made about two months ago concerning American soldiers in combat. He said:

> Our soldiers are GOOD. An Al Quida commander was killed, he was a Chechen national. On his body was a diary that compared fighting the U.S. with fighting Russians. He noted that when you take out the Russian leader, the units stop and mill about, not sure of what to do next. But he added that when you take out a U.S. leader, somebody always and quickly takes his place with no loss of momentum. A squad leader goes down; it may be a private that steps up to the plate before they can iron out the new chain or command. And the damn thing is that the private knows what the hell he is doing. When units came under fire immediately after disembarking from a helicopter, it was not uncommon for two members of squad, without orders, to suppress the enemy and do the buddy team fire and maneuver. No need to fret about the quality of our troops from O-3 on down.

Also, in the same timeframe, Sergeant Major of the Army Jack Tilley went over on his own fact-finding mission. After his return, he sent out an e-mail based on his observations. So let me share with you a portion of that e-mail which I, in a very indirect way, received on my computer.

Sergeant Major of the Army Jack Tilley.
Afghanistan, 6 April 2002.
Photo by PFC Christopher Stanis.

From talking to sergeants who were on the ground in the Afghanistan highlands during Anaconda, I came away again impressed with the importance of the basic fundamentals of soldiering.

I was told their time on the rifle range paid off, as their basic marksmanship skills and the M-4 rifles allowed them to consistently hit targets more than 400 yards away. Their physical and mental stamina also served them well in the steep, barren terrain where the air was thin. One movement by soldiers of the 187th Infantry Regiment was expected to take as long as two days, but these Rakkasans soldiers, as they are nicknamed, did it in about eight hours.

Equally impressive to me was the fact that there were minimal cold weather injuries reported during Anaconda, despite temperatures that plunged as soon as the sun went down and the minimal amount of cold weather gear carried by the soldiers.

All these things–physical conditioning, marksmanship, and cold weather injury prevention–are NCO business, and–if Operation

Anaconda is any indicator–our sergeants know their business quite well.

I was especially proud of the performance of our younger soldiers for another reason. People–including some of us–have been quick to run down the soldiers who have joined the Army in recent years, saying they somehow don't measure up to their predecessors. I wish anyone really believing that could have been with me on that trip, both to hear stories of their performance and see the fire in their eyes. Today's soldiers are as good as any that have ever worn our Army's uniforms. Period.

Most everyone in this audience knows about the story of Flight 93 over a field in Pennsylvania on September 11th. The one hero that emerged, by name, was that of Todd Beamer. He knew that the plane was being hijacked, so he got on his cell phone and he called his wife. And what he didn't know, his wife told him, about what was happening in New York City and at the Pentagon. And he knew what he had to do, so he rallied a few guys together, other passengers, and they made the decision to storm the cockpit, to take back this plane from these terrorists. And we know that his last words on his cell phone to his wife were, *Are you guys ready, Let's Roll!* We know those words, but what a lot of us don't know is that the Federal Aviation Administration was able to recover the *black box* out of that cockpit. They were able to transcribe the Arabic words spoken in that cockpit and translate it into English. And the last two words spoken by a terrorist in that cockpit were, *They're Coming!*

On that note, let me speak a few words of wisdom to our enemy.

Dear Mr. Taliban and Mr. Al Qaeda and any other enemy of freedom wherever you are.

I have a short and simple message for you.

Your first and most critical mistake was to show up to a Jihad with box cutters. Even worse, you wielded your hatred toward America ... and now ... you must deal with the American soldier.

Let me tell you something about my soldiers ...

My soldiers, these AMERICAN DOGS OF WAR, come in all colors, sizes, ages, religions and economic and ethnic backgrounds. They come in both male and female versions. They originate from all corners of the globe, to include yours, and represent the entire color spectrum of the Human Rainbow. Many of our soldiers even come from Texas—and you should know NEVER TO MESS WITH TEXAS. Our Commander in Chief is a Texan. My soldiers are all volunteers, which is another way of telling you that they will all voluntarily engage you on the battlefield.

They are men and women of morals and principles, values and character. Their hearts overflow with the perfect ideals of freedom, liberty and equality ... ideals that have built our great nation. My soldiers have compassion–but they don't have any compassion for you. My soldiers won't forgive you, it's not in their duty description; your God may forgive you, we won't—but it is in our duty description to arrange the meeting.

My soldiers are all leaders. They are brought into our Army as an *Army of One* and then molded into an *Army of One Team*–it is a team based on love and common hardship and common sacrifice, and a shared vision for a better world. It is a military team that you are unable to break, as well as unable to understand. My soldiers' battle record for over 200 years should provide you reason for concern.

My soldiers also possess an arsenal that makes them the best in their business. Let me tell you about a few weapons they have at their disposal.

- They have long-range, precision MORALS.
- And 155MM High-Explosive PATRIOTIC HEARTS.
- They have day/night all-weather LOYALTY.
- They have BRAVERY AND COURAGE set on the *FULL AUTOMATIC* option also known as the *Rock and Roll* selection.

- They have limitless supplies of LEADERSHIP and low-flying, high-performance INTEGRITY.
- My soldiers have highly maneuverable INITIATIVE.
- Their DUTY is battle-site zeroed.
- They have HOOAH–and I-EE-AHH, and other expressions of their WARRIOR SPIRIT, which is something you'll never understand.
- They have total Situational Awareness of their HONOR.
- Their POL [Petroleum, Oil and Lubricants] is SELFLESSNESS.
- The backbone to their Command and Control structure is RESPECT.

They are ready and capable, willing, strong and determined. They are energized by pride and esprit de corps, camaraderie and love of each other and country. These AMERICAN DOGS OF WAR are your worst nightmare and the pride of our nation.

So, next time you want to show up to a Jihad with box cutters: first, read our history. And then look at our soldiers—soldiers just like those here today. Then ask

Infantrymen. These are the men of the 2nd Platoon, B Company, 1-505th Parachute Infantry Regiment, 82nd Airborne Division in Afghanistan, December 2002.

yourself, *Do I really want to mess with the American soldier?* Then remember those immortal last words from your comrade who hijacked Flight 93 over Pennsylvania.

That's right, Mr. Taliban .... WE'RE COMING!

I'd like to close my remarks this morning with a short and simple poem entitled *I am a Soldier*. I don't know who the author is and I provide it without elaboration.

I AM A SOLDIER

*I am a soldier. My blood permeates
the soil of many countries.*

*I have gasped my last breath on many a
desolate stretch of beach.*

*For you ... all of you, the children who play in the parks,
the mothers who watch over them, the fathers who
struggle to sustain them.*

*There are those here who have belittled and reviled me,
who have made a mockery of me and what I stand for. You,
also, have I suffered and died for.*

*I withstood heat, insects and disease so the
right to dissent would be yours.*

*I endured the pain and terror of battle and the maiming of
my body to ensure that you might worship as you please.*

*I died in agony in order that you, no matter who or what
you are, have the freedom to choose your own destinies.*

*AND I WOULD DO IT AGAIN because I believe in the
ideals that made this country what it is today ... FREE.*

*I love her with a deep and abiding love that
transcends mere physical pain.*

I AM A SOLDIER.

*Pray that I will always be there, for if I disappear
from this country, so will you.*

WHY WE ARE HERE		
OCT 1983	MARINE BARRACKS BEIRUT, LEBANON	243
DEC 1988	PAN AM FLT 103 LOCKERBIE, SCOTLAND	244
FEB 1993	WORLD TRADE CENTER NYC, NY	6
JUN 1996	KHOBAR TOWERS DHAHRAN, SA	19
AUG 1998	US EMBASSIES KENYA/TANZANIA	224
OCT 2000	USS COLE ADEN, YEMEN	17
SEP 11 TH 2001	WORLD TRADE CENTER NYC, NY	3000 +
	PENTAGON WASHINGTON DC	
	UNITED AIRLINES FLT 93	

Stenciled Sign. Found on the side of the *USS Iwo Jima* en route to operations supporting Operation Iraqi Freedom.

THE CREATION OF THE MARINE CORPS

In the beginning was God, and all else was darkness and void, and without form. So God created the heavens and the Earth. He created the sun, and the moon, and the stars, so that light might pierce the darkness. God divided the Earth between the land and the sea, and these he filled with many assorted creatures. And the dark, salty, slimy creatures that inhabited the murky depths of the oceans, God called sailors. And He dressed them accordingly.

They had little trousers that looked like bells at the bottom. And their shirts had cute little flaps on them to hide the hickeys on their necks. He also gave them long sideburns and shabby looking beards. God nicknamed them *squids* and banished them to a lifetime at sea so normal folks would not have to associate with them. To further identify these unloved creatures, He called them *petty* and *commodore*, instead of titles worthy of red-blooded men.

And the flaky creatures of the land, God called soldiers. And with a twinkle in His eye, and a sense of humor that only He could have, God made their trousers too short and their covers too large. He also made their pockets oversized, so that they may warm their hands. And to adorn their uniforms, God gave them badges in quantities that only a dime store owner could appreciate. And He gave them emblems and crests ... and all sorts of shiny things that glittered ... and devices that dangled. (When you are God you tend to get carried away).

On the sixth day, He thought about creating some air creatures for which He designed a Greyhound bus driver's uniform, especially for Air Force flyboys. But He discarded the idea during the first week, and it was not until years later that some apostles resurrected this theme and established what we now know as the *wild blue yonder wonders*.

And on the seventh day, as you know, God rested. But on the eighth day, at 0730, God looked down upon the earth and was not happy. God was not happy! So, He thought about His labors, and in His divine wisdom God created a divine creature. And this He called a Marine.

And these Marines, who God created in His own image, were to be of the air, and of the land, and of the sea. And these He gave many wonderful uniforms. Some were green, some were blue with red trim. And in the early days, some were even a beautiful tan. He gave them practical fighting uniforms, so that they could wage war against the forces of Satan and evil. He gave them service uniforms for their daily work and training. And He gave them evening and dress uniforms ... sharp and stylish, handsome things, so that they might promenade with their ladies on Saturday night and impress the hell out of everybody! He even gave them swords, so that people, who were not impressed, could be dealt with accordingly.

And at the end of the eighth day, God looked down upon the Earth and saw that it was good. But was God happy? NO! God was still not happy! Why? Because in the course of His labors God had forgotten one thing, He did not have a Marine uniform for Himself. But He thought about it, and thought about it, and finally satisfied Himself in knowing that, well ... NOT EVERYBODY CAN BE A MARINE!

I now make it
my earnest prayer,
that God would ...
incline the hearts
of the Citizens ...
to entertain
a brotherly affection
and love for one another ...
and particularly
for their brethren
who have served in the field ...

President George Washington

*H*ate war, but love the American warrior.

Lieutenant General Harold G. Moore (Retired)

**U.S. Naval Aviators of the USS Lexington, Pacific Ocean,
World War II.** These pilots just returned from shooting down
17 of 20 Japanese Zero fighters they engaged.

CHAPTER 9

LIBERTY, FREEDOM AND PATRIOTISM

Patriotism is the process of loving, supporting and defending one's nation. American patriots love, support and defend America, with an emphasis on that which makes America great, namely, our liberty and freedoms. This chapter provides insights into American patriotism and the value of our freedoms.

No man is entitled to the blessings of liberty unless he be vigilant in its preservation.

General Douglas MacArthur

Strait is the gate and narrow is the way that leads to liberty, and few nations, if any, have found it.

President John Adams

When President George W. Bush, visiting a New York primary school, was asked to write down why he loved the U.S., he didn't have to think. He wrote, *Because I love freedom.*

USS Kitty Hawk Aircraft Carrier. Sailors spell *FREEDOM*, 18 December 2001. This photo was taken as the *Kitty Hawk* was returning to her base at Yokosuka, Japan, following a deployment in support of Operation Enduring Freedom. Photo by Airman Lee McCaskill.

There are five reasons why we live in a free country and they are the Air Force, the Army, the Coast Guard, the Marines and the Navy. Because of them I am one proud American.

Nikki Mendicino, 14 years old

To attain freedom is mankind's highest aspiration.
To use freedom wisely is mankind's urgent responsibility.
To preserve freedom is mankind's continuing challenge.

Edwin Meese

FREEDOM IS THE VICTOR

Excerpts from remarks at the Brandenburg Gate, Berlin, by President Ronald Reagan, 12 June 1987.

The Brandenburg Gate and the Berlin Wall separate Berlin into East and West. In spite of the changes that are going on in Communist countries, especially the Soviet Union, that wall is a reminder of the difference between freedom and totalitarianism. The people of East Berlin are walled in with barbed wire and booby-trapped explosives. Our advance people had put up speakers aimed at East Berlin, hoping that my speech might be heard on the other side. I could see the East German police keeping people away so that they couldn't hear. They simply don't realize it's going to take more than that to keep out the stirrings of freedom. In the 1950s, Khrushchev predicted: *We will bury you.* But in the West today, we see a free world that has achieved a level of prosperity and well being unprecedented in all human history. In the Communist world, we see failure, technological backwardness, declining standards of health; even want of the most basic kind–too little food. Even today, the Soviet Union still cannot feed itself. After these four decades, then, there stands before the entire world one great and inescapable conclusion: Freedom leads to prosperity. Freedom replaces the ancient hatreds among the nations with comity and peace. Freedom is the victor.

Where liberty dwells, there is my country.

Benjamin Franklin, Statesman, Scientist, Inventor, Diplomat 1706-1790

Freedom from fear and injustice and oppression
will be ours only in the measure that men who value such
freedom are ready to sustain its possession—to defend it
against every thrust from within and without.

President Dwight D. Eisenhower

Freedom—no word was ever spoken that has
held out greater hope, demanded greater sacrifice,
needed to be nurtured, blessed more the giver, damned
more its destroyer, or come closer to being God's will on earth.
And I think that's worth fighting for, if necessary.

General Omar N. Bradley

HUMAN SHIELDS AND HEROES

In March, 2003 the Shelby County Alabama Legislative Delegation hosted a *Stand Up for America Rally*. More than 1,200 people attended including featured speakers Chief Justice Roy Moore, Adjutant General Mark Bowen and Alabama State Auditor Beth Chapman. Below is Mrs. Chapman's speech, which resulted in five standing ovations, tremendous applause and an encore.

I'm here tonight because men and women of the United States military have given their lives for my freedom. I am not here tonight because Sheryl Crowe, Rosie O'Donnell, Martin Sheen, George Clooney, Jane Fonda or Phil Donahue, sacrificed their lives for me.

If my memory serves me correctly, it was not movie stars or musicians, but the United States Military who fought on the shores of Iwo Jima, the jungles of Vietnam, and the beaches of Normandy. Tonight, I say we should support the President of the United States and the U.S. Military and tell the liberal, tree-hugging, Birkenstock-wearing, hippy, tie-dyed liberals to go make their movies and music and whine somewhere else. After all, if they lived in Iraq, they wouldn't be allowed the freedom of speech they're being given here today. Ironically, they would be put to death at the hands of Saddam Hussein or Osama Bin Laden. I want to know how the very people, who are against war because of the loss of life, can possibly be the same people who are for abortion? They are the same people who are for animal rights but against the rights of the unborn. The movie stars say they want to go to Iraq and serve as *human shields* for the Iraqis. I say let them buy a one-way ticket and go. No one likes war. I hate war! But the one thing I hate more is the fact that this country has been forced into war–innocent people have lost their lives–and there but for the grace of God, it could have been my brother, my husband, or even worse my own son. On December 7, 1941, there are no records of movie stars treading the blazing waters of Pearl Harbor.

On September 11, 2001, there are no photos of movie stars standing as *human shields* against the debris and falling bodies … from the World Trade Center. There were only policemen and firemen–underpaid civil servants who gave their all with nothing expected in return. When the *USS Cole* was bombed, there were no movie stars guarding the ship—where were the human shields then?

If America's movie stars want to be human shields, let them shield the gang-ridden streets of Los Angeles, or New York City, let them shield the lives of the children of North Birmingham whose mothers lay them down to sleep on the floor each night to shelter them from stray bullets.

If they want to be human shields, I say let them shield the men and women of honesty and integrity that epitomizes courage and embody the spirit of freedom by wearing the proud uniforms of the United States Military. Those are the people who have earned and deserve shielding!

Throughout the course of history, this country has remained free, not because of movie stars and liberal activists, but because of brave men and women who hated war too. However, they lay down their lives so that we all may live in freedom. After all– *Greater love hath no man, than that he lay down his life for his friend*, or in this case a country. We should give our military honor and acknowledgement and not let their lives be in vain.

If you want to see true human shields, walk through Arlington Cemetery. There lie human shields, heroes, and the BRAVE Americans who didn't get on television and talk about being a human shield—they were human shields. I thank God tonight for freedom–those who bought and paid for it with their lives in the past–those who will protect it in the present and defend it in the future.

America has remained silent too long! God-fearing people have remained silent too long! We must lift our voices united in a humble prayer to God for guidance and the strength and courage to sustain us throughout whatever the future may hold.

After the tragic events of Sept. 11th, my then eleven-year-old son said terrorism is a war against them and us and if you're not one of us, then you're one of them. So in closing tonight, let us be of one accord, let us stand proud, and let us be the human shields of prayer, encouragement and support for the President, our troops and their families and our country.

May God bless America, the land of the free, the home of the brave and the greatest country on the face of this earth!

THIS FLAG MAY FADE,
YET THESE COLORS DON'T RUN

A protest raged on a courthouse lawn,
Round a makeshift stage they charged on,
Fifteen hundred or more they say,
Had come to burn a Flag that day.

A boy held up the folded Flag,
Cursed it, and called it a dirty rag,
An OLD MAN pushed through the angry crowd,
With a rusty shotgun shouldered proud.

His uniform jacket was old and tight,
He had polished each button, shiny and bright,
He crossed that stage with a soldier's grace,
Until he and the boy stood face to face.

FREEDOM OF SPEECH, the OLD MAN said,
Is worth dying for, good men are dead,
So you can stand on this courthouse lawn,
And talk us down from dusk to dawn,
But before any Flag gets burned today,
This OLD MAN IS GOING TO HAVE HIS SAY!

My father died on a foreign shore,
In a war they said would end all war,
But Tommy and I wasn't even full grown,
Before we fought in a war of our own.

And Tommy died on Iwo Jima's beach,
In the shadow of a hill he couldn't quite reach,
Where six good men raised this Flag so high,
That the WHOLE DAMN WORLD COULD SEE IT FLY.

I got this bum leg that I still drag,
Fighting for this same old Flag,
Now there's but one shot in this old gun,
So now it's time to decide which one,
Which one of you will follow our lead,
To stand and die for what you believe?
For as sure as there is a rising sun,
You'll burn in Hell 'fore this Flag burns, son.'

Now this riot never came to pass.
The crowd got quiet and that can of gas,
Got set aside as they walked away,
To talk about what they had heard this day.

And the boy who had called it a 'dirty rag'
Handed the OLD SOLDIER the folded Flag
So the battle of the Flag this day was won
By a tired OLD SOLDIER with a rusty gun,
Who for one last time, had to show to some
THIS FLAG MAY FADE, YET THESE COLORS DON'T RUN.

Author Unknown

Freedom is the result of military victory.

Second Lieutenant R.B. Thieme, Jr., 1972

We are all Americans. And as Americans,
we have a duty to protect the freedoms that make our union the
example and the envy of the world.

Charlton Heston

DEARNESS GIVES EVERYTHING ITS VALUE

These are the times that try men's souls. The summer soldier and
the sunshine patriot will, in this crisis, shrink from the service of
their country; but he that stands it now, deserves the love and
thanks of man and woman. Tyranny, like hell, is not easily
conquered; yet we have this consolation with us, that the harder
the conflict, the more glorious the triumph. What we obtain too
cheap, we esteem too lightly: it is dearness only that gives
everything its value. Heaven knows how to put a proper price
upon its goods; and it would be strange indeed, if so celestial
an article as FREEDOM should not be highly rated.

Thomas Paine

I long for peace. But I also understand that if we do not lead
the world against terror, that your children and our grandchildren
will not grow up in a society that is as free as the society
we have today. Freedom is the precious gift that
one generation can pass to the next. It is a gift and a promise
that I intend to keep to the American children.

President George W. Bush

Every victory for human freedom
will be a victory for world peace.

President Ronald Reagan

I confess that in America I saw more than America;
I sought the image of democracy itself, with its inclinations, its
character, its prejudices, and its passions, in order to learn what
we have to fear or hope from its progress.

Alexis de Tocqueville, French Author, wrote extensively about the
American people and its political institutions. 1805-1859

P atriotism is as much a virtue as justice,
and is as necessary for the support of societies
as natural affection is for the support of families.

Dr. Benjamin Rush

T rue patriotism is of no party.

Tobias Smollett

THE MUSTARD AND THE CREAM

On July 3, 1944, Mr. Elwyn Brooks White, Author, Columnist,
1899-1985, from the Writer's War Board wrote *The New Yorker*
magazine a response to the solicited query, *The Meaning of
Democracy*. Mr. White wrote:

Surely the Board knows what democracy is. It is the line
that forms on the right. It is the *don't* in Don't Shove. It is the hole
in the stuffed shirt through which the sawdust slowly trickles. It is
the dent in the high hat. Democracy is the recurrent suspicion that
more than half the people are right more than half the time. It is the
feeling of privacy in the voting booths, the feeling of communion
in the libraries, the feeling of vitality everywhere. Democracy is
the score at the beginning of the ninth. It is an idea which hasn't
been disproved yet, a song the words of which have not gone bad.
It's the mustard on the hot dog and the cream in the rationed
coffee. Democracy is a request from a War Board, in the middle of
a morning in the middle of a war, wanting to know what
democracy is.

YOU'RE A GRAND OLD FLAG

Tony and Sonny Mayer.
Circa 1918, both grew up to
serve our country in WWII.

You're a grand old flag,

You're a high flying flag,

And forever in peace may you wave.

You're the emblem of, the land I love,

The home of the free and the brave.

*Ev'ry heart beats true 'neath the
Red, White and Blue,*

Where there's never a boast or brag.

*But should auld acquaintance
be forgot,*

Keep your eye on the grand old flag.

Song by George M. Cohan

THE *FOUR FREEDOMS SPEECH*

By President Franklin D. Roosevelt, State of the Union, delivered to the 77th Congress, January 6, 1941.

In the future days which we seek to make secure, we look forward to the world founded upon four essential human freedoms.

The first is freedom of speech and expression–everywhere in the world.

The second is freedom of every person to worship God in his own way–everywhere in the world.

The third is freedom from want, which translated into world terms, means economic understandings which will secure to every nation a healthy peacetime life for its inhabitant–everywhere in the world.

The fourth is freedom from fear, which, translated into world terms, means a worldwide reduction of armaments to such a point and in such a thorough fashion that no nation will be in a position to commit an act of physical aggression against any neighbor–anywhere in the world.

That is no vision of a distant millennium. It is a definite basis for a kind of world attainable in our own time and generation. That kind of world is the very antithesis of the so-called *new order* of tyranny which the dictators seed to create with a bomb crash.

To that new order we oppose the greater conception—the moral order. A good society is able to face schemes of world domination and foreign revolutions alike without fear. Since the beginning of our American history we have been engaged in change, in a perpetual, peaceful revolution, a revolution which goes on steadily, quietly, adjusting itself to changing conditions without the concentration camp or the quicklime in the ditch. The world order which we seek is the cooperation of free countries, working together in a friendly, civilized society. This nation has placed its destiny in the hands, heads and hearts of its millions of free men and women, and its faith in freedom under the guidance of God. Freedom means the supremacy of human rights everywhere. Our support goes to those who struggle to gain those rights and keep them. Our strength is our unity of purpose. To that high concept there can be no end save victory.

HELLO FREEDOM MAN!

President Reagan's 1988 Farewell Speech broadcast live from the Oval Office on nationwide radio and television.

I've been thinking a bit at that window. I've been reflecting on what the past eight years have meant and mean. And the image that comes to mind like a refrain is a nautical one—a small story about a big ship, and a refugee, and a sailor. It was back in the early eighties, at the height of the boat people. And the sailor was hard at work on the carrier Midway, which was patrolling the South China Sea. The sailor, like most American servicemen, was young, smart, and fiercely observant. The crew spied on the horizon a leaky little boat. And crammed inside were refugees from Indochina hoping to get to America. The Midway sent a small launch to bring them to the ship and safety. As the refugees made their way through the choppy seas, one spied the sailor on deck, and stood up, and called out to him. He yelled, *Hello, American sailor. Hello, freedom man.* A small moment with a big meaning, a moment the sailor, who wrote it in a letter, couldn't get out of his mind. And, when I saw it, neither could I. Because that's what it was to be an American in the 1980's. We stood, again, for freedom. I know we always have, but in the past few years the world again–and in a way, we ourselves–rediscovered it. It's been quite a journey this decade, and we held together through some stormy seas. And at the end, together, we are reaching our destination.

Ours was the first revolution in the history of mankind that truly reversed the course of government, and with three little words: *We the People. We the People* tell the government what to do; it doesn't tell us. *We the People* are the driver; the government is the car. And we decide where it should go, and by what route, and how fast. Almost all the world's constitutions are documents in which governments tell the people what their privileges are. Our Constitution is a document in which *We the People* tell the government what it is allowed to do. *We the People* are free.

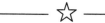

*P*atriotism is that love for country in the hearts of the people
which shall make that country strong to resist foreign opposition
and domestic intrigue–which impresses each and every individual
with a sense of the inalienable rights of others and prepares him to
accept the responsibility of protecting those rights.

American Tribune, March 7, 1890

*T*he Pilgrims came to America not to accumulate riches but to
worship God, and the greatest wealth they left unborn generations
was their heroic example of sacrifice that their souls might be free.

Harry Moyle Tippett

*T*he history of free men is never really written by
chance but by choice—their choice.

President Dwight D. Eisenhower

We've made mistakes along the way, but that's no reason to start tearing up the best flag God ever gave to any country.

John Wayne

WARTS AND ALL

We love this country ... warts and all. We love what it has been ... what it is now ... and even more ... we love what America can be. We're lucky God chose us to spend our lives here ... In return for that, we should pay our dues ... Let's plan our lives in such a way that America will not forget what we chipped in along our ways ...

John Wayne

MY NAME IS OLD GLORY

I am the flag of the United States of America. My name is Old Glory. I fly atop the world's tallest buildings. I stand watch in America's halls of justice.

I fly majestically over institutions of learning. I stand guard with power in the world. Look up and see me.

I stand for peace, honor, truth and justice. I stand for freedom. I am confident. I am arrogant. I am proud.

When I am flown with my fellow banners, My head is a little higher, My colors a little truer.

I bow to no one! I am recognized all over the world. I am worshipped–I am saluted. I am loved–I am revered. I am respected–and I am feared.

I have fought in every battle of every war for more then 200 years. I was flown at Valley Forge, Gettysburg, Shiloh and Appomattox. I was there at San Juan Hill, the trenches of France, in the Argonne Forest, Anzio, Rome and the beaches of Normandy.

Guam, Okinawa, Korea and Khe San, Saigon, Vietnam know me.
I was there. I led my troops, I was dirty, battle worn and tired,
But my soldiers cheered me and I was proud.

I have been burned, torn and trampled on the streets of countries I
have helped set free. It does not hurt for I am invincible.

I have been soiled upon, burned, torn and trampled in the streets of
my country. And when it's done by those Whom I've served in
battle—it hurts. But I shall overcome—for I am strong.

I have slipped the bonds of Earth and stood watch over the
uncharted frontiers of space from my vantage point on the moon.
I have borne silent witness to all of America's finest hours.
But my finest hours are yet to come.

When I am torn into strips and used as bandages
for my wounded comrades on the battlefield,
When I am flown at half-mast to honor my soldier,
Or when I lie in the trembling arms of a grieving parent
at the grave of their fallen son or daughter,

I am proud.

My Name Is Old Glory Long May I Wave.
Dear God In Heaven Long May I Wave!

Author Unknown

Apollo 12. American astronaut erects
Old Glory on the Moon.

SILENT PRAISE

As I face the stately flagstaff,
To give my silent praise.
Old Glory seems to answer,
With every fold that waves.
I hear the ropes a 'clinkin,'
As the breeze stirs their calm.
The only sound to break the hush,
On this early morn.
The birth rays of the day,
Light her colors bright.
She represents our freedom,
And our country's might.
Many think the colors,
Are toys to be waved.
But many have given all,
And lie in forgotten graves.
These and those that follow,
Heroes not intent to be.
Preserve the peace for all,
And our country ever free.

Master Sergeant (Retired) Joe Maddox, USAF

Ceremony at the Pentagon. 11 September 2002.

*Gold is good in its place, but living, brave,
patriotic men are better than gold.*

President Abraham Lincoln

THE GLUE THAT BINDS

*America is a nation of many patriots–ordinary citizens
bound together by the opportunity to give back to a nation that
has given so much to us. Ordinary people fulfilling the promise
of America. We embrace patriotism as both an honor
and a duty–a debt to the nation and to one another. It is a
commitment the diverse people of this great land have revered
since our earliest days of gaining independence because of our
faith in this place we call America. Our patriotism is the glue that
binds the incredible medley of our many heritages into a union
stronger than our many parts–a nation that seeks out great and
noble causes, not just for ourselves, but for the good of all.*

Colin Powell, Secretary of State
General, U.S. Army, Vietnam and Desert Storm

HC-130. The crew and others stand in front of the aircraft
dedicated to Michael F. Lynch, a lieutenant in the New York
Fire Department who lost his life saving others at the World
Trade Center Towers on 11 September 2001. Photo by
Master Sgt. Randy L. Mitchell.

THE BRAVE AND FREE

Years after that historic battle at Fort McHenry between U.S. and British forces, Francis Scott Key told an audience in his hometown of Frederick, Maryland:

I saw the flag of my country waving over a city–the strength and pride of my native State–a city devoted to plunder and desolation by its assailants. I witnessed the

Old Glory. Fort McHenry.

preparations for its assaults. I saw the array of its enemies as they advanced to the attack. I heard the sound of battle; the noise of conflict fell upon my listening ear, and it told me that 'the brave and the free' had met the invaders.

Francis Scott Key, Author of the Star Spangled Banner

Patriotism means to stand by the country. It does not mean to stand by the president ...

President Theodore Roosevelt

Democracy is two wolves and a lamb voting what to have for dinner. Liberty is a well-armed lamb contesting the vote.

Benjamin Franklin, 1759

Patriotism is the love for, or devotion to, one's country. Devotion, in this case, is defined as the fact or state of being ardently dedicated and loyal. Patriotism requires allegiance to the flag, which means obedience and readiness.

Author Unknown

The everyday practice of patriotism makes one a patriot.

Colonel (Retired) William T. Coffey, Sr.

FREEMEN, CONTENDING FOR LIBERTY

Let us therefore animate and encourage each other, and show the whole world that a Freeman, contending for liberty on his own ground, is superior to any slavish mercenary on earth.

General George Washington, New York, July 2, 1776, two days after this General Order all 56 members of the Continental Congress signed the Declaration of Independence

The preservation of the sacred fire of liberty, and the destiny of the republican model of government, are justly considered as deeply, perhaps as finally staked, on the experiment entrusted to the hands of the American people.

President George Washington, First Inaugural Address, 30 April 1789

If we're ignorant of the historical sacrifices that made our liberties possible, we will be less likely to make the sacrifices again so that those liberties are preserved for future generations. And, if we're ignorant, we won't even know when government infringes on our liberties. Moreover, we'll happily cast our votes for those who'd destroy our liberties.

Walter Williams

The founding principles are the road which alone leads to peace, liberty, and safety.

President Thomas Jefferson

Liberty can no more exist without virtue and independence, than the body can live and move without a soul.

President John Adams

The word *patriot* is derived from Greek *patriotes–fellow countrymen, lineage, member, clan (derivative of pater FATHER)*.

The arms we have been compelled by our enemies to assume we will, in defiance of every hazard, with unabating firmness and perseverance, employ for the preservation of our liberties; being with one mind resolved to die free rather than live slaves.

President Thomas Jefferson

MY COUNTRY, 'TIS OF THEE

My country, 'tis of Thee,
Sweet Land of Liberty
Of thee I sing;
Land where my fathers died, Land of the pilgrims' pride,
From every mountain side, Let freedom ring.

My native country, thee,
Land of the noble free,
Thy name I love;
I love thy rocks and rills, Thy woods and templed hills,
My heart with rapture thrills, Like that above.

Let music swell the breeze,
And ring from all the trees
Sweet Freedom's song;
Let mortal tongues awake; Let all that breathe partake;
Let rocks their silence break, The sound prolong.

Our fathers' God to Thee,
Author of Liberty,
To thee we sing,
Long may our land be bright, With Freedom's holy light,
Protect us by thy might, Great God, our King.

*O*ur glorious Land to-day,
'Neath Education's sway,
Soars upward still.
Its hills of learning fair, Whose bounties all may share,
Behold them everywhere, On vale and hill!

*T*hy safeguard, Liberty,
The school shall ever be,
Our Nation's pride!
No tyrant hand shall smite, While with encircling might
All here are taught the Right, With Truth allied.

*B*eneath Heaven's gracious will
The stars of progress still
Our course do sway;
In unity sublime, To broader heights we climb,
Triumphant over Time, God speeds our way!

*G*rand birthright of our sires,
Our altars and our fires
Keep we still pure!
Our starry flag unfurled, The hope of all the world,
In peace and light impearled, God hold secure!

I HAVE A DREAM

Speech by Dr. Martin Luther King, given in Washington, D.C. from the steps of the Lincoln Memorial, 28 August 1963.

I am happy to join with you today in what will go down in history as the greatest demonstration for freedom in the history of our nation.

Five score years ago, a great American, in whose symbolic shadow we stand signed the Emancipation Proclamation. This momentous decree came as a great beacon light of hope to millions of Negro slaves who had been seared in the flames of withering injustice. It came as a joyous daybreak to end the long night of captivity. But one hundred years later, we must face the tragic fact that the Negro is still not free.

One hundred years later, the life of the Negro is still sadly crippled by the manacles of segregation and the chains of discrimination. One hundred years later, the Negro lives on a lonely island of poverty in the midst of a vast ocean of material prosperity. One hundred years later, the Negro is still languishing in the corners of American society and finds himself an exile in his own land.

So we have come here today to dramatize an appalling condition. In a sense we have come to our nation's capital to cash a check. When the architects of our republic wrote the magnificent words of the Constitution and the Declaration of Independence, they were signing a promissory note to which every American was to fall heir.

This note was a promise that all men would be guaranteed the inalienable rights of life, liberty, and the pursuit of happiness. It is obvious today that America has defaulted on this promissory note insofar as her citizens of color are concerned. Instead of honoring this sacred obligation, America has given the Negro people a bad check which has come back marked *insufficient funds*. But we refuse to believe that the bank of justice is bankrupt. We refuse to believe that there are insufficient funds in the great vaults of opportunity of this nation.

So we have come to cash this check–a check that will give us upon demand the riches of freedom and the security of justice. We have also come to this hallowed spot to remind America of the fierce urgency of now. This is no time to engage in the luxury of cooling off or to take the tranquilizing drug of gradualism. Now is the time to rise from the dark and desolate valley of segregation to the sunlit path of racial justice. Now is the time to open the doors of opportunity to all of God's children. Now is the time to lift our nation from the quicksands of racial injustice to the solid rock of brotherhood.

It would be fatal for the nation to overlook the urgency of the moment and to underestimate the determination of the Negro. This sweltering summer of the Negro's legitimate discontent will not pass until there is an invigorating autumn of freedom and equality. Nineteen sixty-three is not an end, but a beginning. Those who hope that the Negro needed to blow off steam and will now be content will have a rude awakening if the nation returns to business as usual. There will be neither rest nor tranquility in America until the Negro is granted his citizenship rights.

The whirlwinds of revolt will continue to shake the foundations of our nation until the bright day of justice emerges. But there is something that I must say to my people who stand on the warm threshold which leads into the palace of justice. In the process of gaining our rightful place we must not be guilty of wrongful deeds. Let us not seek to satisfy our thirst for freedom by drinking from the cup of bitterness and hatred.

We must forever conduct our struggle on the high plane of dignity and discipline. We must not allow our creative protest to degenerate into physical violence. Again and again we must rise to the majestic heights of meeting physical force with soul force.

The marvelous new militancy which has engulfed the Negro community must not lead us to distrust all white people, for many of our white brothers, as evidenced by their presence here today, have come to realize that their destiny is tied up with our destiny and their freedom is inextricably bound to our freedom.

We cannot walk alone. And as we walk, we must make the pledge that we shall march ahead. We cannot turn back. There are those who are asking the devotees of civil rights, *When will you be satisfied?* We can never be satisfied as long as our bodies, heavy with the fatigue of travel, cannot gain lodging in the motels of the highways and the hotels of the cities. We cannot be satisfied as long as the Negro's basic mobility is from a smaller ghetto to a larger one. We can never be satisfied as long as a Negro in Mississippi cannot vote and a Negro in New York believes he has nothing for which to vote. No, no, we are not satisfied, and we will

Dr. Martin Luther King. On the steps of the Lincoln Memorial, 28 August 1963.

not be satisfied until justice rolls down like waters and righteousness like a mighty stream.

I am not unmindful that some of you have come here out of great trials and tribulations. Some of you have come fresh from narrow cells. Some of you have come from areas where your quest for freedom left you battered by the storms of persecution and staggered by the winds of police brutality. You have been the veterans of creative suffering. Continue to work with the faith that unearned suffering is redemptive.

Go back to Mississippi, go back to Alabama, go back to Georgia, go back to Louisiana, go back to the slums and ghettos of our northern cities, knowing that somehow this situation can and will be changed. Let us not wallow in the valley of despair. I say to you today, my friends, that in spite of the difficulties and frustrations of the moment, I still have a dream. It is a dream deeply rooted in the American dream.

I have a dream that one day this nation will rise up and live out the true meaning of its creed: *We hold these truths to be self-evident: that all men are created equal.* I have a dream that one day on the red hills of Georgia the sons of former slaves and the sons of former slave owners will be able to sit down together at a table of brotherhood. I have a dream that one day even the state of Mississippi, a desert state, sweltering with the heat of injustice and oppression, will be transformed into an oasis of freedom and justice. I have a dream that my four children will one day live in a nation where they will not be judged by the color of their skin but by the content of their character. I have a dream today.

I have a dream that one day the state of Alabama, whose governor's lips are presently dripping with the words of interposition and nullification, will be transformed into a situation where little black boys and black girls will be able to join hands with little white boys and white girls and walk together as sisters and brothers. I have a dream today. I have a dream that one day every valley shall be exalted, every hill and mountain shall be made low, the rough places will be made plain, and the crooked places will be made straight, and the glory of the Lord shall be revealed, and all flesh shall see it together. This is our hope. This is the faith with which I return to the South. With this faith we will be able to hew out of the mountain of despair a stone of hope. With this faith we will be able to transform the jangling discords of our nation into a beautiful symphony of brotherhood. With this faith we will be able to work together, to pray together, to struggle together, to go to jail together, to stand up for freedom together, knowing that we will be free one day.

This will be the day when all of God's children will be able to sing with a new meaning, *My country, 'tis of thee, sweet land of liberty, of thee I sing. Land where my fathers died, land of the pilgrim's pride, from every mountainside, let freedom ring.* And if America is to be a great nation, this must become true. So let freedom ring from the prodigious hilltops of New Hampshire. Let freedom ring from the mighty mountains of New York. Let freedom ring from the heightening Alleghenies of Pennsylvania! Let freedom ring from the snowcapped Rockies of Colorado! Let freedom ring from the curvaceous peaks of California! But not only that; let freedom ring from Stone Mountain of Georgia! Let freedom ring from Lookout Mountain of Tennessee! Let freedom ring from every hill and every molehill of Mississippi. From every mountainside, let freedom ring.

When we let freedom ring, when we let it ring from every village and every hamlet, from every state and every city, we will be able to speed up that day when all of God's children, black men and white men, Jews and Gentiles, Protestants and Catholics, will be able to join hands and sing in the words of the old Negro spiritual, *Free at last! Free at last! Thank God Almighty, we are free at last!*

Freedom lies in being bold.

Robert Frost

Patriotism is not a short and frenzied outburst of emotion but the tranquil and steady dedication of a lifetime.

Adlai E. Stevenson, Jr.

THE TRUE PATH TO FREEDOM

The flame that burns the brightest
Is the light of the eternal human spirit:
A beacon of Love, Justice and Peace
That will never be extinguished.
It will triumph over the forces of darkness
And illuminate for the whole world
The true path to freedom,
Through goodness, hope and love.

Author Unknown

We have some incredibly gifted young men.
America's military men and women make up such a patriotic,
selfless, noble culture. God bless 'em all. We should express our
gratitude for their selfless patriotism.

A statement by Defense Secretary Donald Rumsfeld during a press
briefing on the Afghanistan War

SPC Scott Whitlock and SSG Rob Marcinowski. Both,
members of the 101st Airborne Division, fold Old Glory at the
Evening Retreat Ceremony, Afghanistan, 5 February 2002.
Photo by SSG Alberto Betancourt, *Soldiers Magazine.*

WHAT JULY FOURTH MEANS TO ME

The following was written by President Ronald Reagan for Independence Day, 1981. Aide Michael Deaver later wrote: *This 4th of July message is the President's own words and written initially in his own hand.* Contrary to media fiction, President Reagan actually wrote many of his own speeches, commentaries, and other papers.

For one who was born and grew up in the small towns of the Midwest, there is a special kind of nostalgia about the Fourth of July.

I remember it as a day almost as long anticipated as Christmas. This was helped along by the appearance in store windows of all kinds of fireworks and colorful posters advertising them with vivid pictures.

No later than the third of July–sometimes earlier–Dad would bring home what he felt he could afford to see go up in smoke and flame. We'd count and recount the number of firecrackers, display pieces and other things and go to bed determined to be up with the sun so as to offer the first, thunderous notice of the Fourth of July.

I'm afraid we didn't give too much thought to the meaning of the day. And, yes, there were tragic accidents to mar it, resulting from careless handling of the fireworks. I'm sure we're better off today with fireworks largely handled by professionals. Yet there was a thrill never to be forgotten in seeing a tin can blown 30 feet in the air by a giant *cracker*–giant meaning it was about four inches long.

But enough of nostalgia … somewhere in our growing up we began to be aware of the meaning of days and with that awareness came the birth of patriotism. July Fourth is the birthday of our nation. I believed as a boy, and believe even more today, that it is the birthday of the greatest nation on earth.

There is a legend about the day of our nation's birth in the little hall in Philadelphia, a day on which debate had raged for hours. The men gathered there were honorable men hard-pressed by a king who had flouted the very laws they were willing to obey. Even so, to sign the Declaration of Independence was such an irretrievable act that the walls resounded with the words *treason, the gallows, the headsman's axe,* and the issue remained in doubt.

The legend says that at that point a man rose and spoke. He is described as not a young man, but one who had to summon all his energy for an impassioned plea. He cited the grievances that had brought them to this moment and finally, his voice falling, he said:

> They may turn every tree into a gallows, every hole into a grave, and yet the words of that parchment can never die. To the mechanic in the workshop, they will speak hope; to the slave in the mines, freedom. Sign that parchment. Sign if the next moment the noose is around your neck, for that parchment will be the textbook of freedom, the Bible of the rights of man forever.

He fell back exhausted. The 56 delegates, swept up by his eloquence, rushed forward and signed that document destined to be as immortal as a work of man can be. When they turned to thank him for his timely oratory, he was not to be found, nor could any be found who knew who he was or how he had come in or gone out through the locked and guarded doors.

Well, that is the legend. But we do know for certain that 56 men, a little band so unique we have never seen their like since, had pledged their lives, their fortunes and their sacred honor. Some gave their lives in the war that followed, most gave their fortunes, and all preserved their sacred honor.

What manner of men were they? Twenty-four were lawyers and jurists, 11 were merchants and tradesmen, and nine were farmers. They were soft-spoken men of means and education; they were not an unwashed rabble. They had achieved security but valued freedom more. Their stories have not been told nearly enough.

John Hart was driven from the side of his desperately ill wife. For more than a year he lived in the forest and in caves before he returned to find his wife dead, his children vanished, his property destroyed. He died of exhaustion and a broken heart.

Carter Braxton of Virginia lost all his ships, sold his home to pay his debts, and died in rags. And so it was with Ellery,

Clymer, Hall, Walton, Gwinnett, Rutledge, Morris, Livingston and Middleton.

Nelson personally urged Washington to fire on his home and to destroy it when it became the headquarters for General Cornwallis. Nelson died bankrupt. But they sired a nation that grew from sea to shining sea. Five million farms, quiet villages, cities that never sleep, three million square miles of forest, field, mountain and desert, 227 million people with a pedigree that includes the bloodlines of all the world.

In recent years, however, I've come to think of that day as more than just the birthday of a nation. It also commemorates the only true philosophical revolution in all history.

Oh, there have been revolutions before and since ours. But those revolutions simply exchanged one set of rules for another. Ours was a revolution that changed the very concept of government.

Let the Fourth of July always be a reminder that here in this land, for the first time, it was decided that man is born with certain God-given rights; that government is only a convenience created and managed by the people, with no powers of its own except those voluntarily granted to it by the people.

We sometimes forget that great truth, and we never should. Happy Fourth of July, Ronald Reagan, United States President

AN ODE TO AMERICA

By Mr. Cornel Nistorescu and published under the title *Cntarea Americii* meaning *Ode To America* on September 24, 2002 in the Romanian newspaper *Evenimentulzilei* (*News of the Day*).

Subject: Editorial from a Romanian newspaper

Why are Americans so united? They don't resemble one another even if you paint them! They speak all the languages of the world and form an astonishing mixture of civilizations. Some of them are nearly extinct, others are incompatible with one another, and in matters of religious beliefs, not even God can count how many they are. Still, the American tragedy turned three hundred million people into a hand put on the heart. Nobody rushed to accuse the White House, the army, the secret services that they are only a bunch of losers. Nobody rushed to empty their bank accounts. Nobody rushed on the streets nearby to gape about. The Americans volunteered to donate blood and to give a helping hand. After the first moments of panic, they raised the flag on the smoking ruins, putting on T-shirts, caps and ties in the colors of the national flag. They placed flags on buildings and cars as if in every place and on every car a minister or the president was passing. On every occasion they started singing their traditional song: *God Bless America!* Silent as a rock, I watched the charity concert broadcast on Saturday once, twice, three times, on different television channels. There were Clint Eastwood, Willie Nelson, Robert de Niro, Julia Roberts, Cassius Clay, Jack Nicholson, Bruce Springsteen, Sylvester Stallone, James Wood, and many others whom no film or producers could ever bring together. The American's solidarity spirit turned them into a choir. Actually, choir is not the word. What you could hear was the heavy artillery of the American soul. What neither George W. Bush, nor Bill Clinton, nor Colin Powell could say without facing the risk of stumbling over words and sounds was being heard in a great and unmistakable way at this charity concert. I don't know how it happened that all this obsessive singing of America didn't sound croaky, nationalist, or ostentatious! It made you green with envy because you weren't able to sing for your country without running the risk of being considered chauvinist, ridiculous, or suspected of who-knows-what mean interests. I watched the live broadcast and the rerun of its rerun for hours listening to the story of the guy who went down one hundred floors with a woman in a wheelchair without knowing who she was, or of the Californian hockey player, who fought with the terrorists and prevented the plane from hitting a target that would have killed other hundreds or thousands of people. How on earth were they able to bow before a fellow human?

Imperceptibly, with every word and musical note, the memory of some turned into a modern myth of tragic heroes. And with every phone call, millions and millions of dollars were put in a collection aimed at rewarding not a man or a family, but a spirit which nothing can buy. What on earth can unite the Americans in such a way? Their land? Their galloping history? Their economic power? Money? I tried for hours to find an answer, humming songs and murmuring phrases which risk of sounding like commonplaces. I thought things over, but I reached only one conclusion. Only freedom can work such miracles!

The patriotism we celebrate on the Fourth of July is more than an expression of love for our country and pride in its achievements. An appreciation of the origins of the blessings we enjoy is essential for preserving those blessings for ourselves and our children and grandchildren. ... Patriotism is more than a sentiment. It is a necessity.

Thomas Sowell

In the beginning of a change, the patriot is a scarce man, and brave, and hated and scorned. When his cause succeeds, the timid join him, for then it costs nothing to be a patriot.

Mark Twain

DO YOU KNOW A BETTER FLAG?

John Wayne had a deep love for his country. This patriotism is reflected throughout his life. He had wanted to go into the military but an old football injury prevented it. He once stated:

More than anything else, I wanted to go to Annapolis and become an officer in the Navy. It was a terrible disappointment when I didn't make it. John Wayne worked with the USO (United Service Organization) in supporting U.S. troops from World War II through to Vietnam and received many honors. He said, *Sure I wave the American flag. Do you know a better flag to wave? Sure I love my country with all her faults. I'm not ashamed of that, never have been and never will be.*

A TOAST TO THE FLAG

Here's to the red of it—
There's not a thread of it, no nor a shred of it
In all the spread of it from foot to head,
But heroes bled for it, faced steel and lead for
it, precious blood Shed for it, bathing in red!

Here's to the white of it—
Thrilled by the sight of it, who knows the right of it
But feels the might of it through day and night?
Womanhood's care for it
Keeps it so white!

Here's to the blue of it—
Beauteous view of it, heavenly hue of it,
Star-spangled dew of it constant and true;
Diadems gleam for it, states stand supreme for it,
Liberty's beam for it brightens the blue!

Here's to the whole of it—
Stars, stripes and pole of it, body and soul
Of it, O, and the roll of it,
Sun shining through; hearts in accord for it
Swear by the sword for it
Thanking the Lord for it, red, white, and blue!

John Jay Daly, written 14 June 1917

Patriotism is a lively sense of collective responsibility.

Richard Aldington

Guard against the postures of pretended patriotism.

President George Washington

FLAG PROTECTION CONSTITUTIONAL AMENDMENT

Remarks by Honorable Henry Hyde on the floor of the Senate.

We look around this chamber and we see the splendid diversity of America: we see men and women whose great-grandparents came from virtually every corner of the globe. What holds this democratic community together? A common commitment to certain moral norms is the foundation of this democratic experiment.

Human beings don't live by abstract ideas alone. Those ideas are embodied in symbols. And what is a symbol? A symbol is more than a sign. A sign simply conveys some information. A symbol is much more richly textured. A symbol is material reality that makes a spiritual reality present among us. An octagonal piece of red metal on a street corner is a *sign*. The flag is a symbol. Vandalizing a *NO Parking* sign is a misdemeanor, but burning the flag is a hate crime, because burning the flag is an expression of contempt for the moral unity of the American people that the flag symbolically makes present to us, every day.

Why do we need this amendment now? Is there a rash of flag burning going on? NO, happily, there is not, but I believe we live in a time of growing disunity–our society is pulled apart by the powerful centrifugal force of racism, ethnicity, language, culture, gender and religion. Diversity can be a source of strength, but disunity is a source of peril. If you stop and think, the world is torn by religious and ethnic divisions that make war and killing and death and terror the norm in so many countries–Ireland, the Middle East, the Balkans, Rwanda–look around the globe and see what hate can do to drive fellow human beings apart.

This legislation makes a statement that needs to be made–that our flag is the transcendent symbol of all that America stands for and aspires to be and hence deserves the special protection of the law.

We Americans share a moral unity, expressed so profoundly in our country's birth certificate, the Declaration of Independence.

We hold these truths to be self-evident. Jefferson wrote. The truth that all are equal before the law. The truth that the right to life and liberty is inalienable and inviolable. The truth that government is intended to facilitate and not impede the people's pursuit of happiness.

Adherence to these truths is the foundation of civil society, of democratic culture in America.

And what is the symbol of our moral unity amidst our racial, ethnic, and religious diversity?

The flag. OLD GLORY. The Stars and Stripes.

In seeking to provide constitutional protection for the flag, we are seeking to protect the moral unity that makes American democracy possible. We have spent the better part of the past thirty years or so telling each other all the things that divide us. It is time to start talking about the things that unite us—that make us all, together, Americans. The flag is the embodiment of the unity of the American people, a unity built on those *self-evident* truths on which the American experiment rests—the truths which are our nation's claim to be a just society.

Let us take a step toward reconciliation—and toward constitutional sanity—by adopting this amendment. The flag is our connection to the past and proclaims our hopes and aspirations for the future.

Pride. An Air Force crew shows its pride in America after returning to McQuire Air Force Base from a mission supporting Operation Enduring Freedom.

Too many brave Americans have marched behind it–too many have come home in a box covered by a flag–too many parents and widows have clutched that flag to their hearts as the last remembrance of their beloved one to treat that flag with anything less than reverence and respect.

About 187 years ago during the British bombardment of Baltimore, Frances Scott Key looked towards Fort McHenry in the early dawn, and asked his famous question–To his joy, he saw our flag was still there–and how surprised he would be to learn our flag is even planted on the moon!

But–most especially–it is planted in the hearts of every loyal American.

The liberties of our country, the freedom of our civil constitution, are worth defending at all hazards; and it is our duty to defend them against all attacks. We have received them as a fair inheritance from our worthy ancestors; they purchased them for us with toil and danger and expense of treasure and blood. It will bring an everlasting mark of infamy on the present generation, enlightened as it is, if we should suffer them to be wrested from us by violence without a struggle, or be cheated out of them by the artifices of false and designing men.

Samuel Adams

Love your neighbor as yourself, and your country more than yourself.

President Thomas Jefferson

Patriotism itself is a necessary link in the golden chains of our affections and virtue.

Stephen Decatur

A CHANGE FOR THE BETTER

But actually, 9-11 marked a cultural watershed, not an economic one. Although a case can be made that there has been a gradual return to more traditional and virtuous cultural values over the past several years, certainly a new spirit of patriotism and faith arrived in response to the terrorist war against the United States. Just take a quick inventory: American-flag lapel pins by the thousands; heart-felt renditions of God Bless America at sporting events; a measurable increase in the appreciation of friends, family members and co-workers; people more seriously undertaking their daily responsibilities; a greater attraction to the miraculous heritage of the Founding Fathers; once self-full Americans now giving to charities and volunteering for community service. With these have come the duty of courage and the understanding of the clear differences between right and wrong, and between good and evil. Moral relativism is out the door. There can be no doubt that American culture has changed since 9-11. Predominantly, it is a change for the better.

Larry Kudlow

Patriotism is not an outmoded concept. It is not jingoistic. It is not the cause of this war—the terrorists are. But our patriotism will help to keep us united and focused as we face the enemy. Most of us don't love America simply because we are its citizens. Patriotism for us is not some mindless emotional attachment to our nation. While it generates visceral feelings of pride it has intellectual moorings as well. It springs forth from a deep devotion to our founding principles, chief among them being our glorious freedom safeguarded by the rule of law. Patriotism is vitally important because it is about more than mere survival. It emboldens us in our struggle to preserve our distinct way of life, because it understands that peace is not 'so sweet as to be purchased at the price of chains and slavery.'

David Limbaugh, from *The Federalist* newsletter

THE SPIRIT OF A FREE PEOPLE

New York City. A woman near ground zero.

The most visible symbol in New York is the spirit of a free people.

New York City Mayor Rudolph Giuliani

I believe in America because we have great dreams—and because we have the opportunity to make those dreams come true.

Author Unknown

OF ATHENIANS: In the end, more than they wanted freedom, they wanted security. They wanted a comfortable life and they lost it all—security, comfort, and freedom. When the Athenians finally wanted not to give to society, but society to give to them, when the freedom they wished for most was freedom from responsibility, then Athens ceased to be free.

General Omar N. Bradley

The highest patriotism is not a blind acceptance of official policy, but a love of one's country deep enough to call her to a higher standard.

George McGovern

IT'S EASY TO TAKE LIBERTY FOR GRANTED

Author Unknown, 1999.

On my way to work last week, I stopped at a red light behind a purple Geo Metro. It had a National Education Association and a Massachusetts Education Association sticker in the back window. On the bumper was plastered my least favorite bumper sticker ever. It read:

It'll be a great day when schools have all the money they need and the Air Force has to have a bake sale to buy a bomber.

At that moment, I realized who the most undervalued and under-appreciated segment of society is, and it *ain't* teachers. Teachers, I believe, might rank second on the list. Heading the list are the men and women of the United States armed forces, who, throughout our history, have protected our country from the Hitler's and Stalin's and all those others who would have white children marching to the school bus in brown shirts and jackboots and minority children exterminated (at worst) or locked up in experimental laboratories and labor camps (at best).

The U.S. military, the most powerful and influential group of people in the world, hands-down, gets an awfully bad rap these days. Many Americans seem to think simply because communism in the Soviet Union supposedly no longer exists, the world is as safe as Beaver Cleaver's neighborhood. This, of course, ignores three facts:

1. Dozens of countries have nuclear weapons that could take out millions of people with the turn of a key;
2. Leaders of several of those countries (e.g., North Korea, Iraq, Iran, Libya, China, and Russia) would love to see the U.S. and its people blown to pieces; and, most importantly—
3. The U.S. has the greatest collection of human, economic, natural, and technological resources anywhere on earth, making it the world's greatest natural target for military aggression.

Though some would like to fashion the U.S. of the next century as a flowery feel-good fantasy where war and death and violence are mere afterthoughts of a time gone by, that, unfortunately, is not the reality of life and has never been, nor will ever be, the case. As bad as our crime and drug problems are, the U.S. is still considered the jewel of the planet by over half of the world that has yet to make its first phone call.

In ancient Greece, the people of Athens were unparalleled world leaders in art, philosophy and technology. Their rivals in Sparta were not; instead, Sparta built massive, well-trained armies. When the two countries fought, who won? Sparta. Guess who lost their entire civilization because they didn't think it was important to build an appropriate army? *Athens!*

Right now, the U.S. has the best of Athens and Sparta. We are the most cultured and best defended country in the world. But if we continue to lower our defenses by devaluing the military, we open ourselves up to foreign aggression and military attack. Attack the U.S.? *Get real! Ridiculous!* Why does it seem so impossible and unlikely? Because the power projection and protection umbrella of the U.S. military has been so overwhelming in this and the last century that Americans have been free to enjoy a comfort level unlike any in the world. We Americans take it for granted that we will never be invaded by another country, but few other countries in the world can afford to be so sure of themselves. And it's not only Americans who can go to bed feeling safe. Children everywhere from Israel to England, from Brazil to Japan, know that, if their country is attacked, the U.S. will be there to help.

On TV, the military is most often represented by some stiff, buttoned-down General or the occasional Drill Instructor or Chief Master Sergeant who is accused of sexual harassment or some *talking head's* snide or sarcastic remarks about military stupidity or waste. In reality, things in the military are much different. The men and women of the armed forces are, in most ways, just like everyone else in this country: They have a job and are damned good at it. They are mechanics, pilots, cooks, photographers, engineers, secretaries, and X-ray technicians. They work from 8 to 5 (or worse hours) and then come home to their families. The one difference comes when the U.S. or any of its allies is threatened by a foreign power. In that case, military people load it up and ship it out, off to fight and many times die, so the rest of the country, including teachers, can continue their lives without interruption.

So, a teacher's job is to mold young minds into intelligent, independent adults; and, for the most part, they should be admired for the job they do. However, I don't know any teachers who are required to catch bullets or swallow shrapnel if so ordered by the principal.

So, old-fashioned as it may seem, this time of year I pay taxes to provide for the military. I care less about the *social programs!* Now let's tell all the teachers and children to fire up the oven if they want extra dough. Make cakes, muffins, cookies and candy and be happy you're allowed to. Because, as the old saying goes, if it wasn't for the U.S. military, we'd all be speaking German, Japanese, or maybe Cyrillic (Russian) now. It is easy to take liberty for granted, when you've never had it taken from you.

WHAT DOES THE
AMERICAN FLAG MEAN TO YOU?

Michele Giovanni, 14 years old, chose a history class project which asked veterans, *Having served in the military, what does the American flag mean to you?* Her compiled responses constituted her history report. Following are several of the responses she received.

Richard P. Arsenault, Veteran 82nd Airborne Division, Captain, Georgia State Defense Force/Joint Counter-Drug Task Force
> To me, it's a symbol of all that our fathers and fathers before them have fought for throughout our history. What have they fought for? Freedom from oppression, a liberty where the ordinary man is allowed to do extraordinary things and a justice that one cannot be wronged without due process. It is a symbol of our unique way of life, not found elsewhere.

—

George Boddie, Past County Commander American Legion, Otsego County, New York
> What does the American Flag stand for? I could give you the pat answer but I'll give mine. I'm a Vietnam Vet. I joined the service in 1972 when friends of mine were burning the flag and running for the hills. I joined

the army because I realized just what our flag meant to me. It is a rally call for freedom, a treasure and reminder of those who went before so I could enjoy the freedoms paid for by their service, blood, sweat and tears. I realize that to some people it may just be some pieces of cloth and an emblem of our country but to me it's a banner to the rest of the world *FREEDOM HERE*.

Thank You.

—

Name Withheld

I am a retired, 90 percent disabled Army Veteran of Korea [1950-1951, and Vietnam 1966-1967]. The Flag, the emblem of the United States of America is loved and it is reviled, but yet it flies proudly over the greatest nation the world has ever known. What this Flag means to me: poverty, war, chaos, great events, love, purity, recognition of the many, danger and death, freedom and love, security, power and order. It means the three years I spent in Korea, three in Japan, two in Germany and one in Vietnam that our way of life might prosper and grow. In short, the Flag means it binds all of us into a whole nation, under God.

—

Doc Al

The Red stands for the lives given up by Veterans and Citizens alike.

The White stands for the obstacles Americans may face on their climb up the ladder (Red separated by White has a ladder effect).

The Field of Blue represents the unity of Americans, whether they are Veterans, Fireman, Policeman, Hospital Workers, Ground Zero workers, the care takers of the sick, the helpful of the children, the honesty of a company.

The Stars represent our Hero's, the Veterans, the family's, the leaders of our country and the mothers, fathers, teachers, and clergy.

—

Kurt J. Bergstrom, a concerned patriot, former U.S. Army Special Forces SSG

Thank you for the opportunity to express an opinion. I served 1972-80 active Army; 1980-84 National Guard; 1984-87 Reserves, sometimes under 'arduous circumstances.' I am foreign born, from behind the former iron curtain. My opinions are stark, black and white, without any shades. As a child, I remember my grandfather pointing to that beautiful flag and saying *that's the flag of freedom.* My military service, where I witnessed better men than me makes the final sacrifice for that flag, reinforced that viewpoint. It may only be cloth of several colors to those who are superficial, but to those who have fought for it, it is the embodiment of all that we hold dear, it is the symbol of good men who stay forever young in our memories. It is the symbol of personal liberty and freedom that is unmatched anywhere on the globe for over 200 years.

—

Sam Diaz

You ask a question with a very wide answer, Michele. I served in the Navy from 1959 to 1983, and I saw the flag flying in the Cuban Missile Crisis, Dominican Republic, Vietnam, the Six Day War, the world over during the Cold War, and various other places and times. It stands for freedom, equality, the right to believe in whatever I want to believe in, even if I choose to believe in nothing at all. It gives me the right to choose my elected officials, and also the right to criticize them. It stands for a way of life that is unique. It gives me the right to be whatever I want to be, wherever I want to do it, as long as it's within the laws of the land.

—

Leif Dolan, U.S. Army 1977-1987

My flag ... it has brought me to tears ... it has given me pride ... hope ... when I felt I had no honor, there it was to bring me home ... I've seen it perfectly still and best of all ... I have seen it blowing in the wind in all its glory ... I've seen it draped over some of my best friends ... more tears but lots of pride ... an old saying ... for those who served, it has a special meaning that those who didn't will never understand ... there is a price that few who never had to put it on the line can understand ... and I feel sorry for them ... there is a brotherhood/sisterhood with those who put it on the line for their country that civilians don't know about and most don't care about ... when its my turn to go, it will be my honor to go with the flag over me ... taking me home ... *God Bless America.*

Our flag is a sign of FREEDOM. People see that flag and they know that there is a country that has fought and bled for the concept of freedom. Many people have different thoughts about what freedom is to them, and that is OK here in this land. When you see the flag up overhead you should feel proud of what you are living for and where.

Or I might just be wrong, and it is just a red, white and blue piece of cloth.

———

Fred Kossow

The American Flag stands for everything that we have ever fought for and believe in. I'm a pissed off WWII Vet. To think we had a former President that burnt the flag, didn't have enough guts to fight for this country and had a yellow streak up his back a yard wide. I was in the 804th Aviation Engineer Battalion; we built airstrips on Caton, Christmas, Baker, Makin, Saipan, and built and repaired airfields in the Hawaiian Island. And I'm real proud to have served my country in time of need, as my father and son did.

THE SACRED FIRE OF LIBERTY

President Franklin Roosevelt delivered this speech after the military forces of Germany and Japan enjoyed a series of victories over seemingly weakling democratic nations. By early 1941, the German Reich had spread throughout most of Western Europe, while the Japanese Empire covered vast areas of the South Pacific.

The shocking collapse of noble, civilized nations resulted in a creeping erosion of confidence in the future of democracy. To some observers it appeared that Fascism and militarism might be the wave of the future and that democracy with all its inherent problems was in serious decline. In his third inaugural speech, President Franklin Roosevelt turned his attention to this growing misconception and attempted to rally Americans, reminding them of their roots and rekindling the spirit of democracy. President Roosevelt, January 20, 1941:

On each national day of inauguration since 1789, the people have renewed their sense of dedication to the United States.

In Washington's day the task of the people was to create and weld together a nation.

In Lincoln's day the task of the people was to preserve that Nation from disruption from within.

In this day the task of the people is to save that Nation and its institutions from disruption from without.

To us there has come a time, in the midst of swift happenings, to pause for a moment and take stock–to recall what our place in history has been, and to rediscover what we are and what we may be. If we do not, we risk the real peril of inaction.

Lives of nations are determined not by the count of years, but by the lifetime of the human spirit. The life of a man is three-score years and ten: a little more, a little less. The life of a nation is the fullness of the measure of its will to live.

There are men who doubt this. There are men who believe that democracy, as a form of Government and a frame of life, is limited or measured by a kind of mystical and artificial fate that, for some unexplained reason, tyranny and slavery have become the surging wave of the future–and that freedom is an ebbing tide.

But we Americans know that this is not true.

Eight years ago, when the life of this Republic seemed frozen by a fatalistic terror, we proved that this is not true. We were in the midst of shock–but we acted. We acted quickly, boldly, decisively.

These later years have been living years–fruitful years for the people of this democracy. For they have brought to us greater security and, I hope, a better understanding that life's ideals are to be measured in other than material things.

Most vital to our present and our future is this experience of a democracy which successfully survived crisis at home; put away many evil things; built new structures on enduring lines; and, through it all, maintained the fact of its democracy.

For action has been taken within the three-way framework of the Constitution of the United States. The coordinate branches of the Government continue freely to function. The Bill of Rights remains inviolate. The freedom of elections is wholly maintained. Prophets of the downfall of American democracy have seen their dire predictions come to naught.

Democracy is not dying.

We know it because we have seen it revive–and grow.

We know it cannot die–because it is built on the unhampered initiative of individual men and women joined together in a common enterprise–an enterprise undertaken and carried through by the free expression of a free majority.

We know it because democracy alone, of all forms of government, enlists the full force of men's enlightened will.

We know it because democracy alone has constructed an unlimited civilization capable of infinite progress in the improvement of human life.

We know it because, if we look below the surface, we sense it still spreading on every continent–for it is the most humane, the most advanced, and in the end the most unconquerable of all forms of human society.

A nation, like a person, has a body–a body that must be fed and clothed and housed, invigorated and rested, in a manner that measures up to the objectives of our time.

A nation, like a person, has a mind–a mind that must be kept informed and alert, that must know itself, that understands the hopes and the needs of its neighbors–all the other nations that live within the narrowing circle of the world.

And a nation, like a person, has something deeper, something more permanent, something larger than the sum of all its parts. It is that something which matters most to its future– which calls forth the most sacred guarding of its present.

It is a thing for which we find it difficult–even impossible– to hit upon a single, simple word.

And yet we all understand what it is–the spirit–the faith of America. It is the product of centuries. It was born in the multitudes of those who came from many lands–some of high degree, but mostly plain people, who sought here, early and late, to find freedom more freely.

The democratic aspiration is no mere recent phase in human history. It is human history. It permeated the ancient life of early peoples. It blazed anew in the middle ages. It was written in Magna Carta.

In the Americas its impact has been irresistible. America has been the New World in all tongues, to all peoples, not because this continent was a newfound land, but because all those who came here believed they could create upon this continent a new life–a life that should be new in freedom.

Its vitality was written into our own Mayflower Compact, into the Declaration of Independence, into the Constitution of the United States, into the Gettysburg Address.

Those who first came here to carry out the longings of their spirit, and the millions who followed, and the stock that sprang from them–all have moved forward constantly and consistently toward an ideal which in itself has gained stature and clarity with each generation.

The hopes of the Republic cannot forever tolerate either undeserved poverty or self-serving wealth.

We know that we still have far to go; that we must more greatly build the security and the opportunity and the knowledge of every citizen, in the measure justified by the resources and the capacity of the land.

But it is not enough to achieve these purposes alone. It is not enough to clothe and feed the body of this Nation, and instruct and inform its mind. For there is also the spirit. And of the three, the greatest is the spirit.

Without the body and the mind, as all men know, the Nation could not live.

But if the spirit of America were killed, even though the Nation's body and mind, constricted in an alien world, lived on, the America we know would have perished.

That spirit–that faith–speaks to us in our daily lives in ways often unnoticed, because they seem so obvious. It speaks to us here in the Capital of the Nation. It speaks to us through the processes of governing in the sovereignties of 48 States. It speaks to us in our counties, in our cities, in our towns, and in our villages. It speaks to us from the other nations of the hemisphere, and from those across the seas–the enslaved, as well as the free. Sometimes we fail to hear or heed these voices of freedom because to us the privilege of our freedom is such an old, old story.

The destiny of America was proclaimed in words of prophecy spoken by our first President in his first inaugural in 1789–words almost directed, it would seem, to this year of 1941:

> The preservation of the sacred fire of liberty and the destiny of the republican model of government are justly considered ... finally, staked on the experiment entrusted to the hands of the American people.

If we lose that sacred fire–if we let it be smothered with doubt and fear–then we shall reject the destiny which Washington strove so valiantly and so triumphantly to establish. The preservation of the spirit and faith of the Nation does, and will, furnish the highest justification for every sacrifice that we may make in the cause of national defense.

In the face of great perils never before encountered, our strong purpose is to protect and to perpetuate the integrity of democracy.

For this we muster the spirit of America, and the faith of America. We do not retreat. We are not content to stand still. As Americans, we go forward, in the service of our country, by the will of God.

I AM YOUR FLAG

I am your Flag. I was born on June 14th, 1777.
I am more than just cloth shaped into a design.
I am the refuge of the world's oppressed people.
I am the silent sentinel of Freedom.
I am the emblem of the greatest sovereign nation on earth.
I am the inspiration for which American patriots gave their lives
and fortunes. I have led your sons into battle from Valley Forge to

the bloody swamps of Vietnam. I walk in silence with each of your honored dead, to their final resting place beneath the silent white crosses, row upon row. I have flown through peace and war, strife and prosperity, and amidst it all I have been respected.

My red stripes ... symbolize the blood spilled in defense of this glorious nation. My white stripes ... signify the burning tears shed by Americans who lost their sons. My blue field ... is indicative of God's heaven under which I fly. My stars ... clustered together, unify 50 States as one, for God and country.

'Old Glory' is my nickname, and proudly I wave on high. Honor me, respect me, defend me with your lives and your fortunes. Never let my enemies tear me down from my lofty position, lest I never return. Keep alight the fires of patriotism, strive earnestly for the spirit of democracy. Worship eternal God and keep His commandments, and I shall remain the bulwark of peace and freedom for all mankind. I am your Flag.

Compliments of Colonel (Retired) Daniel K. Cedusky, U.S. Army

LOVE IN ACTION

We are clear that in terms of terrorism, you are either with us or against us. We should be just as clear with patriotism—you are either a patriot, one who supports and defends America, or you are not a patriot. The love of a patriot can be known only by acts of a patriot. To understand the love of a patriot, it is important to understand that sacrifice is best defined as love in action. Those who willingly sacrifice, i.e., support and defend, do so out of love.

MG (Retired) Patrick H. Brady, Medal of Honor recipient who served two Tours in Vietnam. He is the chairman of the Citizens Flag Alliance

... In America, justice will eventually triumph and the powerful, searing promise of the founding fathers will come true. I was taught by my parents to always, always, believe in America.

Secretary of State Colin Powell
former Chairman of the Joint Chiefs of Staff

Our flag is ... the symbol of the oldest continuing democracy in the world. It represents that stability of our system of government, the noble ideals to which the nation was pledged long ago and remains pledged today.

President Gerald Ford

Freedom–no word was ever spoken that has held out greater hope, demanded greater sacrifice, needed to be nurtured, blessed more the giver, damned more it's destroyer, or come closer to being God's will on earth. And that's worth fighting for.

General Omar N. Bradley

Freedom is no policy for the timid. And my plaintive plea to all my colleagues that remain in this government as I leave it is, for your sake, for my sake, for heaven's sake, don't give up on freedom!

U.S. Representative Dick Armey

*Liberty is a thing of the spirit –
to be free to worship, to think, to hold opinions,
and to speak them without fear –
free to challenge wrong and oppression with surety of justice.*

President Herbert Hoover

WE FOLLOW THE FLAG

The Republic never retreats. Its flag is the only flag that has never known defeat. Where that flag leads we follow, for we know that the hand that bears it onward is the unseen hand of God. We follow that flag and independence is ours. We follow the flag and nationality is ours. We follow the flag and oceans are ruled. We follow the flag, and in Occident and Orient tyranny falls and

*barbarism is subdued. We followed the flag at Trenton and Valley
Forge, at Buena Vista and Chapultepec, at Gettysburg and
Mission Ridge, at Santiago and Manila, and everywhere and
always it means larger liberty, nobler opportunity,
and greater human happiness; for everywhere and always
it means the blessings of the greater Republic. And so God leads,
we follow the flag, and the Republic never retreats.*

Albert J. Beveridge

FREEDOM IS NOT FREE

*I watched the flag pass by one day. It fluttered in the breeze.
A young Marine saluted it, and then He stood at ease.*

*I looked at him in uniform So young, so tall, so proud,
With hair cut square and eyes alert. He'd stand out in any crowd.*

*I thought how many men like him Had fallen through the years.
How many died on foreign soil? How many mother's tears?*

*How many pilots' planes shot down. How many died at sea?
How many foxholes were soldier's graves? No, freedom is not free.*

*I heard the sound of taps one night, When everything was still.
I listened to the bugler play And felt a sudden chill.*

*I wondered just how many times That taps had meant 'Amen,'
When a flag had draped a coffin Of a brother or a friend.*

*I thought of all the children, Of the mothers and the wives,
Of fathers, sons and husbands With interrupted lives.*

*I thought about a graveyard At the bottom of the sea
Of unmarked graves in Arlington. No, Freedom is not free.*

Cadet Major Kelly Strong, Air Force Junior ROTC, Homestead Senior
High School, Homestead, Florida 1988

*The greatest glory of a free-born people
is to transmit that freedom to their children.*

William Havard

A thoughtful mind, when it sees a nation's flag, sees not the flag only, but the nation itself; and whatever may be its symbols, its insignia, he reads chiefly in the flag the government, the principles, the truths, the history which belongs to the nation that sets it forth.

Henry Ward Beecher

The love of liberty is the love of others; the love of power is the love for ourselves.

William Hazlitt

Liberty will not descend to a people; a people must raise themselves to liberty; it is a blessing that must be earned before it can be enjoyed.

Caleb C. Colton

America will only be the land of the free so long as it is the home of the Brave.

Author Unknown

We too born to freedom, believing in freedom, are willing to fight to maintain freedom. We and others who believe as deeply as we do, would rather die on our feet, than live on our knees.

President Franklin D. Roosevelt, 19 June 1941, this quote is also inscribed on the National Guard Memorial at Normandy Beach, France, at the location that the 29th Infantry Division landed on 6 June 1944

Posterity–you will never know how much it has cost my generation to preserve your freedom. I hope you will make good use of it.

President John Quincy Adams

Every Flag Day I do something a lot of people save for November and Thanksgiving Day: I say a quiet prayer of thanks that this nation is enduring and that there are so many wonderful people, young and old, rich and poor, children of all ages, who haven't yet, won't now, and never intend to give up on America or Americans. This flag has the power to take more than 200 million of us, with all our differences, and make us one people.

Bob Hope

Freedom and security are but opposite sides of the same coin— and the free expression of ideas is not more expendable but far more essential in a period of challenge and crisis ... Through the centuries of crisis the American tradition has demonstrated ... that freedom is the ally of security— and that liberty is the architecture of abundance.

President John F. Kennedy

We pray that peoples of all faiths, all races, all nations, may have their great human needs satisfied; that those now denied opportunity shall come to enjoy it to the full; that all who yearn for freedom may experience its spiritual blessings; that those who have freedom will understand, also, its heavy responsibilities; that all who are insensitive to the needs of others will learn charity; that the scourges of poverty, disease, and ignorance will be made to disappear from the earth, and that, in the goodness of time, all peoples will come to live together in a peace guaranteed by the binding force of mutual respect and love.

President Dwight D. Eisenhower, 17 January 1961
Farewell Address to the American People

The colors of the Great American Seal are the same used in the American Flag, as determined by the U.S. Congress: *White signifies purity and innocence. Red, hardiness and valor. Blue signifies vigilance, perseverance, and justice.*

*The supreme value that our veterans
have fought and died for (with some tragic exceptions) from the
American Revolution to the Civil War to two World Wars is—
freedom. America is the country of freedom.*

Edwin A. Locke

*A man's country is not a certain area of land,
of mountains, rivers, and woods, but it is a principle;
and patriotism is loyalty to that principle.*

George William Curtis

INSCRIPTION ON THE BASE OF THE LIBERTY BELL

*Proclaim liberty throughout the land
unto all the inhabitants thereof.*

*Before God, I believe the hour has come. My judgment
approves this measure, and my whole heart is in it.
All that I have, and all that I am, and all that I hope in this life,
I am now ready here to stake upon it.
And I leave off as I began, that live or die, survive or perish,
I am for the Declaration. It is my living sentiment,
and by the blessing of God it shall be my dying sentiment.
Independence now, and Independence forever!*

President John Adams, 1 July 1776
speaking to the Continental Congress

NOW I KNOW

By Tamara Hall, *The Montana Motivator*, columnist, author and motivational speaker, Bozeman, Montana, www.tamarahall.com, 2001.

I sat in a movie theater, watching *Shindler's List*, and asked myself, *Why didn't the Jews fight back?* Now I know. I sat in a movie theater, watching *Pearl Harbor* and asked myself, *Why weren't we prepared?* Now I know. Civilized people cannot fathom, never less predict, the actions of evil people. On September 11, dozens of capable airplane passengers allowed themselves to be overpowered by a handful of poorly armed terrorists because they did not comprehend the depth of hatred that motivated their captors.

On September 11, thousands of innocent people were murdered because too many Americans naively reject the reality that some nations are dedicated to the dominance of others.

Many political pundits, pacifists and media personnel want us to forget the carnage. They say we must focus on the bravery of the rescuers and ignore the cowardice of the killers. They implore us to understand the motivation of the perpetrators. The major television stations have announced they will assist the healing process by not re-playing devastating footage of the planes crashing into the Towers.

I will not be manipulated. I will not pretend to understand.

I will not forget.

I will not underestimate the intelligence of our adversary who patiently planned and meticulously orchestrated a devastating act of war.

I will not forget that the terrorists desire a world society where women are chattel and freedom is forbidden.

I will not isolate myself from my fellow Americans by pretending an attack on the *USS Cole* in Yemen was not an attack on me.

I will not forget that the Clinton administration equipped Islamic terrorists and their supporters with the world's most sophisticated telecommunications equipment and encryption technology, thereby compromising America's ability to trace terrorist radio, cell phone land lines, faxes and modem communications.

I will not be appeased with pointless, quick retaliatory strikes like those perfected by the previous administration. I will not be comforted by *feel-good, do-nothing* regulations like the silly *Have your bags been under your control?* question at the airport.

I will not forget the liberal media who abused freedom of the press to kick our country when it was vulnerable and hurting.

I will not forget that ABC TV anchor Peter Jennings questioned President Bush's motives for not returning immediately to Washington, D.C. and commented, *We're all pretty skeptical and cynical about Washington.*

I will not forget that CBS anchor Dan Rather preceded President Bush's address to the nation with the snide remark, *No matter how you feel about him, he is still our president.*

And I will not forget the ABC's Mark Halperin warned if reporters weren't informed of every little detail of this war, they aren't *likely–nor should they be expected–to show deference ...*

I will not be influenced by so-called, *anti-war demonstrators* who exploit the right of expression to chant anti-American obscenities. I will not forget the moral victory handed the North Vietnamese by American war protesters who reviled and spat upon the returning soldiers.

I will not be softened by the wishful thinking of pacifists who chose reassurance over reality.

I will embrace the wise words of Prime Minister Tony Blair who told Labour Party conference:

> They have no moral inhibition on the slaughter of the innocent. If they could have murdered not 7,000 but 70,000 does anyone doubt they would have done so and rejoiced in it?
>
> There is no compromise possible with such people, no meeting of minds, no point of understanding with such terror. Just a choice: defeat it or be defeated by it. And defeat it we must.

I will force myself to: –hear the weeping–feel the helplessness–imagine the terror–sense the panic–smell the burning flesh–experience the loss–remember their hatred.

I sat in a movie theater, watching in quiet reverence as the blood of young soldiers turned the sands of Normandy beach red in *Private Ryan* and asked myself, *Where did they find the courage?*

Now I know.

We have no choice. Living without liberty is not living.

———————— ————————

*P*atria Cara, Carior Libertas.

Latin for *Our Country is dear, but Liberty is dearer.*

*N*one who have always been free can understand the terrible fascinating power of the hope of freedom to those who are not free.

Pearl S. Buck, American author and humanitarian

A Village Boy. The child holds an American flag as a sign of friendship between Iraqi villagers and the American soldiers, April 2003.

ON THE SHOULDERS OF A PATRIOT

U.S. Marine. Saipan,
World War II, 1944.

*Despite technical advances and political foolery,
the outcome rests on the shoulders of a patriot with the desire to
fight and a fresh canteen of water.*

Author Unknown

*It is only when the people become ignorant
and corrupt, when they degenerate into
a populace, that they are incapable of
exercising their sovereignty. Let us, by all wise
and Constitutional measures, promote
intelligence among the people, as the best
means of preserving our liberties.*

President James Monroe

The time is now, my fellow Americans, to recapture our destiny, to take it into our own hands.

President Ronald Reagan

Patriotism is the sound of freedom ringing.

Major Bill Coffey

*Educate and inform the whole mass of people.
Enable them to see that it is to their interest
to preserve peace and order ...
They are the only sure reliance
for the preservation of our liberty.*

President Thomas Jefferson

*To sin by silence when they
should protest makes cowards of men.*

President Abraham Lincoln

*America is best described by one word
... FREEDOM.*

President Dwight D. Eisenhower

*To be born free is an accident;
to live free is a privilege;
to die free is a responsibility.*

Brigadier General (Retired) James Seahorn
BG Seahorn was a prisoner of war for six years in Vietnam

CHAPTER 10

TRAINING

The American torch of freedom has been passed from generation to generation for over 200 years. This short chapter addresses the need to pass values and skills from one American generation to the next, especially through the generations of American warriors.

The combat officer must be the combat instructor of his own men;
not only must he know his own tactics, but he must know how to
use the various instruments with which his unit is equipped
to ply its trade, and he must know each better than any of his men.
Further than this, he must have taught and practiced
the use of his complicated instrument, so that it plays equally
well under his hand the simple one-step of the set-piece attack
or the complicated tango of the open-war fight.
He must think, teach, and practice the tactics of his arm.

Major George S. Patton, Jr. of the Third U.S. Cavalry
Writing in the Cavalry Journal, 1922,
about lessons learned from the new tank corps in World War I

The mediocre teacher tells.
The good teacher explains.
The superior teacher demonstrates.
The great teacher inspires.

William Arthur Ward

When the bullets started flying ... I never thought about
half the things I was doing. I simply relied
on my training and concentrated on the mission.

Captain Marie Bezubic, Operation Just Cause, Panama, 1989

THE SHOCKS OF THE BATTLEFIELD

Americans fully understand the requirement of the football field or the baseball diamond. They discipline themselves and suffer by the thousands to prepare for these rigors. A coach or manager who is too permissive soon seeks a new job; his team will fail against those who are tougher and harder. Yet undoubtedly any American officer, in peacetime, who worked his men as hard, or ruled them as severely as a college football coach does, would be removed. But the shocks of the battlefield are a hundred times those of the playing field, and the outcome infinitely more important to the nation. The problem is to understand the battlefield as well as the game of football. The problem is to see not what is desirable, or nice, or politically feasible, but what is necessary.

T. R. Fehrenbach

On the fields of friendly strife are sown the seeds that on other fields on other days shall bear the fruits of victory.

The inscription on a gym at West Point, by General Douglas MacArthur

I was a pre-med student at John Hopkins in civilian life. Now, I do know a little something about anatomy, and I say it's scientifically impossible for the human body to stand up to the training we received. An absolute impossibility. Muscles and tendons and bone structure—it was not designed to withstand that battering. Don't ask me how it happens that we did stand up to it. I don't know. It has no scientific explanation.

From, *Serviceman, The True Glory*, (a War Department film)

It is not big armies that win battles, it is the good ones.

General George Washington

Only the test of fire makes fine steel.

Author Unknown

American Soldiers. Soldiers doing
PT (Physical Training).

*T*he good Lord gave you a body that can stand most anything.
It's your mind you have to convince.

Vince Lombardi

*F*or most men, the matter of learning is one of personal
preference. But for Army officers, the obligation to learn, to grow
in their profession, is clearly a public duty.

General Omar N. Bradley

*A*ll training must stress that every soldier regardless of
assignment has as his primary duty the obligation to fight.

General Jacob L. Devers

*T*raining, the Army's principal activity in peacetime, is
intended to raise individual and unit proficiency to levels
necessary for mission accomplishment.

General E.C. Meyer, former Chief of Staff of the Army

TRAINING–THE ONLY WAY

American Soldiers in Training. *Hit the Ground Running.*

*If we say (maybe in other words) that we love the soldier, and if this comes from not just our mouths but from down deep in our soul, then we really have no choice but to bend every effort, every resource, every activity, and every priority toward his training ...
Not because it is true that 'training is our most important peacetime activity.' Not because it is also true that 'training is what the soldier gets paid for.' Not because it is also true that 'training in peacetime keeps him alive in war.' But because way down deep, beneath all those truths, is the even more fundamental truth that TRAINING is the flat-out only way that the soldier can be what he entered our Army to be ... the only way ... the only way we can meet his expectations ... the only way that organizational and individual goals can both be served, and the only way that we can preclude what really amounts to cheating the man whom we must one day send to perform 'the noblest act of mankind.'*

Colonel Dandridge M. *Mike* Malone

CHAPTER 11

HONOR, HONORING AND PRIDE

This chapter honors those who served and continue to serve our nation and those who have, from their own hearts, shown a level of pride for America and Americans.

Air Force Captain. Capt. Scott F. O'Grady cheers with well-wishers upon his return to Aviano AB, Italy, 9 June 1995. Photo by Sgt. Stephen P. Alderete.

It wasn't the reward that mattered or the recognition you might harvest. It was your depth of commitment, your quality of service, the product of your devotion—these were the things that counted in a life. When you gave purely, the honor came in the giving, and that was honor enough.

Captain Scott O' Grady, the U.S. Air Force officer and aviator who was shot down during a flight mission over Bosnia in 1995 and survived six days being hunted by hostile ground troops before being rescued by U.S. rescue forces

*A nation reveals itself not only by the men it produces,
but also by the men it honors, the men it remembers.*

President John F. Kennedy

*History has shown that personal honor is the one thing
valued more than life itself by the majority of men.*

S.L.A. Marshall

*Whether you be man or woman you will never
do anything in this world without courage.
It is the greatest quality of the mind next to honor.*

James L. Allen

MEDALS

By B.J. Cassady. Mr. Cassady is a Vietnam-era, Disabled Veteran, Writer, Poet, and Author. Dedicated to all whose service has made us free.

Mommy, can I pin the medal on grandpa's uniform today? I asked. *No dear, this is not the time nor the place*, she responded. My young years did not make me understand. I went to my father and said, *Daddy, can I pin the medals on grandpa's uniform today?*

My father looked at me for a long time, as if pondering the weight of the universe and replied, *Yes, you can. But first do you know what the medals mean?* He queried. *I guess it means he served in World War Two and did brave stuff,* I responded.

Let's sit down and I will tell you a story before we go see your grandpa. During the battle of Okinawa he personally attacked a machine gun nest and saved the lives of his company. Then during Truk Island he carried off his wounded commanding officer, during the heat of battle, saving his life. Then during the retaking of some of the other Islands he carried ammo to men that were almost out. During the battle he was wounded and yet still fought because he felt he made a difference. Well he received two bronze stars, a Silver Star, Purple Heart and the Congressional Medal of Honor, given by President Truman himself. Your grandpa, being shy, kept the honors quiet and keeps the ribbons and awards in a drawer to be worn only during special ceremonies.

Now do you understand about your grandpa, my father asked. I was in awe of my grandfather. He always treated me so gentle and with all the love in the world. He told me once he treated me so because of all the anger, evil and hurt he had seen. *Love,* he said, *balances out all the bad in the world.*

Yes. I understand, as I looked at my father. *Then lets go and you can put the medals on his uniform,* stated dad.

We drove for about 15 minutes, the medals weighing heavy in my lap. I tried to think about what it must have been like for my grandpa, but I couldn't imagine how it must have been.

We pulled into the driveway where grandpa was and entered the building. I walked up to the casket where grandpa was dressed in his army uniform and I pinned his country's pride upon my grandpa's uniform.

Thanks grandpa ... thanks. Thanks for your sacrifice and my freedom. I tearfully gave him a Boy Scout salute, then, waited for the service.

We meet here to pay glad homage to the memory of our illustrious dead; but let us keep ever clear before our minds the fact that mere lip-loyalty is no loyalty at all, and that the only homage that counts is the homage of deeds, not of words. It is but an idle waste of time to celebrate the memory of the dead unless we, the living, in our lives strive to show ourselves not unworthy of them. If the careers of Washington and Grant are not vital and full of meaning to us, if they are merely part of the storied past, and stir us to no eager emulation in the ceaseless, endless war for right against wrong, then the root of right thinking is not in us; and where we do not think right we cannot act right.

President Theodore Roosevelt, April 27, 1900

Bury Me with Soldiers

Arlington Cemetery.

I've played a lot of roles in life;
I've met a lot of men,
I've done a lot of things I'd like to think
I wouldn't do again.
And though I'm young, I'm old enough
To know someday I'll die.
And to think about what lies beyond,
Beside whom I would lie.
Perhaps it doesn't matter much;
Still if I had my choice,
I'd want a grave 'mongst
Soldiers when At last death quells my voice.
I'm sick of the hypocrisy of lectures of the wise.
I'll take the man, with all the flaws,
Who goes, though scared, and dies.
The troops I knew were commonplace
They didn't want the war;
They fought because their fathers and
Their fathers had before.
They cursed and killed and wept ...
God knows They're easy to deride ...
But bury me with men like these;
They faced the guns and died.
It's funny when you think of it,
The way we got along.
We'd come from different worlds
To live in one where no one belongs,

I didn't even like them all;
I'm sure they'd all agree.
Yet I would give my life for them,
I know some did for me.
So bury me with soldiers, please,
Though much maligned they be.
Yes, bury me with soldiers, for
I miss their company.
We'll not soon see their likes again;
We've had our fill of war.
But bury me with men like them
Till someone else does more.

Author Unknown

What is life without honor? Degradation is worse than death.

Lieutenant General Thomas J. *Stonewall* Jackson

Whatever you think you'd like to be doing in your life or
with your life, you ought to look in the mirror
and be proud of what you are doing with it today.
If you are wearing the uniform, there is no more noble cause or
calling that could guide your life and your actions than what you
are doing today and the nation needs us more than ever. I am
proud to be wearing the uniform and I hope you are, too.

General John P. Jumper, Air Force Chief of Staff

Your silent tents of green
We deck with fragrant flowers;
Yours has the suffering been,
The memory shall be ours.

Henry Wadsworth Longfellow

Arlington Cemetery.

D-Day Paratrooper Veterans. 82nd and 101st Airborne Division paratroopers gather in France for the 50th Anniversary of D-Day. Many of these paratroopers parachuted into France on this anniversary.

MEN WHO ONCE ACTED THEIR BEST

I now know why men who have been to war yearn to reunite. Not to tell stories or look at old pictures. Not to laugh or weep. Comrades gather because they long to be with the men who, once acted their best, men who suffered and sacrificed, who were stripped raw, right down to their humanity. I did not pick these men. They were delivered by fate and the military. But I know them in a way I know no other men. I have never given anyone such trust. They were willing to guard something more precious than my life. They would have carried my reputation, the memory of me. It was part of the bargain we all made, the reason we were so willing to die for one another. I cannot say where we are headed. Ours are not perfect friendships; those are the province of legend and myth. A few of my comrades drift far from me now, sending back only occasional word. I know that one day even these could fall to silence. Some of the men will stay close, a couple, perhaps, always at hand as long as I have memory, I will think of them all, every day. I am sure that when I leave this world, my last thought will be of my family and my comrades, such good men ... all of them.

Michael Norman, from his book, *These Good Men*

THE LAST PULSE OF THIS NATION'S EXISTENCE

Oliver Wendell Holmes, Jr.

A Memorial Day address delivered by Oliver Wendell Holmes, Jr. on May 30, 1884.

Memorial Day celebrates and solemnly reaffirms from year to year a national act of enthusiasm and faith. It embodies in the most impressive form our belief that to act with enthusiasm and faith is the condition of acting greatly. To fight out a war, you must believe something and want something with all your might. So must you do to carry anything else to an end worth reaching. More than that, you must be willing to commit yourself to a course, perhaps a long and hard one, without being able to foresee exactly where you will come out. All that is required of you is that you should go some whither as hard as ever you can. The rest belongs to fate. One may fall–at the beginning of the charge or at the top of the earthworks; but in no other way can he reach the rewards of victory.

Theirs was a sublime amalgam of patriotism, duty, devotion, acceptance of self-sacrifice, and idealism—above all, idealism. They were the least apathetic people in our Nation's history. And while doubtless many rallied to the colors because they, like their neighbors and friends, were electrified by the summons of the fife and drum, those who found themselves locked in that terrible four-year ordeal persisted to the finish, or to their deaths, out of a sense of idealism–devotion to ideals they cherished more than life itself. Their devotion was a *Transcendence of Self.* I bless and revere them–North and South alike–heroes to me forever. As the poet wrote, *Love and tears for the Blue; Tears and love for the Gray.* May their gallant souls rest in peace, and be honored and glorified, to the last pulse of this country's existence!

A QUIET CONFIDENCE THAT WAS DEAFENING

By Lieutenant Colonel Rick Jones, U.S. Air Force.

I just witnessed something I don't think I'll ever forget. I was down near the cafeteria in the Pentagon meeting a friend for lunch and I see a very large crowd of people inside. I walk in and soon find myself standing less than three feet away from our Commander-in-Chief and right beside the Secretary of Defense (and a bunch of Secret Service folks). President Bush was walking around shaking hands and thanking all of us for what we do. He kept saying to people, *Don't worry*—as if to say, I've got it under control. He must have shaken 1,000 hands or more. What particularly struck me was his presence–not a particularly large man in stature, but he had an aura of a giant–a smile on his face, yet you can sense he was a man on a mission–a man of purpose and conviction–there was just this feeling that he is THE MAN, and he is in charge–he had a quiet confidence that was deafening!

Then, a group of folks just behind me started singing *God Bless America* and, in no time, the entire room–which was packed– was singing the song. It was enough to give anyone goose bumps. If there was a dry eye in the place, I couldn't see it (probably because my eyes weren't too dry). It was just one of those once-in-a-lifetime experiences that I shall never forget.

After *God Bless America*, there were a few chants of *USA! USA! USA!* followed by a lot of applause. When President Bush finally made his way toward the entrance, he turned with his confident smile and waved at everyone, and the room just erupted in cheers and whistles and applause. I've been to professional football games where the noise wasn't that loud. It was just such a wonderful experience–and it made me:

1. So very happy that George W. Bush is our President and Commander-in-Chief.

2. So proud to be an American.

Just thought I'd share. Rick

REMEMBER ME?

Author Unknown.

Some people call me Old Glory, others call me the Star Spangled Banner, but whatever you call me, I am your flag. The flag of the United States of America. ... Something has been bothering me; so, I thought I might talk it over with you. *Because it is about you and me.* I remember sometime ago people lined up on both sides of the street to watch the parade; and naturally, I was leading every parade, proudly waving in the breeze. When your daddy saw me coming, he immediately removed his hat and placed it against his left shoulder so that his hand was directly over his heart ... remember? And you ... I remember you. Standing there straight as a soldier. You didn't have a hat, but you were giving the right salute. Remember little sister? Not to be outdone, she was saluting the same as you with her right hand over her heart ... remember? *What happened?* I'm still the same old flag; oh, I have a few more stars since you were a boy, a lot more blood has been shed since those parades of long ago. But now I don't feel as proud as I used to. When I come down your street, you just stand there with your hands in your pockets and I may get a small glance and then you look away. Then I see the children running around and shouting ... they don't seem to know who I am ... I saw one man take his hat off then look around. He didn't see anybody else with theirs off so he quickly put his back on. Is it a sin to be patriotic anymore? Have you forgotten what I stand for and where I've been? ... Anzio, Guadalcanal, Korea and now Vietnam. Take a look at the Memorial Honor Rolls sometime, of those who never came back to keep this republic free ... one nation under God ... when you salute me, you are actually saluting them. Well, it won't be long until I'll be coming down your street again. So, when you see me, stand straight, place your right hand over your heart ... and I'll salute you, by waving back ... and I'll know that you remember!

A TRUE COMMANDER IN CHIEF

In November 2001, President and Mrs. Bush were on their way to Marine One to leave for Camp David for the weekend. The First Lady led the way into the helicopter with the spaniel dog on the leash, and the president was right behind her with the Scotty on the leash. As the First Lady entered the chopper, the Marine at the gangway saluted and held his salute. The Scottie the president was walking decided it wanted to squat right when he got to the steps. The president pulled on its leash, but the stubborn Scottie persisted in squatting. The president bent down and scooped up the pooch and entered Marine One. After he entered, the Marine cut his salute and returned to the position of attention. Moments later the president reemerged from the helicopter and out onto the steps. The Marine was standing at attention, head and eyes straight ahead. The president leaned over and tapped him on the left arm. The startled Marine turned his body toward the president and received his returned salute! This simple act demonstrated President Bush's respect for our military people. He really *does* get it. Most any

President George W. Bush.

other person of his stature would have just continued his journey, disregarding the neglected return salute. Not George W. Bush. He is earning the respect of the military community, not expecting it— as most would.

FOR PEOPLE THEY DON'T EVEN KNOW

By Eric Dawson, Fairhope, Alabama.

I want to tell you of an experience I had last night flying home from Atlanta. The pilot came on the intercom and went through the usual announcements telling us that *we're just east of Montgomery cruising at 28,000 feet* and *you've picked a beautiful night for flying, just look at the gorgeous southern sunset out of the right side of the plane.* He then, however, said this:

> Please bear with me as I deviate from the script, but I want you all to know that simply by coincidence you have been granted both the privilege and honor of escorting the body of Army PFC Howard Johnson, Jr. home tonight. PFC Johnson was killed in Iraq defending the freedoms we all enjoy, and fighting to extend those freedoms to the people of Iraq. We are also accompanied by PFC Johnson's cousin, Marine Major Talley, who has been chosen by the family to escort PFC Johnson home. Semper Fi!

Private First Class Howard Johnson, Jr.
Age 21, Killed In Action, 23 March 2003, Iraq.

The plane quickly became very quiet, but soon erupted in thunderous applause that lasted for several minutes. It was quite moving, to say the least. As I sat there thinking about what the pilot had said, and visualizing PFC Johnson's dead body riding below me in the belly of that plane, I noticed a couple of things. Two rows in front of me sat a father holding his daughter, an infant, and they were practicing *ma-ma* and in the row behind me was another young boy, probably two or so, learning to count to 10. Now obviously both are too young to realize we're at war, or that one of our dead was with us, but it made me think, and this is the point: These warriors, mostly young, all volunteers, everyday are prepared to give their lives for our future, for a safer, more secure future for people they don't even know, all based on the principle that fighting and dying for this country is worth it. You all know and agree with this, but not everyone does, so I would ask that if you meet anyone that's not *on board* with this philosophy (i.e., the protesters to which Bob refers) that you *correct the situation*. By the way, the flight ended with all of us deplaning only to line the windows of the gatehouse to watch PFC Johnson's body, draped in the American flag, be rolled out of the plane and into a waiting hearse that was surrounded by his family members. Please pray that our soldiers' sight is acute, their aim is true, and that as many come home as God can spare.

IN THE SHADOW OF A GIANT

General John P. Jumper, Air Force Chief of Staff, provided the following remarks at the burial ceremony for Senior Airman Jason Cunningham, Kirtland Air Force Base, NM, September 13, 2002. Senior Airman Cunningham, age 26, from Camarillo, California, was killed in action, March 4, 2002, in an ambush at Takur Gahar, during Operation Anaconda, Afghanistan.

In the frailty of our human existence, we find ourselves ill-equipped to convey to one another the extremes of our emotions. For the peak of our love or the depths of our sorrow, we have only feeble words that never truly capture the peaks or the valleys of our feelings. I stand before you today in a humble attempt to assemble the words to honor a hero, Senior Airman Jason Cunningham, knowing

Senior Airman Jason Cunningham.

in advance that my attempt will fall short of the tribute that is his due. The words you will hear in the citation accompanying the Air Force Cross speak of patriotism, supreme dedication, ultimate selflessness, the very soul of that virtuous task our pararescuemen assign to themselves … that others may live. And I know, and I have witnessed the passion with which Jason and the band of brothers we call pararescuemen, have embraced this creed. I myself, on many occasions, over hundreds of combat missions … I've sat on my heart and throat as I watched the PJ be lowered down through the jungle canopy. And wait for him to ascend again with a downed airman or not ascend again … at all. We have some other heroes with us today, Chief Master Sergeant Joel Talley and Major Tom Newman, both who served in Vietnam at the time that I was there … both winners of the Air Force Cross so that others might live. I have carried around with me for many years a poem that pays tribute to those who were given a second chance, those who were allowed to live because of the heroics of others, a poem written by a soldier. And I'd like to share it with you now:

I ask God for strength that I might achieve …
I was made weak that I might learn humbly to obey …
I ask for help that I might do great things …
I was given infirmity that I might do better things.

I ask for riches that I might be happy …
I was given poverty that I might be wise …
I ask for power that I might have the praise of men …
I was given weakness that I might feel the need of God.

I ask for all things that I might enjoy life ...
I was given life that I might enjoy all things.
I got nothing that I asked for but everything I had hoped for ...
almost despite myself my unspoken prayers were answered.
I am among all men most richly blessed.

Jason did not get a second chance. But he gave a second chance to others. We stand today in a shadow of a giant ... a Senior Airman named Jason Cunningham. And while I and my colleagues flew hundreds of missions in combat, Jason only flew one. And in my hundreds of missions ... I never approached the valor, the honor that Jason did in just one mission. To the family who bears the greatest burden, Jason passes his strength and his courage ... others do live today because of your husband ... your father ... your son ... your brother ... our colleague ... in a great airman ... Senior Airman Jason Cunningham. Thank you all very much.

THE SPIRIT AND PRIDE OF THE UNITED STATES

Letter from Lieutenant Landry, U.S. Navy.

It wasn't until a few days ago though, that we started doing something that I feel may be the first thing I've seen in my short naval career that has truly made a difference. Right now we're supporting the *USS COLE* and her crew in Aden. When the attack occurred we were a day away. Just by luck we happened to be on our way out of the Gulf and headed towards the Suez and could get here in a relatively short amount of time. I know what you all have seen on CNN, because we have seen it too. I just want you all to know that what you see doesn't even scratch the surface. I'm not going to get into it for obvious reasons. But I will tell you that right now there are 250+ sailors just a few miles away living in hell on Earth. I'm sitting in a nice air-conditioned stateroom; they're sleeping out on the decks at night. You can't even imagine the conditions they're living in, and yet they are still fighting 24 hours a day to save their ship and free the bodies of those still trapped and send them home. As bad as it is, they're doing an incredible job. The very fact that these people are still functioning is beyond my comprehension. Whatever you imagine as the worst, multiply it by ten and you might get there.

Today I was tasked to photo rig the ship and surrounding area. It looked so much worse than I had imagined, unbelievable really, with debris and disarray everywhere, the ship listing, the hole in her side. I wish I had the power to relay to you all what I have seen, but words just won't do it. I do want to tell you the first thing that jumped out at me–the Stars and Stripes flying. I can't tell you how that made me feel ... even in this God-forsaken hellhole our flag was more beautiful than words can describe. Then I started to notice the mass of activity going on below, scores of people working non-stop in 90 plus degree weather to save this ship. They're doing it with almost no electrical power and they're sleeping (when they can sleep) outside on the decks because they can't stand the smell or the heat or the darkness inside. They only want to eat what we bring them because they're all scared of eating something brought by the local vendors. Even with all that, the *USS COLE* and her crew are sending a message guys, and it's that even acts of cowardice and hate can do nothing to the spirit and pride of the United States.

I have never been so proud of what I do, or of the men and women that I serve with as I was today. There are sixteen confirmed dead sailors who put it on the line for all of us, and some of them are still trapped here. Please take a minute to pray for their families and say a word of thanks for their sacrifice–one made so that we can live the lives that we do. All of you that serve with me, thank you. All of you that have loved ones that serve, thank you. Please feel free to pass this on to those you think will appreciate it.

USS Cole. Bomb Blast.

A BUILDING BLOCK TO AMERICA

Remarks as delivered by The Honorable Richard Danzig, Secretary of the Navy, *USS COLE* Memorial Service, Norfolk, Virginia, October 18, 2000.

One of the reasons that I love America is because it loves its citizens. In other times, and on this very day in other places, people are regarded as means and not ends, as fodder, stepping stones, dispensable assets. Because we are not like that, we grieve today. We see in the 17 people who died on October 12th, 17 wonders, 17 sons and daughters. We mourn brothers and sisters, mothers, fathers, and those who will never be mothers and fathers. Seventeen unique people. We cherish them. We grieve because we couldn't protect them. Instead, they died protecting us. That we live in America is, in itself, an act of grace. We came to it naturally; we were born into it. Or, we were welcomed as immigrants; we were naturalized. By either route, America has been for every one of us a gift, and what a stupendous gift–a country that was built collectively but cherishes us individually; a country built of the effort of servicemen and statesmen, farmers and factory workers, those who toiled on the railroad and those who bankrolled it. Our philosophers, our politicians, our priests, all together, created something bigger than any of us; and then, they gave it to us. Any true gift is infused with opportunity and responsibility that arises from that opportunity. An inherent talent, a good education, money in the bank–they all cry to the recipient, what will you make of this? What will you do individually? What will we do collectively in light of how many have done so much for us? These 17 answered that question. They didn't opt just for themselves, they didn't stay home, they didn't turn away from their country. They put themselves out there. They joined a family, the United States Navy, and the *USS COLE*–a ship, the very essence of a group enterprise. And think not just of these 17. Think of the 39 who were injured, and then think of the 240 beyond them; the 240 who absorbed the shock of the explosion, who saw the death of 17, the injury of two score, but who turned to and fought on; fought together for their ship and for their shipmates. For two days and two nights, they fought under the most extreme conditions–blood, bent and broken steel, flooding, uncertainty and danger. They saved their ship, their injured–every one of them–and each other. And then their generators failed. The waters rose, and they had to do it all over again. Waist-deep in water, manning bucket brigades by hand, they did it again. Amidst all of that, their captain said to me, *Mr. Secretary, we will save this ship. We will repair this ship. We will take this ship home and we will sail this ship again to sea.* In every gift there is a responsibility. The *Cole* has given us a gift. The 17 join more than 1.3 million service men and women who have given us their lives. Thirty-nine from the *Cole* were injured; 240 fought on. All together, they added a building block to America. Will we, as recipients of this gift, live up to them? I think we will; we're Americans. Thank you, *Cole*.

The nation that forgets its defenders will itself be forgotten.

President Calvin Coolidge

In all that lies before us, may God grant us wisdom, and may He watch over the United States of America.

President George W. Bush, 20 September 2001, Address to a Joint Session of Congress and the American People

It is foolish and wrong to mourn the men who died. Rather we should thank God that such men lived.

General George S. Patton, Jr.

I WILL NEVER FORGET THE SMOKY ODOR

Aboard the *USS Theodore Roosevelt*. The flag that three weary firefighters raised from the ruins of the World Trade Center on September 11 was returned to them Tuesday in a solemn ceremony aboard the *USS Theodore Roosevelt*. (In all, the squadrons flew 2,100 combat sorties.)

The flag had been sent to the aircraft carrier in October as the ship steamed toward waters near Afghanistan, and was given back as the *Roosevelt* headed home. The flag flew on the carrier and six other ships in the war against terrorism. As one sailor sang the Navy Hymn, three other sailors handed the folded flag to two of the three New York City firefighters, George Johnson and William Eisengrein, who hoisted the flag at ground zero. The image was captured in a newspaper photograph seen around the world. *This is truly a humbling experience*, Johnson told the *Roosevelt* crew. Johnson then presented a fire chief's helmet to Rear Adm. Mark P. Fitzgerald, commander of the *Theodore Roosevelt's* battle group, as the crew cheered. The carrier, which was due to return Wednesday to Norfolk, was about 300 miles off the Virginia coast during the brief ceremony Tuesday. About 60 aircraft took off from the deck Tuesday and headed to their bases in Virginia, South Carolina, Florida and Washington State. About 5,500 sailors and Marines are aboard the *Roosevelt*, which departed Norfolk, Virginia, on September 19 in support of Operation Enduring Freedom. *I'm sure they all left with a little trepidation as to what was going to happen out here*, Fitzgerald said. *They rose to the task.* Petty Officer 3rd Class Willie Price, 27, of Oceanside, California, was to be among the first allowed off the ship Wednesday. He is one of about 50 sailors who had a child born while he was at sea. *I can't wait*, Price said. *I don't think I'm going to sleep at all tonight.* The New York delegation in the flag ceremony included police from New York City and the Port Authority of New York and New Jersey. Several New York members of Congress also attended the service, as did House Speaker Dennis Hastert. The third firefighter, Daniel McWilliams, could not make it to the ship because he attended the funeral of a firefighter who died in the attack, said Michael J. Handy, military liaison for New York Mayor Michael Bloomberg.

The flag was signed by New York Governor George Pataki and former Mayor Rudolph Giulani on September 23 before it was presented to Admiral Robert J. Natter, Commander-in-Chief of the Atlantic Fleet. Natter directed that it be sent to the *Roosevelt*. *I will never forget the smoky odor as the flag was unwrapped in my office*, said Captain Richard J. O'Hanlon, the *Roosevelt's* commanding officer. The flag is to be displayed in a place of honor in New York; the location has not been decided, Handy said. After the ceremony, Handy presented another flag to the Roosevelt crew: the flag of New York City. *We are sorely wounded in the city of New York*, Handy said. *And one of the real inspirations has been over the months to watch you go off to sea, to watch you go off to war and protect us.*

BRASSO AND PRIDE

Of the many monuments to the Nation's Fallen there is no other more powerful memorial than the Vietnam Veterans Memorial in Washington, D.C. There is a flag near the entrance of the memorial. At its base are the seals of all the services.

Every morning, the Marines from the Marine Barracks at 8th and I streets polish the Eagle, Globe and Anchor. The other seals have not been touched since the Memorial was built.

TOO MANY BRAVE SOULS

The Military Academy Cemetery rewards the wandering ironist, by Jamie Malanowski, from *Time* Magazine, 17 November 1997.

Walk through the graveyard; cemeteries reward the ironist. The collision between what once was and what is no more, the ineffability of a last impression, the follow-up question that can never be answered—it's all right there. In the cemetery at the U.S. Military Academy at West Point, Veterans Day will pass without formal observation; if the weather holds, the 6,827 men, women and children interred there will spend the day under a cerulean sky and pompon trees, and the living around them will give them the merest thought. Cemeteries reward the ironist.

Start in a bit from the entrance. There is a stone marking the plot of a Colonel Buchwald. It is large but not enormous, and Buchwald probably served his country well. The site would blend unnoticed if his neighbor to the left, lying under a small government-issue marker, wasn't Norman Cota, the general who on D-day rallied the scattered American invasion force on Omaha Beach and pushed it past the German defenses; Robert Mitchum played him in *The Longest Day*. A hundred yards away, under a similarly modest headstone, rests Alonzo H. Cushing, who commanded the federal battery at Gettysburg that stood at the very point Pickett aimed his charge. Cushing, twice wounded, stayed at his guns, firing double canister at the converging Confederates until a third shot got him. Right behind him is buried Judson Kilpatrick, a general considered so profligate with the lives of his men that they called him *Kill Cavalry*. At the end of the row, under an obelisk, lies George Armstrong Custer. Or what may be Custer. When Custer was disinterred a year after the Battle of the Little Bighorn, diggers found that animals had scattered the bones. They took their best guess. Cemeteries reward the ironist.

There are heroes here: Paul Bunker, the only Army player to make Walter Camp's All-America team at two different positions, who died in a Japanese POW camp after smuggling his unit's flag past his captors; Ed White, who walked in space and died in Apollo 1; Joe Stilwell of China; Lucius Clay of the Berlin airlift; George Goethals of the Panama Canal. The biggest monument, however, a large pyramid, belongs to a general named Egbert Viele. An eminent engineer, he helped design the cemetery, which perhaps explains his prominence. The entrance to the pyramid is guarded by a pair of sphinxes. These are not the original sphinxes, which Mrs. Viele found too buxom, and which were then sunk in the Hudson River. Cemeteries reward the ironist.

Walk around. Walter Schulze was assigned to fly the news that the Great War was over to units east of the Rhine; on the way home, his plane crashed and he was killed. Art Bonifas, near the end of his tour, took a group out one day in 1976 to prune a poplar in the DMZ; the North Koreans set upon them and killed him. In Vietnam, Ron Zinn, twice an Olympic race walker, went out on patrol ahead of his unit and stepped on a mine. Bob Fuellhart was advising a Vietnamese battalion; while word was being sent up from the rear that his daughter had just been born, word was being sent back that he had been killed. Cemeteries reward the ironist.

I got interested in this place, says Lieutenant Colonel Conrad Crane, a member of West Point's history department, *when I asked the cadets in my class why they were here. Some said free education or to get a job on Wall Street. I wanted to show them what being a West Pointer is all about*. He shows them a graveyard full of the young, dating from the first man buried here in 1782. Walk along the western edge, and you find the dead of World War II, many of whom perished young. Charles Finley of the class of 1943, killed in Normandy in 1944. Henry Benitez of the class of '42, killed at Falaise in '44. Turner Chambliss, Jr., '43, killed June 6, 1944. And so on, until you turn a corner and start finding George Tow and Samuel Coursen of the class of '49, killed in action in Korea, 1950. Over behind the Viele monument are the graves from Vietnam. There is a row in which 10 of 11 graves are occupied by members of the class of '66, and that does not begin to encompass that class's contribution. When that run ends, you have five in a row from the class of '64. One belongs to John Hottell, III–a Rhodes scholar, twice a recipient of the Silver Star–who was killed in 1970. The year before, he had written his own obituary and sent it in a sealed envelope to his wife. *I deny that I died for anything–not my country, not my Army, not my fellow man*, he wrote. *I lived for these things, and the manner in which I chose to do it involved the very real chance that I would die ... my love for*

West Point and the Army was great enough ... for me to accept this possibility as part of a price which must be paid for things of great value. Walk through the graveyard; cemeteries humble the ironist.

GOT YOUR BACK

I am a small and precious child, my dad's been sent to fight.
The only place I'll see his face, is in my dreams at night.
He will be gone too many days for my young mind to keep track.
I may be sad, but I am proud. My daddy's got your back.

I am a caring mother. My son has gone to war.
My mind is filled with worries that I've never known before.
Every day I try to keep my thoughts from turning black.
I may be scared, but I am proud. My son has got your back.

I am a strong and loving wife, with a husband soon to go.
There are times I'm terrified in a way most will never know.
I bite my lip, and force a smile as I watch my husband pack.
My heart may break, but I am proud. My husband's got your back.

I am a Soldier. Serving proud and standing tall.
I fight for freedom, yours and mine, by answering this call.
I do my job while knowing the thanks it sometimes lacks.
Say a prayer that I'll come home. It's me who's got your back.

Author Unknown

CJTF-180. Soldiers of the Army Space Support
Team and their leaders, Combined Joint Task
Force 180, Kandahar, Afghanistan, October 2002.

STOP TO SALUTE ON MEMORIAL DAY

By Captain John Rasmussen, U.S. Army, 22 May 2002. Eagle Base, Bosnia and Herzegovina. Courtesy of Army News Service.

It was raining *cats and dogs* and I was late for physical training. Traffic was backed up at Fort Campbell, Kentucky, and was moving way too slowly. I was probably going to be late and I was growing more and more impatient. The pace slowed almost to a standstill as I passed Memorial Grove, the site built to honor the soldiers who died in the Gander airplane crash, the worst redeployment accident in the history of the 101st Airborne Division (Air Assault). Because it was close to Memorial Day, a small American flag had been placed in the ground next to each soldier's memorial plaque. My concern at the time, however, was getting past the bottleneck, getting out of the rain and getting to PT on time. All of a sudden, infuriatingly, just as the traffic was getting started again, the car in front of me stopped. A soldier, a private of course, jumped out in the pouring rain and ran over toward the grove. I couldn't believe it! This knucklehead was holding up everyone for who knows what kind of prank. Horns were honking. I waited to see the butt-chewing that I wanted him to get for making me late. He was getting soaked to the skin. His BDUs were plastered to his frame. I watched–as he ran up to one of the memorial plaques, picked up the small American flag that had fallen to the ground in the wind and the rain, and set it upright again. Then, slowly, he came to attention, saluted, ran back to his car, and drove off. I'll never forget that incident. That soldier, whose name I will never know, taught me more about duty, honor, and respect than a hundred books or a thousand lectures. That simple salute–that single act of honoring his fallen brother and his flag–encapsulated all the Army values in one gesture for me. It said, *I will never forget. I will keep the faith. I will finish the mission. I am an American soldier*. I thank God for examples like that. And on this Memorial Day, I will remember all those who paid the ultimate price for my freedom, and one private, soaked to the skin, who honored them.

THEY ARE COMMITTED TO OUR ARMY

By Sergeant Major of the Army Jack Tilley.

I was also privileged to attend the 11th Armored Cavalry Regiment's annual reunion, and it was uplifting for me to be among such great soldiers. I'd ask all of you to take every chance you have to participate in similar functions and thank our veterans for their service.

Although they no longer wear the uniform, they are committed to our Army, our country and our way of life. They will never forget their service, and neither should we–their legacy is an integral part of who we are.

IN SIMPLE OBEDIENCE TO DUTY: A VIETNAM PERSPECTIVE

By Retired Lieutenant General James Link, U.S. Army, former commander of Redstone Arsenal, delivered this address at the breakfast commemorating the arrival in Huntsville, Alabama of the traveling Vietnam Veterans Memorial Wall.

Thank you, ladies and gentlemen, distinguished guests, fellow veterans, and especially fellow veterans of the war in Vietnam. It is indeed a tremendous honor for me to stand before you this morning as we come together to remember fallen comrades, MIAs/POWs and a very important time in our lives. A time of war, a time of conflict not only in Southeast Asia, but throughout our nation. Indeed a time that has shaped our national consciousness, and for we veterans, a time which forged a sense of self that in many ways defines us still today. Lest we forget, how then do we remember? How do we honor those who did not come home, or came home broken and bent in both body and spirit?

I remember when the architectural design of the Vietnam War Memorial Wall was first proposed. Many of us recoiled at the thought of a ditch on the Mall, listing nothing more than the names of those who paid the ultimate sacrifice. Surely, this was yet one more insult hurled at those who had answered the call to serve their nation rather than serve themselves. But that wall has transcended all things political and overcome controversy, as it reaches out to us who served, and even those who did not serve, while deeply touching all of us who lost comrades, friends, neighbors and loved ones during that troubled time. The mystery of the wall is found in its majestic simplicity. Panels of black stone that hold not only the names of those killed, but in its mirror-like finish, the faces of all of us who come to witness its solemn statement. In that reflection, we are made one with the monument, we join its essence, and are consumed by images behind the names. Images of young men, their lives cut short, their personal sacrifices often unrecorded, their selfless service, unflinching courage, and the unique love and caring that is shared by comrades in arms. It is the wound on our National Mall that never heals, but it does serve to soothe the deep scars on those of us who carry heavy memories, and for some perhaps a little guilt for having been the ones fortunate enough to return to *the world*. As this Memorial travels around the country, it invariably brings with it a lot of discussion and perhaps even rekindled old arguments about the Vietnam War. The arrival of the Vietnam Memorial Wall in Huntsville provides an opportunity for us to reflect on this important period in our individual lives and our nation's history. Of course, there are those who might say we veterans are still too close to the heat of battle, too burdened by personal experiences to make objective judgments about the Vietnam War. To that, I say Bull! I've grown weary of those in the media, academia and the entertainment industry, who would purport to speak for us, or to try to define us a bunch of hair-trigger psychopaths on the verge of insanity or some unspeakable violence. We who were actually there know what we saw, and we know what we did. Each of us is just one of the millions who proudly served, having done our duty with honor. I see little of what I experienced reflected in Oliver Stone's movies. I personally think Oliver donated a few too many of his brain cells to his drug use. In my view, movies like *Apocalypse Now* are nothing more than a collection of psychotic experiences made up in Hollywood bearing scant resemblance to the reality we experienced. You and I can certainly recognize the difference between artistic license and a lie, can't we! America's involvement in Vietnam lasted for thirteen years, from 1960 to 1973. Of course, the result was not victory at all. Not even a cease-fire or a demilitarized strip of land between North and South as happened in Korea. Just negotiated terms allowing the United States of America to *withdraw with honor*. Whatever that meant. So we didn't return home to victory parades and kisses in Times Square. Most of us were just another passenger aboard a chartered airliner (mine was a Braniff Airlines Boeing 707) painted a heinous green color. What a beautiful sight! Others came home in Air Force cargo planes to be dumped at some military base usually in the middle of the night. Remember, we came home to antipathy and in many cases to antagonism. We were told to quickly get out of our uniforms in order to avoid confrontations on city streets. No wonder it has taken so long for many of us to even want to talk about the war. But talk we must for we are living witnesses, and if we are silent others will continue to spin a version of the truth that best suits their personal agenda. We must dispel the myths that have grown up around the War, and there are so many. Those of us who served must debunk these myths at every opportunity, and today is one of those.

The first myth is that the armed forces of the United States suffered a major military defeat in Vietnam. Our forces were never defeated in terrible battles where our soldiers and Marines suffered awful casualties, like Dak To and Hamburger Hill, and our airmen suffered too, many killed and captured in the air campaign, but the war was not lost as a result of these battles. In fact, where we found the enemy we defeated him. After the Tet Offensive in 1968, the Vietcong and the North Vietnamese operating in the south were so soundly defeated that they could not launch another major offensive until 1972.

That didn't deter the North Vietnamese, since they were willing to lose the war on the battlefield, they were after victory in the minds of the American people. Perhaps we could have won a military victory, but it would have taken many more than the 500,000 troops we had in Vietnam at the height of the war. Besides, by 1969, public opinion in the United States wanted us out of Vietnam. The role of the media in deciding this issue has been the subject of many books and articles, so I won't go into that here. I will say I don't believe the media caused us to lose the war, although some in the press were trying their best to make it so. Those of you who attended the AUSA Conference in Washington this year will recall General Weyand's remarks while accepting the

George C. Marshall Award. Following Tet 1968, he was interviewed by Walter Cronkite in the Mekong Delta following the resounding defeat of enemy forces there by the U.S. military, including U.S. Navy Riverine Forces. Walter acknowledged the victory, but told General Weyand he preferred to report on the thousands of Vietnamese he had seen being put in mass graves in Hue after Tet. In reporting this rather than any American victory, he said he hoped to bring a quicker end to the war. It didn't seem to bother Mr. Cronkite that the bodies were those of South Vietnamese brutally killed by the North Vietnamese during Tet. Nor did it seem to bother him that he had compromised his own objectivity and integrity in reporting the war. Of course, we who have dedicated our lives defending the Constitution against all enemies foreign and domestic certainly support all its provisions to include the First Amendment. I just hope what we saw in the press in Vietnam and still see today isn't as good as it gets. Our nation deserves better.

The second myth is that somehow the soldiers in Vietnam were very different from those who served in World War II. The myth purports that the Vietnam soldier was much younger, poorly educated, forced to go to war against his will. It is often claimed that they disproportionately came from minority groups, while their better-off social superiors dodged the draft and stayed safe at home out of harm's way. The truth is, of course, different. The average age of the soldiers in Vietnam was just under 23 compared to around 25 in World War II where mass conscription prevailed. The enlisted soldier in Vietnam was actually better educated: 79 percent had completed high school as opposed to just 24 percent in World War II. In Vietnam, 20 percent of the enlisted men had college degrees, three times the number in the Second World War. In a democracy, even your jeep driver may be better educated than you. As far as social representation, studies have shown that blacks and Hispanics were actually slightly underrepresented compared to their percentage of the total population. For instance, African-Americans comprised 13.1 percent of the age group subject to the military; they comprised 12.6 percent of the armed forces, and represented 12.2 percent of the casualties. In 1992 a study looked at the 58,000 Americans killed in Vietnam and found that 30 percent came from families in the lowest third of the income range while 26 percent came from the highest. Not much of a disparity when you look at the facts.

A third myth is that draft evasion was rampant during the Vietnam era and higher than in World War II. Not so. During the Vietnam War about half a million men were draft dodgers, and I bet you know some of their names! Only about 9,000 cases were actually prosecuted, and very few ever served prison time. In World War II, 350,000 were prosecuted for draft evasion and many went to prison. It is interesting to note that during Vietnam 10,000 Americans went to Canada, but up to 30,000 Canadians joined the U.S. armed forces, and of those 10,000 served in Vietnam. We all know cowardice in the face of the draft is not a new phenomenon, but during Vietnam it became an art form. More importantly, draft dodgers made themselves out to be ethical and moral, while those of us who served were made out to be morally inferior, stupid, or just unlucky. The radical left on our campuses had a clear goal of transforming the shame of the self-serving and the fearful into the guilt of the courageous.

A fourth myth is that casualties were disproportionately higher for enlisted men than for officers. Actually, while officers killed in action accounted for 13.5 percent of those who died in Vietnam, they comprised only 12 percent of the troop strength. Proportionally, more officers were killed in Vietnam than in World War II. In Vietnam, we lost twice as many company commanders as we did platoon leaders, confirming in the Vietnam War that leaders led from the front. Another interesting fact you can use to debunk a popular myth is that volunteers, not draftees, accounted for the majority (77 percent) of combat deaths in Vietnam. How many of those do you think were 18-year-olds? Just 101, or less than one tenth of one percent of all those killed.

Well, there are many other myths we could talk about, but instead I'd like to remind you of the humor that accompanied American soldiers in this war, as it has all the others. I suspect many of you remember the time-honored Murphy's Laws of Combat: * Don't look conspicuous ... it draws fire. * If it's stupid, but it works, it's not stupid. * If your attack is going really well, it's an ambush. * When you have secured an area, don't forget to tell the enemy. * Friendly fire ... isn't. * Anything you do can get you shot, including doing nothing. * Never share a foxhole with someone braver than you are. * A sucking chest wound is just nature's way of telling you to slow down. * The buddy system is key to your survival ... it gives the enemy someone else to shoot at. * It's not the one with your name on it you need to worry about, it's the one addressed: *To whom it may concern*.

Remember, nine million men and women served in the military during the 13 years of the war, and three million of those served in the Vietnam Theater. Two thirds of those who saw duty in Vietnam were volunteers and 77 percent of those who died were volunteers. Our American citizen-soldier performed with a tenacity and quality that may never be fully appreciated or truly understood. Should anyone think the war was conducted in an incompetent manner, should look at the numbers: Hanoi admits to 1.4 million of its soldiers killed on the battlefield compared to our 58,000, and about 250,000 South Vietnamese. And if someone tries to convince you that Vietnam was *a dirty little war*, where Air Force and Navy bombs did all the work, you might remind them that this was the most costly war the grunts of the U.S. Marines Corps ever fought—five times as many dead as in World War I, three times as many dead as in Korea, and more total killed and wounded than in all of World War II. To the Vietnam veterans here today, and to all those whose name appears on the Wall, I say you are all heroes. Heroes who faced the issues of this war, including your own possible death, and after weighing those concerns against your obligation to your country, you decided to serve with honor. In the words of a timeless phrase found on the Confederate Memorial in Arlington Cemetery, *Not for fame or reward, not for place or for rank, but in simple obedience to duty, as they understood it*. I ask each of you to treat each other with the dignity and respect you have earned. Reach out and welcome a fellow Vietnam veteran home. God bless each of you, and may God continue to bless this America we love and serve.

A MARINE ON DUTY

I just wanted to get the day over with and go down to Smokey's for a few cold ones. Sneaking a look at my watch, I saw the time, 1655. Five minutes to go. Full dress was hot in the

August sun. Oklahoma summertime was as bad as ever–the heat and humidity at the same level–too damned high. I saw the car pull into the drive, '69 or '70 model Deville, looked factory-new. It pulled into the parking slot at a snail's pace. An old woman got out so damned slow I thought she was paralyzed. She had a cane and a sheaf of flowers, about four or five bunches as best I could tell. I couldn't help myself. The thought came unwanted, and left a slightly bitter taste: *She's going to spend an hour, my damned hip hurts like hell and I'm ready to get the hell out of here right, by-God, now!*

But my duty was to assist anyone coming in. Kevin would lock the *in* gate and if I could hurry the old biddy along, we might make the last half of happy hour. I broke Post Attention. The hip made gritty noises when I took the first step and the pain went up a notch. I must have made a real military sight; middle-aged man with a small pot-gut and half a limp, in Marine Full Dress Uniform, which had lost its razor crease about 30 minutes after I began the watch at the cemetery.

I stopped in front of her, halfway up the walk. She looked up at me with an old woman's squint. *Ma'am, can I assist you in any way?* She took long enough to answer. *Yes, son. Can you carry these flowers? I seem to be moving a tad slow these days. My pleasure, Ma'am.* Well, it wasn't too much of a lie. She looked again. *Marine, where were you stationed? Vietnam, ma'am. Ground-pounder. '69 to '71.* She looked at me closer. *Wounded in action, I see. Well done, Marine. I'll be as quick as I can*, I lied a little bigger. *No hurry, Ma'am.*

She smiled, and winked at me. *Son, I'm 85-years old and I can tell a lie from a long way off. Let's get this done. Might be the last time I can come. My name's Joanne Wieserman, and I've a few Marines I'd like to see one more time. Yes, ma'am. At your service.* She headed for the World War I section, stopping at a stone. She picked one of the bunches out of my arm and laid it on top of the stone. She murmured something I couldn't quite make out. The name on the marble was Donald S. Davidson, USMC, France 1918. She turned away and made a straight line for the World War II section, stopping at one stone. I saw a tear slowly tracking its way down her cheek. She put a bunch on a stone; the name was Stephen X. Davidson, USMC, 1943. She went up the row a ways and laid another bunch on a stone, Stanley J. Wieserman, USMC, 1944. She paused for a second; *Two more, son, and we'll be done.* I almost didn't say anything, but, *Yes, ma'am. Take your time.* She looked confused. *Where's the Vietnam section, son? I seem to have lost my way.*

I pointed with my chin. *That way, ma'am. Oh!* she chuckled quietly. *Son, me and old age ain't too friendly.* She headed down the walk I'd pointed at. She stopped at a couple of stones before she found the ones she wanted. She placed a bunch on Larry Wieserman, USMC, 1968, and the last on Darrel Wieserman, USMC, 1970. She stood there and murmured a few words I still couldn't make out. *OK, son, I'm finished. Get me back to my car and you can go home. Yes, ma'am. If I may ask, were those your kinfolk?* She paused. *Yes, Donald Davidson was my father; Stephan was my uncle; Stanley was my husband; Larry and Darrel were our sons. All killed in action, all Marines.*

She stopped, whether she had finished, or couldn't finish, I don't know. And never have. She made her way to her car, slowly, and painfully. I waited for a polite distance to come between us and double-timed it over to Kevin waiting by the car. *Get to the out-gate quick, Kev. I have something I've got to do.* Kev started to say something but saw the look I gave him. He broke the rules to get us there down the service road. We beat her; she hadn't made it around the rotunda yet. *Kev, stand to attention next to the gate post. Follow my lead.* I humped it across the drive to the other post. When the Cadillac came puttering around from the hedges and began the short straight traverse to the gate, I called in my best gunny's voice: *Tehen Hut! Present Haaaarms!* I have to hand it to Kev; he never blinked an eye; full dress attention and a salute that would make his DI proud. She drove through that gate with two old worn-out soldiers giving her a send off she deserved, for service rendered to her country, and for knowing Duty, Honor and Sacrifice.

I am not sure, but I think I saw a salute returned from that Cadillac.

REFLECTIONS OF THE VIETNAM WALL

By Patrick Camunes, an article published in the *Belvoir Eagle*, November 12, 1998.

Editor's note: The painting *Reflections* of the Vietnam Wall depicts a man standing with his hand on the wall, mourning his father or brother who was killed. What he doesn't see is the reflection from the other side showing that relative with HIS hand on the wall, touching the hand of his survivor. The painting inspired this commentary. There are so many things that are written about the Wall but never anything of being on the other side. That painting inspired this story.

FROM THE OTHER SIDE

At first there was no place for us to go until someone put up that Black Granite Wall. Now, everyday and night, my Brothers and my Sisters wait to see the many people from places afar file in front of this Wall. Many stopping briefly and many for hours and some that come on a regular basis. It was hard at first, not that it's gotten any easier, but it seems that many of the attitudes towards that war that we were involved in have changed. I can only pray that the ones on the other side have learned something and more Walls as this one needn't be built.

Several members of my unit and many that I did not recognize have called me to the *Wall* by touching my name that is engraved upon it. The tears aren't necessary but are hard even for me to hold back. Don't feel guilty for not being with me, my Brothers. This was my destiny as it is yours, to be on that side of the *Wall*. Touch the *Wall*, my Brothers, so that we can share in the memories that we had. I have learned to put the bad memories aside and remember only the pleasant times that we had together. Tell our other Brothers out there to come and visit me, not to say Good Bye but to say Hello and be together again, even for a short time and to ease that pain of loss that we all share.

Today, an irresistible and loving call comes from the *Wall*. As I approach I can see an elderly lady and as I get closer I recognize her ... It's Momma! As much as I have looked forward to this day, I have also regretted it because I didn't know what reaction I would have.

Next to her, I suddenly see my wife and immediately think how hard it must've been for her to come to this place and my mind floods with the pleasant memories of 30 years past. There's a young man in a military uniform standing with his arm around her … My God! … It's … it has to be my son. Look at him trying to be the man without a tear in his eye. I yearn to tell him how proud I am, seeing him standing tall, straight and proud in his uniform. Momma comes closer and touches the *Wall* and I feel the soft and gentle touch I had not felt in so many years. Dad has crossed to this side of the *Wall* and through our touch, I try to convey to her that Dad is doing fine and is no longer suffering or feeling pain. I see my wife's courage building as she sees Momma touch the *Wall* and she approaches and lays her hand on my waiting hand. All the emotions, feelings and memories of three decades past flash between our touch and I tell her that it's all right. Carry on with your life and don't worry about me … I can see as I look into her eyes that she hears and understands me and a big burden has been lifted from her. I watch as they lay flowers and other memories of my past. My lucky charm that was taken from me and sent to her by my CO, a tattered and worn teddy bear that I can barely remember having as I grew up as a child and several medals that I had earned and were presented to my wife. One of them is the Combat Infantry Badge that I am very proud of and I notice that my son is also wearing this medal. I had earned mine in the jungles of Vietnam and he had probably earned his in the deserts of Iraq.

I can tell that they are preparing to leave and I try to take a mental picture of them together, because I don't know when I will

see them again. I wouldn't blame them if they were not to return and can only thank them that I was not forgotten. My wife and Momma near the *Wall* for one final touch and so many years of indecision, fear and sorrow are let go. As they turn to leave I feel my tears that had not flowed for so many years, form as if dew drops on the other side of the *Wall*.

They slowly move away with only a glance over their shoulder. My son suddenly stops and slowly returns. He stands straight and proud in front of me and snaps a salute. Something makes him move to the *Wall* and he puts his hand upon the *Wall* and touches my tears that had formed on the face of the *Wall* and I can tell that he senses my presence there and the pride and the love that I have for him. He falls to his knees and the tears flow from his eyes and I try my best to reassure him that it's alright and the tears do not make him any less of a man. As he moves back wiping the tears from his eyes, he silently mouths, *God Bless you, Dad* ... *God Bless, YOU, Son* ... We WILL meet someday but in the meanwhile, go on your way … There is no hurry … There is no hurry at all.

As I see them walk off in the distance, I yell out to them and everyone there today, as loud as I can, … THANKS FOR REMEMBERING and as others on this side of the *Wall* join in, I notice that the U.S. Flag that proudly flies in front of us everyday, is flapping and standing proudly straight out in the wind today.

CEREMONY HONORS FALLEN FIREFIGHTER

By Master Sgt. Tim Helton, 376th Air Expeditionary Wing Public Affairs. March 14, 2002, OPERATION ENDURING FREEDOM. Courtesy of the Armed Forces Press Service.

In the first official ceremony held at a deployed site in Kyrgyzstan, an American flag was flown, folded and encased for a journey to New York on March 13. The flag will be presented to the family of deceased New York City Fire Chief Peter J. Ganci, Jr. by Brigadier General Christopher Kelly, the 376th Air Expeditionary Wing Commander. Ganci sacrificed his life while saving others as the second World Trade Center tower collapsed September 11. The deployed site has since been unofficially named

Ganci Air Base. *From the moment we made contact with the Ganci family, they have shown an interest and desire to having contact and understanding what we are doing,* Kelly said. *They are a long way from here, so we thought it was a good idea to put something together that brings a little piece of what we have done here to them and therefore them to us.*

After a brief welcome from Chief Master Sergeant David Andrews, 376th AEW Command Chief Master Sergeant, a detail of eight military people marched in and took their place in the center of the fire station here. *This ceremony was about symbolism. We are all visual people. We understand our world by sight,* Andrews said. *It was exceptionally moving to watch.* The ceremony began as the flag was unfurled and held taut while Staff Sergeant Steve Veverica from the 376th AEW Communications Squadron sounded taps on the bugle. *It was a natural addition to the ceremony,* Andrews said. *This was more than a flag-folding ceremony; it was also a memorial service for Peter J. Ganci, Jr. and a chance for us to tell the base about him.* After playing taps, the flag was folded while a room filled with coalition forces stood at attention. The folded flag was then encased in a shadow box made of wood and nails used to build the base. *I could have*

In Memory. An emotional BG Christopher Kelly, 376th Air Expeditionary Wing commander, holds the flag during a ceremony, 13 March 2002, in Kyrgyzstan to honor NYC Fire Chief Peter J. Ganci, Jr., who died in the collapse of 2nd World Trade Center tower Sept. 11. BG Kelly delivered the flag to Ganci's family. Photo by Master Sgt. Jerry King.

brought in some black walnut and let our carpenters make something absolutely gorgeous, Andrews said. *But the idea was to give them something from us, like the wood and nails that make the floors we walk on, like the flag flown over our base, like the vial of dirt in that case. We got more sentimental value from making it. It is truly priceless to the men and women here.*

During the last part of the ceremony, 22 military people lined up and placed one item each into the back of the shadow box. Items included military coins, coalition insignia and unit emblems. The final object to be placed in the box to *signify Peter Ganci's many years of faithful service* was a U.S. Air Force firefighter's badge. *We want each item to represent a little piece of us that we can give Cathy Ganci to show the sacrifice her husband made was not for vain,* Kelly said. *We will carry on, we are here and we will not fail!* As the ceremony ended, Andrews expressed his pleasure. *This was a great ceremony,* Andrews said. *It was our first ceremony of any kind and these men and women did a great job. I will always remember the last line of the ceremony: 'God rest the soul of Peter J. Ganci, Jr., a hero for liberty and freedom.'*

A FIRE CAPTAIN'S EULOGY

From the *New York Times*, December 23, 2001, Week In Review.

The building housing Engine Company 40 and Ladder Company 35 is on the corner of Amsterdam Avenue and 66th Street, and because it is on the West Side, its men managed to get to the World Trade Center disaster sooner than many other units. Of the 13 firefighters who jumped aboard the two rigs that morning, only one survived, Kevin Shea, who was apparently knocked unconscious during the collapse of one of the towers and literally blown out of the building. In the weeks and months that followed, the men of the firehouse attended a series of services for their fallen comrades from this and other units. At the last of these services for the men of 40/35, on December 10, Captain James Gormley, the house commander, paid tribute to his colleague, Captain Francis J. Callahan, a 30-year veteran of the department who was killed on September 11. Captain Gormley eloquently described the complexity of command facing an officer in the New

York Fire Department. His eulogy was delivered, fittingly, at Alice Tully Hall at Lincoln Center, which the firefighters of 40/35 had been responsible for.

Captains and Lieutenants of the New York City Fire Department share a special relationship with other officers of similar rank. When we meet for the first time, we introduce ourselves to each other; we shake hands; we measure each other's resolve and fortitude. At Operations our aggressiveness is based on the trust we share in each other. Firefighters and their officers share a different, but also special relationship. Officers very literally lead firefighters into harm's way. We go first. If things go badly we are required by our oath and tradition to be the last of our command to leave. Accountability for our men is carved into our heart. Responsibility for our men, their wives and children are in the depth of our soul. This is why we are here today. Captain Frank Callahan is the ranking officer killed at the World Trade Center from our firehouse. He leaves last. I cannot say he will be the last to ever leave. We live in a dangerous world, and we put our boots and helmets on every day. Captains, especially commanding officers of companies in the same quarters, have a unique relationship. We know each other as no one else ever will. We are commanding officers of complementary companies. We cannot work successfully without each other. There are not many of us; you could fit us in one fair-sized room. We are not always friends. There is too much at stake, but our respect, and trust in each other, is unquestioned.

Frank Callahan was more than my friend, to simply call him brother would not do

American's Finest. New York City Firemen at Ground Zero. Photo by Paul Morse.

our relationship justice. Frank was my comrade. It's harder to be a comrade than a friend. It's different than being a brother. Friends and brothers forgive your mistakes. They are happy to be with you. You can relax and joke with them. You can take your ease with them–tell them tall tales. Comrades are different. Comrades forgive nothing. They can't. They need you to be better. They keep you sharp. They take your words literally. When a friend dies, we miss them; we regret words unspoken; we remember the love. When a brother dies, we grieve for the future without him. His endless possibilities. If your brother doesn't die of old age, you might never accept the parting. When a comrade dies, we miss him; we regret words unspoken; we remember the love; we grieve the future without him. We are also proud. Proud to have known a good man, a better man than ourselves. We respect the need for him to leave, to rest. Some people equate camaraderie with being jovial. It is anything but. Camaraderie is sharing hardship. It is shouts and commands, bruises and cuts. It's a sore back and lungs that burn from exertion. It's heat on your neck and a pit in your stomach. It's a grimy handshake and a hug on wet shoulders when we're safe. It's not being asleep when it's your turn on watch. It is trust, it is respect, it is acting honorably. You hold your comrade up when he can't stand on his own. You breathe for him when his body's forgotten how. It's lifting a man up who loves his wife and children as much as you love your own. Looking them in the eye for the rest of your life and trying to explain, and not being able to. You kiss them for him. It's laying him down gently when his name appears on God's roll call. It's remembering his name. I'll never forget his name. He was just what he was called: Frank. You never had to chase your answer. He said it to your face. It's at the same time being both amazed and proud that you've known men like him. Looking for your reflection in their image. Seeing it. Knowing you're one of them. There's a song out of Ireland. A line of it says, *Comrade tread lightly, you're near to a hero's grave.* If you ever said that to Frank, he would have given you the *look* and pushed past you in the hallway. Frank was light on his feet but he never tread anywhere lightly. When Frank did something, it was like a sharp axe biting into soft fresh pine, with a strong sure stroke. It was done. It was right. It meant something. It was refreshing. It smelled good. Quite often we discussed history. The successes and failures of political, military and social leadership. The depth and broadness of Frank's historical knowledge was astounding. I've been told Frank enjoyed a practical joke. We never joked together. Rarely laughed. We never sought out each other's company on days off. We never went golfing or fishing. We never went for a hike in the Shawangunk Mountains together. We were often happier apart than we ever were together because we shared the nightmares of command. We shared problems and stress. We shared dark thoughts that are now front-page news. Incredulous at the failures of leadership that have borne fruit, we shared the proposition of a time and place where few would dare to go. He went because it was his turn. He called his wife, Angie, before he received his orders to respond. He told her what was going on. He told her things didn't look good; he told her he loved her. Historically it is said, *They rode to the sound of the guns*:

Capt. Frank Callahan
Lt. John Ginley
Firefighter 1 Gr. Bruce Gary
Firefighter 1 Gr. James Giberson
Firefighter 1 Gr. Michael Otten
Firefighter 1 Gr. Kevin Bracken
Firefighter 1 Gr. Steve Mercado
Firefighter 1 Gr. Michael Roberts
Firefighter 1 Gr. John Marshall
Firefighter 3 Gr. Vincent Morello
Firefighter 3 Gr. Michael Lynch
Firefighter 6 Gr. Michael D'Auria
and Firefighter 2 Gr. Kevin Shea

Kevin, we are joyful that we got you back. Have no guilt. The same goes for the rest of us. I know what you all did, you got your gear on, found a tool, wrote your name or Social Security number in felt tip pen on your arm or a leg, a crisis tattoo in case you got found. We went down there knowing things could go badly. We stayed until we were exhausted, got three hours sleep and went back again, and again. That's what comrades do. Only luck and circumstance separate us from them. It is significant that we are in Lincoln Center for the Performing Arts. The first performance here was *West Side Story*, the story of this neighborhood. This Act is part of that story. It is more than we can absorb in one lifetime; so, the story must be told until it makes sense. It is poignant because the arts have helped mankind deal with reality since stories were told round the fire and we drew on cave walls. The arts help us exercise our emotions. We are surrounded by art and overwhelmed by our emotions. From the pictures children have drawn for us, the poetry, songs, and banners, to the concerts, plays and operas that we have been invited to attend–use the arts to heal your heart. Exercise your emotions. Feel anger, feel hate, feel love and pride. Run the gamut of your emotions until you settle where you belong, as good honorable men, every inch the equal of our comrades, friends and brothers. That's what they want. That's what your families need. That's what you deserve. Frank was a trusted leader, a captain. The best commander I've encountered here, or in the military. It was important to him. We both believed captain to be the most important rank in the department. He was forged by his family, his comrades, every officer and firefighter that he ever worked with. He was tempered by his experience. History, the record of successes and failures of leadership, has caused us to be here. Capt. Frank Callahan did not fail in his leadership. He led his command where they were needed, and he's the last of them to leave. If more of the world's leaders were forged as he was, our world would not be in its current state. Frank Callahan is a star, a reference point. A defined spot on the map of humanity. Guide on him to navigate the darkness. You will not wander, you will not become lost.

BEER DAY #3 AND NYFD LADDER 37 REQUEST

E-mail excerpts from Naval LCDR J.J. Cummings, sent January 25, 2002 from the *USS Theodore Roosevelt* while operating in the Arabian Sea as part of Operation Enduring Freedom:

Beer Day #3 is this Saturday which means that we will have been at sea for 135 consecutive days. NONE on the ship has ever seen a third beer day and that includes all of the salty buggers who have been doing this for 20-25 years. After the accounting collapse of Beer Day #1, the Heavies put in place a rock solid program to ensure that everyone received ONLY TWO BEERS during Beer Day #2 back in November. Unfortunately, their plan worked, thus crushing my long-held belief that it is virtually impossible to keep an ingenuitive American Sailor from getting just two beers on Beer Day. A challenge has been put forth for Beer Day #3 to beat the system and I think we are up for it–there is no way the Man can continue to keep us down. We are also on track to break another record this deployment, one that has been in place for 30 years. If we do not have a port call by February 21, we will break the record of 154 consecutive days at sea without a port call. It appears there are two chances of us having a port call before that date: slim and none–slim was on life support, but I believe his *plug* was pulled this morning. Doing the ENTIRE six-month deployment without a port call is also a distinct possibility at this point which would place this deployment into the Cruise Hall of Fame: epic amounts of flight time, dropping live bombs, four beer days, no port calls. Don't recall seeing those last three items in the brochure at the recruiter's office. Amazingly enough, morale on the ship is still very, very high. People are still smiling, telling jokes and more importantly doing their jobs just as professional as ever. With only eight no-fly days in the last three and a half months, once again, the young enlisted maintainers continue to amaze me at how hard they continue to work up there on the flight deck. Having just reread my *wanking* paragraph, let me set the record straight. Dropping live bombs on a hostile country in the defense of our nation is the culmination of many years of training (11 in my case) and a dream come true for every one of us out here, officer and enlisted alike. Loss of port calls and time away from family is a small price to pay when your country comes calling with the bill!

One last story for you. Just before Christmas, I received a large manila envelope from Ladder Company 37 (Bronx), New York Fire Department. Inside was a collection of wake cards and programs from the funerals of 14 NYC firefighters killed on September 11 as well as a note from LT John Gormley (former F-14 guy) with a special request. He wrote, *I wanted to know if you could do us a favor and spit these wake cards out of your speed brake on one of your flights. We are real proud of these guys and we want to make sure that those greasy Taliban scumbags know exactly who they are dying for ... We know you guys are kicking ass over there and the support of your whole country is with you.*

Be safe and keep up the great work. We are all counting on you.
The note was signed by 15 other firefighters. (I will frame and
hang that letter on my wall when I get home.) Here it was two
weeks before Christmas and I'm looking at the names and faces of
14 firemen, killed in the line of duty on the 11th. Choked up? Oh
yeah. I immediately knew exactly where I would drop these; these
men were bound for Kandahar, the cultural (that word is used
extremely loosely) center of the Taliban movement. On the day of
the flight, I stuffed all of the cards/programs into a big envelope
marked *PLEASE GIVE TO ANY TALIBAN MEMBERS* and headed
up to the flight deck to coordinate getting it tucked under my speed
brake. The speed brake is a 4-foot by 4-foot flight control surface
on the aft portion of the jet that protrudes from the upper and lower
surface of the fuselage. They are deployed anytime you need to
slow down in a hurry (I think Maverick used them to make the
bandit *fly right by* in the movie TOPGUN–sorry, forgive my
cheesiness) or when landing. The key is that they are controlled by
the pilot, so anything placed beneath them will come out with the
flick of a thumb switch. Enough with the F-14 systems lecture. Just
before the Flight Deck Chief climbed up on the back of the jet to
stash the envelope, he opened it to look at the contents. Looking
down from the cockpit onto the flight deck, I witnessed yet another
sight that I will not soon forget: 10 young enlisted men, dirty and
tired, methodically looking at each of the wake cards, gazing at the
faces of 14 fallen heroes, many of whom were the same age of
those Sailors. Judging by the looks on their faces, I would surmise
that they had the same reaction that I did when I first opened the
package. Off to Kandahar. Night hop, so finding the city was easy.
Lights off, just in case any Taliban AAA gunners were up late.
Dropped down to an altitude lower than I probably should have but
I didn't care. Rolled inverted and, while staring *downtown*
Kandahar right in the face, popped open the speed brake. On
December 11, 2001 at approximately 8:30 PM, Kevin Owen
Reilly, CAPT William F. Burke, Jr., Durrell V. Pearsall, Jr.,
Michael Scott Carlo, Nicholas P. Rossomando, Peter A. Bielfield,
Raymond Murphy, Hector Luis Tirado, CAPT Terry S. Halton,
Archie E. Davis, Thomas J. Foley, LT John F. Ginley, Thomas G.
Schoales and Michael Helmut Haub had one last flight, destination

F-14. A *Tomcat* Fighter Jet taking off from the *USS Theodore Roosevelt*, in the Arabian Sea, Operation Enduring Freedom.

Kandahar. If things start heating up again, those names will be on bombs next time.

I want to share one more thing with all of you. One of the pieces of literature now in Kandahar was a pamphlet memorializing the life of Michael Scott Carlo. It contained family photos and a variety of essays written by his mom, dad and brother about their son and sibling; on the very last page was a photocopy of a handwritten note that was hanging over this young man's desk the day he died. Written by Mark Twain, it read: *Twenty years from now you will be more disappointed by the things that you didn't do than by the ones that you did. So throw off the bowlines. Sail away from the safe harbor. Catch the trade winds in your sails. Explore. Dream. Discover.* You can count on it, Michael.

Until next time, JJ

FOR WHAT PURPOSE, I WAS SPARED

By Clifford C. Spencer, Marine, WWII, Memorial Day, 1995.

The guns, the sounds, the smells and dreams of war have long left my conscious and subconscious mind. And yet on this day of remembrance a face beneath an old campaign hat, clearly showing the price of time and memories, stirs me to think back.

The snappy salute to the officer of the deck, again to the colors aft, as I board the quarter deck of the *Ol' Frisco Maru* the loving name given the *USS San Francisco*, heavy cruiser, U.S. Navy. Her size and big guns were awesome to a green country boy from Indiana and Kentucky–16 years old and with nearly all my grey matter unused, this was high adventure of the greatest sort.

Thus started the year in which I lived with fear, bravado, happiness and pain. You are never more alive than when you are in the face of death. Every fiber of your being is vibrating at once with invincible power and—yes, fear.

The guilt for surviving and the eternal sadness does not occur until later.

So, on this day of dedication, I say thanks to all those who died and wonder why, and for what purpose, I was spared.

HIGH FLIGHT

Oh, I have slipped the surly bonds of earth and danced the skies on laughter-silvered wings. Sunward I've climbed, and joined the tumbling mirth of sun-split clouds–and done a hundred things. You have not dreamed of–wheeled and soared and swung high in the sunlit silence. Hov'ring there, I've chased the shouting wind along and flung my eager craft through footless halls of air. Up, up the long, delirious burning blue I've topped the wind-swept heights with easy grace where never lark, or even eagle flew and, while with silent, lifting mind I've trod the high untresspassed sanctity of space, put out my hand, and touched the face of God.

John Gillespie Magee, Jr.

People who say that American kids are not tough have not seen my Marines fighting in holes at three O'clock in the morning. Their spirit, their resolve ... I think I'll stand in awe of that the rest of my life.

Marine Colonel, Operation Enduring Freedom, Afghanistan, 2002, from the video *Enduring Freedom, The Opening Chapter*

To save your world you asked this man to die; Would this man, could he see you now, ask why?

Wystan H. Auden, Epitaph for an Unknown Soldier

A WARRIOR HONORED

At a recent Soldiers' Breakfast held at Redstone Arsenal, Alabama, Sergeant Major of the Army (SMA) Jack Tilley shared the following story. This story was captured by James Henderson, Chaplain to the Association of the U.S. Army Huntsville Chapter.

During the breakfast, SMA Jack Tilley described one of his recent visits to meet with some of our wounded soldiers at Walter Reed Medical Center in Washington, D.C. He noted,

> A Special Forces soldier had lost his right hand and suffered severe wounds to his face and the side of his body [during Operation Iraqi Freedom].

SMA Tilley asked,

> How do you honor such a soldier, showing respect without offending? What can you say or do in such a situation that will encourage and uplift? How do you shake the right hand of a soldier who just lost his?

Finally, he told the audience how he acted as though the man had a hand, taking his wrist as though it were his hand and speaking encouragement to him. But he said there was another man in that group of visitors who had even brought his wife with him to visit the wounded who knew exactly what to do.

> This man reverently took this soldier's stump of a hand in both of his hands, bowed at the bedside and prayed for him. When he stood from praying he bent over and kissed the man on the head and told him he loved him.
>
> What a powerful expression of love for one of our wounded heroes! And what a beautiful Christ-like example! What kind of man would kneel in such humility and submission to the Living God of the Bible? It was George W. Bush, President of the United States and Commander in Chief of our Armed forces, a man who understands and follows his chain of command, a leader God has given us.

ONE MORE ROLL

We toast our hearty comrades who have
Fallen from the skies, and were gently caught
By God's own hand to be with Him on high.

To dwell among the soaring clouds.
They've known so well before, from victory
Roll to tail chase, at Heaven's very door.

As we fly among them there we're sure to
Hear their plea, to take care my friend,
Watch your six, and do one more roll for me.

Commander Jerry Coffee, Hanoi, 1968

Major Coltman, her mother, Gail, and brother, Bill, Jr. Maj.
Kim Coltman from the 366th Medical Group at Mountain Home
Air Force Base, Idaho, places a flower on the casket of her
father, Air Force Col. William C. Coltman, during a burial
service at Arlington National Cemetery on 3 April 2002. Col.
Coltman, an F-111 Ardvark aircraft commander and test pilot,
was buried with full military honors nearly 30 years after he
was declared missing in action during his second tour in
Vietnam. Photo by Tech. Sgt. Jim Varhegyi.

GREATNESS IN THE FLESH

Each Sunday, *The Orange Register* (Orange County, California) recognizes a letter that eloquently expresses a viewpoint or engenders a debate on a topic of public interest. Ann Baker, a real-estate agent who lives in Huntington Beach, won this award on July 9, 2002.

It was our normal Thursday morning business meeting at our real-estate office. No big deal. Before the meeting we hung around the bagel table, as usual, with our coffee. He stood aside, looking a little shy and awkward and very young, a new face in a room full of extroverted sales people. An average looking guy, maybe 5 feet 8 inches. A clean-cut, sweet-faced kid. I went over to chat with him. Maybe he was a new salesman?

He said he was just back from Kabul, Afghanistan. A Marine. Our office (and a local school) had been supportive by sending letters to him and other troops, which he had posted on the American Embassy door in Kabul. He stood guard there for four months and was shot at daily. He had come to our office to thank us for our support, for all the letters during those scary times.

I couldn't believe my ears. He wanted to thank us? We should be thanking him. But how? How can I ever show him my appreciation? At the end of the sales meeting, he stepped quietly forward, no incredible hulk. As a matter of fact, he looked for all the world 15 years old to me. (The older I get, the younger they look.) This young Marine, this clean-faced boy, had no qualms stepping up to the plate and dodging bullets so that I might enjoy the freedom to live my peaceful life in the land of the free. No matter the risk. Suddenly the most stressful concerns of my life seemed as nothing, my complacency flew right out the window with his every word. Somewhere, somehow, he had taken the words honor, courage and commitment into his very soul and laid his life on the line daily for me and us. A man of principle. He wants to do it. Relishes it. And he came to thank us? For a few letters? I fought back the tears as he spoke so briefly and softly. He walked forward to our manager and placed a properly folded American flag in his hands. It had flown over the Embassy. He said thanks again. You could hear a pin drop. As I looked around I

Marine Corporal Michael J. Mendez. Securing the U.S. Embassy, Kabul, Afghanistan.

saw red faces everywhere fighting back the tears. In a heartbeat, my disillusionment with young people today quickly vanished. In ordinary homes, in ordinary towns, kids like him are growing up proud to be an American and willing to die for it. Wow. We'll frame the flag and put it in the lobby. He only came to my office once, for just a few minutes. But I realize I rubbed shoulders with greatness in the flesh and in the twinkling of an eye my life is forever changed. His name is Michael Mendez, a corporal in the USMC. We are a great nation. We know because the makings of it walked into my office. Ann Baker, Huntington Beach

Corporal Michael J. Mendez was assigned to 3/8 Lima Company, 2nd Platoon, Camp Le Jeune, North Carolina. Michael was born on Camp Pendleton, California, 28 June 1981 and joined the U.S. Marine Corps in October of 1999. Michael's best friend growing up, his brother, PFC Matthew J. Mendez, followed his lead and joined the USMC after High School graduation in 2001.

FRANKLIN'S TOAST

Benjamin Franklin, as American minister to France, attended a diplomatic dinner in Paris shortly after the British surrender at Yorktown. The French foreign minister, Vergennes, opened the dinner by toasting his king in champagne: *His Majesty, Louis the Sixteenth, who, like the moon, fills the earth with a soft, benevolent glow.* The British ambassador then rose to give his toast: *George the Third, who, like the sun at noonday, spreads his light and illuminates the world.* Then the aging Franklin rose and exclaimed: *I cannot give you the sun nor the moon, but I give you George Washington, General of the armies of the United States, who, like Joshua of old, commanded both the sun and the moon to stand still, and both obeyed.*

By the rude bridge that arched the flood, Their flag to April's breeze unfurled, Here once the embattled farmers stood, And fired the shot heard round the world.

Ralph Waldo Emerson

These endured all and gave all that justice among nations might prevail and that mankind might enjoy freedom and inherit peace.

An Inscription in Normandy Chapel, Normandy, France

O CAPTAIN! MY CAPTAIN

O Captain! my Captain! our fearful trip is done,
The ship has weather'd every rack, The prize we sought is won ...
My Captain does not answer, His lips are pale and still,
My father does not feel my arm, He has no pulse or will ...

Walt Whitman

Success without honor is an unseasoned dish;
it will satisfy your hunger, but it won't taste good.

Joe Paterno, Pennsylvania State College Football Coach

Behind every Purple Heart is a heart of gold.
Purple Hearts motto

No amount of ability is of the slightest avail without honor.

Andrew Carnegie

A nation that forgets its defenders will itself be forgotten.

President Calvin Coolidge

U.S. Army Nurse.
Comforting a soldier.

Let the generations know that women in uniform also guaranteed their freedom. That our resolve was just as great as the brave men who stood among us. And with victory our hearts were just as full and beat just as fast–that the tears fell just as hard for those we left behind.

U.S. Army Nurse, World War II
Author Unknown

It is in situations like this that Marine Corps training proves its value. There probably wasn't a man among us who didn't wish to God he was moving in the opposite direction. But ... pride helped now to keep us from faltering. Few of us would have admitted that we were bound by the old-fashioned principle of 'death before dishonor' but it was probably this, above all else, that kept us pressing forward.

Gerald Astor, from the book, *The Greatest War*

The highest honor I have ever attained is that of having my name coupled with yours in these great events.

General George S. Patton, to the men of the Third Army, 1945

Grief and tragedy and hatred are only for a time. Goodness, remembrance, and love have no end.

President George W. Bush

U.S. Army Ranger Sgt. Charles Pressburg. Pauses for three fallen Rangers after a memorial service.

A TRIBUTE TO THE SAILOR

This was written by Navy LTJG Juan Mullen on July 4, 2002 as he and his ship, the *USS Belleau Wood* (LHA-3), were headed to the war zone in support of Operation Enduring Freedom.

There is no doubt that today is the proudest day of my life. It is the 4th of July and my sailors are hard at work thousands of miles from their sons, daughters, husbands or wives. The winds blow, the sun beats down and we stare into the eyes of a hurricane. Thousands have come before these; they have sailed through waters that to them have no name. They work hard always, not knowing what day it might be, only hoping to keep their home always free. It is not glory that they search for as they cook, clean, service and maintain–only a livelihood that they wish to sustain. They sweat, toil and bleed; seldom receiving a *thank you* and never feeling the need. They have many names and come from many places; and as they sail into harm's way, you can see the excitement on their faces. They are black, brown, red, yellow and white; if a mission needs to be completed, they willingly work through the night. The Supreme Court has assured that the prisoners in our jails will be more comfortable and have more free time in their cells. They watch older movies and wait for letters from home for a taste of the news. They sleep with a hundred shipmates smelling their dirty clothes and worn out shoes. These sailors say: *Do not feel sorry for me; I am happy to do my duty and sail for months on the sea. Some things are worth suffering, sweating and even dying for, things like knowing that my home will be free forevermore.* So know you, those that they left behind, you are always on their mind. On days like these, they undoubtedly hope and pray that they will bravely do what needs to be done to allow freedom to stay. So to say that I am proud of my sailors today, on the occasion of our Independence Day, is not entirely true–because there is a secret I wish to share with you. There is not a day that passes me by, that I don't look at these sailors and fight back the urge to cry. The Navy has seen fit to place me in a position of authority, but these sailors mean the world to me. Signed, A Grateful Officer

CHAPTER 12

IN GOD WE TRUST

America was founded on Christian principles, and from these principles a country was formed which allows its citizens to proclaim and practice many religions from around the world. America's Christian heritage continues to provide a solid foundation of values by which we, as a government and as a society, continue to prosper and serve ourselves and the world. This chapter celebrates and reflects our Christian heritage.

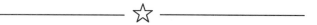

The Founding Fathers believed that faith in God was the key to our being a good people.

President Ronald Reagan

To restore morality we must first recognize the source from which all morality springs. From our earliest history in 1776 when we were declared to be the United States of America, our forefathers recognized the sovereignty of God.

Chief Justice Moore

It is the duty of all Nations to acknowledge the providence of Almighty God, to obey his will, to be grateful for his benefits, and humbly to implore his protection and favor.

President George Washington

The Bible is endorsed by the ages. Our civilization is built upon its words. In no other book is there such a collection of inspired wisdom.

President Dwight D. Eisenhower

There never has been a period of history, in which the Common Law did not recognize Christianity as laying at its foundation.

Justice Joseph Story

I believe no one can read the history of our Country without realizing that the God Book and the Spirit of the Savior have from the beginning been our guiding geniuses ... I believe the entire Bill of Rights came into being because of the knowledge our forefathers had of the Bible and their belief in it: freedom of belief, of expression, of assembly, of petition, the dignity of the individual, the sanctity of the home, equal justice under law, and the reservation of powers to the people.

Earl Warren, Chief Justice, Supreme Court
as quoted in *Time* magazine, 15 February 1954

I proceed ... to enquire what mode of education we shall adopt so as to secure to the state all the advantages that are to be derived from the proper instruction of youth; and here I beg leave to remark, that the only foundation for a useful education in a republic is to be laid in religion. Without this there can be no virtue, and without virtue there can be no liberty, and liberty is the object and life of all republican governments.

Benjamin Rush

We do not need more intellectual power, we need more moral power. We do not need more knowledge, we need more character. We do not need more government, we need more culture. We do not need more law, we need more religion. We do not need more of the things that are seen, we need more of the things that are unseen ... If the foundation is firm, the superstructure will stand.

President Calvin Coolidge

A PRAYER FOR THE USA

By President George Washington.

Almighty God: We make our earnest prayer that Thou wilt keep the United States in Thy holy protection; that Thou wilt incline the hearts of the citizens to cultivate a spirit of subordination and obedience to government; and entertain a brotherly affection and love for one another, for their fellow citizens of the United States at large. And finally, that Thou wilt most graciously be pleased to dispose us all to do justice, to love mercy, and to demean ourselves with that charity, humility, and pacific temper of mind which were the characteristics of the divine Author of our blessed religion, and without a humble imitation of whose example in these things we can never hope to be a happy people.

The morality and values faith implies are deeply embedded in our national character. Our country embraces those principles by design, and we abandon them at our peril.

President Ronald Reagan

Suppose a nation in some distant region should take the Bible for their only law book, and every member should regulate his conduct by the precepts there contained! Every member would be obliged in conscience to temperance, frugality and industry; to justice, kindness and charity towards his fellow men; and to piety, love and reverence toward Almighty God.

President John Adams

Our religion must not alone be the concern of the emotions, but must be woven into the warp and woof of our everyday life.

Booker T. Washington

THANK GOD FOR THE U.S.A.

Our Father who art above,
Inspire in our hearts a greater love,
For whatever Freedoms are left us today,
Before too late, they're all taken away.

Continue to give us our daily bread,
And grant us the wisdom to keep our head,
When Thy enemies rant of a Godlessism,
With which they'd displace our Americanism.

Forgive us for seeming to disregard,
The Rights and Freedoms men fought for so hard,
In all of the wars since the Revolution,
Our Bill of Rights and the Constitution.

Lead us not into wars, except to defend,
The Rights of people, the Freedoms of men,
Whenever the Godless ones seek to kill,
Our Strength, our Faith, our Freedoms, our Will.

Deliver us, our Father, who art above,
From the loss of Freedom we should cherish and love,
So that when our people kneel and pray,
They may always 'Thank God for the U.S.A.'

Amen

It cannot be emphasized too strongly or
too often that this great nation was founded,
not by religionists, but by Christians;
not on religions, but on the gospel
of Jesus Christ. For this very reason peoples
of other faiths have been afforded asylum,
prosperity, and freedom of worship.

Patrick Henry

*When divine souls appear, men are compelled
by their own self-respect to distinguish them.*

Ralph Waldo Emerson

STRENGTH FOR THE JOURNEY

President George W. Bush's address to the National Prayer
Breakfast, February 7, 2002:

Since we met last year, millions of Americans have been
led to prayer. They have prayed for comfort in time of grief, for
understanding at a time of anger, for protection in a time of
uncertainty. Many, including me, have been on bended knee. The
prayers of this nation are a part of the good that has come from the
evil of September the 11th, more good than we could ever have
predicted.

Tragedy has brought forth the courage and the generosity
of our people. None of us would ever wish on anyone what
happened on that day. Yet, as with each life, sorrows we would not
choose can bring wisdom and strength gained in no other way.
This insight is central to many faiths and certainly to the faith that
finds hope and comfort in a cross.

Faith gives the assurance that our lives and our history have
a moral design. As individuals, we know that suffering is

President George W. Bush. Address to the Nation
on the National Day of Prayer, 14 September 2001,
in the National Cathedral, Washington, D.C.

temporary and hope is eternal. As a nation, we know that the ruthless will not inherit the earth.

At the same time faith shows us the reality of good and the reality of evil. Some acts and choices in this world have eternal consequences. It is always and everywhere wrong to target and kill the innocent. It is always and everywhere wrong to be cruel and hateful, to enslave and oppress. It is always and everywhere right to be kind and just, to protect the lives of others and to lay down your life for a friend.

The men and women who charge into burning buildings to save others, those who fought the hijackers, were not confused about the difference between right and wrong. They knew the difference, they knew their duty and we know their sacrifice was not in vain.

Faith shows us the way to self-giving, to love our neighbor as we would want to be loved ourselves. In service to others, we find deep human fulfillment and as acts of service are multiplied, our nation becomes a more welcoming place for the weak and a better place for those who suffer and grieve.

In this time of testing for our nation, my family and I have been blessed by the prayers of countless Americans. We have felt their sustaining power and we're incredibly grateful.

Tremendous challenges await this nation and there will be hardships ahead. Faith will not make our path easy, but it will give us strength for the journey. The promise of faith is not the absence of suffering; it is the presence of grace. And at every step, we are secure in knowing that suffering produces perseverance and perseverance produces character and character produces hope and hope does not disappoint. May God bless you and may God continue to bless America.

I believe the Bible is the best gift God has ever given to men. All the good from the Savior of the world is communicated to us through this book.

President Abraham Lincoln, 1809-1865

Let us once again recommit ourselves to those values which define us. ... Let us renew our commitment to standing for life, and liberty, and peace for all people. Let us renew our commitment to working with all nations to conquer want, and hunger, and disease in every corner of the globe. Let us accept our responsibility to defend the freedom which we are so privileged to enjoy. If terror and tragedy spur us to rediscover and strengthen these commitments, then we can truly say that some good has come from great loss. And in all the trials that may lie ahead, we will carry these commitments close to our heart so we may leave a better world for those who follow. This is our prayer for our Nation and our people. This is our prayer for all Nations and all peoples. Lord, hear our prayer.

Dr. Condoleezza Rice, National Security Advisor, 2003

PARATROOPER'S PRAYER

Kind Heavenly Father, our Great God who invites–*Follows Me*. May we with Stalwart hearts declare Thee Lord of all. We ask Thy Holy blessing to rest upon all paratroopers who are on the path to secure and sustain peace. May we be ready at all times to boldly stand up for Thy truth and ways and be steadfastly hooked up to Thy Law and Gospel. May a primary part of our equipment be a confident faith in Thee as we stand in the door of all missions in life. May the canopy of Thy love shield and keep us now and forever. We go in the name of the Father, the Son, and the Holy Spirit, Amen.

While never willing to bow to a tyrant, our forefathers were always willing to get to their knees before God. When catastrophe threatened, they turned to God for deliverance. When the harvest was bountiful, the first thought was thanksgiving to God. Prayer is today as powerful a force in our nation as it has ever been. We as a nation should never forget this source of strength.

President Ronald Reagan

Alan Keyes.

In this moment, we would do well to remember that there is a God. We are not Him, and neither are the terrorist-murderers who are assaulting us. With our prayers, with our hearts and with all our faithfulness, we should commit both will and judgment to the Lord. Let us trust in Him so that, in this time of tragedy and trial, conscience will not falter, nor prudent courage fail. Let us pray that in His mercy, He will bless America beyond all deserving, as we know and believe He seeks to bless all humanity.

Alan Keyes

While America's military strength is important, let me add here that I've always maintained that the struggle now going on for the world will never be decided by bombs or rockets, by armies or military might. The real crisis we face today is a spiritual one; at root, it is a test of moral will and faith.

President Ronald Reagan

Reason and experience both forbid us to expect that national morality can prevail in exclusion of religious principles.

President George Washington

Almighty and most merciful Father, we humbly beseech Thee,
of Thy great goodness, to restrain these immoderate rains with
which we have had to contend. Grant us fair weather for battle.
Graciously hearken to us as soldiers who call upon Thee that,
armed with Thy power, we may advance from victory to victory,
and crush the oppression and wickedness of our enemies and
establish Thy justice among men and nations.

General George S. Patton, Jr.

Call it mysticism, if you will, but I believe God had
a divine purpose in placing this land between the two great oceans
to be found by those who had a special love of freedom
and the courage to leave the countries of their birth ...
We're Americans and we have a rendezvous with destiny.

President Ronald Reagan, 1976

There is no foundation like the rock of honesty and fairness, and
when you begin to build your life upon that rock, with the cement
of the faith in God that you have, then you have a real start.

Barry Goldwater

A PRAYER FOR STATE GUARD SOLDIERS

Major George H. Heart, National Chaplain Staff College Steering Committee, 1998.

May our common God, the creator of the universe and sovereign of all life, bless all the gallant and noble state guard soldiers who so quietly serve our country and hold this virtuous and worthy *office of honor!* Grant these fine and chivalrous men and women all the good and benevolence they so rightly and justly deserve. We beseech You, Oh Almighty, to shield and protect our brothers and sisters who serve in the various state guards. Bless them with fortitude and comfort and implant in their hearts a steadfast purpose to work as one for the safeguarding of freedom, justice, and peace. Amen.

AMERICA'S ENDURING PRAYER

Defense Secretary Donald Rumsfeld's prayer opening the Cabinet meeting at the White House after the September 11th attacks.

Ever faithful God, in death we are reminded of the precious birthrights of life and liberty You endowed in Your American people. You have shown once again that these gifts must never be taken for granted.

We pledge to those whom You have called home, and ask of You: Patience, to measure our lust for action; Resolve, to strengthen our obligation to lead; Wisdom, to illuminate our pursuit of justice; and Strength, in defense of liberty.

We seek Your special blessing today for those who stand as sword and shield, protecting the many from the tyranny of the few. Our enduring prayer is that You shall always guide our labors and that our battles shall always be just.

We pray this day, Heavenly Father, the prayer our nation learned at another time of righteous struggle and noble cause–America's enduring prayer: Not that God will be on our side, but always, O Lord, that America will be on Your side. Amen.

The First Continental Congress made its first act a prayer, the beginning of a great tradition. We have then a lesson from the founders of our land. That lesson is clear: That in the winning of freedom and in the living of life, the first step is prayer.

President Ronald Reagan

A SOLDIER AND A CHRISTIAN

Many people dismiss Washington's prayer at Valley Forge as sentimental legend. Yet the story is well grounded in the historical record. Our chief source is the eyewitness testimony of Isaac Potts, a Valley Forge resident who shared the following story with the

General Washington. Praying at Valley Forge.

Reverend Nathaniel Randolph Snowden (1770-1851), who then recorded it in his *Diary and Remembrances*.

I was riding with Mr. Potts near to the Valley Forge where the army lay during the war of ye Revolution, when Mr. Potts said:

> Do you see that woods and that plain? There laid the army of Washington. It was a most distressing time of ye war, and all were for giving up the Ship but that great and good man. In that woods (pointing to a close in view) I heard a plaintive sound as of a man at prayer. I tied my horse to a sapling and went quietly into the woods. To my astonishment, I saw the great George Washington on his knees alone, with his sword on one side and his cocked hat on the other. He was at Prayer to the God of the Armies, beseeching to interpose with his Divine aid, as it was ye Crisis and the cause of the country, of humanity and of the world. Such a prayer I never heard from the lips of man. I left him alone praying. I went home and told my wife. We never thought a man could be a soldier and a Christian, but if there is one in the world, it is Washington. We thought it was the cause of God and America could prevail.

Civil War. Army Chaplain Conducts Mass.

*T*he Bible was as much America's founding document as the Declaration of Independence or Constitution. The Founding Fathers' beliefs in liberty, equality before the law and representative government came from Sinai. The Constitution is a covenant reflecting a much older covenant.

Don Feder

*L*ord, hold our troops in your loving hands. Protect them as they protect us. Bless them and their families for the selfless acts they perform for us in our time of need. I ask this in the name of Jesus, our Lord and Savior.

Author Unknown

*L*iberty is a gift from God Almighty, and I believe with all my heart we are obligated to the Author of the Universe to guard it vigilantly and well, with dignity, with honor, with charity–and with energy.

Alan Keyes

World War II. A Wounded U.S. Soldier Prays, Okinawa, 1945.

ALL OUT FOR GOD

By George S. Patton, Jr., Commander, Third Army, World War II.

Urge all of your men to pray, not alone in church, but everywhere. Pray when driving. Pray when fighting. Pray alone. Pray with others. Pray by night and pray by day. Pray for the cessation of immoderate rains, for good weather for battle. Pray for the defeat of our wicked enemy whose banner is injustice and whose good is oppression. Pray for victory. Pray for our Army and Pray for peace.

We must march together, all out for God. The soldier who 'cracks up' does not need sympathy or comfort as much as he needs strength. We are not trying to make the best of these days. It is our job to make the most of them. Now is not the time to follow God from 'afar off.' This Army needs the assurance and the faith that God is with us. With prayer, we cannot fail. Be assured that this message on prayer has the approval, the encouragement, and the enthusiastic support of the Third United States Army Commander.

With every good wish to each of you for a very Happy Christmas, and my personal congratulations for your splendid and courageous work since landing on the beach.

NOW IS THE TIME TO FIGHT

On a warm Sunday morning in 1775, in a Lutheran church in the Shenandoah Valley of Virginia, thirty-year-old Pastor Peter Muhlenberg delivered a sermon on the text: *For everything there is a season, and a time for every matter under heaven* (Ecclesiastes 3:10). Concluding his sermon with a prayer, he added, *In the language of the Holy Writ, there is a time for all things. There is a time to preach and a time to fight.* He paused, then threw off his robe to reveal the uniform of a colonel in the Continental Army. *And now is the time to fight!* He then marched off heading a 300-man regiment that later earned fame as the 8th Virginia.

*R*enewing our knowledge of and faith in God through
Holy Scripture can strengthen us as a nation and a people.

Words from a Joint Resolution of the House and Senate, The *Year of the Bible* was declared in 1983 by a Joint Resolution (House and Senate)

*A*merica was founded by people who believed that
*God was their rock of safety. I recognize we must be
cautious in claiming that God is on our side, but I think
it's all right to keep asking if we're on His side.*

President Ronald Reagan

HE WILL BRING US THROUGH SAFE

Three weeks before the Battle of Gettysburg, a college president asked Lincoln if the country would survive, he responded:

I do not doubt that our country will finally come through
*safe and undivided. But do not misunderstand me ...
I do not rely on the patriotism of our people ...
the bravery and devotion of the boys in blue ...
or the loyalty and skill of our generals ...
But the God of our fathers, who raised up this country
to be the refuge and asylum of the oppressed and downtrodden
of all nations, will not let it perish now.
I may not live to see it, I do not expect to see it,
but God will bring us through safe.*

THE NATIONAL DAY OF PRAYER TASK FORCE

This Task Force exists to encourage and promote events related to the National Day of Prayer, the first Thursday in May. Since the first call to prayer in 1775, when the Continental Congress asked the colonies to pray for wisdom in forming a nation, prayer has been a vital part of our American heritage. In 1952, a joint resolution by Congress, signed by President Truman, declared an annual, national day of prayer. In 1988, the law was amended and signed by President Reagan, permanently setting the day as the first Thursday of every May. Each year, the president signs a proclamation, encouraging all Americans to pray on this day. In 2001, all 50 state governors plus the governors of several U.S. territories signed similar proclamations.

A SOLDIER'S PRAYER

Author Unknown, VFW Post 4051, VFW News, February 2001.

I saw a soldier kneeling down, for this was the first quiet place he had found. He had traveled through jungles, rivers, and mud. His hands were scarred and toil-worn. He had fought for days from night 'til morn. He folded his hands and looked to the sky ...

I saw his tears, as they welled in his eyes. He spoke to God, and this is what he said:

God bless my men, who now lie dead. I know not what You have in mind, but when You judge, please be kind ... when they come before you, they will be poorly dressed, but will walk proudly, for

they have done their best. Their boots will be muddy and their clothes all torn ... but these clothes they have so proudly worn. Their hearts will be still and cold inside, for they have fought their best and did so with pride. So please take care of them as they pass Your way ... the price of freedom they've already paid.

In the days since the attack [September 11, 2001], Americans have been brought back to their faith. I mean this in the literal sense. It has been a time of prayer for us. In this prayer, let us remember that our very existence is a prayer of acknowledgement to the Creator's wise authority. For He has formed and fashioned us with a dignity that we will defend, with the rights that we will preserve and with the hope for human destiny that we will not surrender. Remembering this is a noble cause even–perhaps especially–when we are not at war. Indeed, securing the opportunity to remember it in peace is the reason we now go to war, and will be the fruit of our victory.

Alan Keyes

In 1864, Congress authorized the coinage of two-cent coins. These were the first coins to bear the inscription *In God We Trust*.

DO EVERYTHING IN LOVE

Battle Mass. Dak To, Vietnam

*... Stand firm in the faith;
be men of courage;
be strong.
Do everything in love.*

1 Corinthians 16:13-14

The men who have guided the destiny of the United States have found the strength for their tasks by going to their knees.

President Lyndon B. Johnson

I saw something today which affected me more than anything I ever saw or read on religion. While the battle was raging and the bullets were flying, [Stonewall] Jackson rode by, calm as if he were at home, but his head was raised toward heaven, and his lips were moving evidently in prayer.

Reported by Chaplain Bennett, after the Battle of Cross Keys, Civil War

During the darkest hours of the Civil War, a minister said to President Lincoln that he hoped the Lord was on their side. Lincoln thought for a moment before replying.

I'm not at all concerned about that, for I know that the Lord is always on the side of the right. But it is my constant anxiety and prayer that I–and this nation–should be on the Lord's side.

O'ER THE LAND OF THE FREE

On March 3, 1931, *The Star Spangled Banner* was adopted by Congress as our National Anthem. Francis Scott Key wrote it more than one hundred years earlier, after watching the fierce Battle of Fort McHenry during the War of 1812. Many know and appreciate the stirring words to the first verse of the Anthem, but few are familiar with its inspirational follow-on verses:

O! thus be it ever when free men shall stand
Between their loved home and the war's desolation;
Blest with vict'ry and peace, may the Heav'n-rescued land
Praise the Pow'r that hath made and preserved us a nation!

Then conquer we must, when our cause it is just;
And this be our motto, 'In God is our trust!'
And the star spangled banner in triumph shall wave
O'er the land of the free and the home of the brave!

It is because of this verse that courts allowed to stand the motto, *In God We Trust* on our nation's currency. Had it not been in the national anthem, the courts might have been forced to declare it an unlawful act of the government to promote religion.

Blessed is the nation whose God is the Lord ...

Psalm 33:12a

MAKE ME AN INSTRUMENT

On March 27, 1991, television journalist David Frost interviewed General Schwarzkopf, Commander in Chief of the Coalition Forces in Operation Desert Storm.

Mr. Frost asked him if he had a favorite verse. General Schwarzkopf replied,

Actually, it's a prayer of St. Francis;
'Lord, make me an instrument of Thy peace.'

IN THIS HOUR OF GREAT SACRIFICE

Men's souls will be shaken with the violences of war.
They fight not for the lust of conquest. They fight to liberate. They
fight to let justice arise, and tolerance and goodwill among all Thy
people. They yearn but for the end of battle, for their return to the
heaven of home. Some will never return. Embrace these, Father,
and receive them, Thy heroic servants, into Thy Kingdom. And for
us at home–fathers, mothers, children, wives, sister and brothers,
of brave men overseas, whose thoughts and prayers are ever with
them–help us, Almighty God, to rededicate ourselves in renewed
faith in Thee in this hour of great sacrifice.

President Franklin D. Roosevelt

Our Government rests upon religion. It is from that source that
we derive our reverence for truth and justice, for equality and
liberty, and for the rights of mankind. Unless the people believe in
these principles, they cannot believe in our Government.

President Calvin Coolidge

*Virtue or morality is a necessary spring of popular government ...
Of all the dispositions and habits which lead to political
prosperity, religion and morality are indispensable supports.*

President George Washington

*Our Constitution was made only for a moral and religious people.
It is wholly inadequate to the government of any other.*

President John Adams

*Bad men cannot make good citizens. It is when a people forget
God that tyrants forge their chains.*

Patrick Henry

*Our ancestors established their system of government on morality
and religious sentiment. Moral habits, they believed, cannot safely
be on any other foundation than religious principle, nor any
government be secure which is not supported by moral habits.*

Daniel Webster

*... The man must be bad indeed who can look upon
the events of the American Revolution without feeling
the warmest gratitude towards the great author of the
Universe whose divine interposition was so frequently
manifested in our behalf. And it is my earnest prayer
that we may so conduct ourselves as to merit
a continuance of those blessings with which
we have hitherto been favored.*

President George Washington

Pro Deo et patria.

Army Chaplain Corps motto (in Latin) *For God and Country*

A PRAYER FOR OUR NATION

Lord, we come to You on bended knee,
heads bowed and our hearts filled to overflowing
with so much grief for the many people who have
been injured and killed in our National crisis.

We ask you Lord, to give courage
and strength to those who so bravely
go to their aid. And though their hearts will
be heavy and filled with sorrow we ask Lord
that You give them the endurance needed
to help them through this difficult task.

Please give us the strength Lord,
to get through each difficult and devastating
day that faces each of us and our country.
Protect and guide our Military that
are now being called to duty.

We ask Lord, that You guide the leaders
of our great country in their hour of decision.
The burden that has been placed on their
shoulders during this crisis is overwhelming.
We ask that with Your infinite wisdom You
guide them gently to the right decisions.

And lastly Lord, we ask that You
allow us all to come together as a Nation,
to stand tall and united, so that we might
help each other in our hour of need. Amen

U.S. Soldier with a pocket Bible.

CHAPTER 13

SEPTEMBER ELEVENTH

The terrorist attacks on our nation on September 11, 2001 will forever change America. Some argue that these attacks created a *rebirth of patriotism*. Others contend that these attacks brought out in Americans an expression of love of country that had been residing silently in our hearts all along. Either way, this chapter attempts to capture the emotions and sentiments of our citizens since the September 11, 2001 attacks.

Our free society is inherently vulnerable.

President George W. Bush

ADDRESS TO THE AMERICAN PEOPLE

This morning ... Freedom itself was attacked ... and Freedom ... will be defended.

President George W. Bush, 11 September 2001

President George W. Bush.
11 September 2001.

An Expression of our Gratitude

Author Unknown.

Dear Osama:

Allow me to thank you for your recent visits to our country! I am a 49-year-old male, 4th generation, well-educated, prosperous and yes, a spoiled American.

I have never really understood our nation's history nor the actions of the past generations. You see I grew up in a time period when we had our unpopular war in Vietnam and it wasn't cool to be patriotic. Went through the space generation, the love generation, the me generation and the x-generation without any real appreciation for what went on before my time.

I couldn't understand why men would rush to sign-up to defend our country in the World Wars. Nor could I even really appreciate why we had Veteran's Day or for that matter the Fourth of July.

For my generation, it was merely a holiday, which was a day off from work.

My heroes weren't firemen, policemen, soldiers, or politicians. They were sports figures, business tycoons, movie stars and the like.

Why would anyone take one of those low-paying, dangerous positions when you could have more money, more respect, and have a whole lot more fun as one of these others?

My view of the world was: U.S.A. against the rest of the world because nobody appreciated what we did for them. I was never concerned about the rest of the world or really cared for their well being ... except to dole out money for food and medicine through one of our relief programs (like the $171,000,000 we gave your countrymen last year). All I ever thought about was maybe a vacation to their corner of the world to experience their culture.

Your visit here has changed all that! So I want to tell you *Thanks*! I sincerely mean it too. You have no idea how your visit has changed all that.

You see I realize now what my forefathers fought for and why they risked their lives. I understand what Memorial Day and the Fourth of July are all about.

Upon seeing our Flag, my chest expands; our national anthem brings tears to my eyes. My fellow Americans are truly my brothers and I will defend them with all my might.

As you watch CNN (from our satellite) broadcasting our American family portrait, I am sure you have noticed a different pose. We are all one now.

Racial barriers have been broken, religious barriers are gone, as we believe and trust in any and all religions that support a just and merciful Supreme Being.

My heroes now are firemen, policemen, soldiers and yes, even our politicians. The outside world as I have known it has now embraced us—taking us in during our time of need and giving us the support we so desperately required.

So, you see, Osama, we OWE you. Thank you for realigning our perspectives and values like no one has done before. Your actions have created more goodwill than any one single act I have known in my lifetime. I know you didn't think this would be the outcome, but rest assured this is what you have created! You made us understand a lesson we hope to never forget or take for granted again.

In closing, it is a custom in our country to express our gratitude. So we and a few of our friends (the rest of the world) are going to stop by and deliver a message to you and yours. I hope it comes soon and swift but don't worry if you don't see us right away we won't forget ... not now, not ever.

Artwork by Jeff Grier. *I'll take it from here.*

Aircraft *Nose Art.* Created by U.S. Air
Force Senior Airman Duane White.

*Y*ou can decide to live your life afraid
*of that happening, or you can decide to live your life the way
Americans live their lives, which is unafraid.*

Rudy Giuliani

A LETTER TO BIN LADEN

Author Unknown.

September 27, 2001

This is a personal letter to Bin Laden,

I would like to thank you for taking the time out to send a
few of your willing workers of hate and deception to this country
to attempt to destroy us.

In the process of trying to terrorize us to death, the hand of
God stepped in and still got glory within your evil and deceptive
plan to put fear in the hearts and minds of the American people.

1. Thank you for showing and allowing our President and
past Presidents to worship and pray together in the same
Sanctuary.

2. Thank you for having Congress bow at the feet of Jesus
and ask for forgiveness and ask for the Lord's strength in leading
the nation's people.

3. Thank you for allowing prayer in the schools once more and saving our children across the nation and enabling them to ask God for strength and protection throughout their school day.

4. Thank you for letting employers give workers time to pray and worship our Savior during their work hour.

5. Thank you for showing us that it is the hand of God that allows us to be here day in and day out; we are not just here on our own.

6. Thank you for leading more people back to church in one day to get things right with God than all the witnessing of all the Christians in this country could do in one year.

7. Thank you for waking us up and letting us know that people still care in this country and that we are bigger than the problems in this country.

8. Thank you for reminding us that racial, religious, and cultural hatred is useless and nothing good comes of harboring it.

9. Thank you for letting us again understand why on our money it says *In God We Trust*, why we sing *God bless America* and what true patriotism is.

10. Most of all, Bin Laden, now that the Lord is on our side, thank you for letting him take his rightful place on the battlefield, so you will know that he will have the victory His word says ... If two or three gather in my name it is done.

So in all, we thank you very much for strengthening our faith in God and our love for our fellow American no matter what color, race, creed or religion.

ARRANGE A MEETING

During a question and answer session that followed a lecture on leadership, General Schwarzkopf was asked if he could ever find it in his heart to forgive Osama bin Laden. He responded,

Forgiveness is the Lord's business.
Our business is to arrange a meeting
of the two as soon as possible.

WE WILL PASS THIS TEST

TUESDAY, 11 SEPTEMBER 2001

Following is the transcript of President Bush's second comments on the plane crashes on September 11, 2001. President Bush spoke from Barksdale Air Force Base in Louisiana.

Freedom itself was attacked this morning by a faceless coward, and freedom will be defended. I want to reassure the American people that the full resources of the federal government are working to assist local authorities to save lives and to help the victims of these attacks. Make no mistake: The United States will hunt down and punish those responsible for these cowardly acts. I've been in regular contact with the Vice President, Secretary of Defense, the National Security team and my Cabinet. We have taken all appropriate security precautions to protect the American people.

Our military at home and around the world is on high-alert status, and we have taken the necessary security precautions to continue the functions of your government. We have been in touch with the leaders of Congress and with world leaders to assure them that we will do whatever is necessary to protect America and Americans. I ask the American people to join me in saying a thanks for all the folks who have been fighting hard to rescue our fellow citizens and to join me in saying a prayer for the victims and their families. The resolve of our great nation is being tested. But make no mistake: We will show the world that we will pass this test. God bless.

TOUCHSTONE TO THE AMERICAN SOUL

By Tom Adkins, CommonConservative.com, September 16, 2001.

I met her Thursday. She was a striking young woman, a few years older than my daughter. She hired me to find a home for her and her young son. We talked about finance, her job, the world, and other odds and ends. She had that quiet intelligence that sneaks up on you if you don't pay attention. I remember thinking any dad would be quite impressed if his son brought her home to meet the folks ...

The phone jangled my brain from my sleepy morning. My wife had that desperate urgency in her voice. *Tom, the world is crashing down around us. What's happening?* I stumbled downstairs and flipped on the tube, just in time to see the South Tower collapse. Minutes later, the North Tower fell. In between, the absurd pictures of jetliners plowing into the World Trade Center towers played, they hit the Pentagon, too.

From dreamland to Kafka in two minutes flat.

My friends!

By noon, I contacted everyone I knew in Washington and New York. Are you OK? Are you safe? The responses trickled back over the day. Three, four, five ... finally, all accounted for. But every time I watched those buildings fall, thousands died over and over. The horror wasn't simply the sheer numbers. It was the innocence. Moms. Dads. Sons. Daughters. Husbands. Wives. Grammas. Grampas. Burned, crushed ... gone. This will become an American scar. It will be an historic moment, where everything balanced on a pin. Which way will the world turn?

This just seemed a pivotal moment in her life, like she was taking a pretty big leap ...

I watched an interview with two young men, definitely from the hood. They saw it on TV and couldn't sit around while their fellow Americans needed them. They jumped off their couch and raced down to help. Around them, a million tons of steel, dust, and humanity, laid at their feet. Dead people. In pieces. Right there. Thousands of them. Stepping on them. Search dogs tearing at flesh. In ten minutes, the hood probably seemed like Disneyland. Before the eyes of the nation, these young men became American heroes. A greater cause didn't exist. They made me damned proud to be American.

She'd be gone on a business trip. Next week, she'd be back, and we'd get started. I almost couldn't wait to help her ...

The next day, heartbreak was bitter as the dust on Church Street. Wives looking for husbands. Husbands looking for wives. Parents looking for their kids. Kids looking for parents. Friends looking for friends. A new perspective had dawned. It seemed America finally stopped bickering over trifles. We galvanized.

The young lady with the little boy was the only client I couldn't find. I called her home. Called her office. Called her cell phone. Twice. Three times. Maybe she was watching the news at her mom's house. Finally, I sent off a late e-mail. It came back *...Tom–Do you remember where I said I was going on Monday when I left your office? New York! I was actually in the WTC when the first plane hit ...* My heart thumped. That e-mail sucked me away from the antiseptic perch on my couch, right into the arena. I flushed with concern. I had to call her. I had to hear her voice, hear she was OK. It mattered. She had to know I cared. She'll read this and probably won't understand me. She'll tell this story a thousand times, and we'll never really understand her. But that day, she became my touchstone to the American soul.

She was in the basement train station, heading to her meeting. She got out as the first plane hit the North tower. The rest of the tragedy unfolded during her meeting, blocks away. I think she said the word *surreal* about seven times ...

I knew what I had to do. I would not let these despicable pigs defeat me, my fellow Americans, or my country. I would simply get back to my everyday world. Help my clients. Weed the garden. Basketball on Thursday night.

Somehow, through the tragedy, it seems like America is stitching itself back together stronger than before. Fashionable narcissism? Gone. Attitudes? Gone. We aren't hyphenated anymore. We are Americans. We discovered we aren't quite as selfish as we thought. We don't merely live for ourselves. We live for each other. We live for our family, our neighbors, our nation. And especially for a young lady with a little boy who needs a new house.

Dear Heavenly Father, We are moved by the alarming news and crisis that our country is facing. This, the greatest nation, founded in the belief that 'In God We Trust' and the 'Land of the Free.' Please have mercy on those suffering, hurting and in fear, and give wisdom and strength to those who are assisting. May the forces of evil be broken by your power and may we humble before thee, our strength and refuge. Give wisdom to all, our President and our leaders and bring your comforting peace through the power of your Holy Spirit. Help us here to reach to those that have been affected by this tragedy. In the name of our Lord and Savior, Christ Jesus. Amen.

Author Unknown

YOUR TIME IS SHORT

Poem written by an unknown 16-year-old who reportedly got an A+ from this teacher!

Osama Bin Laden, your time is short;
We'd rather you die, than come to court.
Why are you hiding if it was in God's name?
You're just a punk with a turban; a pathetic shame.

I have a question, about your theory and laws;
'How come you never die for the cause?'
Is it because you're a coward who counts on others?
Well here in America, we stand by our brothers.

As is usual, you failed in your mission;
If you expected pure chaos, you can keep on wishin'
Americans are now focused and stronger than ever;

Your death has become our next endeavor.
What you tried to kill, doesn't live in our walls;
It's not in buildings or shopping malls.
If all of our structures came crashing down,
It would still be there, safe and sound.

Because pride and courage can't be destroyed,
Even if the towers leave a deep void.

We'll band together and fill the holes.
We'll bury our dead and bless their souls.

But then our energy will focus on you;
And you'll feel the wrath of the Red, White and Blue.
So slither and hide like a snake in the grass;
Because America's coming to kick your ass!

In this war on terrorism, we're all in this together.
It's not a situation where you can elect not to be a part of it.
We're all part of it. We're all vulnerable.

General Richard Myers, Chairman of the Joint Chiefs of Staff

WHO NOW IS THE INFIDEL?

The following is a *Letter to the Editor* that the Reverend Charles Stanley of North Carolina sent to every major newspaper in the world, including Pakistan and Iran. An open letter to terrorists and to those who harbor and support you:

I am told by the leaders of my government that you are intelligent people.

In light of your actions, I am having growing difficulty believing that.

Nose Art on a U.S. Air Force Cargo Aircraft.
Operation Enduring Freedom.

At the very least, it has become increasingly obvious that you lack a fundamental comprehension of my psychology as an American.

I hear on our news broadcasts that your rage is fueled by my support of Israel.

It has never been about nationality or religious faith–never about Jew vs. Arab.

I thought you would finally have understood that when I sent my children into harm's way in order to protect the innocent citizens of Arab Kuwait from the savage wolf who would devour them for his own gain.

It has everything to do with the lessons taught to me by my father–and his before him for many generations before the white man came to this land we call America.

I have a vivid memory of coming home, as a boy of about nine years of age, and telling my father of feeling helpless horror as I watched the neighborhood bully unmercifully torment a boy even smaller than myself.

My father reflected for a long moment, then quietly inquired of me as to what I had done about it.

I said that I had watched until it was over and had then come home.

The look in his eyes penetrated me to my core for he had never looked at me in that way before.

He said that he was deeply ashamed of me and he sent me to my room with instructions to think about what had happened?

It seemed hours before he came to my door.

He sat beside me on my bed and, for a painfully long while, he said nothing.

When finally he spoke, he explained,

> There will always be among us dishonorable men who are devoid of humanity and compassion.
>
> They are but naked animals and an empty shell of what truly is a man.
>
> They attempt to fill their emptiness by the exercise of power over others, thinking that it makes them whole men.
>
> Often they are enraged that they do not even understand their own emptiness, what it is that they lack.

When these men are also cowards, they disguise themselves as sheep among the flock and attack from the shadows.

This is the vilest form of subhuman behavior, for even animals attack openly when they must attack.

When humanity and integrity are present in a man, he expresses them as compassion.

When compassion and strength achieve perfect balance within a man, they manifest as wisdom.

The compassionate man feels the pain of others. The wise man protects others from pain.

For, if you watch and do nothing to protect others, who will come to your aide when you alone remain and the bully comes for you?

Some things are far more important than your personal safety and freedom from pain.

If ever again you see someone being hurt, protect him, even if you are certain to be injured in the process. Then I will know that I have truly raised a man.

Anyone who understands the impact of this lesson–and how deeply it runs in the man I have become, will understand my unflinching willingness to sacrifice my children in defense of Arab and Jew alike when they are threatened by the bullies and cowards of the world.

And please do not insult my intelligence with claims of Jewish Treatment of Palestinians.

I am old enough to retain vivid memories of 1948. I remember the excitement of the Jews over the prospect of governing *with* them.

Their reaction, and that of their neighbors, was to attempt to finish what the Nazis could not. Repeatedly.

Intelligent men?

I, for one, am stunned by the monumental stupidity of your arrogance.

Did you actually think that only Americans would occupy the World Trade Center?

You have but fired the first pitiful salvo of World War III for the entire world is now preparing to come after you, your host, your financiers and your supporters.

And please, do not listen to what I say.

You would do far better to watch the sky.

I must say that I owe you a profound debt of gratitude.

Not for what you have done or what you have unleashed upon the world, but for what you have accomplished.

For not one among us could have accomplished it.

On Monday, September 10, 2001, we were a divisive, apathetic nation.

Our young people had nothing by which to identify with our history or heritage; our people were divided by factions of religion and skin color; our government was polarized and paralyzed by political party affiliation, able to agree upon nothing; the military had difficulty obtaining volunteers and most of us simply changed TV channels in response to Red Cross pleas for blood donations.

Your actions have changed all of that in a way that has occurred only twice before in the history of this nation–once in 1776 and again on December 7, 1941.

The worst in the worst of Allah's children has brought out the best in the best of Allah's children and, for this, I thank you.

Since your cowardly act, Muslim, Jew, Christian, black, white, yellow and brown have stood shoulder to shoulder for hours in the hot sun to donate blood for the injured.

Our government has suddenly become totally united in its purpose.

Our military is having difficulty handling the flood of volunteers from among our young people.

Our flag makers report that there is no way humanly possible that they can keep up with the demand–shipments are sold out within minutes.

You have accomplished a miracle that only God could have anticipated.

And, it would seem, the hand of God was present even in the date that you selected for your attack, for you could not have chosen a date more in keeping with a reawakening of American pride and purpose.

There is in America a nationwide system for seeking help in times of emergency.

Every American knows that, when threatened, he can pick up any telephone and dial 911 and help is immediately on the way to assist and protect him.

By selecting September (our 9th month) 11, 2001 to exhibit your cowardice, you unwittingly placed a 911 call that has brought all of America together in a way that brings tears of joy and pride to my eyes.

No longer is our battle cry, *Remember Pearl Harbor!*

Thanks to you and your kind it will now and forevermore be, *Remember 911!* whenever the innocents of any nation find themselves threatened by cowards with guns.

I do not, for a moment, deny that you hurt me.

Far too many parents and children now go to bed wondering where their loved ones are.

And, yes, I am momentarily reeling.

But it is from the sudden realization that I share the planet with anyone capable of such an atrocity against the humanity of so many nations.

In his Inaugural Address in Washington, DC on 20 January 1961, President John F. Kennedy said, *Let every nation know, whether it wishes us well or ill, that we shall pay any price, bear any burden, meet any hardship, support any friend, oppose any foe to assure the survival and the success of liberty.*

He was talking about the liberty of all men, of all faiths, of all nations.

You need to understand that the truth of that statement is the very fabric of who and what I am.

I wish neither to rule nor to inflict injury upon the innocents of any nation.

I am the lion who sleeps with God's lambs to protect them from ravenous wolves that would devour them.

Your 911 call has awakened the lion and now I hunger for the flesh of wolves.

In closing let me state, Mohammed taught that Allah is a God of love–yet you have the unmitigated gall to bastardize Islam to suit your own personal, unholy agenda.

Who now is the infidel?

YOU'RE NO BIG DEAL

United States versus Reid: Final Statements by Judge Young, U.S. District Court. Judge William Young made the following statement in sentencing *shoe bomber* Richard Reid to prison.

January 30, 2003

Judge Young: Mr. Richard C. Reid, hearken now to the sentence the Court imposes upon you.

On counts 1, 5 and 6 the Court sentences you to life in prison in the custody of the United States Attorney General. On counts 2, 3, 4 and 7, the Court sentences you to 20 years in prison on each count, the sentence on each count to run consecutive with the other. That's 80 years.

On count 8 the Court sentences you to the mandatory 30 years consecutive to the 80 years just imposed. The Court imposes upon you each of the eight counts a fine of $250,000 for the aggregate fine of $2 million. The Court accepts the government's recommendation with respect to restitution and orders restitution in the amount of $298.17 to Andre Bousquet and $5,784 to American Airlines.

The Court imposes upon you the $800 special assessment.

The Court imposes upon you five years supervised release simply because the law requires it. But the life sentences are real life sentences so I need go no further.

This is the sentence that is provided for by our statutes. It is a fair and just sentence. It is a righteous sentence. Let me explain this to you.

We are not afraid of any of your terrorist co-conspirators, Mr. Reid. We are Americans. We have been through the fire before. There is all too much war talk here. And I say that to everyone with the utmost respect.

Here in this court where we deal with individuals as individuals, and care for individuals as individuals, as human beings we reach out for justice. You are not an enemy combatant. You are a terrorist. You are not a soldier in any war. You are a terrorist. To give you that reference, to call you a soldier gives you far too much stature. Whether it is the officers of government who do it, or your attorney who does it, or that happens to be your view, you are a terrorist.

And we do not negotiate with terrorists. We do not treat with terrorists. We do not sign documents with terrorists.

We hunt them down one by one and bring them to justice.

So war talk is way out of line in this court. You are a big fellow. But you are not that big. You're no warrior. I know warriors. You are a terrorist. A species of criminal guilty of multiple attempted murders.

In a very real sense Trooper Santigo had it right when you first were taken off that plane and into custody and you wondered where the press and where the TV crews were and he said you're no big deal. You're no big deal.

What your counsel, what your able counsel and what the equally able United States attorneys have grappled with and what I have as honestly as I know how tried to grapple with, is why you did something so horrific. What was in you that led you here to this courtroom today? I have listened respectfully to what you have to say. And I ask you to search your heart and ask yourself what sort of unfathomable hate led you to do what you are guilty and admit you are guilty of doing. And I have an answer for you. It may not satisfy you. But as I search this entire record it comes as close to understanding as I know.

It seems to me you hate the one thing that is most precious. You hate our freedom. Our individual freedom. Our individual freedom to live as we choose, to come and go as we choose, to believe or not believe as we individually choose.

Here, in this society, the very winds carry freedom. They carry it everywhere from sea to shining sea. It is because we prize individual freedom so much that you are here in this beautiful courtroom. So that everyone can see, truly see that justice is administered fairly, individually, and discretely.

It is for freedom's sake that your lawyers are striving so vigorously on your behalf and have filed appeals, will go on in their, their representation of you before other judges. We are about it. Because we all know that the way we treat you, Mr. Reid, is the measure of our own liberties.

Make no mistake though. It is yet true that we will bear any burden, pay any price, to preserve our freedoms. Look around this courtroom. Mark it well. The world is not going to long remember what you or I say here. Day after tomorrow it will be forgotten. But this, however, will long endure. Here in this courtroom and courtrooms all across America, the American people will gather to see that justice, individual justice, justice, not war, individual justice is in fact being done. The very President of the United States through his officers will have to come into courtrooms and lay out evidence on which specific matters can be judged, and juries of citizens will gather to sit and judge that evidence democratically, to mold and shape and refine our sense of justice.

See that flag, Mr. Reid? That's the flag of the United States of America. That flag will fly there long after this is all forgotten. That flag stands for freedom. You know it always will. Custody Mr. Office. Stand him down.

If the 9-11 dead could see how our country is united
to preserve freedom from terror, they'd be proud.
Proud of our unity, proud of our strength, and proud
of the determination to find, root out and deal with the evil
of terrorism and those who seek to terrorize. And we will.
We will remember their lives, and retell their stories, again and
again, so that neither the nation nor the world will ever forget.

Defense Secretary Donald Rumsfeld

AN OPEN LETTER TO TERRORISTS

By Jim Willis, 2001.

I don't know your name, or names–we may never know who you are–so I can't address you personally. Today, you killed several thousands of our friends ... perhaps not people who we knew personally, but people like us. People who worked hard to make a living, who loved someone, who were loved by someone, who worried about making a better life for their children and grandchildren, who believed in God and the American Dream, who criticized this country for its insufficiencies and cared enough to try and change things and ensure a better future, not just for us, but for the world. People who leave behind scores of loved ones, friends, pets, neighbors, coworkers, and members of their faiths. Perhaps even people who derived from your own country and who sought refuge here. Your act was a slaughter of the innocents. You are like an insidious cancer that strikes without warning, ravages bodies, tears families apart, and in the end can never destroy the soul. You are the ultimate coward. You may topple our buildings, collapse our communication systems, disrupt our government, crash our markets, and leave behind the carnage of bodies, but you will never destroy the soul of America.

We made this country from the bits and pieces of the rest of the world; we took the best, the worst of every culture and nationality, race and creed, and made an alloy that may be dented, but not even a trial by fire can melt. I don't know what God you believe in, or what hateful rhetoric you espouse, or what your misguided political beliefs might be that allows you to do what you did today without a fear of eternal damnation. I only know that you may win a battle or two, but you will never win this war! We have the entire history of the world on our side, and no dictator, despot, or madman has survived as long as America has thrived and prospered. If you accomplished anything at all today, it was to give America a wake-up call, and we will now rise up stronger than before. You are defeated before you've even begun, there in your private hell and later in your eternal one. Someday your people may even need our help, and because we are America, we would respond. May God bless the friends we lost, their families, friends, neighbors and coworkers. We will help them rebuild from the ashes. May God continue to bless America, help her to protect us all, and may she continue to shine as a beacon of democracy and hope to the rest of the world.

YOU MISSED AMERICA

By Charles Brennan.

Well, you hit the World Trade Center, but you missed America. You hit the Pentagon, but you missed America. You used helpless American bodies, to take out other American bodies, but like a poor marksman, you STILL missed America. Why? Because of something you guys will never understand. America isn't about a building or two, not about financial centers, not about military centers; America isn't about a place; America isn't even about a bunch of bodies. America is about an IDEA. An idea, that you can go someplace where you can earn as much as you can figure out how to, live for the most part, like you envisioned living, and pursue Happiness. (No guarantees that you'll reach it, but you can sure try!)

Go ahead and whine your terrorist whine, and chant your terrorist litany: *If you cannot see my point, then feel my pain.* This concept is alien to Americans. We live in a country where we don't have to see your point. But you're free to have one. We don't have to listen to your speech. But you're free to say one. Don't know where you got the strange idea that everyone has to agree with you. We don't agree with each other in this country, almost as a matter of pride. We're a collection of guys that don't agree, called States. We united our individual states to protect ourselves from tyranny in the world. Another idea, we made up on the spot. You CAN make it up as you go, when it's your country–if you're free enough. Yeah, we're fat, sloppy, easy-going goofs most of the time. That's an unfortunate image to project to the world, but it comes of feeling free and easy about the world you live in. It's unfortunate too, because people start to forget that when you attack Americans, they tend to fight like a cornered badger. The first we knew of the War of 1812 was when England burned Washington, D.C. to the ground. Didn't turn out like England thought it was going to, and it's not going to turn out like you think, either. Sorry, but you're not the first bully on our shores, just the most recent. No Marquis of Queensbury rules for Americans, either. We were the FIRST and so far, only country in the world to use nuclear weapons in anger. Horrific idea, nowadays? News for you bucko, it was back then too, but we used it anyway. Only had two of them in the whole world and we used 'em both. Grandpa Jones worked on the Manhattan Project. Told me once, that right up until they threw the switch, the physicists were still arguing over whether the Uranium alone would fission, or whether it would start a fissioning chain reaction that would eat everything. But they threw the switch anyway, because we had a War to win. Does that tell you something about American Resolve? So who just declared War on us? It would be nice to point to some real estate, like the good old days. Unfortunately, we're probably at war with random camps, in far-flung places–who think they're safe. Just like the Barbary Pirates did. Better start sleeping with one eye open.

There's a spirit that tends to take over people who come to this country, looking for opportunity, looking for liberty, looking for freedom. Even if they misuse it. The Marielistas that Castro emptied out of his prisons were overjoyed to find out how much freedom there was. First thing they did when they hit our shores was run out and buy guns. The ones that didn't end up dead, ended up in prisons. You guys seem to be incapable of understanding that we don't live in America, America lives in US! American Spirit is what it's called. And killing a few thousand of us, or a few million of us, won't change it. Most of the time, it's a pretty happy-go-lucky kind of Spirit. Until we're crossed in a cowardly manner, then it becomes an entirely different kind of Spirit. Wait until you see what we do with that Spirit, this time.

Sleep tight, if you can. We're coming.

TERRORIST

T is for the times you tried to hurt us

E is for the Evil that implores you

R is for Revenge which you deserve

R is for Reasons America will survive

O is for 'our flag was still there'

R is for recovery that we'll restore

I is for the Ignorance that fuels you

S is for your leader who is Satan

T is for our towers ... they'll be back.

Author Unknown

THE STEEL OF AMERICAN RESOLVE

Terrorist attacks can shake
the foundations of our biggest buildings,
but they cannot touch
the foundations of America.
These acts shatter steel,
but they cannot dent the
steel of American resolve.

President George W. Bush, 9 October 2001

World Trade Center Site. Brooklyn Firefighters,
Dan McWilliams, George Johnson and Billy
Eisengrein. McWilliams said, *Every pair of eyes*
that saw that flag got a little brighter. Photo by
Tom Franklin, 11 September 2001.

WAYS WE'RE DIFFERENT THIS CHRISTMAS, 2001

*Last Christmas we were thinking about
all the things we didn't have.
This Christmas we are thinking about all the things we do have.*

*Last Christmas we were placing wreaths
on the doors of our homes.
This Christmas we are placing wreaths
on the graves of our heroes.*

*Last Christmas we were letting our sons play with toy guns.
This Christmas we are teaching them that guns are not toys.*

*Last Christmas we were counting our money.
This Christmas we are counting our blessings.*

*Last Christmas we were lighting candles to decorate.
This Christmas we are lighting candles to commemorate.*

*Last Christmas we paid lip service to the
real meaning of the holidays.
This Christmas we are paying homage to it.*

*Last Christmas we were digging deep
into our bank accounts to find money
to fly home for the holidays. This Christmas we are digging deep
into our souls to find the courage to do so.*

*Last Christmas we thought a man who could rush down a football
field was a hero. This Christmas we know a man who rushes into a
burning building is the real hero.*

*Last Christmas we were thinking about the
madness of the holidays.
This Christmas we are thinking about the meaning of them.*

*Last Christmas we were getting on one another's nerves.
This Christmas we are getting on our knees.*

*Last Christmas we were wondering how to give our children all
the things that money can buy.
This Christmas we are wondering how to give them all the things
money cannot buy.*

Last Christmas we were thinking about all the
pressure we were under at the office.
This Christmas we are thinking about all the
people who no longer have an office.

Last Christmas we were singing carols.
This Christmas we are singing anthems.

Last Christmas we thought angels were in heaven.
This Christmas we know they are right here on earth.

Last Christmas we were contemplating all the changes we wanted
to make in the New Year.
This Christmas we are contemplating all the changes we will have
to make in this new reality.

Last Christmas we believed in the power of the pocketbook.
This Christmas we believe in the power of prayer.

Last Christmas peace on earth was something we
prayed for on Sunday morning.
This Christmas it's something we pray for every day.

Author Unknown

11 SEPTEMBER 2001

What were you doing when tragedy struck?
When you found out how so many ran out of luck?
Did you cry out in horror, or cry out in pain?
Did this cowardly act make you insane?
I saw the second plane hit the South Tower,
I saw how our country lost some of its power.
Many people's spouses were left all alone,
As we tell children their parents won't be coming home.
In horror I watched as the Towers hit the ground,
I watched the people running, trying not to be around.
Innocent people that died that fateful day,
Left this sad world with so much left to say.
But as we all watched, I saw a great sight.
The people of our country began to unite.

No matter what age, race, gender, or creed,
So many came together to meet this great need.
Out of this tragedy comes a right ray of hope,
As the people volunteer to help our country cope.
I, as well as others, won't forget what was done,
On September Eleventh, Two-Thousand and One.
We shall never forget September 11, 2001.

Christopher Daniel Estrada

I AM THE AMERICAN

I am the American
I am the American you killed on Tuesday.
I have many faces.
I am an airline pilot, I am a secretary,
I am a police officer, I am a flight attendant,
I am a firefighter, I am a street vendor.
I can be all of these things because I am,
first and foremost, an American.

I am also a father, a mother, a sister,
a brother. I am an aunt, an uncle,
a grandmother, a grandfather. I am a child.

Even though I am all of these things,
I am first and foremost, an American.
You can break my body,
you can destroy my buildings,
but you will never break my spirit
nor destroy my essence. Because I am,
first and foremost, an American.

I will live forever in the hearts of loved ones,
and in the hearts of my countrymen.
With every flag that is flown,
with every story that is told, I will survive.
Because I am, first and foremost, an American.

Author Unknown

POINT, COUNTER-POINT

By Major Bill Coffey.

Shortly after the September 11th 2001 attacks on our country, I assembled a slide presentation which I entitled *A Whoop-A-Gram* and e-mailed it to quite a few people. This presentation was directed at Mr. Bin Laden and all his associates; it was a presentation that depicted America's military might, warrior spirit and resolve. Contained in this presentation was some *language of war* which I felt was appropriate given the message and the military audience this presentation was intended to reach. There were some, however, who felt the use of profanity was not appropriate. Below is one response that was sent to me and my response back.

Mr. Coffey:

I appreciate your zeal in presenting a summary of what might happen to our #1 enemy but do you have to use the filthy language to get the point across? A sign of a civilized society is their ability to communicate without resorting to profanity and name calling. You, in resorting to profanity, are bowing to Mr. Bin Laden's level.

Ms. Bocker

—

Ms. Bocker,

Actually, I do not believe Mr. Bin Laden uses *profanity* like I so willingly do—you see, it's probably against his religion.

I appreciate your honesty, but on the point of profanity I have to ask that we agree to disagree. As a soldier I have accepted my duty to our country to fight and win our nation's wars. To do so we must kill people. To fight, kill, and experience war has to be the most vulgar thing one human being can do to one another–and with millions others, I am prepared to engage in this vulgarity so that our nation might survive. One of the symptoms of this vulgarity is the language that accompanies it. I can only imagine that you must be infinitely more bothered by the conduct of war than the language of war.

Here's a question you must ask yourself: If I were to smash you in the face with my fist what would you do? Would you hit me back? What if I hit your mother in the face in front of you? What would be your response? Certainly, you wouldn't hit me back or call me names since that behavior would be contradictory to your standards of a *civilized society*. Really ... what would you do? What if I were to bomb your entire extended family at one of your family reunions and all of your family was killed except you? *Would you call me names? Would you use vulgar language towards me?* Certainly not—at least according to your stated standards and your desire not to *bow* your standards to someone else's. You see, Mr. Bin Laden did bomb my family–it's your family too. I call my family *America*.

I only ask you to consider the language that accompanies such horrific acts as war–especially those committed against thousands of innocent civilians. Yes, according to your definition, we, the U.S.A., are ready to *bow* to the standard of Mr. Bin Laden– we are preparing to kill people–HIS PEOPLE, to blow their bodies apart, to ruin their homes, to make them go meet Allah–it's a nasty reality that we as a nation must do to ensure our survival AND the free speech that allows us to openly have this conversation.

The hell with Mr. Bin Laden, his organization and anyone who wants to attack you, me, our families and our nation, and God Bless you for caring enough to write.

Thank you for your letter.

P.S. Your quote for the day is from Mr. Samuel Adams, spoken circa 1775:

Contemplate the mangled bodies of your countrymen, and then say, 'What should be the reward of such sacrifices?' Bid us and our posterity bow the knee, supplicate the friendship, and plough, and sow, and reap, to glut the avarice of the men who have let loose on us the dogs of war to riot in our blood and hunt us from the face of the earth? If ye love wealth better than liberty, the tranquility of servitude than the animating contest of freedom, go from us in peace. We ask not your counsels or arms. Crouch down and lick the hands which feed you. May your chains sit lightly upon you, and may posterity forget that ye were our countrymen!

Respectfully Disagreeing, Bill Coffey

WHAT A DIFFERENCE A DAY MAKES

On Monday we emailed jokes
On Tuesday we did not

On Monday we thought that we were secure
On Tuesday we learned better

On Monday we were talking about heroes as being athletes
On Tuesday we relearned who our heroes are

On Monday we were irritated that our
rebate checks had not arrived
On Tuesday we gave money away to people we had never met

On Monday there were people fighting against praying in schools
On Tuesday you would have been hard pressed to find a school
where someone was not praying

On Monday people argued with their kids
about picking up their room
On Tuesday the same people could not get home
fast enough to hug their kids

On Monday people were upset that they had to wait
six minutes in a fast food drive through line.
On Tuesday people didn't care about waiting up to
six hours to give blood for the dying

On Monday we waved our flags signifying our cultural diversity
On Tuesday we waved only the American flag

On Monday there were people trying to separate each other by
race, sex, color and creed
On Tuesday they were all holding hands

On Monday we were men and women, black or white, old
or young, rich or poor, gay or straight, Christian ornon-Christian
On Tuesday we were Americans

On Monday politicians argued about budget surpluses
On Tuesday, grief stricken, they sang 'God Bless America'

*On Monday the President was going to Florida to read to children
On Tuesday he returned to Washington to protect our children*

*On Monday we had families
On Tuesday we had orphans*

*On Monday people went to work as usual
On Tuesday they died*

*On Monday people were fighting the
10 commandments on government property
On Tuesday the same people all said 'God help us all'
while thinking, 'Thou shall not kill'*

*It is sadly ironic how it takes horrific events to place things
into perspective, but it has. The lessons learned this week,
the things we have taken for granted, the things
that have been forgotten or overlooked, hopefully,
will never be forgotten again.*

Author Unknown

New York City Mural. *In Memory of All Who Died!*

ONE

As the soot and dirt and ash rained down,
We became one color.
As we carried each other down the stairs of the burning building,
We became one class.
As we lit candles of waiting and hope,
We became one generation.
As the firefighters and police officers fought their
way into the inferno,
We became one gender.
As we fell to our knees in prayer for strength,
We became one faith.
As we whispered or shouted words of encouragement,
We spoke one language.
As we gave our blood in lines a mile long,
We became one body.
As we mourned together the great loss,
We became one family.
As we cried tears of grief and loss,
We became one soul.
As we retell with pride of the sacrifice of heroes,
We become one people.
We are:
One color
One class
One generation
One gender
One faith
One language
One body
One family
One soul
One people
We are The Power of One.
We are United.
We are America.

Author Unknown

Mr. Rumsfeld and his associates are the true moralists in a difficult crisis, who understand that real humanity lies in the often dirty business of ending, not tolerating or ignoring, evil.

Davis Hanson

SHAME ON YOU AMERICAN-HATING LIBERALS

This article comes from a newspaper in England. By Tony Parsons, 11 September 2002.

One year ago, the world witnessed a unique kind of broadcasting—the mass murder of thousands, live on television.

As a lesson in the pitiless cruelty of the human race, September 11 was up there with Pol Pot's mountain of skulls in Cambodia, or the skeletal bodies stacked like garbage in the Nazi concentration camps. An unspeakable act so cruel, so calculated and so utterly merciless that surely the world could agree on one thing—nobody deserves this fate.

Surely there could be consensus: the victims were truly innocent, the perpetrators truly evil.

But to the world's eternal shame, 9/11 is increasingly seen as America's comeuppance.

Incredibly, anti-Americanism has increased over the last year.

There has always been a simmering resentment to the U.S.A. in this country–too loud, too rich, too full of themselves and so much happier than Europeans–but it has become an epidemic.

And it seems incredible to me. More than that, it turns my stomach.

America is this country's greatest friend and our staunchest ally. We are bonded to the U.S. by culture, language and blood.

A little over half a century ago, around half a million Americans died for our freedoms, as well as their own. Have we forgotten so soon?

And exactly a year ago, thousands of ordinary men, women and children–not just Americans, but from dozens of countries–

were butchered by a small group of religious fanatics. Are we so quick to betray them?

What touched the heart about those who died in the twin towers and on the planes was that we recognized them. Young fathers and mothers, somebody's son and somebody's daughter, husbands and wives. And children. Some unborn.

And these people brought it on themselves? And their nation is to blame for their meticulously planned slaughter?

These days you don't have to be some dust-encrusted nut job in Kabul or Karachi or Finsbury Park to see America as the Great Satan.

The anti-American alliance is made up of self-loathing liberals who blame the Americans for every ill in the Third World, and conservatives suffering from power-envy, bitter that the world's only superpower can do what it likes without having to ask permission.

The truth is that America has behaved with enormous restraint since September 11.

Remember, remember.

Remember the gut-wrenching tapes of weeping men phoning their wives to say, *I love you*, before they were burned alive. Remember those people leaping to their deaths from the top of burning skyscrapers.

Remember the hundreds of firemen buried alive. Remember the smiling face of that beautiful little girl who was on one of the planes with her mum. Remember, remember–and realize that America has never retaliated for 9/11 in anything like the way it could have.

So a few al-Qaeda tourists got locked without a trial in Camp X-ray? Pass the Kleenex.

So some Afghan wedding receptions were shot up after they merrily fired their semi-automatics in a sky full of American planes? A shame, but maybe next time they should stick to confetti.

AMERICA could have turned a large chunk of the world into a parking lot. That it didn't is a sign of strength.

American voices are already being raised against attacking Iraq–that's what a democracy is for. How many in the Islamic world will have a minute's silence for the slaughtered innocents of

9/11? How many Islamic leaders will have the guts to say that the mass murder of 9/11 was an abomination?

When the news of 9/11 broke on the West Bank, those freedom-loving Palestinians were dancing in the street. America watched all of that–and didn't push the button. We should thank the stars that America is the most powerful nation in the world. I still find it incredible that 9/11 did not provoke all-out war. Not a *war on terrorism*. A real war.

The fundamentalist dudes are talking about *opening the gates of hell*, if America attacks Iraq. Well, America could have opened the gates of hell like you wouldn't believe.

The U.S. is the most militarily powerful nation that ever strode the face of the earth.

The campaign in Afghanistan may have been less than perfect and the planned war on Iraq may be misconceived.

But don't blame America for not bringing peace and light to these wretched countries. How many democracies are there in the Middle East, or in the Muslim world? You can count them on the fingers of one hand–assuming you haven't had any chopped off for minor shoplifting.

I love America, yet America is hated. I guess that makes me Bush's poodle. But I would rather be a dog in New York City than a Prince in Riyadh. Above all, America is hated because it is what every country wants to be–rich, free, strong, open, optimistic.

Not ground down by the past, or religion, or some caste system. America is the best friend this country ever had and we should start remembering that.

Or do you really think the U.S.A. is the root of all evil? Tell it to the loved ones of the men and women who leaped to their death from the burning towers.

Tell it to the nursing mothers whose husbands died on one of the hijacked planes, or were ripped apart in a collapsing skyscraper.

And tell it to the hundreds of young widows whose husbands worked for the New York Fire Department. To our shame, George Bush gets a worse press than Saddam Hussein.

Once we were told that Saddam gassed the Kurds, tortured his own people and set up rape-camps in Kuwait. Now we are told he likes Quality Street. Save me the orange center, oh mighty one!

Remember, remember, September 11. One of the greatest atrocities in human history was committed against America. No, do more than remember. NEVER FORGET!

TWO THOUSAND ONE
NINE ELEVEN

Two thousand one, nine eleven
Six thousand plus arrive in heaven
As they pass through the gate,
Thousands more appear in wait.

A bearded man
with stovepipe hat
Steps forward saying,
'Let's sit, lets chat.'

They settle down in seats of clouds
A man named Martin shouts out proud
'I have a dream!' and once he did
The Newcomer said, 'Your dream still lives.'

Groups of soldiers in blue and gray
Others in khaki, and green then say
'We're from Bull Run, Yorktown, the Maine'
The Newcomer said, 'You died not in vain.'

From a man on sticks one could hear,
'The only thing we have to fear ...'
The Newcomer said, 'We know the rest,
Trust us sir, we've passed that test.'

'Courage doesn't hide in caves
You can't bury freedom, in a grave'
The Newcomers had heard this voice before
A distinct Yankees twang from Hyannisport shores.

A silence fell within the mist
Somehow the Newcomer knew that this

Meant time had come for her to say
What was in the hearts of the six thousand plus that day.

Back on Earth, we wrote reports,
Watched our children play in sports
Worked our gardens, sang our songs
Went to church and clipped coupons.

We smiled,
we laughed,
we cried, we fought
Unlike you, great we're not.

The tall man in the stovepipe hat
Stood and said, 'don't talk like that!
Look at your country, look and see
You died for freedom, just like me.'

Then, before them all appeared a scene
Of rubbled streets and twisted beams
Death, destruction, smoke and dust
And people working just 'cause they must.

Hauling ash,
Lifting stones,
Knee deep in hell
But not alone.

'Look! Blackman, Whiteman, Brownman, Yellowman
Side by side helping their fellow man!'
So said Martin, as he watched the scene
'Even from nightmares, can be born a dream.'

Down below three firemen raised
The colors high into ashen haze
The soldiers above had seen it before
On Iwo Jima back in '44.

The man on sticks studied everything closely
Then shared his perceptions on what he saw mostly
'I see pain, I see tears,
I see sorrow—but I don't see fear.'

You left behind husbands and wives
Daughters and sons and so many lives
Are suffering now because of this wrong
But look very closely, you're not really gone.

All of those people, even those who've never met you
All of their lives, they'll never forget you.
Don't you see what has happened?
Don't you see what you've done?
You've brought them together, together as one.

With that the man in the stovepipe hat said,
'Take my hand,' and from there he led
Six thousand plus heroes, Newcomers, to heaven
On this day, two thousand one, nine eleven.

Author Unknown

WITH PRIDE AND DETERMINATION

We're American; we don't walk around terrified.
We're going to move forward with pride and determination.

Colin Powell, Secretary of State

America appears to have a president
(more precious than gold) worthy of its people ...
One man with courage is a majority ...
Backbone is not an average gift ...
Guts are not an average gift ...
There are things you just know ...
There was always another America ...
America can and will stand and fight for a cause ...
It's beautiful to see Americans stand up.

Peggy Noonan

AND WE WILL RISE ...

They didn't know what they've started.
But they are about to find out.
In the weeks and months to come, as Americans,
we will weep, we will mourn, and
we will rise to defend all
we cherish and all we hold dear.

President George W. Bush

CLOSING THOUGHTS

My fondest hope is that
Americans will travel the road
extending forward from the arch of experience,
never forgetting our heroic origins,
never failing to seek divine guidance
as we march boldly and bravely into a future
limited only by our capacity to dream.

President Ronald Reagan

Think of your forefathers! Think of your posterity!

President John Quincy Adams

THE SHINING CITY

And that's about all I have to say tonight, except for one thing.
The past few days when I've been at that window upstairs, I've
thought a bit of the 'shining city upon a hill.' The phrase comes
from John Winthrop, who wrote it to describe the America he
imagined. What he imagined was important because he was an
early Pilgrim, an early freedom man. He journeyed here on what
today we'd call a little wooden boat; and like the other Pilgrims,
he was looking for a home that would be free. I've spoken of the
shining city all my political life, but I don't know if I ever quite
communicated what I saw when I said it. But in my mind it was a
tall, proud city built on rocks stronger than oceans, windswept,
God-blessed, and teeming with people of all kinds living in
harmony and peace; a city with free ports that hummed with
commerce and creativity. And if there had to be city walls, the
walls had doors and the doors were open to anyone with the will
and the heart to get here. That's how I saw it, and see it still.

Excerpts from President Reagan's Farewell Speech, 1988

I know that for America
there will always be a bright dawn ahead.
I see America,
not in the setting sun of a black night of despair ahead of us,
I see America in the crimson light of a rising sun fresh from the
burning, creative hand of God.
I see great days ahead,
great days possible to men and women of will and vision ...

President Ronald Reagan

We're Americans
and we have a rendezvous with destiny ...
No people who have ever lived on this earth have fought harder,
paid a higher price for freedom,
or done more to advance
the dignity of man than Americans.

President Ronald Reagan

American Avenger Fighter-Bomber. 1942.

THAT IS ALL

Bill Ott was just one of thousands of fliers during World War II who died for their country. He kept his *heart* right to the end. This is the U.S. Navy's description of Ott's final moment:

On his way back, Ott was attacked by Japs and shot up. Running out of gas, he called the *Yorktown*, said he could fly only fifteen minutes more. His radioman was dead, and he himself had only one good arm and one good leg. Finally, his last report came,

I am out of gas. That is all. Good luck and God be with you.

*Let us set for ourselves
a standard so high
that it will be a glory to live up to it,
and then let us live up to it and
add a new laurel to the crown of America.*

President Woodrow Wilson, 28th President of the United States

Union Field Hospital. Gettysburg, Pennsylvania,
July 1864. Doctors are preparing to amputate the
leg of a soldier.

A young Union sergeant, whose leg had been shattered during the Battle of Fredericksburg, December 13, 1862, had fallen while carrying his country's flag. Refusing to relinquish the banner, he had clung to it through the amputation of his leg. Now he lay dying, still wrapped in the Stars and Stripes. Those attending him saw his lips move and they stooped to hear his last words:

Come on, boys! Our country and our flag forever!

They then asked him,

Is the Savior with you?

He whispered,

Do you think He would pass by and not take me? I go, I go.

I am grateful for America's glorious past; I am awed by its unbelievable present; I am confident of its limitless future.

William Arthur Ward, Writer

518

ABOUT THE AUTHORS

Colonel William T. Coffey, Sr. resides in Plainville, Connecticut and is retired after a total of 43 years in the U.S. military as an Infantryman and seven years as a State of Connecticut employee. During the Korean War, Colonel Coffey (then Corporal Coffey) was mobilized with his National Guard division serving in Germany from 1950-53. Colonel Coffey also served as an Infantry Battalion S3 and XO with the 4th Infantry Division in Vietnam during 1969-70. He served in the Pentagon while assigned to the National Guard Bureau from 1974-78 and at the Combined Arms Center and Command and General Staff College, Fort Leavenworth, Kansas from 1978-1982. Colonel Coffey is a graduate of 31 Army, Air Force and Joint service schools including the Command and General Staff College and the U.S. Army War College and holds a Masters degree in Management and Supervision.

Colonel (Retired) William T. Coffey, Sr. (right). At Camp Eagle, Bosnia-Herzegovina, 13 December 2001 with Squad Leader, Company B, 1st Battalion, 102nd Infantry Regiment, Connecticut Army National Guard.

Colonel Coffey serves as a Research and Marketing Analyst for Purple Mountain Publishing & Books and is the co-author of this book. Colonel Coffey remains actively involved with the Employer Support to the Guard and Reserves (ESGR) supporting the service men and women from his home state. He also remains active with the Association of the United States Army (AUSA), Veterans of Foreign Wars (VFW) and the American Legion.

Colonel Coffey is married with one son and two daughters and has six grandchildren.

Major William T. Coffey, Jr. resides in Colorado Springs, Colorado where he is a full-time defense contractor supporting the U.S. Army Space and Missile Defense Command.

He served as an Active Reservist with the U.S. Northern Command (NORTHCOM) and the North American Aerospace Defense (NORAD) Command from 2002-2003 as a Military Intelligence officer, serving on their J2 staff as a National Systems Officer and Senior Intelligence Planner. Major Coffey spent 10 years on active duty from 1984 to 1993, serving in tactical units in Germany, Korea and several locations throughout the United States.

Major William T. Coffey, Jr.

Major Coffey is the Sole Proprietor of Purple Mountain Publishing & Books. He is also the author of the book *Patriot Hearts* and the co-author of this book. He writes and speaks publicly on the topics of patriotism, service, character and leadership and has several of his articles published nationally.

Major Coffey is married with one son and one daughter.

PERMISSIONS

Every effort has been made to ensure that required permissions for all materiel were obtained. The editor and employees of LJ Editing LLC cannot take responsibility for any errors or omissions. Those sources not formally acknowledged here will be included in future printings of this book. Grateful acknowledgment is made to the following to reprint previously published and unpublished material:

Articles:
America (Like It or Leave It). Article by Barry Loudermilk, reprinted with permission. Letter dated 20 December 2002.
An Open Letter to Terrorists. Article by Jim Willis, reprinted with permission. Letter dated 10 January 2003.
A Tale of Eight Americans. Article by Tom Segel, reprinted with permission. Letter dated 16 December 2002.
A Tribute to a Sailor. Article by LTJG Juan Mullen, reprinted with permission. Letter dated 30 December 2002.
Bear Day #3. Email by LCDR JJ Cummings, reprinted with permission. Letter dated 3 December 2002.
Blinding Flashes of the Obvious about Leadership. Article by Major General (Retired) Perry M. Smith, reprinted with permission. Letter dated 8 January 2003.
Breath of the Dragon. Article by Tom Clancy, reprinted with permission. Letter dated 4 February 2003.
Dear Brother Bob. Excerpts from a letter from Corporal John Tanney, reprinted with permission of his brother, Tom Tanney. Letter dated 17 December 2002.
For People They Don't Even Know. Article by Eric Dawson, reprinted with permission. Letter dated 5 May 2003.
Freedom Is Not Free. Poem by Kelly Strong, reprinted with permission. Letter dated 9 June 2002.
From the Heart of a Hero. Letter from Colonel (Retired) David Hackworth, reprinted with permission. Letter dated 23 February 2003.
From the Heart of the Seventh. Article by Major Robert L. Batemen, reprinted with permission from Vietnam Magazine. Letter dated 11 February 2003.
Greatness in the Flesh. Letter from Ann Baker, reprinted with permission. Letter dated 13 December 2002.
Heroes. Poem by Ms. Amy Konigsberger and her 2nd Grade class at Washington Elementary School, Canton, Ohio, reprinted with permission. Letter dated 21 January 2003.
I Am a Soldier. Article by Daniel Cedusky, reprinted with permission. Letter dated 13 December 2002.
I Am Your Flag. Poem courtesy of Daniel Cedusky, reprinted with permission. Letter dated 13 December 2002.
In Simple Obedience to Duty: A Vietnam Perspective. Speech by LTG (Retired) James Link, reprinted with permission. Letter dated 10 February 2003.
I Serve Because. Article by Captain Clemens S. Kruse, reprinted with permission. Letter dated 6 January 2003.

It Came Down to One Ship and One Marine. Article by Vin Supreynowicz, reprinted with permission. Letter dated 27 August 2002.

Loyalty to Our Country. Letter by Paul Pritchett, reprinted with permission. Letter dated 12 December 2003.

Medals. Article by B.J. Cassady, reprinted with permission. Letter dated 21 February 2003.

My Month with the Military. Article by Dan Juneau, reprinted with permission. Letter dated 7 January 2003.

Now I Know. Article by Tamara Hall, reprinted with permission. Letter dated 5 February 2002.

Reflection of the Vietnam Wall. Article by Patrick Camunes, Belvior Eagle Magazine, reprinted with permission. Letter dated 14 January 2003.

Sometimes I Forget. Article by Airman First Class Joshua Wilks, reprinted with permission. Letter dated 17 December 2002.

Soldier Actions in Combat. Response by General (Retired) Barry McCaffrey, as posted on CommanyCommand.com, reprinted with permission. Letter dated 13 December 2003.

Struck Down, But Not Destroyed. Speech, given by Brian Shul, reprinted with permission. Letter dated 6 December 2003.

Ten Great Reasons to Celebrate. Article by Dinesh D'Souza, reprinted with permission. Letter dated 30 September 2002.

They are the Real Heroes. Email by LCDR JJ Cummings, reprinted with permission. Letter dated 3 December 2002.

They're Just Not in Step with Today's Society. Benediction by Pete Peterson, reprinted with permission of the Daedalians Society. Letter dated 15 January 2003.

This Ranger is Lone in His Ways. Article by Sally Jenkins, reprinted with permission from the Washington Post, letter 7 February 2003.

Thoughts from a Father's Heart. Article by Bob Hager, reprinted with permission. Letter dated 20 April 2002.

Too Many Brave Souls. Article by Jamie Malanowski, Time Magazine & Tribune Media Services, reprinted with permission. Letter dated 8 January 2003.

Touchstone to the American Soul. Article by Tom Adkins, reprinted with permission. Letter dated 8 January 2003.

We will be the Next Patrol. Speech by Ms. Nikki Mendicino, reprinted with permission. Letter dated 22 December 2002.

We'll Fight Till the Last 50-Year-Old. Article by Jeff Ackerman, reprinted with permission. Letter dated 14 January 2003.

What Does The American Flag Mean To You? Responses collected by Ms. Michelle Giovanni, reprinted with permission. Letter dated, 20 September 2002.

What is an American? Article by Peter Ferrara, reprinted with permission. Per telephone conversation, 17 April 2003.

What It Means To Be An American. Article by Lauren Provini, reprinted with permission. Per telephone conversation 11 January 2003.

Who Are Americans? Email from Major David Balmer, reprinted with permission. Letter dated 5 December 2003.

Why Mom Still Wears the Uniform. Article by Colonel (USAF) Cheryl Zadlo, reprinted with permission. Letter dated 15 December 2002.

Photographs and Artwork:

I'll Take It From Here. Artwork by Jeff Grier, reprinted with permission. Per telephone conversation, 14 January 2002.

ACKNOWLEDGMENTS

In addition to all those who authored and contributed items to this book, special thanks is humbly given to the many folks who have freely shared stories, letters, their comments and opinions and other items included in this book. In no particular order, a very special thank you to:

MG (Retired) George Buttery, MG (Retired) Carroll Childers, LTC (Retired) Don Schneider, Mr. Tom Tanney, Mr. John Ables, Mr. B.J. Cassady, COL (Retired) Tommy Brown, Mr. Trent Loucks, LTC (Retired) Tim Mishkofski, COL (Retired) Robert Reed, Mr. Ray Bryant, Ms. Karen Popovich, Mr. David Woodruff, Ms. Erika Lishock, MAJ Jeffrey Williams, Mr. Guy Fucci, SFC (Retired) Elijah Murphy, LTC (Retired) Dave Linder, COL Kate Kasun, LTC Doug Lobdell, LTC (Retired) Gary Wilson, Mr. William Proctor, LTC (Retired) Neil Garra, LTC Lloyd Leitz, CSM (Retired) Lon Hardy, Mr. Randy Threet, MAJ Robert Zaza, MAJ Cory Steinke, MAJ (Retired) Dick Mortensen, LTC James Stockmoe, Mr. Bill Hutchinson, Mr. Rodney Smith, LTC Donald Morris, MAJ Jeff Williams, MAJ Ron Stimpson, Mr. Mark Choiniere, Mr. Akshai Gandi, LTC (Retired) William Gessner, LTC (Retired) Tom Gray, Mr. John Maney, Mr. John Choby, Mr. Darren Woodward, Mr. David Woodruff, MSG (Retired) John Lamerson, Mr. Rex Burton, COL (Retired) Daniel Cedusky, CPT Kone Faulkner, MAJ (Retired) Henry 'Duke' Boswell, Mr. Robert Larsen, Mr. John Dodson, LTC (Retired) Collin Agee, LTC Rolfe Bott, MAJ Mike Doyle, LTC (Retired) Warren Silva, LTC (Retired) Lewis Vasquez, CW4 (Retired) Rudolph LaLiberte, Sergeant Mike McKenzie, Laurie Findlay, COL (Retired, USMCR) Carl Vinditto and SGM (Retired) Bernard Morgan.

INDEX BY
AUTHORS, TITLES, PHOTOGRAPHERS, SUBJECTS

This index provides a quick reference guide to all items in this book including: authors, titles, photographers and subjects of photographs and articles. *Italics* indicates titles of individual articles, letters, etc.

ORDERING INFORMATION

To order copies of *Patriot Hearts* or *More ... Patriot Hearts* using check or money order, write to:

Purple Mountain Publishing & Books
P.O. Box 77019
Colorado Springs, Colorado 80970-7019

Telephonic orders, using a credit card (Visa, MasterCard, Discover) can be made by calling 719-351-8321 (cell phone). To order online using a credit card, visit the Purple Mountain Publishing & Books website at http://www.patriothearts.com.

Price for *Patriot Hearts* softcover is $16.95 and the hardcover version is $23.95. The price for *More ... Patriot Hearts* is $25.00 for the hardcover and $18.00 for the softcover version (Please check for availability of softcover version of *More ... Patriot Hearts* before ordering–check website or call). Please add $2.95 per book for shipping and handling. This S/H cost applies to U.S. addresses including APO/FPO, Puerto Rico, Guam, American Samoa, and other U.S. Protectorates. Shipping and Handling for international addresses is $7.00 per book. Please make checks or money orders payable to *Purple Mountain Publishing & Books*.

Similar to this book, *Patriot Hearts* is a collection of true and inspirational stories, letters, speeches, poems, quotes and stories about Americans and American values. *Patriot Hearts* is 440 pages and contains over 750 items.

For additional information about either book or to contact the authors, please visit our website (http://www.patriothearts.com).

Purple Mountain Publishing & Books continues to solicit letters, speeches, stories, quotes, poems, and other items similar to those found in this book for future publications. These items can be mailed to the book ordering address listed above, or emailed directly to the authors via the link provided on the website http://www.patriothearts.com.